# MARADONA

## The Boy. The Rebel. The God.

## GUILLEM BALAGUÉ

**W&N**

**WEIDENFELD & NICOLSON**

First published in the UK by Weidenfeld & Nicolson 2021

1 3 5 7 9 10 8 6 4 2

ISBN Hardback  978 1 4091 5775 5
ISBN Trade Paperback  978 1 4091 5776 2
ISBN eBook 978  1 4091 5778 6
ISBN Audio 978 1 4091 8640 3

A CIP catalogue record for this book
is available from the British Library.

Typeset by Input Data Services Ltd, Somerset

Printed and bound in Great Britain by Clays Ltd, Elcograf S.p.A.

Weidenfeld & Nicolson

The Orion Publishing Group Ltd
Carmelite House
50 Victoria Embankment
London, EC4Y 0DZ
An Hachette UK Company
www.orionbooks.co.uk

To my niece Alba, who has brought so many laughs to this confused world, and to Juan Carlos Unzué, who constantly reminds us of the value of inner strength and a smile.

# CONTENTS

# PROLOGUE

Francis Cornejo, the coach of a youth side affiliated to Argentinos Juniors that he called *Cebollitas* (little onions), had to travel to Villa Fiorito to check the boy's age on his ID. Goyo Carrizo had brought along his friend Diego Maradona for a trial at Parque Saavedra. As Cornejo watched him play, he was stunned: 'He's tiny, there's no way he's eight.'

As soon as Francis got in the back of José Trotta's orange Rastrojero pickup truck, doubts overcame him. 'Ah, Fiorito.' The shanty town of Villa Fiorito, in the outskirts of Buenos Aires, was where some of his young players lived, but it was also a neighbourhood that regularly featured in police reports of fights, shootings and murders. With a bit of luck, they would be back home before dusk. First of all, he would drop off eight or nine boys along the way and then take Goyo, Diego and the others to Fiorito. José Trotta, Cornejo's assistant and team chauffeur, knew how to get there, but *El Pelusa*, Diego, would then have to direct him to his house.

The truck had to cross some railway tracks and Francis was surprised to see wells, horse-drawn cart tracks and even a stream of dirty water that soaked into the rotting piles of rubbish. 'It's there,' said Diego, pointing to the left. Cornejo crossed the road and knocked on the door. Doña Tota opened it, with one of her daughters standing behind her. They seemed taken aback.

'We're putting together a team at Argentinos Juniors and we need to confirm your son's age . . .' The other boys had got off the Rastrojero and gathered around the door.

'Come in,' she said kindly before swiftly showing Francis her son's birth certificate from Evita Hospital, confirming that his date of birth was 30 October 1960. That kid really was eight years old.

Francis had discovered a rare gem who could slot into his side. In fact, he did more than that. From March 1969 onwards, he helped the team get an unheard-of 136-game unbeaten run.

In his book *Cebollita Maradona* – the story of his relationship with that 'little onion', tinier than the other kids, big hair, round faced, little fast-moving legs – Cornejo recalled dozens of standout moments. 'He received the ball to the right of the box, scooped it up with his left foot on to his head . . . That's when everyone's jaws dropped: he ran through the area from right to left, with the ball glued to his head, and when he was in front of goal, he suddenly stopped, dropped it from his head to his left foot, turned and unleashed an incredible strike that thumped the right post, with the goalkeeper motionless, as if he had been hypnotised by the play. The ball came back out and Polvorita Delgado got there first to tuck it home. Crazy.' The entire stadium applauded that move, opposition fans included.

One day, while training at Parque Saavedra, an old man, who had stopped playing *bocce* to enjoy watching Maradona, gave him his bicycle. 'No, sir. Thank you, but I can't take it.'

'Do take it, son. It's yours. I want you to have it. You're a demon with your dribbling. Remember me when you're in the national team.' Francis nodded his consent and a grateful Diego, shocked by the reaction his football produced, accepted the offer. Maradona remembered him when he eventually became an international but never knew how to get hold of him, or even if he was still around.

Diego's parents started to travel to the games in José's pickup truck. Don Diego and Doña Tota sat with the driver in the cab, while Francis enjoyed being with the boys in the back: 'I had the wind blowing against my face and the racket from the lads around me, singing, making jokes, getting themselves psyched up for the match.'

That talented *Cebollita*, who made his first-team debut at fifteen, wasted no time in winning over the Argentinos Juniors faithful, while the club's board got him and his family out of the slum of Fiorito by renting a flat for him in Villa del Parque near the training ground. Diego lived at number 2,750. There was a shy girl called Claudia who lived at number 2,046. One day he glimpsed her from behind in her yellow trousers and immediately fell in love. She didn't know who he was. Maradona, though, told the story rather differently further down the line.

Don Diego and Doña Tota didn't have enough money to pay their rent every month and ran the risk of being evicted, but the club helped out by buying Diego his first property. He was eighteen. It was a standard home on two floors with a courtyard in the modest neighbourhood of La Paternal, three blocks from the Argentinos stadium. His parents, siblings and even some of his brothers and sisters-in-law lived there. Maradona slept in his own bedroom, but he needed to walk three steps to the next level for the toilet, on the same floor as the roof deck.

At nineteen, long before turning into the 'dirty God and sinner' described by the writer Eduardo Galeano three decades later, he became an U20 World Cup winner in Japan. By then, the Rastrojero pick up truck had been left behind and Maradona was already turning into a petrolhead, with his wheels acting as a calling card, an Argentine trait that would always be with him. The fans wanted to thank *El Pelusa* for the joy he gave them so they decided to raise funds to buy him a car, a lordly red Mercedes-Benz 500 SLC, with a respectable horsepower of 237. Another gift of gratitude.

His salary gradually allowed him to save up to buy his first car and he gave himself a Christmas present in the shape of a functional Fiat Europa 128 CLS, straight and rectangular as if designed by a child. A collector still keeps it near Buenos Aires and has turned down offers from Italian museums to exhibit it.

If you're a star, and Maradona already was one at twenty, you can't really drive a Fiat Europa, so he bought his first sports car from Porsche, which arrived from Germany, a dark grey 924 with brown leather seats. It was his first treasure before getting rid of it prior to leaving Boca Juniors for Barcelona. Thirty years later, while in charge of the national team at the disappointing World Cup in South Africa, you could buy it for half a million dollars, but two years later the price dramatically plummeted, just as the then manager's stock did, to $77,500.

Maradona's Barcelona contract included a car, a red VW Golf, from which he emerged by the Camp Nou's entrance one afternoon in 1983. The door to access training was shut though. 'See that, Diego! They say the early bird catches the worm, but it's the first time you've arrived early and it's shut.' Fernando Signorini, a young fitness coach, wondered if he'd made a faux pas with that sardonic comment, his introduction to the player. Diego's half-smile left room for doubt.

Maradona knew about Signorini, as he was one of the few people with the authority to attend manager's César Luis Menotti's training sessions. 'So, you're the coach? We're playing tomorrow, then I'm off to Argentina on holiday, but when we're back for the pre-season in Andorra, I'd like to speak to you because my agent Jorge Cyterszpiler and I are thinking about setting up a football school in Barcelona.' Later on, Diego asked *El Profe* (the Prof) to become his personal trainer, which was unprecedented at the time in the world of team sport. They would spend, on and off, almost ten years together.

The first great downturn in his life came after Argentina's victory in the World Cup in Mexico in 1986. After reaching the glory he had dreamed of as a child, Maradona entered a state of depression. His life as a multi-millionaire prisoner of fame in the city's Posillipo neighbourhood weighed heavily on him. When that happened, someone was there to offer some magic powders and Diego, already by then elevated to the category of hero and myth, did not hesitate to use them. And as the depression passed it was replaced in a few heartbeats by a state of mania. With his chest puffed out once again just as it had been when he heard the refrains of the Argentine national anthem, he felt ready and prepared to take on anything.

Lifted to near divinity status in 1987 after winning the first of two Scudetto titles with Napoli, he decided on a whim he needed a Ferrari. He said to his agent at the time, Guillermo Cóppola, that he wanted a black Testarossa instead of the usual Rosso Corsa, the most famous red in that elevated world. Cóppola was not your typical agent. He took charge of Diego soon after his arrival in Italy and managed to propel him into the global footballing stratosphere. He also stood by him during the player's cocaine hell, an addiction that they both shared. The pair discovered a high level of mutual love along the way. And Guillermo would do anything for his friend.

'It was worth $430,000,' Cóppola explained on TyC Sports. 'I passed over double the cost to Napoli ... and added $130,000 for the paint. Club president Corrado Ferlaino ended up accepting because I promised him that he'd make the money back with a friendly. And there it was, a black Testarossa. The two of us got inside the car for the first time and Diego started looking around. I asked if there was an issue. "What about the stereo?" he asked. I said, "What stereo? It doesn't have one. It's a racing car, with no stereo or air conditioning. It doesn't have anything." He responded, "Well, they can shove it up their arse in that case." Ferlaino couldn't believe it.'

Maradona eventually kept the black Ferrari. In that vehicle, he often had to escape from Vespas that followed him from his house to the training ground. At the end of the session and as long as nobody screamed, touched his hair or grabbed his shoulder, Maradona would normally stay behind to sign whatever he was given.

Diego, the boy from Fiorito who looked at the world with his nose pressed up against the glass that separated him from it and yearned for a life of luxury, fell in love with Maradona, the adult, because he was able to have all he wanted and more: cars, women and jewellery. And constant adulation.

In Naples, just like in Barcelona, there were visitors to his house at all hours. Food was always available for everyone, including some journalist friends, who were part of the select group that could enter the hermetic but, if accepted, generous Diego world. The ghostwriter of two of his autobiographies, Daniel Arcucci, is one of them – they met one Christmas Eve and he was invited to spend the following day with Diego, a relationship that never ended.

Years later, at the end of May 1990, with Napoli on the verge of sealing a second Scudetto, Arcucci was sent by *El Gráfico* to cover the build-up to the Lazio game, which was a potential title-clincher. He decided to walk around Forcella, which was one of the Neopolitan areas that was controlled by the dominant Mafia group headed by Carmine Giuliano.

Signorini was the guide for the journalist and his photographer, Gerardo 'Zoilo' Horovitz. As soon as they went into Forcella, they found themselves surrounded by menacing men. At first it was subtle, and then they were suddenly trapped with no escape. 'Let me go and talk to them,' said the fitness coach.

'Everything is fine,' he said on his return. He had explained that they were friends with Diego. 'But we have to have a drink with someone.' They left the crowded street via an alley, followed by another smaller one and another one even darker. The normal sounds of the city were growing distant and voices sounded echoey. They entered a café, feeling both fascinated and frightened. The customers quickly got up. The sound of chairs moving gave way to silence. Arcucci recognised him from the pictures in the newspapers, the man sitting at the back: Carmine Giuliano.

'Vuoi café?'

'Yes, yes, of course. Thank you.'

'Do you need anything?' Carmine asked. Like El Gráfico, Argentine TV channel Telefe didn't have anyone in Italy so they asked Arcucci if he could send some filmed reports of the city. The problem was they had not sent him any equipment.

'Maybe a camera, since you're asking,' he ventured, half-jokingly.

Carmine clicked his fingers: 'A camera for the gentleman.'

That evening the journalist had dinner at Maradona's house. As the domestic staff had been given the night off, Doña Tota prepared some pasta while they watched television. Don Diego sat at the back and Diego's partner Claudia was coming in and out of the living room as they talked about the possibility of Napoli wrapping up the league the following day. It was almost midnight when somebody rang the doorbell. Diego let Claudia answer and she muttered something into his ear.

Maradona, who was in flip-flops, suddenly got up and put some shoes on. 'Come, Dani, let me show you the real Naples.' Doña Tota, Claudia, Diego and the journalist headed down to the car park. There were two Ferraris, but they all got in a Combi, that popular Volkswagen van with a curved design which in the sixties became such an icon of hippy culture. Diego was at the wheel as always. At the end of the ramp, there were views of the Bay of Naples – and a red Lancia sports car. Carmine Giuliano emerged from it, dressed in a tight suit, and went over to greet Maradona with a kiss on each cheek before both vehicles set off for the city.

The Lancia was leading the way, with the van following behind. As they approached the sea, there was a sudden swarm of Vespas, ridden by young men who had been waiting for hours for something to happen. 'Maradona, Maradona!' they shouted as they followed their idol through the empty streets of the city. 'This life!' Doña Tota said with a frustrated sigh. 'You can't go anywhere with my son.'

Dalma Salvadora Franco, who gave birth to eight children, was known to everyone as Tota: she was everyone's mum. Above all, she was Diego's protector, idealised mother, hoarder of affection and a key character in the story of her son's very public and very well documented adventures. His dad, Don Diego, or *Chitoro* as his friends called him, was born in 1927 in Esquina, in Corrientes province, north-east Argentina, or so it has been said. In his youth, he took a river boat that moved cattle from village to village and later on, when the whole family moved to Buenos Aires, he went to work in a chemical factory where he barely earned enough to make ends meet. One day Diego asked him to stop working and keep him company. His barbecues and his silences were legendary – Don Diego, a man of perhaps Indian ancestry, was happy being invisible.

At the peak of his professional career, Diego married Claudia Villafañe, his long-term girlfriend, when their daughters Dalma and Gianinna were two years and six months old respectively. There was a spectacular party at the Estadio Luna Park, Buenos Aires, and the guest list included Fidel Castro, the Argentine president Carlos Menem, Silvio Berlusconi and the president of Fiat, Gianni Agnelli. None of them could or would attend, but there were plenty of politicians, singers, actors, models and celebrities, and the full Napoli squad was also present. The eight-layer cake had a hundred ribbons hanging off it, with ninety-nine gold rings for guests to take home and one more with a diamond. But before it all kicked off, they had to wait with drinks in hands for longer than expected, because

Maradona, as usual, arrived late. He had something to do first.

Diego's friend Néstor was driving the elegant green Dodge Phantom that took the bride, groom and Guillermo Cóppola from the Sheraton Hotel to the Luna Park. The train of Claudia's dress occupied the whole back seat and Diego's head stuck out on one side against the mountain of whiteness. Suddenly he asked Néstor to turn right towards Córdoba street. 'Why? That's not the way,' Cóppola said as the walkie-talkie that connected him with the organiser at the party venue was losing signal.

'Turn here, into Sanabria. Go left after three blocks. Castañares street. That big door, number 344, stop there,' indicated Maradona after twenty minutes of directions.

'But what are we doing here? We're running very late.' Cóppola was getting angry now.

'Knock on the door, Guille. Ask for Don José.'

A woman of about seventy opened the door. 'Señora, could you tell Don José that Maradona is here?'

Twelve years earlier, a young Maradona had to travel to the headquarters of Puma in Germany with his agent Jorge Cyterszpiler to sign his first contract. The kit sponsor had sent them three first-class air tickets. Diego invited Claudia. That inspired Don José, the local ironmonger, to contemptuously say something like, 'Those Villafañes shouldn't let the girl go with that footballer! Who does he think he is?'

Don José, who was wearing light-blue pyjamas and slippers, found Maradona outside his door. He took a step back, his eyes wide with astonishment. '*Buenas noches*,' he managed to say.

'*Hola*, I'm here with the girl that you said I shouldn't take to Germany when I was sixteen. She's my wife now and the mother of my daughters, Don José. Watch the wedding party on television . . . Now, Guille, we can go.'

Debt settled.

Those years at the end of the eighties were not a calm period. Maradona's philosophy was that we are all born with a date stamp on us, so best to savour every moment because we don't come out of this life alive. Hedonism should have its limits, however. Instead, Diego never accepted half-measures – he embodied excess, a messianic character who often spoke of himself in the third person, a man who lacked boundaries. We all watched a lot of those transgressions, as multiple cameras kept rolling or taking pictures next to him: we saw him kissing girls and men, drunk, high. Joking with his two girls. Funny. Followed, surrounded. Asphyxiated. Sharp, clever. Lost. Cheeky.

Once, in London, his inseparable Cóppola suggested going to see a nearby Range Rover dealership because he coveted one. As they were leaving their Park Lane hotel the particular model he fancied happened to pull up right in front of them. 'Two guys got out' explained Cóppola on Argentine television show *Pura Química.* "'Maradona, Maradona! Can we take a photo? Can we get an autograph?" "Sure. Go to the reception and ask for a pen and paper."' While they did that, Maradona and Cóppola looked at each other. Diego smiled. 'Shall we . . .?'

'We got in the Rover and drove away, went to a sports bar nearby, parked anywhere,' Cóppola remembered. Two hours must have passed since they'd borrowed the car. 'We went back and the two men were just sitting on the steps where we'd left them. There were more hugs, they took photos, gave us some shoes, shirts and pullovers that were in the boot and they came to pick us up the next day to take us to the airport.'

When he returned to Boca in 1995, still endlessly hunting for the ultimate sensation, he purchased two visually arresting Ferrari F355 Spiders, red this time and with dainty noses. He had collected quite a few automobiles which he used on alternate days. He'd drive a Porsche sports car on Mondays. On Tuesday, he would talk to journalists sticking his head out of the window of a tall Mitsubishi pickup truck. On Wednesdays, he would turn up for training in a proper lorry, a blue Scania 360.

Eventually Maradona hung up his boots in La Bombonera. The sending off, the evening where he let Diego the footballer go, was in 2001, years after he had played an official match for the last time. He told the packed-out stadium, which included many of his former teammates, that in spite of everything, 'the ball remains unstained'.

But he was not really going anywhere.

A new challenge had started – keep being Maradona, and, as Arcucci once said, keep scoring a goal against England. His narcissistic and manic-depressive personality, defined in psychiatric classifications as bipolar, dominated his decisions. After retirement, he decided he wouldn't allow the man he inhabits the possibility of enjoying a good life. He preferred to be the man everybody wanted him to be. Depression was followed by near-death experiences, resurrection and new falls, all of which were multiplied and accelerated when his parents passed away in the second decade of this century. Then the floor became muddy, unstable.

And when there are stimulants at hand, that inability to say 'enough' became a danger to Diego himself and to those who occasionally surrounded him. His life became a street without an exit. A drug addict, when quitting, presents a neurobiological vulnerability that makes them sensitive to relapse. 'Perversion' is how psychoanalysts label his strong inclination to write his own rules and break them too, which accounts for the many incidents that have occurred in different public places where he was invited and then ordered, or finally forced, to leave, often with some form of violence by Diego, whether verbal or physical.

His Argentina teammate Jorge Valdano once said that 'many people think that Maradona's problem has been his friends, but I believe that the problem of his friends is Maradona'. His friends either paid due homage to him or split from him. Among those who chose the second option there was a legion of ex-friends and ex-lovers who tried to advise him for his own good but were fired. He fought against everyone, even the closest – Cyterszpiler, his wife Claudia, Cóppola. And in a very public way. The judicial wars were endless; there are still many outstanding claims.

His health deteriorated in the last ten years of his life, but the biggest hurt was to realise that, in Arcucci's words, 'he did not feel Maradona any more'. And clearly, when you look back at his last managerial roles in Mexico with Sinaola or Argentina with Gimnasia y Esgrima, nobody managed to convince him that it was not necessary to continue trying to be Maradona. He spent his life looking for peace but when he found something that could resemble it, he ran away from it.

Diego abused his body. He stopped using cocaine and other substances that made it possible for him to believe he was above anything, but he never stopped being addicted. To alcohol. To sleeping tablets. To adulation. To the destruction of his own life.

He spent his final few days in the dimly lit house he had rented during his last health scare. His bed, placed in the kitchen so that he wouldn't have to negotiate the stairs, would become his bier.

Death became the only limit he could not transgress – he passed away just after he turned sixty from an acute secondary lung oedema due to exacerbated chronic heart failure. But it could have been anything.

Diego only lived nineteen years without the ball.

A Chevrolet pickup truck of the Scientific Police of Buenos Aires took him to the hospital for an autopsy. An ambulance, a white Fiat Doblo van, drove him to the Casa Rosada, the presidential residence that hosted a massive vigil, a continuous parade in front of his coffin of all types of Argentinians, some arrived from hundreds of miles away, eager to pay him homage. They were not saying goodbye; they were enthroning him. Authorities and Claudia decided to close the doors of the Casa Rosada too early. Prevented from getting close to the Diego of the People, the crowds rioted. Violence broke out and there were arrests.

A dark grey Peugeot hearse drove him to the Jardín Bella Vista cemetery, where he was buried next to his parents by those who were with him at the start, or those few left anyway – Claudia, Dalma, Giannina, Cóppola.

Peace had finally found him.

If only we could have warned him, when he posed for his first photos, shy and clean, with a ball in his hand, what was coming, if only we were able to push him in a different direction.

How to explain Diego Armando Maradona, the footballer? The two goals against England in Mexico 86 could be enough. A whole book is surely not sufficient. It is a story that can be seen in big headlines, but is better understood when read between the lines – a chronicle of epic feats and anecdotes, paradoxes and mistakes, contradictions and rebellions. What you have in your hands is the path walked by the player, from his origins to that day in which he left the ball behind in La Bombonera.

In order to write it, I had to go back to where it all started, outside Buenos Aires, to that Villa Fiorito shanty town, but nobody wanted to take me. It was my last day in the Argentine capital in early 2020. My plan was to pay a visit before setting off for Ezeiza airport to fly home. 'Do you really want to go?' one driver asked me several times before reluctantly accepting the request.

We exited the motorway and went around a couple of round-abouts. Neither of us was speaking. I didn't know what awaited, although I did have an idea. As the roads were becoming narrower and less smooth, the houses started to be small boxes with half-finished fences and some with neglected plants. Bags of rubbish rotted outside tired looking gardens, a man passed steering a horse-drawn cart piled up with cardboard. Children were kicking a ball about barefoot in the uneven dirt road we were driving through and women carried enormous bags that were filled with God knows what. I guessed possibly not much had changed since Francis Cornejo's first trip there.

There was not one sign en route to the place where Maradona's foundations were laid, to the street where he learned those things that are not taught, to that *potrero* paddock, the waste ground where he played football for days without end – in fact, today it is a land where other shacks with sheet metal roofs have been built.

It was halfway through the afternoon of a warm December. We slowed up behind a man in shorts and no top on who was walking down the middle of the unpaved road to avoid mountains of rubble. Without stopping and having barely wound down his window, the taxi driver asked with an apologetic tone for Diego's house. 'Over there, 200 metres away.'

'There it is, OK? Can we go now?' my intimidated friend asked.

We were finally outside Maradona's first home, the engine kept running. The garden was overgrown but, towards the back, you could make out a heavily shaded bungalow. In front of the door that Doña Tota once opened to Francis, a man in a white vest swiftly got off his rocking chair.

'What are you looking for?'

'Nothing, sir. My friend here just wanted to see the . . .' responded the taxi driver while putting the car in gear and driving off. On the left, we passed a dirt pitch with no markings and a single goal.

Just after Diego's sixtieth birthday, the local authority of Lomas de Zamora, which has authority over Fiorito, declared his first residence 'cultural patrimony' after they promised its occupant a new home. The day Maradona died an artist contracted by the town hall painted Diego's face with a yellow aura around it on the wall of the bungalow. 'God's house', it read underneath.

# Part I

# El Pelusa

# 1
# DON DIEGO, THE FATHER

'Don Diego's father went barefoot.' That is the expression that people used, even those who never knew him, to describe the humble origins of Diego Armando Maradona's grandfather. It's not a derogatory description. Rather, it's an acknowledgement of a simpler lifestyle, one that harks back to the indigenous peoples of Argentina, a forgotten Argentina. Don Diego Maradona never got involved in those discussions – maybe he went barefoot, maybe he didn't.

In reality, very little, if anything, is known about Don Diego's father. He was born into an impoverished community and fathered many children, some of whom were known to him, others not. His life was unconventional. Nominally a Catholic, he viewed life through his own particular lens. He had 'faith' but would have been hard pressed to discuss what that faith meant and to whom it was directed.

'It seems as if he descended from indigenous people,' stated Fernando Signorini on WhatsApp. 'I was told that by a friend of Diego's dad from Esquina, a city in the province of Corrientes.' Nothing in the Esquina civil registry indicated the indigenous origins of Don Diego's family branch. What makes complicated any research in that direction is that he took his mum's surname (Maradona), as his dad disappeared from their lives very early.

What we know is that Don Diego, *Chitoro* to his friends, was born on 12 November 1927. The surname is not Italian, despite the way it sounds: Mara-do-na. It certainly has that Italian rhythm, particularly when Neapolitans say it with an emphasis on the 'n'. In fact, the surname seems to come from Lugo in the Spanish region of Galicia, possibly from a town south of Ribadeo or Barreiros. It could be Arante, Vilamartín Grande or Vilamartín Pequeño, where many Maradonas live.

There was a Francisco Fernández de Maradona, born in the northern Spanish village of San Pedro de Arante, who in 1745 or 1748, depending on which document you read, headed down to north-west Argentina and established himself in San Juan de Cuyo. He was, we know, the first Maradona in Argentina. During the 1920s, a relation of Francisco Fernández, an engineer called Santiago Maradona, was the governor of the province of Santiago del Estero and was the only Maradona in town. Santiago did not marry, but he did have children who kept the surname, including *Chitoro's* mother, the footballer's grandmother. Based on the odd photo that survived over the years, Diego's maternal great-grandfather, the engineer, looked like Don Diego and by extension like Diego as well, with a round face, prominent chin and chubby cheeks.

A descendant of that first Maradona in Argentina recently received a law degree from the University of Buenos Aires. José Ignacio Maradona told the website *Enganche* some more details about the footballer's roots: 'As there are few of us Maradonas, we know exactly where we come from. When Diego broke through, however, nobody knew to which branch of the family tree he belonged. So my father went up to Don Diego during a match. Don Diego didn't know his own father and his surname came from his mother, who was from Santiago del Estero. At a very young age, he went with her to Esquina, in the province of Corrientes.'

It had always been said that Don Diego was from Esquina, but it turns out that he was born an eleven-hour car journey away. Back then, however, it would have taken much longer, even days, for Don Diego and his single mother to make that trip. What were they escaping from? Why such a long journey?

So Don Diego was born in Santiago del Estero, the capital of the province with the same name, that stands on the banks of the Dulce river in the north of the country. Maradona's paternal grandfather left only a very small visible trace, which *Chitoro* could not help fill.

Maybe, just maybe, he was a member of the indigenous people that had lived there for centuries and who had been subjugated and evangelised by the Spanish conquistadors. Exploited. Impoverished. Ignored. In fact, they were practically exterminated as the plains were colonised, and their natural habitat was gradually destroyed as colonisers arrived on the newly laid railways.

The indigenous communities found work as lumberjacks and demolition workers in the Santiago mountains; there were very few other opportunities. They lived by their own rules. They did not register their children and often moved home. While they definitely knew where they had come from, they did not know where they were going.

Don Diego, now a teenager settled in Esquina, met Doña Tota, whom he was destined to marry. And that is where it all started for him. He would discuss little about his past before that encounter, as if everything before his wife came into his life (living without a dad, the moving around, the starting over) were clothes that did not fit him.

Far away from Esquina, something that was going to shake Don Diego's world took place. Juan Domingo Perón was elected president of Argentina in 1946. He had been swept to power on a populist mandate that promised a new industrial age and work for all. His socio-economic policies improved the lives of workers and imposed increased state control on the economy. He and his wife Evita fought for emigrants' rights.

In the fifties, Buenos Aires became a magnet for the rural poor, particularly from the north of the country, who flooded the capital in response to Perón's rhetoric. Diego Armando's parents were among them, drawn to the capital by the prospect of work.

In fact, Doña Tota had already lived in Buenos Aires during her youth working at a family member's house, but loneliness had caused her to return to Esquina to be near Don Diego again. When her sister later moved to Villa Fiorito, Doña Tota convinced her husband that they could not survive on *changa* (seasonal short-term work) with their small boat with which *Chitoro* transported livestock and materials to the islands around their town.

They decided to leave everything behind, but Doña Tota was to go first to check things out. She left for Buenos Aires with their daughter María and her mother, Salvadora Cariolicci. Once established, she wrote to ask Don Diego to join her; she had found a place they could move to in a town called Villa Fiorito. The day arrived to say goodbye to his small boat, which he sold for 3,500 pesos, and his old life. He shed silent tears. A large boat transported him and his second daughter Rita over 1,000km down the Paraná River with their two suitcases and an oversized blanket that held some clothes, pots and pans. Everything else was left behind.

*Chitoro* soon discovered that Villa Fiorito was a derelict neighbourhood filled with houses made of cardboard, wood and sheet metal, with unpaved dirt roads. It was a destination for migrants and a ghetto for the marginalised. Not too far away, separated by the black waters of Argentina's most polluted river, lay the city of Buenos Aires.

There was a house earmarked for them, but when the Maradonas went to move there, they found that it had already been rented out. There was another one not too far away at 523 Azamor which, like the rest of them, had neither electricity nor gas. Don Diego had to head out to look for some sheet metal for the roof and something to sleep on for the first night. It was not what he had envisaged, but he accepted it stoically. It was no moment for the 'Indian inside him to burst out', as his friends would say when he emitted the odd swear word, a sign that someone had overstepped the bounds of decency.

Soon after, *Chitoro* found a job at Tritumol, a bone-crushing factory in the chemical industry. He would leave home at five in the morning and get back completely shattered at ten at night. Even so, his salary did not cover everything, but there were other people around helping out – Doña Tota's sister, or the beloved Uncle Cirilo. Don Diego's brother, short in stature and hence called *Tapón* (small cork lid), had been an amateur goalkeeper and lived nearby in Fiorito. Everyone had something to share.

Doña Tota and Don Diego had already had four daughters – Ana, Rita, María Rosa and Lili – when Diego Armando was born on a sunny 30 October in 1960 at the Evita Polyclinic in Lanús. Diego's first memory was of his mother looking for him to take him to school and of hiding among the cornfields that grew on the border of Villa Fiorito until it was time to go back home.

The house had a kitchen, but no running water. There was a bedroom for the parents and grandmother and another for the siblings, of whom there were eight in the end. 'On days when it was absolutely pouring, the rain would perforate the sheet metal roof and the dirt floor would get filled with dark patches that looked like little bugs,' was Diego's description to Gabi Cociffi on *Infobae*. 'Mum then shouted, "Go and get the buckets!" and we'd all run around the house putting buckets under the leaks until they were full and we'd then throw the water out the window.'

Some evenings, *Chitoro* would drink tea, maybe have a slice of bread and let his children eat at the table. Many times he was seemingly not hungry. Neither was his mum.

The kid played football for up to ten hours sometimes, sometimes on his own, hitting the ball on the kerb, or against plant pots, unconsciously creating neuroreceptors during those many hours of practice that were shaping his brain and his talent. 'We used to play on the *potrero*, no markings anywhere, with dirt flying all over the place, from dawn till dusk. I would then go home completely filthy. What a mess I looked! And of course my dad would then want to whack me as you are not supposed to do that with your clothes, and I'd escape from him and dodge his reach . . . which helped refine my dribbling.' As a kid, Maradona never spoke much to his father and if he was ever hit by him, Diego would say, it was because times were different back then.

Diego remembered how he used to like doing things with the ball that others found difficult. 'It's not my fault, is it? I can control the ball with my heel and when my teammate wanted to do so, it hit his knee. I don't get that from my old man because he was a terrible footballer. My uncle said to him, "*Pelu* certainly didn't get his football skills from you!"' *Pelu* is short for *Pelusa*, 'Big Hair', as he had, from a child, an abundance of hair.

The day Francis Cornejo came home to check Diego's age, *Chitoro* was out working in the factory, even though it was a Saturday – he always said yes to any extra work. The coach got to meet him one day when he came to training with his son, after a journey that involved a train and a couple of buses.

'My dad would take me on a bus to train and he'd be absolutely exhausted,' said Diego on *Infobae*. 'He'd hold onto the handrail and I'd be under his arm on my tiptoes to support him because he'd fall asleep standing up. That's how we travelled, supporting each other.'

Cornejo discovered a man of few words but strong convictions. From early on, Don Diego and Doña Tota went to all the games with the Cebollitas group, sitting in the cab of José Trotta's pickup truck, while coach Francis travelled with the boys in the back.

Those trips allowed the family to discover the world. Maradona remembered walking over the Alsina bridge about a hundred metres from the house, looking down at the dirty river water between the wooden planks. On the other side the market of Pompeya belonged to others: toy shops, shoe stands, shirts hanging from rails ('with shirts that my sister wanted, that I wanted', Diego recalled). Going shopping was not something they did often.

There was instead an age rotation. Today, María can buy shoes. A couple of weeks later, it is your turn, *Pelu*. What do you want?

'A little wooden horse.'

'Don't be daft, something to wear.'

'Ah, *papi*, a shirt then.'

'Which one?' And the chosen shirt will be with them for ever, as it moved from one kid to another till it became only useful as a dish cloth.

'Dad, do you have a pair of underpants to spare?' Diego would ask when in need.

Once Maradona was asked by the journalist Diego Borinsky if he ever thought of stealing, as many of his contemporaries did. 'No, no, my old man would have kicked the shit out of me. He taught me the best way he could. Whatever I did afterwards is because I learned to do bad things; it had nothing to do with him.'

In Diego's Cebollitas years and before making it into the first team at Argentinos Juniors when he was a fifteen-year-old, his father washed and polished his boots until they looked like new, quite a contrast with the others, worn and unkempt.

Even when, aged eighteen, Diego became the breadwinner for the family and asked his dad to stop working, his parents were still in charge at home. Diego needed that to be the case, always searching for guidance and clear, unquestionable reference points to cling on to.

His dad's quiet nature allowed Doña Tota to prattle away until Don Diego grew tired of it or something bothered him. Short in stature, he became a giant when he wanted to be heard. And then even Doña Tota had to be quiet. Sometimes a glance sufficed. If the fitness coach Fernando Signorini needed to set Diego straight, he would often defer to Don Diego. If he was there, the larking around soon stopped.

It wasn't fear he commanded, but respect. All the bravura that he would display later in life, challenging and mocking those in power, was a rebellion not against authority per se, but rather a protest at the abuses of power that overlooked the hardships of people like them and the half a million who lived cheek by jowl in Villa Fiorito and whose plight was mirrored in some 800 settlements dotted around Buenos Aires.

Maradona the child was always sensible, polite, attentive, even if a little cheeky. Once Doña Tota found out that her son's bad marks at school had magically improved – somehow he had paid off a teacher. She told her husband. Don Diego banned him for training for almost two weeks. Anybody breaking rules drove *Chitoro* mad. He was meticulous and a pedant. If he said, 'We're going fishing in Corrientes tomorrow morning at five,' he would be in his car at that time and would wait for no one.

It was the only way to maintain order in a sheet metal and cardboard world.

Many years later, after living first in a house near the Argentinos Juniors stadium, Don Diego and Doña Tota moved to a flat purchased by their son in Villa Devoto, a residential neighbourhood in Buenos Aires, with a large courtyard, a television that was almost always on, cigarettes always lit in both parents' lips and, of course, a barbecue of which Don Diego was the king. It was easier to get Diego off the pitch than Don Diego away from it.

The journeys to see Cebollitas matches continued at the first team of Argentinos, Boca Juniors and also in Barcelona. The Maradona home in the upper part of the Catalan capital had a huge kitchen in which Doña Tota would spend hours making food for all the people coming and going without any sort of schedule. Don Diego watched everything from a corner, invisible but omnipresent. The devotion they both felt for their son was undying. The more they watched him entering his artificial paradise, the more they sensed his weaknesses and felt a deep allegiance beyond anything they felt for anything or anyone else, maybe trapped in an asphyxiating feeling of responsibility, lack of control and sharing a life with a different being.

Whenever *Chitoro* was asked what it was like to be Diego's father, he struggled to keep his composure. 'When I go down the street, everyone stops me. "Congratulations on your son," they say. And I don't know how to answer that,' and by then the voice would break. 'I know that he's the best of all time, but I assure them he's a better son than a footballer.' He would then shed tears.

'He's a cry baby,' is how his son often described him, while struggling not to end up breaking down himself. 'I'd like to be one per cent of what my old man is. He's noble and he has dignity. He fought during his whole life to feed us. I wanted to be like him when I was little and I still do as an adult. I only want one hour of the tranquillity my old man has in his head. Then I can die happily.'

The law of life usually dictates that one day the father, Don Diego, has to depart this world.

After a long convalescence with respiratory and heart problems and over a month at Los Arcos hospital in Palermo, Buenos Aires, Don Diego said his final farewell at eighty-seven.

Guillermo Blanco, who had known the teenage Maradona, travelled to Buenos Aires and arranged to meet Fernando Signorini so both arrived at the same time at Don Diego's wake. They travelled very late at night to avoid the media, although there were still many people there. A very overweight Diego was sitting down, having just flown in from Dubai, where he was living at the time.

'Diego, *El Profe* and Guille are here,' his secretary told him. Guillermo looked for the real Maradona in his eyes. After five decades of adventures, Blanco saw his tiredness, but there was little sign of the child he was convinced had ended up trapped inside.

It had been many years since he had seen either of them. Diego slowly got up off his chair, his girth apparent, his sad face setting the tone. He slapped Signorini on the chest once and then again. It felt like an eternity between each slap, almost as if it were the exaggerated and defining scene of a theatre production.

Maradona not Diego, the character not the boy, was brushing his grief under the carpet with the performance. Signorini and Blanco were sure he would suffer even more later, when he was alone. He would then remember his father cleaning his boots. Falling asleep in the bus that took them to training. He would ache with sadness and loss. But at that moment, at the wake, Maradona was acting and in doing so he was delaying the pain.

'I was thinking of you today, you son of a bitch', he told Signorini. 'Remember that day we went to face Roma in our first year at Napoli. I couldn't sleep and I called you into my room. You came and we sat on the floor. I told you that I'd prefer to die myself than see my mother or father die, but they'd both already passed away. Do you remember what you said to me?'

Signorini tried to smile, but grimaced instead. 'I said that you were being a pussy because it's the natural way of life. In no way should you prefer your parents' suffering over your own.'

Don Diego's wake lasted all night and the party left around midday to attend the private burial ceremony at the Jardín Bella Vista cemetery on the outskirts of Buenos Aires.

Diego Armando Maradona, at the age of fifty-five, had become an orphan.

# 2
# THE MOTHER, DOÑA TOTA

'He's coming.' The packed-out stadium was chanting his name again.

*Dieeeegooooooooooo, Dieeegooooooooo . . .*

Far in the distance, you could see a group of people getting just behind the huge inflatable wolf's head with an open snout from which Maradona would emerge into the stadium. Amongst them, a white cap with the number 10 on it. 'He's here!'

Like a Roman gladiator entering the arena, the silhouette of the new Gimnasia y Esgrima La Plata coach began to materialise. Slowly, with the pace allowed by knees which had recently been operated upon and carrying excessive body weight, it was a warrior that had seen better days. A fifty-seven-year-old Maradona had found a new theatre where he could act out the next few years of his faltering career, in fact his last one. As leader and coach he promised to lead Gimnasia y Esgrima La Plata to great things. The club knew they were in for a busy, public and interesting journey and that was all that mattered to them.

After retiring as a footballer, he had taken project-management roles in the UAE, for Mexican club Sinaloa and even with the Argentina national team. Often his teams sensed the envy of others and their desire for him to fail. Whatever. It certainly beat anonymity.

*Dieeeegooooooooooo, Dieeegooooooooo . . .*

Every step he took towards the pitch of his new stadium, encouraged by the swelling noise from the stands, awoke a pain or a memory. Brutal tackles on pitches in Spain and Italy had left an indelible mark on him. His prosthetic knee was protesting, same as a painful shoulder, and the anxiety that he treated with sedatives had left him in a perpetual state of weariness. On the inside, cocaine had redesigned his interior landscape, and on a host of occasions his heart had reacted adversely to the historic abuse.

Maradona was not embarrassed by admitting to other cosmetic touch-ups. Gastric bands, hernias and kidney stones had all left their mark. The reconstructive surgery on his upper lip from when his dog bit him also stood out, and that was just what you could see. There were other items of personal baggage that provided relief or generated sorrow depending on the day: he acknowledged that he had a minimum of five children and six more paternity suits were proceeding. He had fought with Claudia inside and outside court-rooms and television studios. He had dozens of court cases pending at any time.

And he'd lost his parents.

'Diego, my son, my eyes, my boy.'

He thought he heard those words in the wolf tunnel and felt a tightness in his throat. Did he just see what he thought he had seen? Then, looking confused, he emerged blinking into the sunlight of the crowded stadium.

*Dieeeeeegoooooooo!*

Diego Maradona hid his face while hugging club president Gabriel Pellegrino as he tried, unsuccessfully, to compose himself. He was unable to hold back the tears.

'When I was coming out of the tunnel, my mum suddenly ap-peared,' he later stated. 'I think there's a reason for everything.'

Plunged into the deepest emotion, yet soaking up the jubilation, he took another painful step forward, as if carrying the weight of the entire universe on his shoulders. Easing himself into a golf buggy, the driver, off script, handed him an Argentina jersey to sign.

'I don't think I ever stopped being happy,' Diego had previously said. 'The issue is ... both my parents passed away; that's my only problem. I'd give everything I have today for my mother to come through that door.'

And that day in the stadium she reappeared.

La Tota, the people's mother, had passed away eight years earlier, aged eighty-one.

It was national news, something unprecedented for a footballer's mother. A minute's silence was observed ahead of every fixture on matchday 15 of the Torneo Apertura. The Boca players wore black armbands, while Napoli fans chanted her name and displayed a flag saying, 'Rest in peace, Mamma'. A newspaper even went with the headline 'The mother of football has died'.

Maradona spent twenty-eight hours travelling from Dubai to try to get there in time to bid her farewell. 'Come straight back,' was the message from family doctor Alfredo Cahe. Doña Tota was in intensive care at Los Arcos hospital in Palermo. She was in and out of medical care in the final months of her life, as she suffered from kidney and heart failure. During a previous visit to Buenos Aires, before a relapse, Maradona showed her his new tattoo on his back, a turquoise rose, with words in italic script: 'Tota, I love you'.

But Diego did not arrive in time: still on the plane, Dr Cahe told him Doña Tota had died. Numb with shock, he travelled directly to the wake house in Tres Arroyos. Wearing a white shirt, dark tie, black jacket and hiding his puffed eyes behind sunglasses, arm in arm with his new partner, Verónica Ojeda, he spent the following hours crying next to the coffin. Nearby, he could find the comfort of Claudia Villafañe, Dalma, Gianinna, his seven siblings and Don Diego.

'My girlfriend, my queen, my everything has gone,' Diego repeated as La Tota's remains were buried in the Jardín Bella Vista cemetery on a hot November day in 2011.

Son of a culture dominated by immigrants from southern Italy and Spain, with their strong religious beliefs and adulation for the self-sacrificing and incomparable mother who always forgives the wayward son, he had lost the woman that never made a mistake, the one who defended him 'from windmills'. Maradona, who never overcame the Oedipus complex, used to say jokingly that his mother married his father because she met him before meeting Diego himself.

His mum admitted something unspeakable: Diego was the son she loved the most. 'She had a soft spot for me,' Maradona admitted. 'The day I turned forty-six, I looked at her and said, "You're the first woman of my life, my eternal girlfriend. I owe everything to you, Tota, and I'll always love you more and more.'"

She was the idealised mother of hundreds of Argentine folk songs, of Tangos, Milongas or Chacareras, all cultural symbols whose sources are real feelings but also constructed realities. In the popular '*Cómo se hace un tango*' (how to do the tango), the following is sung to *Her*: 'Ears at the ready, the person who loves you is going to speak/today, tomorrow, at any time because, for me/you aren't just my mother, but my girlfriend.'

'Singer Joan Manuel Serrat said once that you stop being a son in order to be a parent when your own parent dies,' explains Guillermo Blanco, Maradona's press officer during his time in Barcelona and the first years in Naples. 'Diego was deeply affected by both parents' deaths, especially his mother's. There was a very special kind of love between them.'

His siblings accepted Diego's special status in their mother's eyes and in the world's. Some still live close to the Argentinos Juniors ground, having been bypassed by destiny, mere mortal relations of a demi-god. You can't escape that, whatever you do. Lalo and Hugo decided to challenge perceptions and wanted to have a career in football, but they never set the world alight and remained as the 'brothers of'.

Doña Tota, comfortable with the role of mother not just of the Maradonas, but of the People, was the sun around whom everyone orbited. She was the head of the pack. 'When Doña Tota said something, it was gospel and nobody, not even Diego, dared argue,' recalled Fernando Signorini. She was more loquacious than Don Diego unless she was watching television or was bustling in and out carrying plates and trays to an always laid table.

Although she spent long periods of time with him in Europe, the ever-loving mother needed to feel wanted and loved in return. She was jealous of Claudia and all the other girlfriends, which made life a bit difficult for them, and Diego's absences left her feeling frustrated. She often complained that he had 'left her behind' in Buenos Aires. One day, Diego remembered hearing on the phone from Doña Tota how lonely she was. In the background you could hear family and friends, constantly surrounded by people.

La Tota thought she had prepared herself for the inevitable: that as her son grew up and his talent became a high-value commodity, the Old World would take him away from her. That is just what FC Barcelona sporting director Nicolau Casaus wrote about her in his report during the initial negotiations to sign Maradona: 'I imagine she must be a similar age to her husband, but given her dishevelled appearance, it's difficult to say. When I talk to her about her son potentially joining Barcelona, she just says, "God willing."'

Football was a source of joy and trouble for Doña Tota. It was the bicycle chain that allowed her to get away from Villa Fiorito and accelerated life at a previously unimaginable speed, but that also caused accidents. 'When we were watching on TV the Under-20 World Cup in Japan, Argentina went 1-0 down against the Soviet Union,' recalls Guillermo Blanco. 'What did La Tota do? She was suddenly no longer in the kitchen with us, she went to bed, she could not handle the emotions. She then came back, Argentina scored through an Alves penalty and she celebrated. There's even a photo in *El Gráfico*. She then went back to bed. She came back again and Argentina scored a second through Ramón Díaz. She went to bed once again before coming back in time for Diego to score a free-kick. It was total euphoria. Everyone was shouting and hugging.'

Maradona's parents did have a passion for football, rather than it being imposed on them. Don Diego even had a playing career as a right-winger for some local teams in Esquina, although not a particularly successful one. 'Football was one of the few things that the poor had,' states Blanco. They rarely missed a match that *El Pelusa* played, going right back to his Cebollitas days. *Chitoro* used to make all sorts of adjustments to the shift rota at the factory to be able to watch him. Seated in the cab of José Trotta's pickup truck, they often went off to socialise and have barbecues with middle-class families, which most of the Cebollitas youngsters belonged to, with residences near the Argentinos Juniors pitch, an hour and a world away from their home.

Maradona took his mother to a pizzeria in Pompeya after receiving his first pay cheque as a footballer. 'Just the two of us alone, like a couple. All the salary went,' explained Diego years later.

At home Doña Tota and Don Diego set the limits. If he was the punishing father with moments of fire in his belly, she was more often than not the conciliatory mother. One day, Diego ignored La Tota's request not to leave the house. He went off to play football and returned home with his recently acquired Flecha trainers broken and filthy. It had taken his parents weeks to save up for them. Don Diego's rage turned into physical force. Doña Tota heard what was happening and ran in pointing her finger and shouting, 'If you touch my son, I'll kill you tonight when you're asleep.'

She would get Diego to buy some slices of pork or beef to add substance to meals that had to feed eleven people: the eight siblings, both parents and the grandmother. But on those celebrated occasions, Diego would have the biggest piece and the sisters were served plenty of salad. 'The poor girls chewed lettuce like crazy,' recalled Maradona in his autobiography, *Yo Soy El Diego*. They were not the only ones. La Tota would sometimes complain about a stomach ache at mealtimes and she would not eat, so she could distribute whatever she had among her children. His dad often did the same.

'Sometimes I'd be washing the only socks that the children had until five in the morning so they were clean for school,' Doña Tota told *Gente* magazine. 'I remember I had to wash six school overalls. Six! Just imagine. When it rained, I had to dry them on the heater and I'd also get up at any time to iron them.'

When it rained and the roof leaked, they collected some of it as there was no running water. If there was not enough, Diego was in charge of filling the empty twenty-litre oil cans from the communal tap, which was the start of his weight training. That water was used for cooking, drinking and washing. If it was cold, hair washing was left for another day.

As there were so many of them they lived in a state of perpetual chaos. But when Doña Tota had the television on in the room that served as the lounge, dining room and kitchen, smoking her untipped cigarettes, the children all retired to the back of the room and maintained silence. Her own mum watched on without batting an eyelid, while smoking a pipe, almost a part of the furniture.

In the morning, Diego would walk from Calle Azamor to Remedios de Escalada de San Martín school, which he attended just because he had to. He was biding his time until football could relieve him of other responsibilities and obligations.

Out of school he spent his time on the dirt pitches next to his house, playing with friends, or competing in matches for Estrella Roja, which his old man had founded. He fell asleep embracing the first ball that he'd been given at the age of three from his cousin Beto, whom Diego adored.

At the age of thirty, Doña Tota left home with a swollen belly and contractions to make her way to the Evita clinic in Lanús with her husband and sister-in-law, Ana María. They walked three blocks towards the single track at Fiorito station and took the tram to Lanús. They got off two and a half blocks from the hospital. La Tota was experiencing sharp pains and could not stand. Before entering, she saw something shining on the kerb by the pavement and bent down. It was a star-shaped brooch, shiny on one side and dark on the other. A metaphor for the future perhaps. She pinned it to her blouse. Fifteen minutes later, at 7.05am on 30 October 1960, Diego was born 'with hair all over'.

Diego was her fifth child and first son. La Tota had arrived from Esquina five years earlier, in search of a better future, alongside daughter Ana and her mother, Salvadora Cariolichi, the daughter of Mateo Kriolić, who was born on 29 September 1847 in Praputnjak, a town near the city of Bakar, 150km from Zagreb in west Croatia.

From all these confluences had just emerged Diego Armando Maradona.

# 3
# GOYO CARRIZO, A FRIEND STILL IN VILLA FIORITO

Goyo leans back in his wicker chair, smooths his hand over his bald head and gives a tired smile. He glances at the house opposite, his own house, where he has lived since he was born and where three generations of his family have slept and died. He had told the journalist Diego Borinsky from *El Gráfico* to come to his son's house, where he now sits. It's still unfinished, but the patio is bigger than his.

Was he doing the right thing? Talking now? Goyo had always felt uncomfortable with the attention he received because of his close association with Diego Armando Maradona. Yes, they were friends, yes he took *El Pelusa* to the trial that began his stellar career, but now? Such a distance had grown between them. And what of his own journey? The story of the child who could have been a very good player but did not fully make it had some merit, but it was his adulthood that he didn't want the world to see.

Gregorio Salvador Carrizo, Goyo, is short, slim and appears older than his age – he was born nine days before Maradona. He and Diego were in different classes at school. One day he spotted *El Pelusa* kicking a 'ball' made out of a bag filled with biscuit wrappers. He'd taken over a small, flat area of grass which a floral border denoted was strictly out of bounds. Goyo went up to him and called for the improvised ball. The two boys, no more than seven, started kicking it about until they were called back into their classrooms. Soon after, Goyo bumped into Diego at the station and they started chatting.

'Where do you live?'

'On Calle Azamor,' Diego replied.

'Ah, just a few blocks from my house,' Goyo told his new friend.

'I'm going for a kickabout, my dad is taking me, are you coming?' *El Pelusa* said to him one day, and from that moment on they were inseparable.

'Here, on this pitch?' asked Goyo.

'Why not?'

Well, one might think, because cows and horses passed by and somebody had marked off that area with wires, so in theory you were not allowed. And on top of that the grass was very tall. Nobody had ever seen anyone around those parts, so, Diego suggested, if the grass was somehow cut or more likely stepped on often enough, they could mark the area out and make a goal using thick cane.

Today there is a pitch fifty metres away from Goyo's house. Sometimes it is a mass of mud and rusty tins, just like the path leading to it. The *potrero*, symbol of a life where you have to avoid problems and debris, is used often by local kids, who learn very quickly that to overcome the obstacles you get better results when you join forces.

As Maradona said back in his day, everything is a struggle in Villa Fiorito and not much has changed in five decades. During their childhood, if they were able to eat, they ate. If not, that was that – it was not even worth talking about. With no running water, Goyo and Diego would go together to fetch water from the standpipe. They were up and down in their Flechas or Pamperos trainers, which they wore every day until they literally fell apart.

There was a cesspit full of all kinds of things not far from where Diego lived. He must have been under ten on the day when he fell and ended up in excrement up to his neck after chasing the ball. Once in it, he kept looking for the ball and going deeper and deeper. Where was the ball? His uncle ran to save him, half-submerged in the mud, stretched out and grabbed Diego's arm. Goyo, of course, never let him forget it.

*El Lalo* and *El Turco*, Diego's younger brothers and early sparring partners in the games at the *potrero* or in the streets, discovered early on that the world is unfair and that if you are tiny, you cannot get the ball from the older kids – not from *El Goyo* and *El Pelusa* anyway. The Maradonas used to be a large but harmonious family, but for a long time Diego had no longer felt close to his two brothers, and they stopped talking. Despite wanting to include them in many things, he lost them and that often moved him to tears. *El Turco* lives in Naples, *El Lalo* remained in Argentina. The death of their parents brought them much closer, although contact with Diego was never easy.

If there was a match, Diego and Goyo played to win, be it as team-mates or on opposing sides. Goyo was a classic two-footed number 9, with great instinctive movement, his link-up play was impressive and he did not think twice in the opposition box. Maradona did not know his best position. He started as a sweeper, with the whole pitch ahead of him, as he could then decide how to build the play – he enjoyed being in charge.

Goyo Carrizo played for Argentinos Juniors. A bricklayer from Villa Fiorito who worked near the Argentinos ground took him to a trial. The small pitch looked huge and the whole team was just the player that was nearby. While he was changing to go home, Francis Cornejo, the coach who was putting together a team of eight- and nine-year-olds for the club, touched him on the head. 'You're staying.' Just a few months passed when Goyo told the coach there was a better player than him in his neighbourhood. 'It's full up,' responded Francis, before eventually changing his mind.

So Goyo went running after Diego and breathlessly informed him, 'They want boys. Come on Saturday.' Diego ran off to tell his mother. 'Ask your dad,' she said. He waited for his father by the door to the garden. 'Will you take me on Saturday?' Don Diego, who was dead tired after work, did not even answer. The following day, Diego insisted and the pair went to Goyo's house to speak to his father about Cornejo's team.

On the walk back home, Don Diego said to him, 'OK, I'll take you.' It was raining on that Saturday and when they arrived in the Malvinas neighbourhood, where the trials were scheduled to take place, they were told that the venue had changed. They had to go to Parque Saavedra instead. They needed two bus tickets, but Don Diego did not have any money with him.

Meanwhile, in the park, Francis Cornejo was laying out jump-ers for goalposts near a row of eucalyptus trees and picked the two teams. Don Diego persuaded a man to take him and his son to the Parque in his lorry. Francis put Diego and Carrizo on the same team and immediately saw that they linked up well. Goyo recalls that his friend performed decently, and Francis did not have to think about it for long. 'You're staying.' Diego felt he was touching 'the sky with his hands'.

Maradona told the story of how he and his dad got the 28 bus which crossed La Noria Bridge, and both walking from there in silence the twenty blocks that took them home. They were happy. That was not, however, how it happened.

Francis was not sure that little Diego was eight. As he had no ID on him, they went on the Rastrojero pickup truck belonging to José Trotta, who was the father of one of the boys, to ask Doña Tota. It turned out Maradona really was eight and was given the final green light. It was the start of a long list of happy moments at Cebollitas.

As Don Diego worked late during those first few years, it was easier for Goyo's father to take them from Villa Fiorito to training in Malvinas and back. Given he did not have a car, the journey took almost two hours each way. In order to have some leftover money to be able to buy a slice of pizza for the three of them, they would sneak on to the train in Fiorito that would take them to the stop on Alsina Bridge. Then they would get a bus.

On the way back, the children would fall asleep. On certain Fridays when they were playing the following day, they would stay the night at the house of Jorge Cyterszpiler, near the Argentinos ground. He had quickly become a friend of theirs, a generous young man with an eye for opportunity, who took the role in the team of helper and man for all occasions, which led to him to become a sort of adopted older brother to Diego.

'Goyo had a magic understanding with Diego on the pitch,' recalled Francis Cornejo in his book about those times. They did things that were not common at their age: '"Kings of the unpredictable" is how their coach put it.'

Diego 'once controlled the ball on his chest, let it drop at his feet and he was off,' wrote Cornejo. The tiny player dribbled around everyone on his way and walked the ball into the goal. 'Roberto Maino ran over to hug and kiss Diego inside the goal,' Cornejo added. 'I said to him, "That looks bad. You're the referee!" He said to me, "What he did was enough to get the game suspended right then."'

They played just like they danced, as Don José and Francis once observed at a kids' party – with the same audacity and synchronisation of soulmates. That was how they won game after game after game, going 136 matches unbeaten.

In September 1971, the first article about *El Pelusa* was published in the national newspaper *Clarín*, after he had showcased his skills during half-time of Argentinos Juniors matches. The newspaper called him Diego 'Caradona': 'The 10-year-old earnt rapturous applause during the half-time of Argentinos Juniors' clash with Independiente after displaying a rare ability to perform tricks with his instep and even with the outside of his boot.' There was also a photo of Diego with a large, floppy fringe doing kick-ups wearing an enormous T-shirt.

Goyo played for his father's team, Tres Banderas, just as Diego did for his – Estrella Roja it was called. Those were games on some good pitches marked out with white lime. That was their life – the two friends competed in the neighbourhood and played together for Cebollitas.

They sometimes plugged gaps in the men's teams. One was short on players and despite being only thirteen, the two teenagers filled in. The match ended all square and went to penalties. The coach asked Goyo to take one. '*Pelu* is a better penalty-taker,' he responded. Maradona tucked his penalty away and they were crowned champions. The players received some prize money, which went down well. As it was Father's Day, Goyo bought his old man a bottle of coffee-flavoured liqueur. Don Diego liked gin, but Maradona did not have enough to get some. 'Here you go, *Pelu*.' Goyo gave him what he had left.

'I want to make it big in the top flight,' Diego used to tell Goyo, who would usually look away because he knew that each step in that direction would likely drive his friend further away from him. The first piece in the famous magazine *El Gráfico* about Cebollitas came out in August 1973. 'These boys are tearing it up,' wrote Horacio del Prado.

'*Pelusa*, go and buy a soda siphon,' Doña Tota asked Diego one afternoon. 'Let's go, Goyo.' They ran, of course. When they turned a corner, Diego fell over and the siphon cut his hand open. He had seven stitches at hospital and his whole arm was bandaged up. 'What will Francis say?' they asked each other, more out of respect than fear. 'You won't play for a month,' decided the coach when he saw him. Diego's head dropped and Goyo took Diego's number 10 shirt as a modest tribute to his missing friend. 'Goyo, tell him that I want to play, we're going to be champions,' Maradona said tearfully. 'How can he play like that?' asked Cornejo, who called Don Diego. 'Dad, let me play, I won't clash with players! I want to be involved and celebrate our league title.' With his arm in a sling, Cebollitas won 7-0, with Maradona, back in his 10 shirt, notching five goals.

At seventeen, Goyo started training with the Argentinos Juniors first team, a year on from Diego's debut. After being part of the youth national team that was crowned world champions under César Luis Menotti, Diego said to him, '*El Flaco* [The Thin Man: Menotti] wants you!' The message stuck in his mind. An agent promised that he would get him out of Villa Fiorito. In a bid to help him take a step forward in life, Argentinos wanted to rent a flat for him near the stadium, but it only had one bedroom. His sister had children and he did not want to leave her on her own. So he stayed in Fiorito, where he received invitations to play in matches for cash, typically 500 or 1,000 pesos – in today's money, five or ten pounds. That was easier than having the discipline needed to become a first division professional.

Goyo was selected in the Argentinos third team to play away to Huracán, but he twisted his ankle the previous night in a paid match. Another day, he was on the first-team substitutes' bench. He just needed one decision by the coach or one injury to a teammate to make his debut, but it was not to be. In 1981, he himself suffered a serious injury playing a game – he reached the touchline and crossed the ball, but his opponent made contact with his supporting leg and ruptured his knee ligaments. The injury still troubles him today.

That was when Maradona was on the verge of going to Barcelona from Boca. Argentinos let him go, so his friend took Goyo to a gym and paid for six months' rehabilitation.

He kept playing until he was thirty because he did not even know how to lay a brick or anything else. Football or football was his only possible choice, but what about after football? He had to go skip-diving: he would open bags of rubbish with a friend, they would get bottles, cardboard and if there was any copper, it was time to celebrate. On Saturdays and Sundays, they would sell locally what they had rescued.

In 1980, on Children's Day, Diego came to Villa Fiorito with Guillermo Blanco in a lorry full of toys. They joined a barbecue for a bit. Fiorito was, more or less like today, a town of 50,000 inhabitants with the same pizzerias and poorly stocked shops that cater to their sense of hopelessness. Some say that another time he returned with a limousine and ended up drinking whisky in the back seat with some guys.

Others tell the story of the day he stopped in the tram station and signed his autograph in one of the Os of the Villa Fiorito sign, that bit cut out the next morning with an electric saw and taken away. The most recent stop-off from Diego in Fiorito occurred in 2005 as part of the documentary on his life filmed by Emir Kusturica. He was besieged – hugged, pulled and cheered.

Goyo missed the real and also the fictional visits, but he saw his friend three times after he moved to Europe. When he joined Napoli, *El Pelusa* got his cousin to call Goyo, who travelled to his house, always full of people. His old friend was the only one Maradona took to the kitchen. 'Take care of yourself, Goyo,' he told him there. 'Speak to my sister Lili if you need anything.' Gregorio never ever asked for anything.

During preparations for the 1994 World Cup, Goyo discovered through someone in the neighbourhood that at an event for famous people, Diego was so drugged up that he wanted to throw himself off a balcony. His friend found out where Maradona was training and went to see him, but was not allowed to enter the premises. He had written a letter which he managed to give to someone who was going inside in a van. 'Give it to Diego, please,' he begged. Soon after, another van came steaming out towards the entrance, with the driver honking the horn. 'Goyo, Goyo!' It was *El Pelusa*. They exchanged a hug and cried. Diego said, 'Don't cry, we're together now, aren't we?' They spent four hours in a room chatting.

Then they saw each other at a distance on a television programme in 1997, which was a surprise tribute to Maradona with friends from different eras.

'Here we are, sir,' he tells the journalist Borinsky, who has just arrived. 'We're still in the same house where we've always lived. Diego used to sleep just opposite, there, in my house, and the pitch we played with Tres Banderas, my dad's team, used to be right there. The land was then bought and they built houses . . .'

# 4
# FRANCIS CORNEJO AND CEBOLLITAS

Francis Cornejo, also known as *El Negro* or *El Zurdo*, was a talented footballer with a good shot in him, but he never played professionally, and didn't feel that he had missed out at all. He was much more comfortable paving the way for those starting out and correcting technical mistakes or attitudes. He was one of those anonymous heroes who manages children dreaming of hitting the big time. In 1969, he was putting together a team of under-9s for Argentinos Juniors. He almost had what he needed, but on a Saturday in March he was going to try out a new kid.

He almost cancelled training that day due to pouring rain, but decided to stick all the players on his friend and assistant José Trotta's pickup truck in order not to ruin the pitch at Las Malvinas, and took the group to Parque Saavedra, which was around twenty-five blocks away. Soon after, a short thin boy arrived on another pickup truck, wearing long light-brown trousers, worn trainers and a faded green jacket which he peeled off while running towards the group.

In the open park, Francis got a nine-a-side game going (or maybe eight-a-side, he cannot recall) and Diego placed himself in midfield without anybody telling him to do so. In that trial, he hardly heard a word from him, but he started doing things that only the chosen few are capable of: he controlled one of the early passes with his left foot and effortlessly flicked the ball over an opponent without letting it touch the ground before driving towards goal.

'There's no way he's eight. He must be a dwarf,' the coach said to José Trotta.

However, something was lacking in Diego then. In order to be successful as a player you need to be both mentally and physically ready. A few days after the trial, Cornejo took him to see Dr Roberto Paladino, who decided he had to put on weight and bulk up a bit. He had a healthy but scrawny body, decently fed, even more so than others, but in need of some supplements, which the doctor gave him.

Without going through the period of adaptation and acceptance that Francis Cornejo always asked of others, *El Pelusa* broke into the line-up and stayed put, though occasionally the coach decided to mess with the opposition. In a match against a Boca Juniors youth side, one of the most respected academies in the country and a hotbed of talent, he registered Maradona with a made-up surname, Montanya, and put him on the bench. Boca raced into a 3-0 lead, before the miniature wizard was brought on. He transformed the team and turned things around with a brace to help them get back on level terms. The opposition coach provided a fitting match report when he went up to Cornejo – 'You played Maradona, you son of a bitch!'

'His ability is innate,' is Signorini's analysis. 'He's an instinctive guy and he's dribbling through life all the time, just as he does with the ball.' At the age of eight, he was already 'putting defenders on their backsides', as Cornejo put it. And he did things not usually seen in young kids: he could slam on the brakes and leave opponents behind, applying the pause in the games, the thinking.

When a player's talent is so obvious, his teammates want to give him the ball. Without any boisterousness and always generous with his efforts, he was aware that he had something that others lacked, but also that he was part of a squad that was already good. Diego, Goyo and the rest were insatiable youngsters who liked winning, even in training, and that was something Francis promoted. After fitness drills, there would be a small-sided game, with the winners getting a Coca-Cola or a sandwich, or an ice cream if it was hot.

There were ferocious fights among short-term enemies who afterwards kept discussing and laughing all the way to the cinema or to the river for fishing. Cornejo created activities and taught them the virtues of competing but also of sharing, all of which was reflected on the pitch. He bought Diego his first pair of Fulvence boots, fashionable at the time and tough, and when they were battered and bruised, *El Pelusa* gave them to Don José, who has kept them till this day.

Diego listened to, and followed, Cornejo and José's instructions on the pitch, but he would also come up with shooting techniques, make accurate passes and dribble for fun. He enjoyed talking in detail with the coaches about players, matches and moves. In those exchanges, young Diego showed his admiration for Independiente's Ricardo Bochini, whose runs with the ball and dribbling he wanted to emulate.

When Goyo Carrizo and the others got ready to go home after practice, *El Pelusa* liked to stay behind to take more penalties, improve his shooting with his right foot, although it was already a rocket, and work on his heading. Cornejo tried to teach him how to take free-kicks with his primed left foot, but Diego could take them better on his own.

Physical changes did not take long to appear. Diego was bursting with energy in training, supported by the supplements that Doña Tota and *Chitoro* now had somehow to pay for. He discovered his place in the team, as a number 10 out on the left, but gradually earned his freedom to roam all over the pitch. At ten, he played passes that only he could see. By eleven, he even dared to play a *rabona* cross towards Carrizo. He rarely overdid it with his skills; they tended to make sense instead of being merely showing off. More often than not, he preferred to pick out a well-placed teammate than finish himself.

'Give *Pelu* an egg, Mum,' said Daniel Delgado, another talented Cebollitas player. Diego started kicking the raw egg about with consummate ease. Delgado went through a few dozen eggs that week in a bid to replicate his teammate's immaculate skills.

'I started dreaming the day I went to train with Argentinos Juniors,' explained Diego. 'I knew football was going to give me a better life because I could see how I could gobble the best players up for dinner, but I wasn't blowing my own trumpet. And I owe a lot to my old man. He would polish my boots before every game. The other players' footwear was in a pitiful state: they were filthy and caked in mud . . . My father helped me shine.'

Cornejo claimed that '*El Pelusa* transformed that team into a moon-bound rocket'. The retired man at Parque Saavedra who offered Maradona his bicycle was joined by other fans. Coaches, supporters and players at different levels at Argentinos also followed the team. Invitations were flooding in from clubs all over the country who wanted to rack up a prestigious victory. In some villages, they were even welcomed by a local band, as another Cebollita, Mauro Mongiardini, recalled. In 1971, the team had to venture outside Argentina for the first time for a trip to Uruguay, but Diego was unable to take part because he forgot to take his documents. An increasing number of unfamiliar faces, including scouts from other clubs, came to watch them.

Football is like Janus, the two-faced Roman god of doorways. It opens up a new world with the potential for glory and subsequent failure in equal measure. Diego started to be man-marked and his ability forced defenders to take him out with strong tackling. Opposition fans would shout all sorts at him and *Chitoro* nearly came to blows with the perpetrators on more than one occasion. Diego, who did not complain, discovered that he was capable of ignoring them, back then at least. He also found it easy to swiftly conjure up a moment of magic to silence them all.

But the inevitable happened. On a Saturday in 1971, a big, slow player marked him. In the second half, while jumping for the ball, the defender stretched out a leg, but as he fell, he made contact with Diego's right supporting one. It was a serious incident and Maradona was in tears. His knee swelled up and one hour later his temperature went as high as 40°. He had to be taken to hospital the next morning and the doctor removed some black blood from his knee with a large syringe. En route to recovery, Diego went through the various phases of annoyance, impatience, fear to compete for the ball and eventually forgetting the injury.

Cebollitas were officially founded in 1973 in the Trofeo Evita. We have been calling them that, but they didn't really have a name before then. On the registration day, Cornejo wanted to call the team Argentinos Juniors, but while he waited to hand in the form, he heard the other sides' names: Villa Tachito, Los Soles, Lucero. The players in his team, who were born in 1960, seemed smaller than the rest. 'Let's give them a name that sounds little: Los Cebollitas.' That document ended up framed in José Trotta's house.

They finished runners-up in that tournament, with Diego inconsolable after losing the final. A run of 136 wins on the bounce (or 142 or 151 depending on whom you ask) made it much harder to accept the few defeats. When losing is such a rarity, each episode seemed like a small death. 'He was full of hatred and felt guilty,' Francis recalled.

Maradona had scored a memorable goal against River Plate in which he dribbled past seven players (or possibly eight or six), so the interest grew. His local fame had seen him appear on *Sábados Circulares*, a popular family television programme, performing the skills that he still showcased at half-time at the Argentinos stadium. 'I have two dreams,' he said into the camera. 'My first is to play in the World Cup and the second is to be champion, that is, win the eighth division and whatever follows [with Argentinos Juniors].'

'It might sound ridiculous, but Diego would understand this,' explained Cornejo. 'If Maradona is at a party in a white suit and a muddy ball flies through the air, he'll control it on his chest.' That is the coach's description of pure football, where dominating a ball is the most essential thing. Diego, whose existence as a teenager already revolved around training and the next match, was living the life that he would later yearn to recreate.

To make it as a professional in the top flight, however, many factors have to fall into place. You need the right family that understands the openings offered by football, patient mentors in training, the right culture, country and a suitable club. Argentinos Juniors, which looked for local boys with good technique, certainly ticked that box.

Based in La Paternal, Buenos Aires, a neighbourhood of modest working-class families where everyone knows everyone, Argentinos was founded in 1904 by a group of lads with socialist and anarchist beliefs. Its story is one of battling against the tide and reaching the top without accepting any handouts. The club has one of the country's most prestigious academies and the first team has proudly had at least one player from the youth setup every year since 1979.

At the age of thirteen, it was not yet time to make a living from football, that did not happen back then. Diego was only earning what he was given to play in games with the bigger boys, so he had to look for a job and got one at a disinfection company. He would get on a bus at 7am to San Martín Bridge. He would be given packets of cockroach poison that he would then spread on the grates and in the corners from the basement to the top floor of buildings.

What about school? It seemed to be a hindrance to *El Pelusa*'s relentless ascent. One afternoon, José Trotta, the assistant coach, headed to Fiorito to talk to his teacher, who confirmed that he was not doing well because he often did not show up and only ever thought about football. Ever since that conversation, the details of which have never been made known, the teacher never mentioned Diego's absences again and he finished primary school without any problems.

On matchdays, a boy from the La Paternal neighbourhood who suffered from polio from a young age, started appearing in Las Malvinas. His brother Juan Eduardo had played for Argentinos before dying from cancer very young. With a complex name, broad shoulders and an abundance of curly hair, Jorge Cyterszpiler redis-covered his desire to enjoy football when he came across Diego, who was almost two years younger than him. He became friends with the players, went to training, travelled with Cebollitas on the pickup truck, could be heard during matches, went on walks with them and helped conjure up childhood mischief.

Cyterszpiler also learned from what he heard. Representatives from more than one club made overtures to try to convince the Maradonas to move teams. First, the Racing president spoke to Don Diego, but it came to nothing. River Plate adopted a similar direct approach. A former player of the Buenos Aires club talked to *Chitoro* while Francis Cornejo was coaching the kids and offered him a size-able sum of money. It must have been an amount worth thinking about because that is exactly what Don Diego did, when in the past he had immediately rejected other proposals. He asked his wife, the parents of other players in the team and finally Cornejo.

'I'll keep it short and sweet for you: I think Argentinos Juniors will be the cradle and springboard to fame for Diego,' the coach told him. Thirteen-year-old Diego was sitting quietly on the floor. He begged his dad in a broken voice to 'stay with Don Francis'. There was silence. Don Diego frowned, everyone expectant.

'The Maradona phenomenon was written all over the wrinkles on his father's head and his cracked hands,' Fernando Signorini says. 'At other houses in Fiorito, the father would have beaten the son up if he didn't go to work with him. Instead he saw Diego had a bright future and was desperate to help him.'

At that point, Don Diego was of course the one who made the big decisions.

'It's OK. You're staying with Francis,' he proclaimed. It was perhaps the last time he could shape his son's career.

In 1974, a fourteen-year-old Maradona and his team were already Argentine champions of his age group. During the following year, just before his top-flight debut, the club gave him a flat with electricity and running water in Villa del Parque, near the ground, so that his parents and siblings could be more comfortable. The family pyramid had definitively been inverted: the son was now the provider, and in charge of his own destiny.

Seven years later, Diego Armando Maradona gave the shirt from his farewell Argentinos match to Francisco Cornejo.

After being admitted to Bancario Hospital in the Argentine capital, in March 2008, Don Francis passed away from leukaemia at the age of seventy-six.

# 5
# FIRST-TEAM DEBUT FOR ARGENTINOS JUNIORS

The year was 1972 and the whistle had just blown for half-time in the Argentinos v Boca game. An eleven-year-old Diego took to the empty pitch and began showing off some of his ball-juggling skills, the ball never touching the ground for the full fifteen minutes while walking from goal to goal. That was the first time in what was to become a regular feature and the crowd lapped it up. In 1974 his Cebollitas team won the championship in their age bracket as well as the national Trofeo Evita in the city of Embalse (not in Río Tercero as his autobiography erroneously reported). It was that same year when Cebollitas left coach Francis Cornejo behind to integrate the team in the under-14s of Argentinos Juniors, the first age in which players could be registered with the Argentine federation.

By then Jorge Cyterszpiler was the team co-ordinator. Those Fridays when Diego stayed at Jorge's house on Calle San Blas, near the team stadium, they would play Scrabble or watch television, his first experience of one. One afternoon, Cyterszpiler took Diego on a visit to *El Gráfico*, the most prestigious sports magazine in Latin America, known as the 'Bible of Sport'. It was not without intent. Jorge wanted *El Gráfico* to learn about the team. But more than that, he wished them to give Diego coverage and put him on the publication's front cover.

His tenacity started paying dividends. The magazine sent a reporter and a photographer to an Argentinos game. For the first time in *El Gráfico*'s history, a lower division player appeared in its pages, such was Diego's spellbinding skill. In exchange, Jorge had to promise the magazine he would give them the exclusive on a rumoured upcoming first division debut.

Still fourteen, he started playing games, five in total, with the under-16s. 'Waiting's almost over,' Jorge told *El Gráfico*. It was now 1975 and conditions were ripe. Professional footballers were on strike, demanding better pay and conditions, and the youths would have to step up and don the colours. Argentinos were to face a River team on the cusp of clinching the title, albeit the game was to be played at Club Atlético Vélez Sarsfield's stadium, also in Buenos Aires. 'It could be today,' Cyterszpiler cautioned the magazine.

Diego was selected, but as a ball boy. One of Argentinos' executives was watching the game and spotted Diego sitting atop a ball. He shouted down from the stands: 'Diego, Diego, what are you doing on the sidelines? How are you going to pass the ball to those donkeys on the pitch when you're sat there? Get on the pitch and show them how to play!' Diego laughed.

Rejection can bring anxiety to many teenagers when a door of opportunity is slammed in their face. Not for Diego. Challenges never ceased to arrive and be overcome. He was picked to play some friendlies for Argentinos Juniors' third team. Coach Juan Carlos Montes had just been signed to bring order to the misfiring Firsts, trying to steady the listing ship through the last few games of the season. The new boss asked Diego to train with them. First-team captain Ricardo Pellerano was warming up with his teammates at the multi-sports complex Club Comunicaciones when Diego arrived: 'He was overdressed and sweating a lot, possibly just amazed at how the whole situation was turning out.' Along with three other youth players, he got ready for the training session in the changing room with the rest of the team.

Heading back out to the now floodlit ground, the captain spotted the smaller boy standing on the pitch. The veterans looked at him, bemused. What happened next would stick in Pellerano's mind. In one play, Diego drove forward with the ball at great speed, then braked immediately to a standstill. Before anyone could react, he'd gone back to full speed, leaving players in his wake.

'He totally dazzled me,' Pellerano says. 'But there were other players who didn't like him, and they were hard on him. I told them, "We are going to look after him. I have the impression he's a little different from the rest of us . . . and we might need him.'"

The training session was scheduled to last ninety minutes. It took coach Montes just five minutes to comprehend the talent he was witnessing. Montes told Diego that because of his age, now fifteen, he would continue in the Thirds but he might get a call from time-to-time. The Thirds travelled with the first team to play some friendlies in La Plata. As Diego stepped off the bus, Montes informed him he'd be on the Firsts' bench for the next game. Five minutes against Estudiantes was followed with a half-hour against Atlanta. The official debut was surely just around the corner.

In September 1976, the under-18s faced a crucial match against Vélez – Diego was asked to play. Some dubious refereeing calls didn't exactly ingratiate him with the players. Diego addressed him at the end of the match. 'What a top man you are, you should referee some international matches.' He was admonished with a bracing look for his cynicism, but before he got to the changing rooms, Diego couldn't resist: 'You are a disaster!' Misconduct after the final whistle – a red card and five-game suspension. The meteorite's trajectory had been impeded.

One Monday, Juan Carlos Montes informed Jorge Cyterszpiler that if Diego trained well on Tuesday, he would make his debut the next day in Argentinos' home game against Talleres de Córdoba at La Paternal stadium. Diego knew nothing of these developments. It had been fourteen months since Jorge had first called *El Gráfico* about the wonder kid's possible official debut against River Plate. Despite that false alarm, he called again. The magazine agreed to extend its deadline to be able to include the game.

Diego shot back to Villa Fiorito. The club had rented the Maradonas one of Argentina's famous 'chorizo' apartments in a long and thin sausage-shaped building. All the residences were laid out in a straight line and accessed via a narrow corridor that ran the length of the building. This one was in Calle Argerich in Villa del Parque, a few blocks from Argentinos' stadium. But the Maradonas and their possessions were still ensconced at the old Villa Fiorito family home;

this included Mamá Dora, Diego's grandmother, who had no intention of moving out of the shanty town. They would have to find an ingenious way to get her out of there.

Diego could barely breathe as he told his mother about his debut. Doña Tota started to cry and hug him. Don Diego looked away from his son, biting his lip. Doña Tota wiped her eyes while admonishing her husband. 'Cry! Can't you see that your son is going to play for the first team?'

'And you can imagine . . .' Diego said much later. 'Within two seconds, all of Fiorito knew the news.'

Diego, *El Pelusa*, told his cousin Raúl and then went to see the person that gifted him his first football, his adored cousin Beto. Raúl and Beto used to watch Diego play for the juniors, as and when they had money to catch the *colectivo* bus to the stadium. Now, Beto and Diego couldn't stop hugging and crying. And that was the moment that Diego fully realised the effect his football had on others. He understood he was at the start of something very big.

Don Diego went to work that October Wednesday, the day his son would sit on the bench for the Firsts of Argentinos Juniors. He asked permission to leave early so he could attend the game, but had to wait for his answer. Diego prepared to travel solo to the stadium. Despite it being a hot and sultry day, he dressed in a white shirt and his only pair of trousers, bell-bottomed turquoise corduroys, the type that gauchos wear in winter.

Doña Tota walked Diego to the door. 'I'm going to pray for you, son,' she said.

The openness of the *chorizo* home layout meant one could peer into other apartments from certain windows. Claudia lived in the same building and could see Diego when he left to go to training. 'I played dumb to her when she looked at me, but I was always watching her, intently but covertly. I didn't encourage anything until almost eight months passed,' he wrote more than twenty-five years later in his autobiography, changing his previous fascination for a girl with yellow trousers to actually him being the object of desire.

He took the train, then buses 44 and 135, meeting some Argentinos players en route. The team met up at El Rincón de los Artistas restaurant on the corner of Jonte and Boyacá streets, adjacent to the stadium. His new teammates exchanged quizzical glances after seeing Diego in his lambskin trousers. 'They were thinking, "This guy's made a serious wardrobe error." But . . . we didn't even have a wardrobe!' Maradona would remember years later.

Steak and mashed potatoes were followed by coach Monte's tactical team chat. Among the players, there was talk of a win bonus. Diego thought: 'Well, the sub will get something at least, and if I get on the pitch, a little more.' He did some calculations. 'I'll get some new trousers.' After their meal, the team walked to La Paternal stadium. By 2pm, six journalists from *El Gráfico* were in attendance, including writer Héctor Vega Onesime, in charge of the match report, and photographer Humberto Speranza.

The game was due to start early in the afternoon. The day was getting hotter and much more humid; the public searched for shade while waiting for the ground to open. Numerous Talleres de Córdoba fans sat on the pavement, sharing bottles of wine, having made the 700km journey from Córdoba to Buenos Aires to support their team. In fact, an unusually large crowd was building up; word had been spread by the coaches that someone special might play. The official Argentina Football Association (AFA) lists 7,737 as the official attendance for that match. It was probably higher, with many getting in without a ticket. Whatever the final count, it will never be as high as the numbers suggested by those who claimed they were there on that day.

Argentina's national coach, César Luis Menotti, was present, a fact unearthed by journalist Diego Borinsky. Early that same week, Montes had met with Menotti and gushed about this fifteen-year-old kid who was 'a *crack* [superstar]'. The national coach half-joked: 'If he's such a *crack*, why don't you put him in with the Firsts?'

'That's why I'm here to see you,' Montes replied. 'On Wednesday, I'm giving him his debut.'

'Diego, your old man has arrived,' someone yelled at the players at they entered the stadium. Maradona smiled, thankful for the information.

'When we got into the changing rooms, I felt like I was touching the sky with my hands,' Diego recalled. He was part of the sixteen-man squad and actually wore the number 16 shirt. He held it reverently before putting it on, raising it as one gently lifts a baby, taking great care not to mark or harm it. It engulfed him when he put it on, making his little legs seems even smaller and thinner. 'Being in the changing rooms, the warm-up, the boss talking to you ... you don't know whether to lace your boots or ... it was all new to me. Absolutely new.' Joy and tension accompanied him onto the pitch for the warm-up and back to the changing rooms. A few moments later he was sitting on the bench as far away as possible from the coach. And he waited.

Talleres de Córdoba dominated the first half and took the lead after 27 minutes. Just before the break, Montes locked eyes with Diego and raised his eyebrows. 'Yes, I'm prepared,' the kid transmitted back, as he held his coach's gaze.

On that day, 20 October 1976, Diego Armando Maradona was about to make his official debut at the start of the second half, replacing Rubén Aníbal Giacobetti. He was the youngest player ever to do so in the Argentine top flight.

Montes asked him to play as he knew ... and if he could, to nutmeg someone. Diego got the ball with the back to his marker, Juan Domingo Patricio Cabrera. With a light touch, he passed the ball between his legs. 'Clean and quick,' Maradona described it, chatting to TyC. 'Right away, I heard the "ooooole" of the crowd, as if they were welcoming me.'

Diego, through years of playing in front of older players, had learned how to avoid the kicks and shoves of his fully grown opponents. His survival manual included dribbling, riding and jumping tackles and most importantly, driving forward with the ball, without fear. From the moment he made his debut in the first division, as he was seen as the talented one, he got kicked around and his pain was masked by painkilling injections or tablets. It is easy to become dependent on them, as it is the way to keep playing. And playing was the thing that defined him.

Miguel Ángel Bertolotto was the only *Clarín* journalist present at the game – his newspaper had not been given any tip about the potential debut. He wrote: 'The entrance of the Maradona boy gave the attack greater mobility, but he wasn't the solution to the requirement of more possession in the Cordoba half. Maradona showed great skill, but he had no one to play with.'

The game ended in a 1-0 defeat for Argentinos and it was, according to Diego, all 'very nice'. Maradona would say much later, 'Our rivals should have scored 18 goals.'

Héctor Vega Onesime wrote in *El Gráfico*: 'Argentinos were buried by their lack of offensive capacity. Not even the introduction of the surprising, skilful and intelligent former "Cebollita" Maradona managed to resolve the problem.' He was given seven out of ten by the magazine.

A couple of weeks later, Diego scored two goals and provided two assists as Argentinos won 5-2 away at San Lorenzo de Mar del Plata. The team were travelling back by bus and Alberto Pérez, a director at Argentinos, was sitting opposite a sleeping Diego. Fellow director Reinaldo Mediot, in his late sixties, commented: 'Look at this boy, not even he knows how far he can go. I may not get to see him reach his full potential, but you are definitely going to enjoy it.' Diego had just turned sixteen.

Just two days before, Diego had been called up for the first time by César Luis Menotti for the national team and was included in the national coach's list of players that couldn't be transferred abroad. 'Everything happened too fast,' Diego admits to *Clarín* in his first interview with journalist Horacio Pagani, just a month after his debut. 'I have to take it all with a pinch of salt because if I really think about it, it could drive me mad ...' During the interview, Diego says he felt he had done well with two goals plus the three nutmegs. 'What?' asked Pagani. 'You count the nutmegs?'

'In the first team, yes, because I've only played a few games. I nutmegged Cabrera from Talleres on debut, another one to Gallego, but then he got me back with one. Sunday I got Mascareño a good one ...'

The article ends with Pagani's frank recognition that 'his story is the adventure of a little boy. Dangers await him. But there is hope in his football. And Argentine football is in need of hope.'

'Get ready, Jorge, I need you.' At the beginning of 1977, Diego asked Jorge Cyterszpiler to represent him. Jorge was becoming the first-ever manager of an Argentine player and negotiated his first professional contract in May that year. It was a logical step – Jorge was already taking care of Diego's dealings and he had envisaged what they could do together.

A year and a half later, aged eighteen, Maradona renewed his contract at Argentinos. The club president, Prospero Cónsoli, recognised Maradona's value and wanted to show his star player some love. Cónsoli upgraded the *chorizo* home to a six-roomed, two-storey house with a patio and upper terrace, located closer to the stadium. Maradona was still considered a minor, so the deeds were in the name of his father, Don Diego. *El Pelusa* shared the 130 square metres with his two brothers and four of his sisters; the eldest, Ana, had already married. And his grandmother. They had found a way to bring her: Diego and others gave the old woman a big scare before running away as she was half-asleep on the patio of the bungalow of Villa Fiorito. Some possessions had also disappeared. It was time to join the rest of the family.

The new house's only toilet was above Diego's room, on the terrace. Not for Diego the door and stairs route to get to it; keeping true to his scamp *'villero'* ('slumdog') character, he would climb out of the small window of his room, just to save a few steps.

# Part II
## DIEGO

# 6
# A DOMINANT FORCE AT ARGENTINOS JUNIORS

In 1958, under the leadership of President Arturo Frondizi, a lawyer and journalist, Argentina had to follow a strict austerity plan agreed with the International Monetary Fund, a strategy that had sparked dozens of nationwide strikes. He had pursued policies to help the automobile, steel and petrochemical industries grow and compensate for those strict measures. The military felt at the time that they were loaning authority out till they needed to recapture it. They imposed severe restrictions on Frondizi's plans and forced him to establish even tougher economic policies, which led to further civil unrest, with thousands arrested and many more sentenced to prison in summary courts martial. They were confusing times – six coups took place between 1958 and 1963, each faction clamouring for power and their *inalienable* right to lead the country, with each coup imposing new conditions on the people.

Diego Armando Maradona was born in 1960, in the middle of that uncertainty.

The 1963 elections promoted Artur Umberto Illía to the presidency. It was a weak administration characterised by a populist agenda and, yet again, Illía was deposed in a military coup after just three years. The consequent military dictatorship oversaw a decade of tension, with revolts by workers and students coupled with an exodus of scientists abroad. The popular former president, Juan Perón, was in exile.

In 1973, the military dictatorship began to disintegrate, imposing a reduced and conservative state before they called elections. Through it all, Maradona and his Cebollitas team were enjoying fame locally.

Perón, outlawed for the elections, backed Héctor Cámpora as a candidate. Cámpora duly won and within months called for a new vote, with Perón back on the ballot paper. The ageing Perón was backed by more than 60 per cent of the electorate. His death a year later meant his wife and vice-president – María Estela Martínez de Perón ('Isabelita') – succeeded him as president. She was not well versed in politics. Chaos filled the power vacuum, driven by hyper-inflation and a lack of leadership skills. Congress voted through legislation that allowed the military and security forces to 'annihilate' anyone throughout Argentina considered to be 'non-conformist'.

The armed forces, police and vigilante groups abused their new powers and, without trials, killed anyone they deemed subversive. Many say it was a deliberate plan, and one that wilfully included the extermination of a generation of progressive thinkers, called the 'disappeared'.

With Perón gone, Church leaders and armed forces united and took control on 24 March 1976, placing María Estela Martínez de Perón under house arrest. The pretext was to stabilise the economic chaos and help the fight against guerrilla cells; the subtext was much broader. There were other coups across South America around the same time: Pinochet in Chile, Bordaberry in Uruguay and Banzer in Bolivia. Brazil had endured a dictatorship since 1964, and Stroessner continued to rule Paraguay with a strong arm, as he had since 1954.

Meanwhile, large, North American multinational banks pocketed the surplus from the oil boom in Arab countries. These same banks lent money to Latin American nations. The high interest rates drained the country's coffers until they ruptured, generating what at the beginning of the eighties was called 'External Debt'. Many were unable to service this debt, and their own growth was curtailed in what is now known as the 'Lost Decade'.

Maradona, aged sixteen, made his debut for Argentinos Juniors' first team against this tumultuous political backdrop. Maradona's unifying skill was what journalist Horacio Pagani meant when he wrote that Argentina needed new dreams. Politics did not enter the Argentinos changing room. It was football and girls, and the sport of *getting* them. Diego didn't smoke or drink, he loved to train, staying behind to practise, even when they'd turned the stadium lights off. He'd convince goalkeeper Carlos Munutti to participate in penalty competitions for money involving other players. If no one was willing, they'd take penalties against each other; Diego shooting first, then Munutti trying to score past his diminutive teammate. More often than not, the caretaker – who had to take two *colectivo* buses to get home – would have to hound them from the pitch.

There is no television recording of Maradona's first goals for Argentinos, but there are photos of his brace from that 5-2 win at San Lorenzo de Mar del Plata in November 1976. The game was Maradona's fifth official match, and he started on the bench. Nothing could separate the teams at half-time; *El Pelusa* came out for the second half, wearing 15 on his back. His first goal, and the team's fourth that day, came 42 minutes into the second half. He eluded three opponents then played a quick one-two with his teammate Lopéz before dispatching a low, left-footed shot across from an angle into the goal.

'From his first involvement, he demonstrated his tremendous ability and football intelligence.' *La Capital* published a photo of Maradona completing the scoring that day, Argentinos' fifth goal and his second. Julio Macias' analysis of the game and of Maradona read: 'He came on for the second half, but was the most important part of the game's development ...' 'Under Maradona's influence, Argentinos dominated the game and ran out worthy winners,' concluded Segundo César Cheppi in *La Capital*. Maradona kept a copy of that publication, but that memento, like so many others, got lost in the dozens of house moves during his career.

Benicio Acosta was the coach at San Lorenzo. After the game, he rebuked his own player, Alejandro Edelmiro Mascareño, saying: 'It's shameful this little lamb danced rings around you.'

His teammates were far more curious to know more about the young *Pelusa* on the return trip from Mar del Plata than on the way there. 'We started taking care of him because we realised what we had in the squad. The rest of the team became, little by little, just ten people running for him,' recalls Ricardo Giusti, a World Cup winner at Mexico 86 and another young player at Argentinos Juniors at the time.

There was talk of how, in one training session, Maradona had flicked up an orange with his foot, then flipped it up to his leg, his shoulder, his chest and finally launched it into the air and balanced it on the back of his neck. 'He put ten balls in the middle of the pitch and pointed to the crossbar,' says Giusti. 'No less than seven hit the crossbar. Without exaggerating, I tried and didn't even reach the goal.'

Argentina's national coach César Luis Menotti had seen enough. In February 1977, Diego made his national team debut aged sixteen. Days later, Maradona insisted that nothing had changed: 'When I was younger, I trained once a day. Now I train all the time. I don't want people to think that I've abandoned my friends, but since they called me up to play against Hungary, I haven't had a free moment to visit my neighbourhood. I don't want it ever to be said that I got too big for my boots. Everyone is on top of me. Magazines, television, newspapers, all asking me the same thing. It's tiring. In reality, I am nobody, and the only thing I can talk about is my childhood and my idol, Bochini.' The boy was beginning to gauge the price of fame.

His relationship with Claudia Villafañe, the girl in yellow trousers who gazed at Diego clandestinely from her window, began in the summer of 1977. He would stop by Claudia's house for a walk after training two or three times a week. It seemed the whole country would accompany them on the walk, with journalists taking shots of the moment. That attention never diminished.

The following season was Maradona's first full one with the first team. It is remembered for a goal he scored at Huracán's Buenos Aires ground, of which there are only a few images of the final phases. He picked the ball up in his own area and drove forwards then played a clever one-two with a teammate to take four opponents out of the game. Intelligence and talent had brought Maradona to the dream situation – a one-on-one with the goalkeeper. Talent and impudence took over. He nutmegged the goalie.

Yet he never forgot the unwritten codes of street football after all the years playing with the Cebollitas. He needed it against River Plate when he came up against the then thirty-seven-year-old Marshal Perfumo, considered the best defender in the history of Argentine football, and a firm fan's favourite.

'Maradona comes in and dribbles, dribbles, dribbles,' recalls writer Sergio Levinsky. 'Perfumo knew how to whack players, but oozed class when he did it. He would just appear, like James Bond, implacable, without a hair out of place. Well, Perfumo jumps up and gives Maradona an absolute whack! And on the way down Maradona lashes out at Perfumo's foot, leaving both needing treatment from the doctors and physios. Maradona is up first and out of respect for the legendary veteran, asks Perfumo, "Marshal, your foot's fine, right?" To which Perfumo replies, "Don't worry, Diego, I'm fine."' There were countless more hard tackles for Diego to endure, yet he learned to live with what was meted out, and rarely protested.

*El Pelusa* helped a squad short on talent win games. The press speculated that Diego's youth and growing influence affected the rest of the players. 'We win matches together, all eleven starters and the five substitutes,' Maradona stated. 'If Ríos doesn't score, if Fren doesn't perform, then Maradona is useless. It's disrespectful that journalists write Maradona 2 such-and-such-team 0, it hurts the players.' Teammates made similar statements, but it was telling and slightly odd that Diego had begun to refer to himself in the third person.

Diego started to share more of his time with a press pack for which he had increasingly contradictory feelings. With the help of Jorge Cysterszpiler, and perhaps subconsciously, Maradona was creating his own media and marketing image. He began telling journalists about the cars he bought and his love of imported clothes and perfumes while lamenting his inability to 'be able to spend two weeks relaxing with my girlfriend and my family'.

'What caught my attention was that his relationship with the press had an obvious character very early on,' surmises Lalo Zanoni, who studied Maradona's public life in his book, *Living Among the Media*. 'When he played for Cebollitas, Horacio del Prado interviewed Diego for *El Gráfico*. Del Prado found a twelve-year-old who was very mature for his age, a very free spirit. At fifteen years old, he was playing for the first team at Argentinos Juniors, and at sixteen he was already a man. Look at the photos of him in the media, he was really a boy, but his posture and his way of standing are that of an adult. Soon they would make him captain of the team, surrounded by older players. He was the first player in Argentina, if not the world, to have an agent, and that was before he was even famous. Björn Borg had an agent, but it wasn't prevalent in the 1970s.'

At first, word of his exploits did not really cross borders, and only those who lived in or travelled to Argentina heard the tales. Stories of a boy who not only broke into the Argentinos first team and from the age of eighteen was the top scorer in the Metropolitano Championship (1978, 1979, 1980) and Nacional Championship (1979, 1980), but who was also the youngest to achieve the feat and, to this day, the only footballer to be top scorer five times. At seventeen Diego was already the leader and dominant force at Argentinos Juniors and it was only the fact that the dictatorship, on the suggestion of Menotti, prohibited his sale to a foreign club that kept him a total of five years at this modest club.

Argentinos Juniors is renowned not only for developing football players but also for instilling in them a team ethos and leadership skills. Many captains of Argentina came through their ranks, including Juan Pablo Sorín, Juan Román Riquelme and Esteban Cambiasso. Diego felt that leadership was a natural step forward, particularly when there was a vacuum to fill, whatever your age. 'We went to play in Brazil,' recalls teammate Rubén Favret, who, like the rest of the squad, played midweek friendlies in Argentina and abroad to earn the cash to pay for the material comforts that come with success. It made all the difference having a special player in the squad. 'It was the era of the colour television and we all wanted to bring one back. But we had not been paid our bonuses. Diego, who was eighteen years old, stood up for everyone and told Cónsoli [the president of Argentinos] that if they didn't pay us, he wouldn't play.'

In the new Maradona house, Doña Tota would watch a black-and-white TV, emptying packets of tobacco. Diego brought his mum a colour set from Brazil.

A month after the U20 World Cup, *El Pelusa* played in a friendly for Argentinos against San Martín de San Juan in Argentina's mid-west. Things were not going well. The team trailed 3-0 and Diego was grumbling to himself as he entered the changing rooms at half-time. 'Plenty of time for revenge,' his teammate Quique Wolff told him. Diego returned to the pitch a new man. He dragged his team back into it. As the game was drawing to a close, he eluded five opponents and was up against the goalkeeper with a chance to win the game. He saw Wolff free in the six-yard box, drew the keeper and popped the ball to Wolff to poke home. Wolff, open-armed, froze on the spot. The ball grazed his ankle and went out of play.

'What happened?' Diego asked. Wolff couldn't look him in the face.

'Your play was so spectacular that I couldn't react. I couldn't believe what was happening. I was left watching and admiring, just like a fan.'

# 7
# THE MEETING WITH PELÉ

Maradona solved football puzzles where there was neither the time nor space to do so. He viewed his surroundings like a freeze-frame photograph, elected the best strategic option then performed the necessary action, possible or seemingly impossible. His decisions derived from a fusion of analysis and intuition, from football intelligence as well as innate ability, combined in an extraordinarily sophisticated way – topped with a dusting of genius – and all in the service of a humble football.

Why genius? Diego not only answered questions on a pitch at a pace that nobody could match, but there was more. He didn't just master dribbles, passes and tricks; he created his own. In 1979, everything was primed to propel him to a level above all other players. His firework displays lit up the year with moments of spectacle beyond any expectations. And then another rocket went off, and then another. Argentina was unanimously astonished at his skill; international glory beckoned.

Before that perfect year of 1979, Maradona had vacillated between the highest peaks of praise and a new feeling of dark descents into deep catacombs of rejection. He began to feel addicted to this emotional rollercoaster which every day seemed more his new norm.

Having played eleven games in the first division, Diego made his international debut under César Luis Menotti in February 1977. It was a friendly against Hungary played at the Bombonera, home to Boca Juniors. 'After this, go to the Los Dos Chinos hotel and focus,' Menotti had told him at the end of a training session. 'If the game works out favourably, you might play. You can tell your parents, but only your parents.' They were 5-0 up with 20 minutes of the second half remaining. Menotti fulfilled his promise. Maradona is still the youngest debutant for the national team. Veteran midfielder Tolo Gallego gave him a fatherly hug at the final whistle.

He was called up again six months later for a couple of friendlies. The 1978 World Cup was to be played in Argentina and Menotti was getting his squad sorted; he had to trim three from the original twenty-five players he had selected. On 19 May, Admiral Emilio Eduardo Massera, a member of the military junta that governed Argentina, went to the team hotel, accompanied by Vice-Admiral Carlos Alberto Lacoste, vice-president of the dictatorship's entity charged with organising Argentina's World Cup. Both officials were met at the hotel by Menotti and Alfred Cantilo, president of the Argentina Football Association, and they were introduced to the players, who were then sent to the hotel for a meal and a rest. They were to be notified of the World Cup squad later in the afternoon.

A bus took the players to a football pitch a couple of miles from the hotel. Menotti gathered the team on the halfway line. He read out the names of the twenty-two to make the cut; Víctor Alfredo Bottaniz, Humberto Bravo and Maradona were left out. Striker Leopoldo Luque looked at a distraught Diego and, as the manager kept talking, tried to console him in a quiet voice: 'Dieguito, I thought I had chances to go to the World Cup in '74, when I was playing for Unión. When I was left out, I started working towards '78, and look, it's happened for me. You are seventeen years old, you have five World Cups left.'

'Stay if you want,' the coach told the omitted players. Maradona left the group crying. He knew he was better than some of the footballers going to the tournament. He requested permission to play for Argentinos against Chacarita Juniors that same day and promptly scored a hat-trick in a 5-0 win. Chacarita defender Hugo Pena told Diego: 'I was wearing the Chacarita shirt, but when you scored that last goal, I almost hugged you.'

'Anyone can see Maradona is a great player,' César Luis Menotti recalls today. 'I apologised for taking him out of the squad . . . I know it hurt him a lot. I didn't pick him because I was thinking about the Under-20s in Japan the next year. He was very young, and there were more experienced players in his position – Kempes, Villa, Ardiles

– not necessarily better than him, but more experienced. If I'd taken him, he would more than likely have made an impact, but at that time I preferred to keep him back.'

In Argentina, the land of the *coup d'état*, people are accustomed to broken promises and disappointments; nothing is what it seems. Football is tarnished with the same paint. A popular tale surrounds Norberto Alonso, the much-loved River Plate midfielder whom Menotti was allegedly going to exclude from the '78 squad. The story goes that, in that visit to the hotel where the squad stayed, Vice-Admiral Lacoste, a River fan, pressured Menotti to include Alonso into what became a World Cup-winning team. Menotti retorted, 'No one influenced me. I didn't know Lacoste and only met him twice in my life. Cantilo, the president of the national team, was completely committed – Lacoste couldn't get within a block of Cantilo, let alone earshot.'

Maradona wanted to quit football. He couldn't take a rejection like that one.

Jorge Cyterszpiler used his growing influence to act as emotional support. 'How are you going to quit football?' he said. 'All this will pass, you will play other World Cups, the Under-20s one in Japan . . .'

The goals of Mario Kempes, Osvaldo Ardiles' vision and the technical skills of Ricardo Villa lit up a summer of sporting success for the national team. Was it that relaxed atmosphere that led to Maradona almost being sold to Sheffield United for $1.5m that summer? Had the dictatorship and Menotti, wanting to keep the talent in the country to help the national sides, changed their stance about players being forced to stay in Argentina? Domingo Tessone, director at Argentinos, had the chance to do a deal for Maradona with the English side while club president Cónsoli was away. Or so the tale has been told until now.

Sheffield United manager Harry Haslam had convinced Alejandro Sabella, a skilful number 10, and midfielder Pedro Verde to sign for the Blades, at that point in the second division. During the celebration of the 1978 World Cup, Haslam travelled to Buenos Aires with chairman John Hassall to close the deals and to explore the talent in the Argentine market, a rare move in those days. The *Sheffield Star* journalist Tony Pritchett accompanied them.

Tottenham Hotspur manager Keith Burkinshaw and some club executives of the London club were on the same plane. Harry Haslam was also in advanced talks to sign Ricardo Villa and Ossie Ardiles, two top-drawer international players. During the flight, it became clear to Haslam and Hassall that Tottenham, newly promoted back to the first division after a spell in the second, held a better bargaining position. Villa and Ardiles moved to White Hart Lane, where they enjoyed a decade of success, paving the way for more overseas footballers to play in England.

A former reserve team player at Aston Villa, Oscar Arce had recently started work as a coach at Sheffield United and picked up the Sheffield entourage at the airport, helping out as a translator. They ran into the legendary Boca Juniors footballer Antonio Rattín at some point, and history begins to meld into legend. Sheffield's account mentions watching Boca Juniors train on the outskirts of Buenos Aires, but Diego was still playing for Argentinos Juniors at the time of the visit. Whatever the truth, the fact is that Haslam was spellbound after witnessing Maradona in training. 'How much does he cost?' he asked.

Other versions swirl around. Lalo Zanoni says in his book *Living Among the Media* that the English club offered almost a million dollars for Maradona, a high figure for the time. President of Argentinos Juniors, Prospero Cónsoli, and one of the club's directors approved. Contracts were drawn up, but bureaucracy stepped in. The official line was: 'The AFA prohibited 40 youths, including Maradona, from playing abroad ... so as not to hinder the plans of coach Menotti and achieve qualification for the World Youth Championship in Japan.'

'You don't know the money I lost!' Maradona declared to journalist Horacio del Prado for *Goles* magazine, talking about that potential move to England.

In Sheffield, there is yet another explanation. Argentinos director Domingo Tessone suggested a $200,000 price tag. Haslam didn't feel the fee to be exorbitant and was going to accept it, as he believed he had discovered a jewel to take back. During the evening, there was an authoritative knock at Haslam's hotel door. A military police officer demanded another $200,000 to let Maradona leave the country. The amount was still affordable, but Haslam was not sure how to make the payment, or even if it was a good idea. He spoke to the Sheffield United board and was told to leave the country immediately, and without Maradona. Argentinos president Cónsoli learned of the demand and, according to the Sheffield version, put the brakes on the deal anyway.

Maradona was already a marketing machine, the hard currency that crushes football's spirit. Yet Diego retained his own dreams, kept afloat with the same boyish enthusiasm and curiosity of his youth. One of his big idols was Pelé.

'Diego, eighteen then, was playing in South America's under-20s competition in Uruguay, trying to qualify for Japan 1979,' says the journalist Guillermo Blanco, organiser and chronicler of that historic meeting. 'Menotti had given the team the day off. We spent the day with Diego and Jorge's [Cyterszpiler] families on the beaches at Atlántida . . . there, Diego confesses for the first time that one of his dreams is to meet Pelé.'

Argentina qualified for the Under-20s World Cup (then known as the World Youth Championship) in Japan and Diego's performances put him finally on the front page of El Gráfico, the first of many splashes. Blanco proposed that the prestigious magazine arrange a Pelé–Maradona meeting. 'But when Diego could, Pelé couldn't, and vice versa,' explains Blanco. 'Diego's behaviour was curious. One Monday, Pelé could meet so I ran to Diego to tell him, and he said, "I can't." A week later, another Monday, the same answer: "I can't." I said to myself, "But he was so anxious to meet Pelé." He wouldn't tell me why he couldn't meet on a Monday.' It took three months for the meeting to materialise.

On 8 April, after Argentinos Juniors had just played at Huracán, the green light arrived. Maradona and Blanco went to Buenos Aires' international airport, Ezeiza. Waiting for them was Don Diego and Jorge Cyterszpiler. Diego, whose body was pulsing with pain after a hard game, said he would settle for only five or ten minutes because he knew how busy Pelé was. They arrived at their hotel in Rio de Janeiro; it was after midnight, and having eaten something light, Maradona put ice on his leg.

At eleven o'clock that morning, Pelé was waiting for all of them in Copacabana, in a friend's apartment where the Brazilian was staying. He received them 'with outstretched arms, a wide smile, wearing a yellow open-necked shirt with white flowers,' wrote Blanco in *El Gráfico*. Pelé first gave Don Diego a hug, then greeted Maradona. Presentations made, they all sat down with a somewhat nervous photographer in front of them. Colour photography was nascent, and photographer Ricardo Alfieri was having some technical issues. Blanco remembers almost every word of what was said in what is one of football's most famous meetings:

'But what a sacrifice, travelling after playing on Sunday to come and see me. You should have stayed at home, I am not worth the trouble.'

'Please, what sacrifice? No, no . . .'

Diego could barely string two sentences together. It felt as if he'd waited a lifetime to meet Pelé.

'I'm annoyed [Pelé said]. I have to leave soon. I didn't think you were going to come here after the game. I've arranged with my lawyer Samir to go to Santos to sort some tax and revenue papers, you know? And now you're here I want to stay for lunch with you. Tell me, how's your team doing?'

'Top of the league, we're having a good season. Delem's the boss, he sends you his greetings. Yesterday we beat Huracán three-one, we scored some great goals, and the fans are getting behind us, following us everywhere.'

'So, Diego, the other day you scored a goal with your hand? [against Newell's Old Boys]. Don't worry, that's the referee's problem.'

Blanco dedicated a special insert of his *El Gráfico* report for other wisdom Pelé was imparting to Diego:

'Accept applause, but do not live for the applause.'

'Contracts: every player has their own problems. It is a very personal matter, but always keep in mind that you must fight for what you are really worth. Always respect yourself and never give yourself away. When you sign your contract, afterwards do not protest or ask for more. Your signature is your word.'

'This talk in Argentina of you moving abroad . . . decide only after you have properly analysed the situation. You tell me that you have eight brothers and your mother and your father. Take that into account when you make your decision.'

And a premonition: 'The body is your tool kit. From what I see, you have a very good physique; take care of it. In life, there is time for everything. There is time to go out, to have a drink, smoke a cigarette, go to bed late, eat whatever you fancy. But everything requires balance. If not, it's over too soon.'

Pelé's lawyer came over to remind him that the driver was waiting outside. Pelé looked up and asked for a little more time. He spotted a guitar and played a few chords. 'I can't sing, I have a very coarse voice. You know what, though? I recently made an album for kids.'

'Pelé, are you going to play any more games?' Diego asked. Because I only saw you against Huracán, in Buenos Aires, do you remember that game?'

'Yes, yes, I think it was my last match in Argentina. Well, I'm sure I'll be playing benefit games quite often.'

Suddenly, Pelé took Diego's hand. Ricardo Alfieri was gazing at them both, the power of the moment making him forget himself.

He suggested heading out onto the balcony to take some more photographs using the bright tropical noon light. Pelé gave Diego a Brazil top and signed a ball for him. Cyterszpiler also asked him to sign the shirt he was wearing.

'Take this watch,' Pelé insisted. 'It's not a good one, you can't go into the water with it. Give it to one of your brothers, and take this medal for yourself. They made it for my farewell from [NewYork] Cosmos.'

'I'll keep it my whole life.'

It was all over in an hour. 'It was wonderful,' said Blanco. 'We were going to the airport, and we had the Christ the Redeemer statue above us. I said, "Diego, one thing still bothers me . . . why the hell didn't you want to go on Monday?"'

'Guille, Mondays belong to Claudia.'

'I knew he was a god as a player; now I know he is a god as a person,' Diego told his teammates in the next Argentinos training session. 'How many kids like me want to see Pelé, touch him, exchange a few words, and I . . . It was Pelé who came and gave me a hug, but first to my dad, he treated my old man as his own. Every time I would grab his hand, my mouth would just drop open, gawking at him. I saw how my old man cried when Pelé was giving me advice. Meeting Pelé is the World Cup I didn't have.'

The meeting merited only a small corner of *El Gráfico*'s cover, pushed to the side by boxer Víctor Galíndez's World Light Heavy-weight title victory.

# 8

# THE 1979 WORLD YOUTH CHAMPIONSHIP IN JAPAN

In January 1979, just after Argentina had confirmed its presence at the World Cup for Under-20s in Japan via the South America qualifying tournament held in Uruguay, Diego took his family to the Uruguayan coast to fulfil a long-discussed dream: to sit on the white sand beaches of Atlántida. He also wanted to take his dad aside and convince him to stop working. 'He was fifty years old, and he'd already done more than enough for us. It was my turn,' Maradona would say years later.

Diego became the head of the family, but 'he didn't lose a father', Néstor Barrone, a close friend of *El Pelusa*, says when talking about the footballer's new position. 'It's one thing to buy a house, help your siblings or ask your father to stop working. Another one is everyone's personal space within the family unit. Diego always felt the need to distinguish between the two. After that, some folk may grow and some might not, but at least everyone was given a chance.'

While Diego's brothers Lalo and Hugo played some games in Argentina's first division and their football careers took them to Spain, Japan and Italy, his sisters hardly ever entered the stage to be part of the Maradona story.

From very early on, the Argentine state wanted to own Maradona and his successes. In 1972, when Argentina was chosen to host the '78 World Cup, the country was already under a dictatorial regime. In 1976, a civil–military coup, led by Jorge Rafael Videla, ended the brief government of President María Estela Martínez de Perón. The junta used Argentina's World Cup win in June 1978, the organisation of which was taken from the hands of the football federation, to legitimise its existence and extend its powers.

Also, 'there was a lot to steal, plus you could manipulate things and show joy to the outside world, while washing away any mud that might stick,' recalls the writer Sergio Levinsky. Many people were kidnapped at la Escuela de Mecánica de la Armada (Navy Mechanics School), situated just half a mile from Monumental de River Plate stadium. 'While the goals are being celebrated, its noise covers up the shouts of the tortured and killed,' said Estela de Carlotto, president of *las Abuelas de Plaza de Mayo* (the Grandmothers of Plaza de Mayo), who was among many that waited daily for information about their missing children and grandchildren, news that would never come.

The state tendrils reached the under-20s national side through compulsory military service, short haircuts and the obligatory photo. Most of the young players went for only a couple of hours a week, never standing guard or holding a weapon. Their mere presence was manipulated for the press. Conscription was nicknamed *colimba*, a composite word made from the first syllables of Spanish verbs *correr* (to run), *limpiar* (to clean) and *barrer* (to sweep) – because that was exactly what they did during service. 'I spent a total of nine and a half hours in the *colimba*,' explained Maradona, whose brief interlude in military service started in March 1979 in a building in front of the seat of government, the Casa Rosada. He wasn't even taught how to salute a higher-ranking officer.

He continued training with Argentinos Juniors and both the full and youth national teams throughout. Before travelling to Japan for the World Youth Championship, Maradona played with the senior national side in various Argentine provinces as well as in Switzerland, Italy, Ireland, the United States and Scotland. It was in a friendly at Hampden Park on 2 June that he scored his first international goal in a 3-1 win against Scotland. Put through on goal, he cheekily sold the goalkeeper a dummy with a feigned pass to a teammate, then stroked the ball home from a tight angle.

'It's not for nothing he's Pelé . . . he even gave me advice, what a privilege,' Maradona repeated to his teammates on the way to Tokyo, a tale no one could escape.

National team manager César Luis Menotti and Diego were re-united for the tournament in Japan. Diego was the leader of the team that represented the essence of Argentine football: talent, commitment and competitiveness. 'Better than that of 1978,' according to Menotti himself, who chose to lead the under-20s in Japan.

The military junta gave Menotti everything he wanted while he was in charge of the national team. It was he that suggested no player could leave the country to play abroad until the end of the 1978 World Cup. Special dispensation was given to Mario Alberto Kempes because he had already arranged a deal with Valencia. Menotti also demanded that the youngsters should leave their clubs to join up with the national side for a pre-tournament training camp in Japan.

*El Flaco* Menotti created a tight-knit group from the outset, mixing advice with toughness but always showing faith in the players. 'Should we just get together for a few weeks and see how it goes?' he said. 'Or do we focus and you do what I say? If you give your heart and soul, maybe we'll be champions.' Needless to say, the team went with the second option.

Gabriel Calderón, who would go on to develop his career at Real Betis and Paris Saint-Germain, recalls being awestruck at having a World Cup-winning manager in the changing rooms. 'Menotti told us, "I'm going to Japan to be world champion, not to finish second."' His methodology required cerebral application: training exercises involved physical and mental concentration to complete. Alliances were built, and a group of boys became a unit, a team that garnered public support and filled stadiums even for friendly games, including one against Franz Beckenbauer's New York Cosmos.

The most common starting line-up was Sergio García, Carabelli, Simón, Rubén Rossi and Hugo Alves; Barbas, Osvaldo Rinaldi and Diego Armando Maradona; Escudero, Ramón Díaz and Calderón. The championship featured heavily in the Argentine media, and many people would wake at five in the morning to follow the games.

Maradona took on the role as figurehead of the team. 'One day we scored eleven goals against [Buenos Aires club side] San Telmo,' midfielder Osvaldo Rinaldi told Argentine newspaper *La Nación*.

'During the game, he told me: "I'm going to try and go past every-one." And he did. . . It was like being at Disney every day. And he was the most humble person, a stupendous companion and a funny, protective captain.'

On the field, Maradona's personality pushed them onwards. 'He said just enough at the right time and was the leader on the field. If you lost the ball he would say, don't worry, keep going, come on, keep it up,' said Calderón. 'And he was the quickest with the banter. You had better not get involved in a battle of words with him; he always had the last say, sharp and streetwise.'

The group stages saw three matches in six days. Indonesia was dismissed 5-0 in the opener, with Maradona scoring two. Yugoslavia battled hard in the second match. 'Why the fuck did you come to Japan?' Menotti yelled at his team during the break, demanding they play to their standards. A second-half goal gave them the victory, followed by a routine 4-1 win over then European Under-20s champions, Poland.

In the quarter-finals, Algeria was thumped 5-0, Maradona scoring the opener then complaining and breaking down in tears when he was substituted before the final whistle. The semi-final was the River Plate *clásico* against neighbours Uruguay under the Tokyo rain, two goals from the lethal duo, Díaz–Maradona, ending the Uruguayan resistance.

'Do you know who taught Ramón Díaz to finish?' Diego explained jokingly years later in *La Nación*. 'Me, daddy, me! I got it into his head that to score goals he did not need to make a hole in the goal-keeper's chest. He listened and learned. My pleasure, Ramón.'

'Wake up happy, Argentina!' was the endless message on national radio and across the media. The government suspended classes so that everyone could see the final. Military junta representatives and celebrities alike wanted to travel to Japan to see it live – President Videla began choreographing a victory photo of Menotti and Maradona.

'You've already fulfilled my expectations,' Menotti told them in the last training session before the final against the Soviet Union. 'I am going to tell my children, when they grow up, that this team was the one that came closest to what I want from a team. You gave me everything I wished for. There's nothing else I can ask of you.' The coach got his desired response immediately, taking some pressure off the team but provoking a reaction.

'We've still got the final to go!' players protested. Menotti kept up the psychology: 'The final doesn't matter to me. Anything can happen – a chance goal, and we might lose. I want you to know that whatever happens, you are the best team I've ever managed.' Maradona agreed with the statement in his autobiography, *Yo Soy El Diego*. 'That was by far the best team of the whole of my career.'

The final was played on a sweltering and stuffy night in Tokyo. After a goalless first half, the Soviets scored early in the second. Argentina hadn't hit their early tournament groove. Eight crazy minutes brought glory: first, a penalty, converted by Hugo Alves, then a goal from Ramón Díaz followed by a free-kick from Maradona to make it 3-1. With a goal tally of twenty scored and only two conceded, Argentina were worthy world champions. Diaz's strike made him the tournament's leading scorer with eight goals, two ahead of Diego, who was player of the championship and scored in five of their six matches.

'The truth is, taking my daughters out of the equation and speaking only of my career, it is difficult for me to find anything that gave me so much joy,' said Maradona two decades later. Back at the Takanawa Prince hotel, the squad sang, 'Maradona is not for sale, Maradona is not leaving, he is national heritage, Maradona is Argentinian...'

Two days later the victors flew, with several stopovers, to Buenos Aires, except Menotti who had to join the senior team in Europe. Maradona's military service call-up meant he wasn't allowed to join the men's national team. He and five other World Youth champions still had several months' conscription to complete. At Rio, they boarded a military plane to Buenos Aires, then took a helicopter to C.A. Atlanta's pitch.

'From there, we travelled all the way down Corrientes [one of Buenos Aires' principal avenues, some five miles in length]. The route was inexplicable,' recounted midfielder Osvaldo Rinaldi. 'Much later on we found out it was to parade us in front of the emissaries from the Inter-American Commission on Human Rights, who'd arrived in the country the day before. On the street, it was a massive party. We didn't have a clue what was happening.'

The Commission had come to investigate crimes carried out by the dictatorship. They had been meeting the Grandmothers of Plaza de Mayo and visiting prisons. The junta encouraged people to show their unity in the street, proclaiming 'Argentinians are Humans, and we are Right', a play on words around the Commission's official title. The bus ended up at the Casa Rosada, where President Videla would receive them.

'We all went with long hair,' Maradona recalled years later. 'Claudia said, "Cut your hair." ... "Forget it! I am a world champion," I said. Well, we were on our way to meet the Commander in Chief, and someone came along and said, "Cut it all off." You know how they left us? As smooth as hard-boiled eggs ... they had this little machine ...' All the recruits, including *El Pelusa*, were forced to change their civilian clothes to military fatigues. Diego's hat was too small for his head. 'It looked like a paper boat floating on top of a big head,' recalls his teammate Sergio García.

A few streets away from the celebrations at Casa Rosada, a woman was registering the disappearance of her son to the Inter-American Commission. She was Jorge Piaggio's aunt. Jorge was one of the celebrated under-20s world champions, and the missing person was Guillermo Mezaglia, Jorge's cousin.

Before the presentation of the victory plaque and commemoration photo, the young players were given a half-hour briefing on how to perform the military salute, to prepare for meeting the Argentine dictator, President Jorge Rafael Videla, and Roberto Eduardo Viola, Commander-in-Chief and the future president. When it came to it, Maradona, who had been pushed by the group to the front of the queue to meet the top brass, only shook the hand of Viola.

'Ermmmm ... General Videla ... one thing ...' Maradona asked for him and his five teammates to be discharged from their military service. Within a month, all of them were stepped down apart from Juan Barbas, the only one not to be pardoned. 'If you bring me Maradona, I'll liberate you,' a lieutenant-colonel told Barbas. 'No drama,' said Jorge Cyterszpiler when asked to take *El Pelusa* to the lieutenant-colonel, and Maradona went, of course.

A few days after the celebrations, the Commission concluded that 'the problem of the disappeared is one of the most serious human rights issues facing the Republic of Argentina'.

'Power has always tried to get close to Maradona,' says sports commentator Victor Hugo Morales. 'And, when very close, it is difficult to push it away.' The dictatorship and then the democracy that followed would go on to use Diego and football, all wrapped up in a demagogic discourse from which a branch of the Maradona legend would grow: a nationalist myth, the defence of the best player in the world, who of course is Argentinian.

The media had also found a new idol. Diego treated journalists well if he felt they understood him and reported him fairly. Guillermo Blanco was one such journalist. Every day something was written about Dieguito, *El Pelusa* from the slums of Villa Fiorito; the boy from the neighbourhood, the kid with charisma, a humble winner, a good lad, concerned about his family, who is still with his teenage sweetheart. And who also looked after his best friend from childhood. Jorge Cyterszpiler had been in Japan, too.

Diego knew that the rushing, cascading waterfall of a life whose current carried him unstoppably forwards was the reward for his remarkable ability, and fame on a scale that had crossed frontiers. The praise pleased him, even though he rejected the pressure from those who would make him an idol.

When Maradona said he never wanted to be held up as an example of anything, it always sounded like he was simply asking not to be judged. He felt he was starting to move in uncharted, swampy waters.

# 9
# JORGE CYTERSZPILER

A nation's emotional map, whether real or imagined, is drawn from its myths, its history and its beliefs, creating an ever-shifting, subjective narrative landscape. Very early on, Argentina became the paragon of street football, its jinking dribbles and tricks an antithesis to its British creators' vision of the game with their emphasis on physical prowess and aerial skill. *El Gráfico* magazine, founded in 1919, takes credit for nurturing the idea that Creole football added Argentine touches and panache to the original. The image triumphed abroad as more and more players were successfully exported, often shouldering the hopes of an entire family.

Argentina circa 1979 saw a mischievous, skilful and illusory young Creole breeze into Argentina's sleeping consciousness in an era of political confusion and lack of reliable references. He was becoming the embodiment of the spirirt of Argentina. What great timing. The nation had been waiting for him. Maradona's early play was epitomised by a daring, streetwise streak, the football poet with the game as his muse and with the amateur spirit that does not need a financial incentive to perform. He was a boy, a *pibe*, a kid who conjured new tricks and pulled new feints just to hear the applause and to bare his soul to the public.

The problem is that when, as is natural, he stops being a child, the tendency remains to keep asking him to reproduce his childlike ingenuity. As such he will be denied the normal developmental phases of growing up, smoothing off the rough edges and becoming an adult. The journey of this type of player creates a flawed man – always a kid on the pitch, but when he behaves as such off it we feel disturbed. Like Peter Pan, some of his choices were unexpected to say the least, like standing Franz Beckenbauer up when Cosmos played in Buenos Aires. He just did not fancy meeting him that night.

Meanwhile, Argentinos Juniors understood that Maradona was a cash cow, and the income he could generate would allow them to keep him a little while longer. They became the first Argentine club to have a shirt sponsor. 'We are going to look after this *pibe*, he's going to show us the world,' used to be the joke between his teammates as they travelled to a midweek friendly in Colombia or Ecuador. In December 1979, the team went to Barcelona to play at the Camp Nou. Jorge Cyterszpiler, in full flow as the first football agent, only let Maradona do interviews for money.

'Maradona is the best player right now,' Hugo 'El Loco' Gatti, Boca Juniors' goalkeeper, told *El Litoral* newspaper. 'But do you know what worries me? His physique ... in a few years he will struggle with his tendency to be chubby.' Diego, who was already captaining Argentinos at the age of twenty, got wind of the comments via friends and also Cyterszpiler. 'He has called you a fatty,' he was told by his agent, adding fuel to the fire just before both teams were about to face each other.

'I was thinking of scoring a couple of goals, now I aim for four,' Diego told him. 'And by any means ...' Gatti apologised to Diego before the game and warned him his words had been misconstrued. *El Pelusa* accepted his apology. And then the kick-off arrived. He scored a penalty, a free-kick and added one more, a '*vaselina*' lob – he controlled the ball on his chest then chipped the ball over Gatti for his hat-trick. It was not enough. Bearing down on goal again, Maradona was pulled back and from the resulting free-kick, larruped home his fourth to seal a 5-3 victory.

The game finished in unusual circumstances, with the rival Boca crowd shouting 'Maradó, Maradó!', the beginning of a love affair. Cyterszpiler, who spent most matches in the stands mimicking his friend's tricks and techniques despite his own physical challenges, was rapt as he watched the events unfolding. He kept note of that evening.

One day Jorge, always in awe of the talent of *El Pelusa*, asked him how he knew his marker was behind him. 'I hear it,' he said.

Somehow Diego had developed a sixth sense. Things were clearly going as planned.

Jorge Horacio Cyterszpiler was the youngest son of a hard-working Polish family that arrived in Argentina in the early 1970s. They owned a shoe factory situated just 200 metres from the Argentinos ground, meaning Jorge would never stray too far from his love of football. His brother, Eduardo, was a full-back who made his Argentinos debut in the first division, but he was diagnosed with cancer and died six months later aged twenty-three. The blow left Cyterszpiler reeling, and for the first time in his life he put his football dream in the locker and closed it, ostensibly for good. He was unable to move on until the club told him about a group of young footballers who were going to be something special. That team helped Jorge reconnect to the world.

'Jorge couldn't be what he wanted to be,' explains Guillermo Blanco. Jorge's right leg had been weak since he was two years old after a severe polio outbreak in Argentina in the 1950s. Although he wore a prosthesis that supported it from the knee down, he lacked muscle strength and limped. His physical affliction belied a fighting spirit that sometimes bordered on being vengeance against the world.

Jorge Cyterszpiler had a magnetic force, and Fernando accompanied him wherever he went, often since that early invitation, to see the Cebollitas team. At other times they would go to La Tablada Jewish cemetery so Jorge could speak with his deceased brother, Eduardo. If it was closed, he would talk to him through the walls.

'What do you do on Saturday mornings?' Jorge asked his schoolmate Fernando García one day. 'Nothing? Then come with me to a match. There's a team with a new Pelé. I bring the lemons and water. You will be surprised.' Jorge, two years older than Diego, could already foresee the footballing destiny of the nine-year-old. 'There was also a very good number 9, Goyo Carrizo, who played like the gods,' remembers Fernando García. 'He was from another planet. But his life's circumstances meant he never made it.'

Before his illness, on Fridays Eduardo used to invite two or three teammates to the spacious Cyterszpiler house, which had an open-door policy. If they were playing at home, then the stadium was at hand. If they were away, the buses left from Argentinos' ground so it was still a good meeting point. Jorge emulated his brother; five or six Cebollitas, including Diego, would stay over at the family home instead of getting the different buses back to Villa Fiorito. On those Fridays if you opened the Cyterszpiler fridge, a kid would come out. Dinner, of course, was included. Toncha, Jorge's mother, made a Milanese everyone loved. Diego, always one to push boundaries, would sneak down and raid the refrigerator at night.

Thus began their relationship; Jorge was able to process the grief from the loss of his brother into love for football and the Cebollitas. He would bring not just lemons, but also balls and bibs, and was always at hand. On one occasion, shortly after winning the league, their manager Francis Cornejo, suffering from gallstones, left his post to Cyterszpiler: 'I ask only one thing, Jorge. No in-fighting – and have fun.' It would end in a pitch battle and a closely guarded secret.

Diego and Cyterszpiler's relationship started becoming an occasional business partnership when Diego made his debut for the first team in 1976. The following year, Jorge followed the Argentina under-20s to Venezuela where they played in the South America Cup youth tournament. He displayed entrepreneurship in Caracas, scraping money together by selling leather and shoe samples given to him by a friend. Argentina didn't get past the group stage, a blot unremarked upon in Diego's autobiography. Still, it taught him that not every game is a victory and not every step is forwards, as Jorge had been telling him.

Cyterszpiler had been studying economics but ended up taking very few lessons, such was his confidence in an intuition that was confirmed after the tournament. Diego asked his friend to represent him full-time and Jorge promised to protect him and make him enough money to facilitate a better life for him and his family. Don Diego and Doña Tota knew that Diego was in good hands. He and Argentinos agreed Diego's first professional contract that included the rental of a house on Calle Argerich and a monthly salary of $400.

Footballers negotiated their own contracts in those days, their pockets being picked while they signed because of a lack of know-how about football finance. Jorge looked to the tennis world and its system of agents to help understand the issues; image rights, accountants, lawyers and advertising all needed to be considered. His older brother Silvio was studying law and proffered advice too. Jorge wanted the most professional structure possible for Diego, someone he saw not only playing for the national team but reaching World Cup finals and winning them all on the way to becoming the best football player in the world.

But on the way, there were things for Diego to do off the pitch. Jorge developed a relationship with Roberto 'Cacho' Paladino, a doctor who looked after boxers, and with another consultant, Dr Alfredo Cahe, who became, from then on, the Maradona family doctor. It was he who, many years later, called Diego to inform him of the death of Doña Tota. He created a medical team away from the club, another first in football.

Jorge always understood what Diego, who trusted his friend implicitly, needed. He knew that the promising footballer was more temperamental than cerebral, so their personalities complemented each other. Cyterszpiler used his charm, backed by intelligence, wit and intuition, to woo those that needed to be wooed. These two kids from the streets of Buenos Aires started 'Maradona Producciones', Jorge's idea, a ground-breaking commercial endeavour, despite having no professional training, to produce films, bring sponsors, and develop and monetise the image of Diego. Cyterszpiler looked ahead and saw absolutely nothing getting in his way with the same spirit he showed playing in goal in kickabouts with friends.

These were the actions of a confident nineteen-year-old Jorge and the equally cocksure seventeen-year-old Diego, confronting the world head-on as they started life's journey. It wasn't easy, but Jorge managed to get Diego a Mercedes-Benz, three ever-more valuable contracts at Argentinos within just five years, a coveted cover shot on the front page of El Gráfico and, of course, public exposure and adulation. As Maradona's agent, Jorge looked after the rapport he had been building with the media. He would do everything for them at Argentinos, even serving them Coca-Cola during breaks. He was particularly ebullient when Diego did not have a good game.

Italian journalist Pier Paolo Paoletti is a connoisseur of the world of Maradona. He described Jorge and Diego's relationship in Sergio Levinsky's book, *Rebel With a Cause*: 'What can you say about Jorge? He's sort of a graceful gnome, but also a man of immeasurable inner wealth and values, crowned by a great passion and identification with Diego. During matches, Cyterszpiler would walk from goal to goal without seeming to notice his bad leg. He would stare at Maradona in ecstasy. Every movement Diego made, he copied. The connection was absolute. . .'

In the same book, Bruno Passarelli, Italian correspondent for *El Gráfico*, explained: 'If Diego had training or a game the next day, something important to do, Jorge would sleep on the floor next to Diego's bed, to stop him from going out at night and doing his thing.'

'Jorge had an eternal love for Diego. Eternal,' says Néstor Barrone, part of their inner circle in Barcelona. 'And from wherever he may be, I suppose he must still love him.'

'Everything was tranquil, healthy, promising,' explains Fernando García, Jorge's friend. 'In all honesty, the real sport was chasing women. During the day, think about how to make their football career more professional and then during their free time, think about girls. They were a couple of teenagers who matured very quickly. For me, Diego was at his purest when he was at Argentinos Juniors and hand in hand with Jorge.'

Cyterszpiler had brought home a professional camera from the World Youth Championship in Japan with the idea of breaking into the vast, untapped market of the United States. He wanted to make a film about how *Dieguito*, as he was called by journalists, was on his way to becoming the new Pelé. Cameraman Juan Carlos Laburu was hired and would travel with them everywhere, continuing when the caravan moved on to Barcelona and later Naples.

After Argentina won the youth tournament in Japan, Cyterszpiler had the idea of organising a show during the Christmas holidays. It was dubbed *Maradona's Christmas*, with proceeds going to a national children's trust, El Patronato de la Infancia. More than two thousand people attended the Luna Park Pavilion, the same boxing and event venue in Buenos Aires where Maradona would celebrate his wedding. There were some ball games, raffles, music and a variety show where, among others, Diego appeared and also Menotti who spoke to the crowd. This served too as the unveiling of Maradona Producciones, with the event brochure declaring the entity to be 'one man, one company'.

Some of the more cynical media hacks were suspicious of the motives behind the function. Maradona told them, 'Do I need to advertise myself? Did you forget to mention that all the proceeds go to El Patronato? It's hurtful. I was a poor kid too once, and I know what it's like not to have a number 5 ball [a full-sized football].'

But in reality, from that moment on, multiple advertising contracts materialised. Diego signed with Coca-Cola and then with Puma, his first sports sponsor whose clothes and shoes he wore for many years. Jorge Cyterszpiler asked sponsors for relative fortunes for that time, and many accepted: AGFA Gevaert, Maurizio de Souza Producciones, TSU Cosméticos, Della Penna . . .

Jorge was in charge of brokering Diego's first transfer from Argentinos. It was not the last one he would work on, but by 1985 and with Diego in Naples the relationship, even the friendship, was over. 'I loved Diego, I love him, and I will always love him,' Cyterszpiler declared in 2015. 'I won't speak ill of him: he is the very concept of what friendship is. A word against him will never come out of my mouth.'

In 2002, he celebrated twenty-five years as an agent, and the entire Argentine football royalty attended his party, from AFA president Julio Grondona to the many contacts he made throughout his career, including Maradona's parents, but not the player. 'He is Diego's best friend, always has been,' Tota said of Jorge that day.

Without Maradona, Cyterszpiler knew how to reinvent himself. He temporarily moved away from representing players to organising events in the entertainment world, as well as a successful tour for the national team. When former footballer and then manager Miguel Ángel Brindisi decided to look for an agent, he contacted Jorge, who then took charge of more than 200 international transfers. He linked up the Argentine football market with Russia, made a fortune and also a few mistakes.

Maradona and Jorge met again in 2011, away from the cameras, when *El Pelusa* was coach of Al Wasl in the United Arab Emirates. Diego wanted to buy one of his clients, Juan Ignacio Mercier, so invited Jorge to visit his home on the Arabian Peninsula. It was a friendly meeting and the transfer was agreed. They did not see each other again.

The well-oiled representation business was not filling him with the necessary happiness to look forward to each new day. His divorce hurt him deeply, sending his world into a spiralling turmoil that he was unable to control. Jorge's therapist kept a close watch on him, as there was a time where nothing got him out of bed and nothing could change his tendency to see everything as dark, very dark. In 2017, he travelled to Europe and went to Málaga to have lunch with one of his clients, former Manchester City player Martín Demichelis. 'Not at your house, Martín,' said Jorge. He didn't want the footballer's wife to see the state he was in. 'Today, joining all the dots together, I think Jorge already knew what he was going to do, and that lunch was a farewell,' Demichelis told journalist Diego Borinsky.

Twenty days later, on 7 May 2017, on a slow, lazy Sunday, Cyterszpiler was staying in room 707 in a hotel in the Puerto Madero neighbourhood of Buenos Aires. Once alone, he threw himself from the balcony of his seventh-floor room. He was fifty-eight years old.

When Maradona heard the news, shaking his head, he tried to find a reason: 'A woman makes you suffer, but she should not kill you . . . I think with Jorge we all fell asleep at the wheel.'

1980. Diego with his parents, Dalma Salvadora Franco (Tota) and Diego Maradona Senior. The rocks. The mutual devotion.

Diego idealised his past. He tried to recreate the feelings inspired by this photograph wherever he went. The old village. The emotional links.

A young Maradona (centre) relaxing with his family. He promised he would take them to a beach. He was always generous to the people in his inner circle.

April 1978. Maradona with the Argentinos Juniors T-shirt. His first professional club had a history and philosophy which were very close to his heart.

1979. Maradona waves to the crowd, watched by his brother Hugo, after an Argentinos match. The two brothers, Hugo and Lalo, made it as professional footballers, but not at a very high level.

11 November 1980. Maradona in action during a match between Argentinos Juniors and Guadalajara (Mexico). Argentinos 0-1 Guadalajara. The club raised money with foreign trips.

1981–82. Maradona in Boca Juniors, where he got his only title in Argentine soccer. A special relationship was created with the club that lasted forever.

26 August 1982. Maradona and Bernd Schuster during the European Winners' Cup final between FC Barcelona and Standard de Liège (2-1). Allies and misunderstood misfits.

2 June 1986. Maradona is fouled by South Korea's Kim Young-Se during their first-round World Cup match in Mexico City. He got a kicking wherever he played . . .

22 June 1986. Maradona used his hand ('the hand of God') to score the opening goal against England at the Mexico World Cup quarter-final.

29 June 1986. Maradona holds aloft the World Cup trophy on the shoulders of Roberto Cejas, an unknown fan at the time.

# 10
# THE TRANSFER TO BOCA JUNIORS

As early as 1979, FC Barcelona had reached a preliminary transfer agreement with both Argentinos and Maradona, and their vice-president Nicolau Casaus travelled to Buenos Aires to tie up both contracts. He wrote a short report after his first meeting with *El Pelusa*:

> The house is located in the same neighbourhood as the club and was given to Maradona by Argentinos Juniors. It is a very simple construction and consists of one floor. Upon entering, there is an atrium in the Creole style, which serves for everything: dining room, living room and children's playroom. Maradona's mother welcomes us along with Maradona's brothers. The whole family are decent, good people, but they could not be from a more humble background. Maradona, extremely simple despite his great popularity, retains a charming modesty. He always dresses like an athlete. Nice but very shy. He prefers to listen than speak, and when he does speak it is with a lot of common sense. He has a girlfriend.

The following year, 1980, started with Maradona, with abundant hair, crossing himself before getting onto another pitch and then dribbling and passing with his now nationally famous silky left foot. By the end of that year, he had turned into the most effective, artistic and desirable player on the market. There was already talk of him being the best in the world. Diego had scored forty-three goals in forty-five games, two of which came against River Plate at their

Monumental stadium in a match that ended with the opponents trying to sign him. He had become captain of Argentinos, knew how to handle the media and was making his own decisions about his future. After that one year, Maradona looked very different from the Diego that Casaus had seen.

'We were a poor team technically, but with him in 1980 we were runners-up, two points behind River Plate,' recalls Ricardo 'Gringo' Giusti, Maradona's former teammate. That second place, three years after his debut, remains *El Pelusa*'s greatest success at Argentinos. In the careers of many of the finest footballers, there is often a moment of realisation that the player has outgrown the club that nurtured him. When it happens, managing that dynamic is not easy.

Argentinos improved Maradona's contract and wages several times during his time there, making him the highest-paid player in the country, albeit helped with controversial top-ups from the Argentine federation (AFA). In 1980, the government assigned the AFA a budget for maintenance and promotion expenses, and some of it found its way into Maradona's salary. 'It is an exceptional case,' proclaimed the federation's executive committee. Argentinos also covered part of Maradona's wages thanks to Austral, one of the two Argentine state airlines, an arrangement facilitated by General Carlos 'Pajarito' Suárez Mason, an influential member of the dictatorship. With foreign teams hovering around Maradona, the government and the AFA wished to demonstrate their desire to retain their prized possession, whatever the cost.

Diego wondered if it were legal to keep hold of a player who wanted to play abroad. The dictatorship took Menotti's idea to stop players from leaving Argentina before the 1978 World Cup and established it in law. If a player wanted to leave the country, they had to deal directly with the dictatorship's strongman, Vice-Admiral Carlos Alberto Lacoste.

The press, closely monitored by the dictatorship, begged Diego to stay put, suggesting that – perhaps overzealously – his departure could precipitate the death of Argentine football. River Plate tried to use the same arguments by offering a reasonable offer to Argentinos. Juventus president Giampiero Boniperti travelled to Buenos Aires prepared to pay $1.3m for a one-year loan deal. It even included a clause to return Maradona four months before the 1982 World Cup so he could join the preparations with Menotti's squad. However, club owner FIAT had financial difficulties and union strife to contend with, and Boniperti eventually put the brakes on the idea.

And, at the age of twenty, Diego decided that he wanted to play for Boca Juniors, his dad's team. Unwittingly, Diego's spirit was drawn to a club that would stoke his myth in Argentina and elevate him above the level of a simple footballer.

The Boca neighbourhood is located south-east of the centre of Buenos Aires, at one of the mouths of the River Plate. It is home to a large contingent of Italian immigrants and has been famous for its intense cultural identity since the early twentieth century. It is not just a place, it is the very root of social identity, almost a miniature independent republic brimming with working-class expatriates. Emir Kusturica, while he filmed his documentary *Maradona* with Diego, said, 'I discovered the greatness of the poor in cities when I filmed [*Do You Remember*] *Dolly Bell?* I saw that the noble spirit had disappeared from the houses of the rich and transferred to the houses of the poor. There, the rules are respected, and sacrifices are made. When Maradona had to choose between River Plate, which offered more money, and Boca Juniors, Diego chose Boca for these noble reasons.'

At Boca Juniors, the working class and the poor from the local neighbourhoods, Maradona's dad too, shared a collective dream – to play in front of their friends at the Bombonera stadium. If it goes well for you at Boca, to paraphrase sociologist Pablo Alabarces, the media will write about your successes as an *Epic of the Poor*. Maradona was very comfortable with that bigger picture.

And so, the first great media-led transfer in history had kick-started.

The transfer out of Argentinos Juniors seemed irreversible. The negotiations and even the names of other clubs waiting in the wings in case it failed were all in the public domain, but the last step, the confirmation of his next club and the signature, was being delayed. What stopped the inevitable? In an interview for *El Gráfico* in July

1980, Maradona recognised his predicament: 'I am in the middle of everyone, arms folded as if I were at an auction and the gavel is raised, and they're saying . . . "Who offers more?"'

The government let Maradona know they preferred him to keep quiet while everything was being sorted, but they knew he wasn't the docile type. 'I am not a commodity, I am a football player,' Diego stated at the time. 'By staying in this country, I'm taking a big risk because if something happens to Maradona, he will stop serving a purpose. Then no one is going to offer a penny for him.' The third person again.

Fernando Signorini said that Diego, whose oratory always played to the cheapest seats, started speaking in the third person 'because sometimes he himself does not believe that this is all happening to him. He thinks that this happens to Maradona, while he remains the humble, family-minded, salt-of-the-earth Diego.'

Cyterszpiler held informal talks with River Plate, looking for a trade-off to benefit everyone. After Maradona scored those two goals at the Monumental, the president of River, Rafael Aragón Cabrera, asked how much Argentinos' president wanted for *El Pelusa*. 'We're not selling,' Prospero Cónsoli replied. River's efforts didn't let up, and they pushed for an answer at the beginning of 1981. Cónsoli began to accept that he could no longer hang on to his star. 'Thirteen million dollars.' River offered half that amount plus a player, a counter-offer that left Diego cold when he found out. In February, Maradona and his family went to Monumental to watch a youth match. During the game, he was repeatedly and disdainfully reminded by some fans of his declared adulation of Boca, River's greatest rival. 'I'm not going to set foot in that stadium again,' he told Claudia. River raised its offer to Argentinos, but inserted a new clause: Diego's salary cannot exceed that of Ubaldo 'Pato' Fillol, River's best-paid player. Diego took this as yet another slight.

A year after scoring four goals past Hugo Gatti and *that* ovation from the Xeneize (Boca fans are also known as Xeneize – Genovese – because the team founders were from Genoa), and despite FC Barcelona's having agreed a pre-contract, Maradona decided to sign for Boca. 'How could I do it?' he wondered.

Unlike today, the football gossip universe in the 1980s revolved around a few media outlets: an influential magazine (*El Gráfico*), a large radio station (*Rivadavia*) and a few newspapers (*Clarín, La Nación, La Razón* and *Crónica*). Diego chose *Crónica*. He leaked to one of its journalists, Cayetano Ruggeri, that he was in advanced negotiations with Boca. Fake news – well, at that point anyway. Cayetano most likely already knew, but he played his part, publishing the story in the newspaper as either a favour or part of a deal with Diego.

The winds of change were blowing through Boca. The new president, Martín Benito Noel, appointed Silvio Marzolini as manager, bringing in strong and talented players such as attacking midfielder Miguel Ángel Brindisi and Carlos Morete. It was a good moment to be part of the club.

*Crónica*'s article, suggesting negotiations between the Xeneize and Maradona were going well, excited fans and left the club with little wiggle-room. The directors at Boca called Cyterszpiler to talk about the message Diego had sent them.

The agent confirmed the player's interest in the move, but insisted that speed was of the essence as there were other options. The club lacked the funds, but they promised to make a bid. What began as a straight purchase for the not inconsiderable sum of $10 million became a last-minute loan using six Boca players, some cash and what Maradona described as 'dodgy flats' and also cheques as collateral.

To start with, the owner of a Buenos Aires newspaper pledged the $10 million Argentinos wanted for the player and he also helped put pen to paper to contract terms for Diego and Cyterszpiler. Newspaper, radio and television networks assumed it was a done deal, or close to it, creating dedicated reporting teams for coverage of every detail, saturating the news from 13 to 20 February.

But a fly wandered into the ointment. The investor's rival newspaper ran a story claiming the Revenues and Customs office wanted to know how Boca could afford such a transfer and where the money was coming from.

Businessman '*Cacho*' Steinberg, the former representative of the boxer Carlos Monzón, tried to take advantage of the confusion and offered to remove any obstacles in the way. If done through him, everything could be sorted, he told everyone. Steinberg tried to speak directly to Diego, and the player warned Jorge, 'Hey, bighead – they're trying to go over yours.' These are the moments that quantify and solidify relationships.

The Boca board couldn't back down in the face of public pressure, but the first investor finally decided not to get involved, so the club had to devise an alternative, urgently. Maybe a loan deal of some kind? Maradona was going to help again.

On Saturday, 14 February, Maradona travelled 400km south from Buenos Aires to the seaside resort city of Mar del Plata, to play for Argentinos against Hungary in a summer tournament. *El Gráfico* tried to convince Maradona to do a photoshoot with him wearing the Boca shirt. Diego thought about it, but concluded it would just muddy the waters further. Having said that . . . He also knew that being seen in the blue and gold Xezeine colours could force every-one's hands. Maradona donned a Boca shirt while a few teammates – only their hands showing – stretched the shirt outwards. It was a photo that would be splashed on the front page of the magazine's next edition.

That was the last full game he played for Argentinos. The follow-ing Thursday, and after many long meetings that went into the early hours, an agreement was reached between Boca and his club. For $4 million, he would move to Boca Juniors on loan until the start of the 1982 World Cup in Spain, sixteen months later. After the tourna-ment, another $4 million would be paid for the full transfer. On top of the cash, four Boca players would move to Argentinos and a fur-ther two would go on loan. Boca also promised to pay Argentinos' debts with the AFA (money that the federation had loaned to pay some extra wages to Diego) and also some bank loans, all of which amounted to a further $1.5 million.

Another businessman smoothed various issues to ensure the deal came to fruition. Federal Bank employee Guillermo Cóppola had convinced the six Boca players to complete their side of the bargain and move across to Argentinos – Maradona was impressed and commented on Cóppola's vibrant energy. For his friend Jorge Cyterszpiler, he saved a genuine 'Thank you, bighead'.

Years later, Diego defined the contract with his new club as 'a little strange'. He wrote in his autobiography, 'To complement the deal, they gave me some apartments built by businessman Tito Hurovich. They looked like they were made of cardboard, there were no papers for them, we couldn't register the deeds, nothing.' But he'd got what he wanted – to play for Boca Juniors.

The media frenzy culminated in Maradona signing his contract in front of the TV cameras – Channel 13 had bought the live broadcast television rights. On Friday 20 February, an injured Diego played in a friendly between Argentinos and Boca at his new home, the Bombonera stadium. He wore an Argentinos shirt in the first half, which he later gave to his old coach Francis Cornejo, and Boca's in the second.

It had been twelve years since that trial at Parque Saavedra and four and a half since his debut in the Argentinos first team for whom he scored 116 goals in 166 games. Maradona now left behind friends in the squad, the stadium and lots of memories.

Argentinos, thanks to the transfer money and some good signings, were proclaimed first division champions in 1984, won the Copa Libertadores in 1985 and were finalists in the Intercontinental Cup the same year. In 2003, their stadium was renamed 'Diego Armando Maradona', although many fans would have preferred it to retain its original neighbourhood moniker, La Paternal.

The official Boca debut came two days later, in the opening Torneo Metropolitano league match against Talleres. Maradona scored two penalties in a 4-1 home win. The first one 'dropped like a tear', according to the poetic account of legendary radio and television commentator Víctor Hugo Morales, who likewise was making his debut as a commentator in Argentina. 'That day I was inspired,' Víctor Hugo recalls. 'But it was easy to let the imagination fly when you are watching Diego, especially on that stage, the Boca stadium, *la bombonera*, the box of chocolates, with that noise so special and unique.'

The match raked in around a million dollars, fulfilling Boca's economic forecasts and helping them start to comply with the transfer demands. River Plate had missed out on the star they coveted, so they brought prolific striker Mario Alberto Kempes, the hero of Argentina's 1978 World Cup win, back home from Valencia. However, the dollar soared against the Argentine peso while government policies dramatically affected the financial clout of both River and Boca. The cheques used to pay Maradona's transfer were no longer backed by sufficient reserves.

'The agreement was that Boca would pay four million dollars at first, a million at a time,' explains Alberto Pérez, who was then the secretary-general at Argentinos Juniors. 'They soon told us, "We cannot pay what you are asking, the dollar has got a much higher value today compared to when we reached the original agreement."'

With the devaluation of the peso, Boca couldn't in fact pay for Maradona, even if they filled the whole stadium four times over. Nor River Plate for Kempes, who went back to Valencia after winning the Argentine league with them. At the end of the year, Diego had to leave Boca and return to Argentinos, but before he could play he joined the national side preparing for the World Cup in Spain.

In the middle of that confusion, Barcelona, using the pre-contract they had agreed in 1979, knew their moment had arrived.

# Part III
---
# MARADONA

# 11
# THE STAY AT
# BOCA JUNIORS

During his fifteen months at Boca, Maradona's world changed. Fame meant lots of doors opened and, full of testosterone and bravado as he was, he happily walked into new rooms. He was conscious of being the highest earner and also the player who could accumulate and wield the most power, an influence he applied to sensitive causes. For example, Boca charged the younger players for the club shirts they wore. Diego demanded the board give the entire squad one free shirt for every game. On Friends' Day, in July, he gave away branded watches, always a status symbol, to his closest friends.

Roberto Mouzo holds the record number of appearances for Boca. 'Diego lent me his BMW to go to Morón [a city within the Buenos Aires province] to buy *La Razón* on Saturday nights,' he told Diego Borinsky in *El Gráfico*. 'The first time we did it, we won, and then it turned into a superstitious ritual.'

The weekly magazine *Somos* published Maradona's assets in a report: two chauffeured Mercedes-Benz, a BMW, a black Ford Taunus, a house on Calle Cantilo valued at $800,000 and another on Calle Lazcano. There was a piece of land in Moreno, a city in the province of Buenos Aires, and the Maradona Producciones office housed in an impressive building in the centre of the city. 'He has 40 pairs of shoes, 50 Italian shirts and he wears Paco Rabanne perfume,' the magazine stated.

Diego liked to go to the cabaret and revue theatres and didn't mind having his photo taken with the *vedettes*, the main female leads. His image was immortalised as he was snapped leaving famous restaurants where he would meet actors, politicians and well-known businessmen. To satisfy his new lifestyle, he rented an apartment in the northern quarter of Buenos Aires for friends and footballers to visit. Carlos Salinas, one of the players who moved to Argentinos Juniors as part of the Maradona deal, was among them. 'After the move, we met Diego several times in an apartment that he had on Santa Fe Avenue,' he told Diego Borinsky for *El Gráfico*. 'Right downstairs, there was a nightclub, Dover it was called, and we took the women from there up to the apartment. Guillermo Cóppola, Carlitos Randazzo were also involved . . . they were like a walking rock and roll band, and they knew how to throw a party.'

It was Randazzo who introduced Diego to Cóppola just before the bank employee got involved in his transfer to Boca Juniors. 'It was like hooking up a couple,' said Randazzo, born in La Boca and one of the players transferred from Boca to Argentinos in the Maradona deal. 'One day we did an advert for Flipper Jet together, some new electronic game,' Randazzo explained in *El Gráfico*. 'Diego invited me to his apartment. It was evening and when I went up . . . there were already girls, many girls in there.'

When, years later, drugs became part of Maradona's story, Randazzo was often included in the same breath. 'Every time anyone mentioned drugs . . . they always pointed at Diego and me,' he told Borinsky. 'But nobody talked about when we were 17 or 18 when the doctors at the campuses gave us, and many others, injections to help us play. And then the day they offered me cocaine, I said, "This is nothing, this is crap compared to the injections." That's why we got so hooked.'

According to Randazzo's claims, doctors also provided some players with amphetamines across the football academies, because 'if the one in front of you is being helped, then we want help too'. The footballer insisted that, as a consequence, many suffered from sleep problems and needed regular detoxifying immersions in baths and saunas.

Diego played the friendly between Argentinos Juniors and Boca carrying a knock and then spent several days trying to recover, but he felt fit enough for April's *Superclásico* against River at La Bombonera. It was a rainy night, but that didn't stop Maradona displaying memorable moments. Attacking midfielder Miguel Ángel Brindisi scored Boca's first two goals. The opener came when Diego picked the ball up in his own half and pushed forwards. He was felled not once but twice by wild tackles, both worthy of yellow cards, but the referee played on because Diego got up and played on. He skipped past three more defenders and tussled with goalkeeper Pato Fillol for possession. The ball squirted out to Brindisi who stroked home. Brindisi scored again, and Boca added a third to win 3-0 on the night. That final goal became an iconic one.

'*Cacho*' Córdoba, the Boca number 3, made an uncharacteristic surge up the right wing and spotted Maradona free around the penalty spot. Córdoba cut back inside and floated the ball to Diego, who subtly controlled the ball that then stopped dead on the muddy pitch. Fillol rushed from his line to block, Diego feinted left and jinked out to the right, leaving Fillol floundering on the floor. The dance took less than a second, and in less than one square metre of space; Fillol had been completely outsmarted. Tarantini, a defender, was on the line and swooped towards Maradona's feet, like a goalkeeper. 'I was going to dummy him, I assure you,' recalled Maradona. 'But I saw a side open and "tac", I put the ball there.' The scoring touch was a soft, controlled, sand wedge of a shot, the ball lofted between the flailing Tarantini's outstretched hand and the right-hand post. A press photographer sprang from behind the goal-line and tracked Maradona's celebratory run, comically falling into the mud as the flash of his camera lit up the scorer's face.

Maradona and Brindisi each scored seventeen league goals for Boca that season, the lethal duo helping the team win the Metropolitano title – Maradona's only senior club success in Argentina.

He was enjoying his football: the rivalries, the raucous stadiums, the celebrations and his love affair with the ball. But inside, the first cracks of something fragile breaking could be heard. Doubts swirled about the Xeneize club's ability to make the transfer payments almost as soon as their newly acquired star had scored those first goals for his new team. He was back on other clubs' radars.

In the extreme way he understood life, the incessant focus of the media started to choke him. He decided he wanted to quit football, to get away from the monster of his own creation, always in search of a magic gateway to fresh pastures. He mixed nights out in Buenos Aires with periods of introversion. Or he simply hid away with his family, who were caricatured in *Humor* magazine as a group of tourists who bought everything with Diego's money. 'I cannot be quiet anywhere,' he complained.

Boca was flanked by government tax collectors and had its 'Sports City' complex, one of its biggest assets, seized. The Central Bank threatened to disqualify them when it was confirmed that its leaders issued cheques without having sufficient funds. It was even written in the press that Maradona, oblivious to the club's shenanigans, had stopped paying his taxes and could even wind up in prison. The pressure was immense, as these matters filled the sports and the general papers.

Eight months after signing, Boca organised a world tour to raise money to be able to pay their golden boy. It was in October, and an overwhelmed Maradona was en route to the Ivory Coast when he confided in Roberto Passucci, Boca's legendary defender. 'When he turned the lights off, he couldn't sleep,' Passucci told the Boca website, 'and he tells me: "Passu, I can't sleep. I can't handle the fame, I can't relax anywhere. If I want to go and buy a T-shirt today, Cyterszpiler has to juggle all sorts of arrangements so that people don't see me. It's terrible."'

Hundreds of Ivorian boys wearing T-shirts emblazoned with Maradona's image welcomed the team as they disembarked at Abidjan airport. It was a choreographed move set up by his agent. Diego had never seen anything like it. 'The kids rushed past these machete-carrying police officers and just dangled off me, chanting "Die-gó, Die-gó!"' he wrote in his autobiography. 'Later, when we went to have lunch at the hotel, about twenty kids came up to me, and one calls me *"El Pelusa, El Pelusa"*. A Black boy from the Ivory Coast knew the name, *El Pelusa*!

'Abroad, I was treated like a king; at home . . . the least said, the better.'

Diego felt overwhelmed, and even raised the subject with his father, a rarity. Part of him wanted to go back and be the boy from

Villa Fiorito. But he soon discovered nowhere welcomes you back completely. So he had a sense of dislocation, a kind of vertigo.

'I want to quit football,' he told Guillermo Blanco during the flight back to Argentina from Africa. Maradona's first-division debut had been five years previously, and he was about to turn twenty-one. He wanted to 'play a game with kids, against kids, with the kids in the stands, with kids as goalkeepers, with kids as policemen . . . just with kids . . . with the innocent'.

'Maradona could not allow himself any weakness,' said Fernando Signorini in Asif Kapadia's documentary *Diego Maradona*. 'One day, I told him that with Diego, I would go to the end of the world. But with Maradona, I wouldn't even take a step. He said to me, "Yes, but if it hadn't been for Maradona, I'd still be in Villa Fiorito."'

'Sometimes, I hear that I have to score one thousand goals like Pelé and I don't understand why,' Diego told Guillermo Blanco in 1981 on the plane that brought them back to Buenos Aires from the Ivory Coast. 'Is that going to give me peace and quiet? . . . I want people to forget about Maradona, and for the newspapers to stop writing rubbish. The last thing they invented was about a yacht, printing that I had bought one. Lalo, my brother, came and asked me about it. I said no, and he replied, "But in the article it even says the name of the guy who is going to take care of it! Are you sure it's not true?"'

There was only one possible solution to that frenzy.

# 12
# THE 1982 WORLD CUP
# IN SPAIN

From the moment he mentioned openly that he wanted to leave football, Maradona had to climb up from a very deep place. Wounded and frustrated, he went on holiday to Las Vegas with his family. He even skipped national team get-togethers – a banishment offence in Menotti's book, who nonetheless noted Maradona's mood. Diego missed another Argentina training session when he decided to spend the night caring for his ill mother, Doña Tota. At twenty-one years of age, his emotions were on the verge of boiling over.

'After we made the sale,' explains the general secretary of Argentinos Juniors, Alberto Pérez, 'I told [Josep Lluís] Núñez, "Look, I don't know if Diego will adapt to Barcelona." He looked at me, surprised. "I am telling you . . . Catalans are quite formal, Diego comes from a different background . . ."' The president of Barcelona had received his first warning.

'When we finished negotiating the whole thing, Jorge Cyterszpiler said to me, "Barcelona gave Diego a car,"' continues Pérez. 'And he tells me to ask Núñez to pay for the petrol as well. "He will go crazy, Jorge, you tell him." "No, no, you tell him." So, I tell Núñez that there was one detail left, a very small one, sooooo . . . Barcelona had to pay for the petrol of the car . . . He got up and started to shout, "The petrol? The petrol? With the millions of pesetas that . . . and you ask me for the petrol!"'

Jorge and Diego, two boys from a Buenos Aires neighbourhood, went together to conquer Europe. They were about to land in Barcelona with all their mistrust and anxiety equalled by the suspicion and hostility of their hosts, ready to defy the First World that the club and Spain represented.

But before that adventure, there was the small matter of the World Cup in Spain. What goes up, must come down and time resolves almost everything. Once the Barcelona transfer got on the right track, peace of mind and focus returned for Maradona, allowing him to prepare adequately for the 1982 World Cup. Menotti started them as early as 14 February, four months before the opening match. He mixed world champions (Fillol, Passarella, Ardiles, Kempes) with some of the youngsters from Tokyo (Ramón Díaz, Calderón, Barbas and, of course, Maradona). Friendlies were played in Argentina against Bulgaria, where the crowd whistled at them, and Poland, in a game where Diego's team leadership stood out for the first time. 'I hope our fans understand this is a type of football that has to be protected. The whistles the other day hurt me,' admitted Diego.

His brilliance was beginning to outshine and overwhelm everything, including the coach. 'Do you compete with Diego?' journalists asked Menotti at a press conference. 'I don't play, and he is the best player in the world, how can I compete with Maradona?' he answered. The transfer of pre-eminence first had to be dealt with in the national side's European tour. Menotti argued that 'silence is healthy' after banning his main star from having chats with the media when he learned that Maradona had asked for $2,000 to give an interview during the visit to London. Diego, who was not used to being told what to do, became impatient. Neither was he accustomed to having filters to deal with the public, his eager audience. Cyterszpiler also asked him to moderate his statements, which the Argentine government had also suggested. It seemed the free spirit could not be sufficiently harnessed.

In interviews, Maradona insisted that he was the same as always, that nothing had changed since he'd left the shanty town, but that speech became formulaic and repetitive.

The national team stayed at Hotel Benidorm in Alicante during the first group phase of the World Cup. Maradona was one of the tournament's superstars, along with the Brazilian Zico and Karl-Heinz Rummenigge of West Germany. It was Diego that was splashed on

the magazine covers and the poster pull-outs, his face on the advertisements in Spanish streets. The Argentine press served up the idea
that he was the chosen one, from whom the most was expected, in
various dishes: 'He is no longer a child . . . he must fulfil "what he
promised us".' Pelé, whose football transcendence was under threat,
aired his doubts about whether Maradona had 'sufficient greatness
to justify the honours paid to him by the world'.

Teammate Ossie Ardiles believed Diego needed more normality
and that he should be sporadically withdrawn from the artificial
empire being built around him. They slipped off to visit a church
at the nearby coastal town of Villajoyosa. Ardiles told the story to
Andrés Burgos, for his book *El Partido*: 'When the guards at the rally
realised that we were missing, all the alarms went off. There were
rumours of possible armed action or kidnapping by the SAS [Brit-
ish Army special forces] against the team. Diego was at Mass, with
me, watching a bunch of kids making their first communion, when
suddenly guys dressed in suits and dark glasses came in, sighing because they had found us.'

The World Cup champion wanted to look after the delicate young
man, hungry for success with the senior national team and with
outstanding technique. '[In the warm-ups] he would stand in the
middle of the pitch and start juggling the ball,' Ardiles told the *Daily
Mail*. 'Then he would kick it in the air and chat to you, as though he
had forgotten it. "Ossie, how are you today?" And then, "boom!", the
ball would fall on to his foot again. Most of the time, the opponents
stopped their warm-up to watch, knowing that ten minutes later
they would be playing this monster. He knew that . . . For the other
team, it was, "Cor blimey!" And for us, "Hello, he's playing for us."'

On the other side of the Atlantic Ocean, Argentina was in turmoil,
in the midst of a conflict with the UK over the Falkland Islands, a
British Overseas Territory whose sovereignty has long been contested
by Argentina, who call the remote island group Las Malvinas. On
2 April 1982, Argentine soldiers occupied the islands' capital, Port
Stanley, triggering a favourable reaction around the country. The
military junta translated the response as universal support for the

campaign, delivering an opportunity to negotiate with the United Kingdom about the islands' disputed sovereignty. Cyterszpiler and Maradona, like many other celebrities in the day, raised funds for the campaign.

The war invaded the national side's changing room: some players had relatives involved, others felt indignant towards the junta and a few more bought the patriotism sold by the dictatorship. There was no agreement to come up with a single voice, but the government wanted to control what came out. A civil servant gave the team a document with instructions of what to say about the conflict. Menotti was very clear about it: he told him that there was no form in the world that could stop courageous men saying what they felt.

'We wanted to beat Belgium for our country, which is suffering so much,' said Maradona of Argentina's first group game, but in reality not much more was said publicly about the war situation as, in any case, the players were not getting reliable reports about it. Years later, in El Gráfico, Menotti explained their apparent emotional distance from the tragic events: 'It was an awful time. The players were talking to their families in Argentina, and they were all telling us that we were winning the war 4-0. In Spain, we found out little by little that it was actually a massacre.'

The day after Argentina's World Cup debut ended in a 1-0 defeat to Belgium, the junta accepted the humiliating cessation of hostilities. Spanish journalist Paco Aguilar, who followed the Argentine team during the World Cup, tells a story of that convoluted time: 'Ramón "Pelado" Diaz had gone to a nightclub on a bender after the game, despite the instruction that no one should go out. Ardiles' cousin, José Ardiles, an Argentine army pilot, had died that same day. When the captain Daniel Passarella heard about José and realised Diaz had gone out, he went to look for him, found him, punched him, threw him to the ground then took him back to the hotel.'

On the pitch, Menotti used Maradona as an out-and-out striker, while Mario Kempes, in reality a fox-in-the-box type of player, was deployed further back to help build play. Menotti's plan meant Diego didn't get the ball in the areas he could do most damage. He was not a pure goalscorer, but a finisher of moves he manufactured for himself or teammates. Additionally, the older players failed to integrate him into the team.

The lack of synergy in the squad and the tactics did not stop him trying to display leadership. 'For him a match was [a] show. At his best, he didn't need to warm up or concentrate,' Ardiles told the *Daily Mail*. 'But before a game he would almost be in frenzy, using swear words to motivate himself and us. He would transmit just how much it meant to him.'

Diego started ignoring Menotti's instructions and sought to initiate attacks, but lacked the maturity to choose the optimum moment. At the Camp Nou, the Belgians had aggressively man-marked him, annulling his threat, and then a single goal had given the three points to the Europeans. 'Maradona cannot complain,' wrote Pelé about Belgium's stringent tactics. The Brazilian, in a cosseted relationship with FIFA, was seemingly not courageous enough to demand protection of artistic ball-players.

Argentina won their two subsequent group matches and qualified from the first stage, despite looking more like a group of eleven individuals, a team that was not fusing. Maradona's best moment was a brace and an assist in the 4-1 win over Hungary.

Next was a three-team, knockout group phase with two of the strongest teams of the competition, Italy and the favourites Brazil, to be played in the Sarrià stadium, Barcelona, with only one qualifying for the semi-finals. The first match was against the Europeans and is considered a turning point in football. Claudio Gentile, Italy's famous hard-man defender and enforcer, clamped down on Maradona throughout. The Italian committed twenty-three fouls on the Argentinian, one every four minutes and the highest number in the history of the competition to date. The two played a game in parallel, a sashaying sprite trying to evade the crashing of the ironmonger's hammer in an engrossing yet unpalatable dance.

'Gentile?' Maradona was asked at the end of the game. 'Good, good, he marked me well.'

Marco Tardelli, who played in the midfield that day, said, 'To stop Maradona you have to use your hands, your feet, kick him, because otherwise there is no way to stop him. I would have treated him the same.'

Antonio Cabrini, the Italian left-back said, 'We had to anticipate his movements, get there before him and commit fouls, make him nervous, not letting him play, stopping him from receiving the ball ... And above all, we had to prevent him from turning to face our goal. A player like Maradona does not have the same effect if he cannot face the rival box.'

Maradona said, 'The only one I have complaints against is the referee. I really don't know what he wanted to do.'

Gentile said, 'The Argentines shouldn't complain. It is obvious that when you lose, you look for excuses. Tarantini, Passarella, Gallego were not angels. Bah! It is better to forget about it.'

Tardelli said, 'I think that in today's football it would have been an even bigger story, because no one can commit as many fouls nowadays as we did in 1982.'

Gentile was booked in the forty-second minute. Italy won 2-1, and the defender's work was praised back home. The near-perfect display of the transalpine country's defensive football culture provided a shot of confidence to a team that went on to win the competition. Maradona still had a career of criminal fouls waiting for him, but after such a public pummelling the first calls from media and commentators to protect football's showmen were finally heard.

Argentina needed to win against Brazil to have any hope of advancing to the semi-finals. Timing is everything in football and the ideal platform was not created to encourage the talented Diego. He seemed to amble around the field again, unable to grasp what the match required. The team was three down in what would be a 3-1 defeat when Maradona was sent off for a lunge into Batista's midriff. 'All I know is that I raised my leg with my boot level to protect myself, without any intent,' a still het-up Maradona said afterwards. 'Sometimes you get tired of receiving fouls.'

Affronts and a desire for vengeance accumulated throughout Maradona's life, but this was the first time it manifested itself so strongly. The 1982 World Cup created a platform for his anger and a new source of rebellion. The World Cup was over for Argentina after Menotti had failed to mix two talented generations. In *Yo Soy El Diego*, the player cited insufficient physical preparation and the ignoring of his revolutionary request for individualised training as factors in his performances. 'You can't make assessments based on a kid like me having to sprint 150m to join attacks – I'd just played a long tiring season!' The legendary coach, who had renewed Argentine football and built it into a successful team with an overarching philosophy, decided to leave the federation.

Back in Argentina, Diego barricaded himself in his villa in Moreno with Claudia, his family and his friends, away from the glare of the media. He needed to process his sorrow and regain his strength for his return journey over the Atlantic Ocean. A farewell dinner was organised with former colleagues from Argentinos, Boca, celebrities and artists. On 26 July, dressed in a white suit, Diego and Jorge Cyterszpiler went to Ezeiza airport. Claudia, Diego's parents and his brothers accompanied them, giving them an effusive send-off; they would travel to Barcelona later.

Maradona was flying to a club down in the doldrums and in need of a pick-me-up and some prestige. Barcelona had just won the Cup Winners' Cup but had not triumphed in La Liga for eight years and had only registered one title in twenty-two seasons. In the eyes of the president, Josep Lluís Nuñez, Maradona was primarily a strategic signing; he had just extended the Camp Nou's capacity from 90,000 to 120,000 spectators. It was easier to fill it, acquire business partners and secure loans with the best player in the world in the team.

Núñez, discreet in appearance, held the Barcelona presidency for twenty-two years. He made the club financially independent thanks to his vision for creating income from television rights and merchandising. That enabled the acquisition of big stars, two stadium renovations and the purchase of land for what is today the Joan Gamper Sports City. He never had a sporting director and dealt directly with coaches and players.

In that earlier trip of Maradona from Alicante to Barcelona, Nuñez had signed all five of the contracts related to the transfer: two with Argentinos, one with Boca, one with Maradona Producciones (some of the wages were paid via his production company) and one with the footballer himself. Diego agreed a six-year deal and would be paid less than German coach Udo Lattek, but more than Barcelona's other German star, midfielder Bernd Schuster. He would, in fact, be the best-paid player in the world, earning the equivalent of €421,000 a year through salary, bonuses and publicity arrangements. Barcelona inserted a sale release clause should they not be happy with his performances.

Maradona landed at Barcelona airport on 27 July. It was a 'cold welcoming', according to Spanish media, as only a dozen fans and a bunch of journalists waited for his arrival. There was no plan for an individual presentation so as not to upset other members of the squad. When asked about what he expected to find in Spain, he sent a first message: 'I know there are many Gentiles, but I trust Spanish referees.'

He rang his mum when he got to the hotel and director Joan Gaspart's driver took him to a restaurant where he had dinner with Osvaldo, a former Argentinos Juniors teammate who was on trial with Barcelona Atlético, FC Barcelona's second team. The next morning the squad was going to be presented to the fans in the Camp Nou.

Maradona forgot his boots and also missed the short Mass that was officiated in the chapel in the tunnel on the way to the pitch. Barcelona was in the middle of a conflict with Spanish television companies, so only one private camera filmed the event. He and the team were welcomed by 60,000 fans, certainly more than usual, but they made more noise for Bernd Schuster, recently recovered from months of injury. The manager Udo Lattek had to choose two foreign players, the limit imposed by UEFA at the time, and decided to keep the German midfielder ahead of the Danish forward Allan Simonsen, who was sold.

The arrival of Maradona suited the image Spain wanted to give the world in 1982. Colour TVs were replacing the old black and white ones, just as the streets were also being tinted in hundreds of ways. Seven years after the start of the post-Franco democratic transition and only eighteen months since a failed *coup d'état*, the World Cup had left the impression of a country wanting to fit in.

A memorable Rolling Stones concert under the Madrid rain, and the music and art that was being created in hubs in the main cities, were signs of a national awakening. The victory of the socialist party (PSOE) and the elevation to the presidency of young and eloquent Felipe González, and the realisation that within the State were other nations that wanted recognition for their historic needs, gave the Spaniards the feeling of being alive and relevant again.

But there were reservations. The suspicion about the transfer fee and the adaptability of the new arrival could be felt in the national media. Enrique Castro 'Quini', the team striker, admitted 'no player is worth that money', referring to the record-breaking $7.3 million transfer, at a time when the average annual salary was $10,200. The president of the Spanish football federation, Pablo Porta, also considered the figure 'exorbitant' and asserted that 'football here is different and marking is harder, we will see if he overcomes that'.

Journalist Lluis Canut remembers Maradona's first off-the-pitch flashpoint, which arrived early: 'He was about to play his first pre-season friendly in Bordeaux. Before the game started, Maradona asked club vice-president Nicolau Casaus for one million pesetas [around €6,500] to play the match. Núñez was gobsmacked and, of course, refused to pay. Maradona was like a cyclone. When he went to the president's office, normally to ask for more money, Núñez would hide from him.' What did the president have to fear?

The president's way of operating the club gave birth to an appellation still in use today: *Nuñismo*. The Catalan journalist Frederic Porta explains, 'Let's say the Olympus of football is formed by Di Stefano, Pelé, Kubala, Maradona, Cruyff and Messi. Four of them played for Barça. Isn't that something to be happy about? Nuñez managed to make it look like Maradona wasn't at Barça, like he does not deserve to be considered a *culé* [Barcelona fan]. It reminds me of the photos of Stalin with Trotsky erased. But why? Instead of being proud of having had him at the club and according to *Nuñista*'s way of looking at the world, Maradona's personal behaviour in the city didn't match the club's alleged "lofty" values.'

The eternal battle between a free spirit and a censorious establishment was about to begin a new chapter.

# 13
# FC BARCELONA: HIS TEAMMATES AND THE MEDIA

Critical moments showed Diego's real character; put a lion in his path, and he would face it down. But sometimes he couldn't do everything on his own. This was where the help of his support team of Jorge Cyterszpiler, Guillermo Blanco and Fernando Signorini really showed its worth.

After Argentina's disappointing 1982 World Cup, Diego faced the Barcelona challenge head-on. Things started well. In a European Cup Winners' Cup tie in October, most of the 100,000 fans packed into Belgrade's Marakana stood to applaud Diego's *vaselina* lobbed goal, a delightful, arcing chip over goalkeeper Red Star's Stojanović from the 'D' of the penalty area following a thirty-yard run. It was, perhaps, the best goal he would score for Barcelona.

After that promising start, by the end of 1982 there was, as Blanco recalls, 'an enormous lion to face. Diego had hepatitis. Cyterszpiler called me from Spain saying that he needed people to give Diego some TLC. He explained that I knew what Diego was like, his needs and what brings him positivity. He asked how was I for work, if I could give him a hand . . .'

Blanco accepted the proposal, more the request of a friend than a job offer at that time. He bought a ticket to Spain with a loan from someone close and lived between Valencia and Barcelona. At Cyterszpiler's behest, Blanco worked at *Match* newspaper and in May 1983, when César Luis Menotti came to manage Barça, Blanco moved permanently to Barcelona, coinciding with Signorini's era as

Diego's personal trainer. Now writing for *Sport* and *Don Balón*, he became a reference point in Catalan journalism because of his close ties to Diego and Cyterszpiler.

Signorini also grew leaps and bounds as he helped Diego to create his own individual training regime, something unheard of then. On the first day of their collaboration, the trainer took him to the Montjuic athletics track. 'Let's see how far we can run in twelve minutes,' he told Diego. Signorini fitted him with a heart-rate monitor, one of the first times it had been used to measure a footballer's fitness. After ten minutes, the footballer couldn't run anymore. 'Enough. Stop, stop, stop.' Maradona looked like an angry little jug, with his hands on his hips, trying to get his breath back. Signorini was thinking to himself, 'I'll give him the whole lot now: this work was developed by Dr Cooper at the University of California to determine, blah blah. . .'

'And how long do you run in the twelve minutes?' Signorini was in good shape when he was thirty-two, and could run faster. Maradona looked him in the eye and grabbed a fizzy drink he had nearby: 'Well, on Sunday you play.' It was Signorini's first lesson in how physically to prepare a footballer. 'That is not how you run on a pitch,' the fitness coach admits. 'No one had ever said that to me through all those years of study. It made me re-think everything.'

When Maradona travelled to Buenos Aires to recover from his 'Goikoetxea' fracture (of which more shortly), Blanco accompanied him. He promised to help him with everything he needed, from playing tag to simply lending an ear. Alongside Don Diego, Blanco organised a reunion of the Cebollitas at Maradona's.

Eventually, Cyterszpiler offered Blanco a salary to run Diego's media affairs, becoming the world's first press officer for a footballer. Maradona wanted to direct the narrative he felt others were channelling, particularly when the criticisms began.

In Barcelona, Blanco went training daily with Maradona, and spent long hours at his house, with Claudia, Doña Tota, Don Diego and the brothers when they were there, which was often. He had his own family needs, but helping Maradona was all-encompassing. And everyone wanted a piece of Maradona, so Blanco organised media interviews and told those who were interested, off the record, about Diego, his thoughts, his desires.

Blanco captures the intensity and unpredictability of a day with *El Pelusa* in this account he gave to Signorini: 'Diego sends a letter to the Spanish King – I wrote it for him. He wanted to meet him. The King answers, invites him along and starts telling Diego little anecdotes, as if he was not a king at all, like how he used to escape on a motorbike so no one would see him at night. And Felipe González enters the meeting and says, "Excuse me, I would like to know if you could sign a shirt for my son . . ."'

There's no doubt Maradona electrified the great and the good in Barcelona and across Spain, but how did his new teammates take to him in the autumn of 1982?

'He was hailed as the saviour,' says Juan Carlos Rojo, a forward in the FC Barcelona squad that welcomed Maradona. 'We hadn't won La Liga since the Johan Cruyff era some eight years earlier, and we believed that Diego could help us win the league again.' With only one league title in twenty-two seasons and no European Cup to their name, Barça was not a European powerhouse. It was merely a club with a prestigious name, burdened, as so many before, with the heavy weight of potential.

At *El Pelusa*'s first meeting with the squad and the coaching staff, he dressed in a Puma tracksuit and calmly greeted them one by one. 'You said to yourself . . . this is Maradona,' remembers Jaume Langa, the club's physiotherapist. 'With the hair, he was short, he looked a bit . . . stubby. He had a very strong lower body.'

Diego sat near the full-back Julio Alberto and the winger Marcos Alonso. 'Hey, if you need anything, just let me know,' suggested Julio. 'He suddenly picked up some badly-folded socks, made them into a ball and just started keepy-uppies, pam pim pam . . .' One more touch, another and another. 'He got to about two hundred,' remembers Marcos, 'and we were all sitting around the dressing room and looking at him: "What is this?"'

Marcos whispered to Julio Alberto: 'Best we don't train, he's going to make a fool of us.' That was how Diego announced his arrival at the team. A few days later, he did the same conjuring trick with a lemon, flicking it onto his shoulder or his head. People were surprised to see he didn't tie his bootlaces. 'His feet were very wide, and when he tied his boots they hurt,' explained club physiotherapist Angel Mur. 'During warm-ups and whenever he could, the laces went to the wind.'

The winger Lobo Carrasco became one of Diego's hosts, explaining the city, the club and the Catalan culture to him. Lobo was from Alicante, in the south-east of Spain, but sometimes outsiders can better observe a nation's idiosyncrasies. 'Diego was very humble on arrival,' the former Barcelona player remembers. 'He carried the balls to and from training. It might seem irrelevant but it showed us he wasn't above his station.'

*Los Culés*, Barcelona fans, would arrive half an hour early to games just to watch Maradona's warm-ups. As a child Pep Guardiola was among their number and said, 'Diego would stand in the middle of the pitch, grab a ball and kick it high in the air. As it came down, first time and without it touching the grass, he sent it back up into the sky. Over and over, six or seven times, and he never left the centre-circle. I didn't even try. I know my limitations.'

Once games started, Maradona showed a mastery of the ball that had not been seen in the Camp Nou before, able to control it as though in slow-motion. He could accelerate or brake instantaneously, and his sprints and pace intimidated any defender he ran at. He put pinpoint passes to advantageous positions for his teammates. Marcos Alonso's goalscoring record owes much to Diego's assists. Pass him the ball poorly, and he returned it like a polished coin. When things were going badly, he demanded the ball, using his will to drag his team back into it. Nobody was angrier after a defeat. It wasn't long before he became a leader on and off the field.

The club organised friendlies when the season had started; they needed to squeeze their signing and that way be able to pay for him. Those extra games, which forced the club to field Maradona, were not in the contract with the player, who often had to play through back pain due to the lack of rest. Two hours before kick-off in one such friendly against Fiorentina in Florence, Maradona asked teammate

Jose Vicente *'Tente'* Sanchez if the squad were being paid extra to play. They weren't. 'If you don't get paid more, I don't play. I am not joking,' was his categorical answer.

When *Tente* told Nicolau Casaus of the demand, the vice-president 'had to call the club and speak to the president', the footballer recalls. 'Nuñez said not to worry, that the matter would be settled when we returned to Barcelona.' Diego insisted, 'It has to be sorted out now.' Once it was confirmed everyone would be recompensed, the team took to the field, albeit a little late. On another occasion, Maradona heard that bonuses were to be negotiated and he immediately volunteered to help. Logically, in his second season, Diego was appointed as one of four team captains.

The other foreigner and leader of the team was the quiet but strong-willed German, Bernd Schuster, a midfielder of huge intelligence, capable of the most accurate long passes. 'Two such different mentalities, and we slept in the same room,' Schuster explained to Lluis Canut for Catalan channel TV3. 'But we understood each other perfectly, even if our biorhythms were not synchronised. Diego liked to get up at midday. I was used to starting the day by raising the blinds, opening the windows, turning on the light . . . I soon noticed that this was a no-no. So I would go quietly to the bathroom.'

'There was one small problem . . . and it was the team's fault as well as mine,' Schuster observed. 'We thought that Diego was going to solve all our problems on the pitch because of his quality and because he was a leader. The rest of us backed off a bit, and it showed.'

Maradona shone in his first few months, in particular inspiring a 2-0 victory over Real Madrid at the Bernabéu. During the match, a group of Madrid fans hurled insults at Maradona, including one pertaining to his mother. Sitting next to them was Diego's family and friends; verbal abuse was traded and backed up with physical confrontation, forcing the police to step in to calm the situation. The Catalan press reported the fracas and the Diego roadshow had a new act: the Maradona clan.

His first lodging in Barcelona was the Hotel Avenida Palace, owned by club director Joan Gaspart. Curiously, the hotel features a Beatles suite, so named after the band slept there following their concert at the nearby Monumental. There is no mention of Maradona's stay at the Palace. Later, he moved to a large detached house in the upper part of the city on Avenida Pearson de Pedralbes, along with Claudia, his parents, in-laws, more family and friends.

'The first thing he did was put the Barça coat of arms in the middle of the swimming pool,' says one of his Catalan friends, Marc Bardolet. 'The house was immense, with three floors, a lift and 6,000 square metres of grounds, really something impressive,' said Fernando García, Cyterszpiler's friend. 'Diego had a gym built, too. When he trained, he was like a wild animal.'

There were a lot of schools in the area, and children would go to the house during their midday break. Diego would come out and sign autographs or give them postcards with his photo, and occasionally took part in an impromptu street kickabout.

Doña Tota always had a batch of gnocchi ready for anyone dropping in unexpectedly. 'The kitchen was huge, the tablecloth was made of plastic. At any time, you might find a group of people making an *asado* [barbecue],' recalls journalist Pepe Gutiérrez, who had an excellent relationship with the family. The patio had a barbecue grill, and there was also a tennis court, which was often used. Maradona put effort into tennis, but none of his football magic transferred to a racket.

He was the ultimate friend – he set up a gazebo so everyone could enjoy themselves, always a sense that time had stopped and every day was a holiday. 'Diego brought a little bit of "over there" over here,' according to his Catalan friend Marc Bardolet. A piece of Buenos Aires in Barcelona.

'They added some columns, like those on the porches of American houses, Romanesque,' says Josep María Minguella, who had been an intermediary between FC Barcelona and Boca Juniors during the transfer negotiations. A photographer from *El Periódico* and *La Vanguardia* went to Diego's Pedralbes house for a job and, shocked, told Lluis Canut what he had seen: 'All the friezes and columns of that house, a fantastic house, they had been covered with plaster and painted with some crazy colours ... They'd asked for permission, paid what was due and destroyed the house. At lunchtime, twenty people were sitting down, suddenly Maradona walks out from the corridor, carrying two trays of chips and food, and playing keepy-uppy with a ball. A crazy house.'

At just twenty-two years old, he had planted himself atop a mountain, viewing life's possibilities from the best vantage point. But some roots gnarl and twist and crack the earth. Some of his friends were starting to appear in media forums too often, and in December it was confirmed that Maradona was suffering from hepatitis, putting him on the sidelines for three months. The doubts about his illness appeared straight away.

'There was always the question of whether the hepatitis was real or actually a sexually transmitted disease,' says Lluis Canut. Barcelona club physio Jaume Langa defends the official version: 'One hundred per cent – it was hepatitis. I was going to his house to give him the treatment. I won't say the name of the medicine though.'

'Ah, the hepatitis . . .' says Fabián Ortiz, Argentine sports journalist and psychologist based in Barcelona. 'I know this because my partner at the time was working within what was called The First Champions Production, the official name of Maradona Producciones. Hepatitis was in fact a venereal disease Diego contracted through careless sexual practices. That could not be told to the media, it was intolerable and so the club generated the hepatitis story to explain away the time needed for rehabilitation.'

'When Claudia or the parents were in the house, everything was under control,' Lobo Carrasco concludes. 'I went twice, and I never detected anything that purely affected sporting behaviour. But of course, there may have been ten or twelve people waiting in and around the house . . . and they had access to money. One thing can easily lead to another.'

Maradona's friends practically lived with him. 'It was crazy from day one,' explains Lluis Canut. 'It was like an Argentine clan invasion, there were about twenty folks around him. At Camp Nou, they took over the changing rooms area, and you felt you took your life in your hands passing through them. It was different from what we were used to.'

Anonymous journalists, nightclub owners and doormen all offer their own 'clan' stories. Some say that while waiting for Maradona's flights to land, friends would race around the airport. 'The clan's Mercedes drove down Rambla Catalunya to pick up sex workers. Then they took them to Diego's house,' claimed others, who do not want to be named. The clan, apparently, was forbidden entry to the famous Up & Down nightclub. 'They walked in like the Mafia,' said one. 'They were intimidating,' said another. 'They overdid it with the nightclub's PR woman.'

Journalist Alex Botines had a programme on the Spanish radio station SER at the time. One show included an illuminating interview with an anonymous girl. '*Ay*, if I talked about the nights with Diego,' she shared with the audience.

'The clan were pretty angry when they heard that,' Canut says. 'They came down to the station and waited until the show was over, they had a score to settle with Botines. Cyterszpiler whacked him on the head.' The Spanish Association of Sports Journalists reported the aggressive act to FC Barcelona.

Diego wanted to buy a luxury house in the suburbs of Maresme, a coastal area just north of Barcelona where club director Joan Gaspart and team coach Udo Lattek lived. He needed the approval of the neighbours, but the story goes that they rebuffed the application, citing the fame that preceded the footballer.

'Maradona's attitude – and anything he did with his friends – was now criticised harshly by the media,' explained Lalo Zanoni in his book *Vivir en Los Medios* ('Living Among the Media', subtitled 'Maradona Off the Record'). 'Almost daily, this superstar had to answer those criticisms about his behaviour, clarify and retract statements or simply start a new fight.'

'The journalists in Europe lambasted foreign players that earned a lot of money,' explained Argentine journalist Carlos Ares in Zanoni's book. 'And if they happen to be proud and vain, as Maradona was, it's worse. The Russian [Cyterszpiler; he was of Polish heritage] was a good friend, but it all got out of hand; he thought he was this great businessman, but he didn't know how to give good advice. The clan were out of their depth . . . They made money living off his name. And Maradona needed to be surrounded by all this to feel empowered.'

Ramón Miravitllas, the executive editor of the Spanish magazine *Interviu*, claims in Bruno Passarelli's book *La Caída de un Ídolo* ('The Fall of an Idol'), 'My relationship with Maradona during his time at Barcelona was limited to having to listen, with scepticism, to a lot of statements from young women. Young women with tired, sad old eyes, who in exchange for some money were happy to tell me how and with whom they fucked at parties organised by the clan.'

Something was changing for Maradona. The shadow of the shy and straightforward Japan World Youth champion Diego seemed to be distancing itself from the confident and brash leader Maradona of Barcelona.

But was he a leader? The team needed one, so of course he took on that role. The outside world, with a booming football industry in search of idols, identified him as such too. Was he confident? He certainly was very assured of his possibilities, something that unnerves many Catalans who struggle with New World cockiness. And how about brash? Could it be that Maradona didn't want to become what everyone else wanted him to be?

'His personality didn't fit in with the Catalan idiosyncrasies,' explains the Barcelona-born journalist Emilio Pérez de Rozas. Perhaps they didn't want to understand him or empathise because he didn't satisfy the stereotype with which a part of Catalan society felt most comfortable – he refused to be the submissive and grateful South American footballer.

Maybe he was too much of a 'Southerner', too much the 'uncivilised outskirts' boy for those in Barcelona who were desperate to be considered European and orderly, respectful of the establishment.

And in the face of perceived injustices, for Diego there was only one response: rebellion.

# 14

# HIS FRIENDS IN BARCELONA, THE 'CLAN'

Angel *'Pichi'* Alonso often sat next to Maradona on the team bus to matches. It soon became apparent to the Spanish forward that the newcomer 'was very nostalgic'. Paraphrasing Uruguayan writer Mario Benedetti, Diego probably didn't realise that sentimentality is the price you pay for enjoying good times. He had found the solution to being maudlin by bringing 'over there' 'over here'.

'It was Thursday,' Maradona recalled with laughter on Argentine TV channel TyC Sports. 'I was in bed with Claudia, fast asleep, I was due to play my first game against Real Madrid two days later. And Loco Galíndez says to me, "I'm going out, Diego, I'm going to see some girls."' Loco Galíndez is Miguel di Lorenzo, a legendary physio of the national team in the 1986 and 1990 World Cups. Maradona was aged fifteen when the two met at Argentinos Juniors and he made Galíndez a member of his close team while in Barcelona.

'At one o'clock in the morning, Claudia wakes me up, "Diego, they're beating up Galíndez!" I pick up the phone. "Hello, Diego, they're pummelling me, they're killing me, they're beating me to shit, please come!" I grab the phone, get up, put on a hoodie and slippers, and say to Gabriel ['the Walrus'], who was at home, "Come on, they're killing Galíndez!" We picked up another friend who lived around the corner. Claudia meets up with Chino Vallejo, and we call all the Argentines and tell them to go to the club. I arrive, and I tell the doorman, "Hey, wasn't there a fight here just now? Didn't they hit . . .?" "Noooo, he's having a drink at the bar." We go in, and I see Galíndez with a glass in his hand, and he's laughing. And I say to him, "Galíndez, are you an idiot or what?" "Boss, I did well, eh?

See how close-knit we are, you came out for me." And I said, "I was sleeping, you son of a bitch! I'm going to kill you." There I was, in a disco on a Thursday night when I was playing against Real Madrid on Saturday. As we left, we could see the rest of the Argentinians arriving.'

Loco Galíndez, Gabriel *El Morsa* (the Walrus), *Chino* Vallejo, Diego's brothers and parents, the in-laws, the 'clan' ... Maradona had quickly recreated his own little Villa Fiorito in Barcelona. But who would put their own lives on hold to join this clique? And what was in it for them? Néstor *'Ladilla'* ('Hanger-on') Barrone was one of the members of this selected group of friends.

'I come from a humble family and neighbourhood in Buenos Aires. I went to see the 1982 World Cup – César Menotti and [Julio] Grondona, the president of the AFA, helped me and one of my friends. We travelled with the national team entourage in a separate bus to the players. The World Cup was very short for us, so I just stayed on in Spain.'

Barrone used to play football and had some trials, including with Barcelona Atlético. He even took part in a testimonial match for FC Barcelona's Peruvian forward Cholo Sotil, a game that featured Sotil's former teammate Johan Cruyff. Time passed, he got to know people and adapted to his new country; returning to Argentina was off the table due to the political and economic turmoil. He started working in an Argentine restaurant, Corrientes 348, with Jorge Vallejo, the *Chino*. One day Cyterszpiler, Diego and four or five other Argentinians went to eat there.

'Well, let's go back to my place, come have a drink,' suggested Diego to everyone. It was getting late, and he even invited Barrone, who was twenty-seven at the time, to stay over. 'I slept on a huge couch that was nicer than a bed. "I'm fine here," I told Diego. I think three or four other guys stayed, José Luis *'El Gordo'* (Tubs) Menéndez, for sure.' Shortly afterwards, Jorge Cyterszpiler suggested that he join the group of friends who had Diego's back.

'Diego trusted us a lot, and he was very supportive of us. Nobody had a specific task, we were a group of friends, and he had his privacy. Nobody actually lived with Diego. We were in a flat with

Jorge, which was in the district of Pedralbes, too. José Luis, *el Pato*, Osvaldo, Nando and I were all of similar ages. We spent much of the day at Diego's, eating, playing cards, talking about the previous day's game or the next, just meeting up. That's why it was often said that we lived with him, but we didn't.'

It was a group forged from the same furnace. They shared similar childhoods, ideologies, sense of humour and customs. Néstor Barrone was streetwise from the off and survived on his wits; as a kid, he always had enough to pay the bus to get to training in the amateur clubs he played for, but not always for the bus fare home. He always got home, though. He was that type of guy.

They loved football, and considered the nutmeg the highest art form, the definitive representation of what the game was all about – trickery, fun. Maradona's rascally play on the pitch came to symbolise the group. 'An intelligent football player who showed solidarity and with a clear notion of responsibility, this is how I describe the man in simple terms,' Néstor says.

'We needed him. None of us was doing well in Barcelona for a variety of reasons and circumstances. We'd come to work, but none of us was particularly bright. We were the kind of people that had learned more in the school of life than at school. It was difficult to get a break.'

The closest members of the clan, the ones that Néstor Barrone is talking about, lived about ten blocks away from Maradona. If Diego had a famous guest, one of the group would show them the sights of Barcelona to ease the strain on his time. 'There was always a car available. The white Mercedes-Benz coupé was one of the favourites. Maradona himself could hardly venture out and that obviously really annoyed him. It was very difficult to be Maradona. We used to accompany Diego wherever he went, and people annoyed me, getting in our faces, knocking our glasses off, so imagine what it was like for him.'

The group went with Diego to events, publicity shoots, matches and training sessions. Some days they wanted to satiate their yearning for home. Someone would head to an Argentine restaurant to get a *pastafrola* (a sweet tart), a *medialuna* (small croissant) or some *dulce de leche* (sweet, boiled milk, similar to caramel), usually from El Seis restaurant. Diego went out wearing a wig once. 'That's how we managed to all go and get an afternoon *factura* [a sweet pastry],' Barrone says.

'He had a room that was like a clothes shop, plenty of stuff from his sponsors, so he would just give us some. And he had a lot of cars. He had brought a BMW from Argentina, imagine.' It hadn't occurred to anyone that the cars brought over from Argentina would be seized at the port's customs office. They would be treated as illegal imports. But Diego wanted his cars with him and Josep María Minguella helped him get them in, with a little help from other friends.

It wasn't the only jam Diego's friends had to escape from. 'Once, I ended up with that BMW in Germany,' Barrone remembers. 'I had to pick up some bags of clothes Puma had given Diego. The car had Argentine plates, and of course, I was stopped by the police.'

Néstor went with Maradona to Monaco after the player received a call from Prince Rainier: 'From the balcony of my hotel room in Monaco, I looked down and saw two hundred yachts, and we had a thirty-metre table for lunch. How things change, I thought. But the economic and larger powers weren't interested in a guy like him making many people happy. Or they were interested in him but from a different viewpoint. Why did Prince Rainier call Diego to go to the palace in Monaco, or King Juan Carlos and Felipe González ask him to see them, and Pope John Paul II, and King Fahd of Saudi Arabia . . . What do these people have in common with Diego? They wanted to touch his aura of indestructible glory.'

In among the perceived chaos, Diego was playing and practising a lot, taking care of himself and his skills. He installed a goal on his tennis court and bought a metal barrier in the silhouette of a players' defensive wall so he could practise his free-kicks. Diego loved to recreate *portero* football, impromptu street football played on any field or road. Mondays saw everyone come over to his house, including Menotti. They would go to play on the small pitch at San Juan Bosco School in Sarriá, a block from where the clan lived. They would play until it got dark and then head home for dinner.

'He liked to be among his own people partly because he's never been prepared for any other type of gathering,' recalls Fernando Signorini. Maradona was never a reader, but he was a curious and sensitive soul and liked to be informed; if a subject piqued his interest, he enjoyed asking questions and finding out more. 'He was a very spontaneous guy, who caught things on the fly, astute and intelligent,' Signorini adds.

'Cristiano Ronaldo has five bodyguards, Diego had us,' says Barrone. 'We looked after him as a friend, we protected him. All these distortions and lies . . . They called us "The Clan" in a derogatory way – we were bothering a specific part of Catalan society. Not all of it, it must be said.

'Diego was fit and lived healthily. People attributed the things that happened at night to him, but it was us, not him. Unfortunately, this halo we built for him helped a lot of people construct a certain image of him.'

Fernando Signorini spent many an hour among Diego's friends: 'I remember coming across them for the first time during the final of the Copa del Rey. One of Diego's mates, a very athletic guy, was drinking a beer. This guy was calling him a *sudaca* [disrespectful term for South Americans], so the friend walks up to this guy, with the beer in his hand and . . . boom! Shouting, blood . . . These guys were all . . . kids from humble origins.'

'They were mostly Argentinians,' Signorini recalls. 'People would call them bums, barflies, layabouts. They'd say Diego wasn't a sportsman and didn't live a sporting life, he was living only for the night . . . Bullshit! Diego was not stupid. He went out, yes, like everyone else. How could he not? Did he have to live in a convent? He couldn't lead a reclusive life because he would have been unhappy.'

That group of friends, chatty, cheeky, young, were successful with the girls. 'These guys talked differently, the sweet Argentine accent must have helped,' reflects Signorini jokingly. 'They were triumphant in Barcelona, where people are a little more withdrawn. But it also caused irritation and rubbed people up the wrong way. More than once they were all thrown out of the Up & Down nightclub.'

*

Maradona's relationship with the press wasn't always tense, or not with all of them. The negativity surrounding him and the clan appeared in print when Diego began to come into conflict with the club and he always defended his friends to the end. 'While Diego was playing and scoring goals, dribbling past eight players and putting the ball in the net from all angles, he was considered a phenomenon, untouchable,' says Néstor Barrone.

Some Catalan journalists did approach the clan and, Barrone says, 'loved and protected us a lot. Pepe Gutiérrez and Paco Aguilar, they were with us at important and intimate moments. They did get to know us.'

'We used to travel with the team in those days,' recalls Aguilar, whose long career was spent mainly at *Mundo Deportivo*. 'When training was over you would go and have an aperitif with the players or wait in the car park for them. Sometimes you could meet for lunch or dinner, including Maradona.' Paco, a defender of old school journalism, picked up Doña Tota at the airport on one occasion and brought her a bouquet of flowers. She never forgot it: 'You could go to their house, and if Diego wasn't there, they would invite you in to chat for a while. One day there could be fifteen people at home; another day nobody, it just depended.'

'There were no mobiles then,' says another veteran and respected journalist, Quique Guasch, who worked for TVE during the Maradona era. 'I had to call the house and use a code so that he would know it was me – he never picked up. He would ask me to call at a certain time. And if I called and he didn't want to talk, they told me he was asleep.'

Guasch has a dozen stories that paint a very different picture to the ones being depicted by club sources. 'Diego saw a medical programme on TVE International, and he asked me for the video,' says the journalist. 'It was about what a couple of his friends were suffering from. He ended up paying for their kidney transplants in Barcelona.'

Not all journalists understood the beast they tracked. Argentine sociologist Sergio Levinsky reasons, 'Most of them were used to ever-grateful idols who never swore or broke the rules. They were facing a different kind of icon – one that took the first step forwards and carried a spear. He was the first to tell the truth, or his truth, come what may.'

Barcelona directors were mistrustful of their players, seen often as money-grabbers with not enough respect for rules and not fearful enough of authority. 'The head of security, Iglesias, was a national police officer and was well-connected with people of the night,' recalls Pepe Gutiérrez. 'He had friends in bingo halls, discos, restaurants . . . There was no party a player could attend without him knowing the next day. And all the players went out for drinks. We, the press at the time, had more of a footballer's mentality than that of a journalist. We handled information without damaging their image.'

The club also had Maradona spied on.

'Actually, Diego wasn't a guy who went out much,' says Gutiérrez, who stepped out with Maradona on more than one occasion. 'He would drink a whisky and Coke, he called it a "whiskycola", and stand by the bar. At Up & Down, the waiters didn't charge him. When Claudia arrived in Barcelona, he mainly stayed at home, watching movies or whatever all night long, then got up late.'

'These big *fiestas* at Diego's house, don't believe it was all drinking. It was people watching videos until three in the morning,' says Josep María Minguella. 'Every Monday they went to Videos Vergara to rent new releases and spent the whole night watching them. There would be ten or twelve young people sitting on the floor or leaning against the wall, in front of a big TV showing films by [French comic actor Louis de] Funès, [Italian singer and actor Adriano] Celentano, Westerns, everyone laughing . . . But, really, it was not the life of a top professional sportsman.'

'The TV programmes used to finish early, they'd play the national anthem, and then the screen was just noisy,' explains Barrone. 'Then we would put the video on, two or three films in a row, more when Diego was sick or injured.'

When he contracted 'hepatitis', Diego often stayed in a house loaned to him by a friend, on the coast north of Barcelona, between Lloret de Mar and Blanes. He was joined for days by Barrone and the rest of the group. Cyterszpiler came almost every afternoon, and journalist friends like Paco Aguilar dropped by to witness what were long and tedious days of recuperation.

Nobody ever saw Diego take cocaine in Barcelona. 'It's something that has grown legs and runs like truth, because Diego said it and because it's in his official biography – but it's a lie,' says Argentine journalist Fabián Ortiz. 'When Maradona went out, he used to drink one or two "whiskycolas".'

Maradona recorded an anti-drug commercial as part of a Catalan government campaign. *Just Say No* was the slogan he repeated while surrounded by kids. But did he try cocaine? 'Not here. Not here. No, no, not here. Here, while he played at Barcelona, he never took anything,' says the *Chino* Vallejo, another member of the clan.

In 1999, Catalan public television channel TV3 wanted to pay homage to Diego in its programme *Aquest any cent!* When he was asked about drug-taking in Barcelona, he answered with a resounding 'No, no', different to the version that he would write later in his book. The conversation moved to the famous 'clan' and the suggestion that Diego was always surrounded by people and lived in a chaotic environment, leading an irregular life that included much partying. Maradona hotly denied this: 'If I had done all that has been published, I wouldn't be here. I wouldn't have kept my wife or had two daughters. I'm not an example to anyone . . . but if I hadn't had an organised life or took no responsibility, I probably wouldn't have played for Barcelona.'

'Maradona was living the life of any young man,' says Paco Aguilar. 'At that time, Catalan society was very racist, and Maradona was a *sudaca*, a spic. I am talking about the Catalan bourgeoisie, the Barcelona media, even the *gauche divine* – the city's intellectuals. They had the best player in the world, but they didn't know how to best use him or celebrate him.'

Also Diego felt constrained on the pitch. Udo Lattek was an orthodox coach who limited his freedom with his tactics. Cyterszpiler passed titbits to receptive journalists to expose Udo's old-fashioned training techniques. 'Training with medicine balls – you can't shoot them, can you?' Maradona told his manager once.

The 1982–83 season had started with Udo Lattek at the helm but ended with César Luis Menotti in charge. After recovering from his illness, Maradona failed to rediscover his best form, but he helped the team win the Copa del Rey, defeating Real Madrid 2-1 in the final, and finish fourth in La Liga, six points adrift of champions Athletic Club de Bilbao.

Not good enough.

# 15
# CLAUDIA VILLAFAÑE

'In Diego's house there were many men and only one woman,' says Fernando García, the then secretary to Jorge Cyterszpiler. '[Claudia] was the villain in the film – and she was Diego's partner! People got invited regularly to the house, and almost daily there were eleven, twelve of us at the table. An Argentine boxer was stranded in Barcelona, and he was told to come along. Or a player with nowhere to go, it was "come", and the long table busy with young men. Diego would go to bed and come down the next day, and he'd say "Who's this?" and then carry on. Until one day Claudia says, "Hey, this isn't a football club." She was trying to create a married life, but none of us took much notice really.'

Néstor Barrone tries to find some perspective: 'His private life was upstairs on the first floor of the house, and leisure time downstairs. But looking at it now, I would say, Christ, we must have been so annoying, sitting at the table and Claudia waiting on us.'

Years later, on more than one occasion, Claudia, perhaps sentimental for a time and a place, has been heard to say, 'That Barcelona house should never have been sold.'

Claudia, Diego's 'ideal companion' according to Signorini, stoically coped as a hostess, determined as she was at that time to accompany Diego on his journey. She gave everything she had, 'no matter how much it bothered her that so many people were living there,' *El Profe* points out. Diego was not ashamed to hold her, kiss her in front of everyone, be attentive as well show her off, possess her: 'Claudita, my love . . .' Maradona was grateful for his partner taking the submissive role.

Claudia followed Diego when he moved to Barcelona, along with both sets of parents. Her mother, Ana María Elía, was a dressmaker who gradually lost her sight after sewing for years, while her father Roque Nicolás Villafañe, known as *Coco*, was a taxi driver. They took turns escorting the couple. Running the house and handling domestic affairs filled most of Claudia's day.

In her free time, she updated her own newspaper cuttings library that she had begun when she was sixteen, sorting them into envelopes, one for each month. Featuring in columns of newspapers was confirmation of their elevated status. She gathered up the cuttings like confetti from a wedding, a collection of beautiful and ephemeral moments.

Their relationship had started early in the summer of 1977, when it seemed to be on an equal footing. It quickly developed into the roles of a footballer with potential and a working-class girl, slightly younger in age, from the San Rafael School for Girls in Buenos Aires. The crush was mutual, but Diego enjoyed retelling the love story with a slightly different narrative. 'He was my neighbour,' said Claudia many years later on Telefe, a TV station in Argentina. 'He says he fell in love because he saw me from behind, when I was wearing some yellow trousers. He hadn't seen me face-on, poor thing! I didn't know who he was, he had just made his debut for the first team of Argentinos. He explained later that of course I knew who he was, that I pretended not to know him, a typical macho-man story.'

Maradona must have surely sensed that, as a first-team footballer, he wouldn't lack female admirers. His teammates were dating singers and models, but Diego was always attracted to people faithful and close to the world he grew up in, to his early neighbourhoods and their idiosyncrasies and aesthetics. There were no aristocratic or petit-bourgeois pretensions about his partner, none of the supposed refinement of other footballers' wives. Claudia graduated in business studies but abandoned her dreams to be Diego's partner, the girl next door. Just as he wanted.

Diego declared his love to his *mina* (woman) at Club Parque in Buenos Aires while they danced to Roberto Carlos' song 'I Propose to You'. Which he duly did, years later. He saw her without fail every Monday, the team's day off, even when he moved to a bigger house in Lascano street that the club provided for him. From the start,

Claudia was his accomplice, mother-figure and confidante, whether she wanted to be or not. He made the rules.

'One day,' wrote journalist Any Ventura in *La Nación*, 'Diego's father confronted her: "The boy can't be going so late to bed. You have to look after him more, he has to go to training." Claudia bit her tongue; it was the first she knew about it. That night, she had gone to bed early, and Maradona had gone off somewhere without her knowledge. She understood then that her life was going to be different.'

Diego was asking her for unconditional support. According to Dalma, the elder of their two daughters, Claudia couldn't continue with her business studies because Diego was 'jealous'. He begged his wife not to come to watch him play. 'He said it made him nervous,' Dalma explained in her book *La Hija de Dios* ('The Daughter of God'). 'He couldn't play if he knew my mother was by herself in the stands, that he was afraid something would happen to her – how dense.'

Claudia wasn't part of the contract discussions when Diego moved from Argentinos to Boca but she helped stabilise him when he thought about quitting football. She could picture very easily settling in Barcelona. She made the house at Avenida Pearson an oasis of comfort, often supported by her mother and Doña Tota.

Her influence on Diego had its limits, so Claudia used those around her to keep him on track, people like the physio Galíndez: 'Diego had a fever, and I remember that I took my mattress to Claudia and Diego's room and put it on the floor on Diego's side of the bed. He was known to escape at night sometimes, and that's why Claudia asked me to look after him.'

She was the one continuous presence. Claudia was in the ambulance taking Diego to hospital after Goikoetxea's notorious tackle and watched from the sidelines of the tennis court as Maradona followed Dr Rubén Dario Oliva's revolutionary recovery work under the supervision of Fernando Signorini and Guillermo Blanco.

Maradona needed to feel that his wife cared about him, but his insatiable carnal appetites meant that from the beginning Claudia was not enough. 'Maradona's power is in his body, and it is a body that must exhibit itself,' suggests the Argentine philosopher and historian Gustavo Bernstein. 'The mind is subordinate and a consequence of that all-conquering body. His body devastated everything that it met, on the pitch and in life,' he continues, saying that Maradona's energy is Dionysian – sensual, spontaneous and emotional – 'And that implies all the darkness, too.'

Bernstein's own theory dismisses the conception of two personalities: Diego the child and Maradona the myth: 'We cannot pretend Maradona leaves the stadium and, like a bank employee who works from eight to five, returns home and drinks tea. On the pitch he is asked to transgress, to play-act, to cheat . . . he cannot then pretend to be a gentleman afterwards.'

Maradona never sought to hide or inhibit his morals or ethics. He allowed himself to be carried away by his own personality, changing opinions at will. So why the adulation from so many? His emotions pushed him to act beyond the norm, and therefore he embodied freedom. 'His rules are made up of exceptions – he always demanded exceptions to everything,' explains Bernstein.

He was not an example of anything and – says Bernstein – he cared not who judged him. What he wanted was to have his cake and eat it. He was not a hero nor wished to be one because he knew that he was not a paragon of virtue. Perhaps that was why he represented Argentinians, the best and the worst of them, the absurd, the arbitrary, their restlessness and arrogance. Yes, arrogance. Who really thinks they can dribble past all the opposition team on the way to the goal? Only the arrogant and the brave. Look at photos of Diego the kid, at Argentinos Juniors and then at Barcelona, standing with the ball, sticking out his chest. Plenty of those attributes can be found there already. Many of us are drawn to this shiny Maradona, vicariously enjoying Maradona the rebel.

Few would want or be able to break this indomitable colt, especially any that depended on it running freely, or any that loved him deeply and without limits, like Claudia in Barcelona. Meanwhile, nobody thought of looking into her soul and writing her story, not even herself, as she continued collecting newspaper cuttings.

Diego loved Claudia in his own way: as a woman and as a mother.

He wanted her to forgive his carelessness and also permit it, to be a hostess to all and at the same time, invisible. But the innocence or ignorance required to keep that type of relationship going doesn't last for ever. Maradona didn't see the cracks appearing; he ignored or misjudged the damage he was doing as he bartered his love for more and more exceptions.

The couple first's child, Dalma Nerea, arrived in the world in 1987, a year after Diego won the World Cup and while he was the star of a great Napoli team. Two years later, Claudia gave birth to their second daughter, Giannina Dinorah. Both were born at the Clinica del Sol in Argentina, and for both births Claudia had only Coco and Ana María by her side. Football matches got in the way of life.

Claudia and Maradona, after twelve years together, decided to get married shortly after Giannina's arrival. They threw a memorable party at Luna Park in Buenos Aires, and all Diego's former and present companions, from Cebollitas to Napoli, were invited. Before the celebration, Maradona went off-piste to show off his soon-to-be-wife to an old neighbour.

Claudia always sought normality within the midst of the madness of Maradona's world. She took her daughters to school every day and wanted the other mothers to treat her equally, getting involved in school matters, meetings and parties. She obtained special discounts for end-of-year trips (there are some things that nobody minds being a bit special about) and shared out meat she was gifted. Cameras often followed her in public, much to her chagrin, and she always apologised to everyone whose privacy was invaded.

But after years of sacrifice and suffering, Claudia began to question her life. She decided she needed her own space, and immediately Maradona wanted to restrict and belittle her – a typical male chauvinist reaction. Claudia gradually moved away from the media circus and, back in Buenos Aires, dared to make herself distinct from Diego as her daughters became balanced teenagers.

She discreetly organised her own property and business portfolios, wore slightly tighter-fitting clothes, visited the hairdresser more often and was almost always on a diet. No more did she desire to be known as 'the wife of' someone – she wanted to be loved for being

Claudia Villafañe. Her rare media appearances were usually provoked by tiring of Diego being the public narrator of her life. Finally, her patience snapped, and Claudia told the world what it was like to have an unfaithful husband who had fathered several children by several women.

The inevitable separation came after Claudia reported Diego's abandonment of the family home. It came in the year 2000, some twenty-three years after her yellow trousers were first spotted by the cheeky young player. But when Diego retired from football at the Boca stadium in November 2001, Claudia was in the VIP box. She had promised herself not to abandon him completely. Although she could never influence the route he was sailing, she would use whatever little – but important – influence she still had to coax him to safer waters. There would be no reconciliation, and she was no longer in love with him.

On that day of his send-off at the Bombonera, Diego gave a farewell speech. He forgot to mention Claudia.

Three years after the divorce, Maradona appeared on Argentina's Canal 9 TV channel. As he had expounded many times previously, he still needed to count on the woman of his life: 'Claudia has her own life, she has built her life, her business. Claudia deserves all the good things that happen to her. She does. I haven't finished the relationship yet. She finished it, with good reason.' That little morsel gave reams of content to voracious relationship magazines and TV shows. Meanwhile, quietly, Claudia continued to rebuild her own separate life, with her two daughters close by.

This new life had to be kept secret; she knew Diego's defects and shortcomings, and so was in some way always destined to be his wife. Despite his own infidelities, Maradona kept picking away to find out if a rumoured affair between Claudia and producer Jorge Taiana was real. Claudia managed to keep it under wraps for a decade before Diego winkled out the truth. When he did, he accused his whole family, not just Claudia, of treason. In public, he called her a thief. He started a series of legal actions against her for fraud and irregularities in the distribution of goods; that is, for not returning his career mementoes.

On Dalma's thirty-second birthday, Diego's congratulations were sullied with new accusations against Claudia. But this was a freshly forged Claudia, a woman with a strong family base, tired of the allegations and pain each new tongue-lashing induced. She went to the police and denounced Maradona for the psychological abuse she had suffered since he'd discovered her affair with Taiana.

It was all a far cry from the Claudia who felt the insults hurled at her husband were stains on her own name. 'We were playing with Barcelona against Manchester United,' recalled Menotti on *Fox Sports*. 'The first half I told Diego to play just in front of the midfielders . . . he started to drop deeper and deeper, and I got annoyed. So I took him off fifteen minutes before the end. After the game, I had already forgotten it. Diego had this serious face on, he wouldn't speak to you, but he never made any ugly gestures. Next, I found Claudia, crying, "What the hell did you do to Diego?"'

Claudia, always Claudia. The Wife, even after the divorce. The woman in charge of his funeral.

# 16
# CÉSAR LUIS MENOTTI AND ANDONI GOIKOETXEA

Diego Armando Maradona has always required a tacit agreement with the public: for his art, he desires appreciation. The relationship with fans is usually temporary and oscillates, but with Maradona, the pact is permanent. He needs and stipulates eternal devotion in exchange for his lack of everyday life. Should he ever feel the love is not undivided, the reaction is vehement.

There was never this level of adulation at Barcelona, starting with the club leaders. President Josep Lluís Nuñez ran the club from the main office at his construction company, Nuñez y Navarro. Not a single step was taken without his permission, including sporting decisions, albeit he didn't interact much with the players. Day-to-day management he handed to a person he trusted – Antón Parera – and he deployed Joan Gaspart as executive vice-president and negotiator. Nicolau Casaus was the friendly face that spoke for the club.

The president had a powerful and stubborn personality. There was no one more important in the club, or at least with more authority than Nuñez. His economic triumphs glossed over sporting mediocrity and if Barcelona didn't win the league, there was always a new project about to begin under his watch. Nuñez conducted a discreet social and family life and demanded the same of those who worked for him. 'A player must not only play football but also lead an acceptable personal life ... If he does not understand this, there is no point in punishing him; the best thing is for him to leave the club,' he said in November 1982, Diego's first season. The message, clearly addressed to the Argentinian, received this response from the player: 'I don't programme anyone's life, and I don't want anyone to programme mine.'

Hoping to please their star, Barcelona decided to hire César Luis Menotti months before firing Udo Lattek. 'When the problems between Diego and Lattek started, as they had not clicked at all, Cyterszpiler realised that the right coach for Barcelona was Menotti,' explained Guillermo Blanco to Roberto Martínez in the book *Barçargentinos*.

In fact, the Catalan club had already tried to sign Menotti after his successful 1978 World Cup campaign – indeed, a contract had been signed. AFA president Julio Grondona convinced him to stay with the national team. 'Stay, and we'll change Argentine football,' Grondona told him so he stayed and did transform it. Menotti always felt there was a genetic and cultural memory in football. He believed Maradona wasn't born out of nothing, because he was partly the son of Mario Kempes and other legends of Argentine football like Omar Sívori or José Manuel Moreno. So, he worked to implant it in the national team while he tried to decipher the game. 'Football is a great mystery that only great footballers can solve, and sometimes even they can't,' he once said.

The relationship with the Catalan club continued. Menotti produced a detailed report about the seventeen-year-old Diego for them: 'He has prodigious technical qualities, dribbles easily, always from deep. He has a laser-beam eye for goal but knows how to pick a ball for the benefit of a better-placed teammate. Extraordinary reflexes. He protects the ball very well and can play it immediately and effectively. His short passes and shots are a pure wonder. Wonderful changes of pace.'

Despite this glowing appraisal, he had still left Maradona out of his 1978 World Cup squad. Even though Menotti did not make the most of the squad he had in the 1982 World Cup, Maradona agreed he was the perfect coach for what was needed at Barcelona. Nuñez got rid of Udo Lattek after losing 2-0 at home to bottom club Racing Santander. For the Argentinian manager the Camp Nou was like Milan's La Scala opera house and he was going to have 'a Schuster and a Maradona, two spectacular soloists, and I only had to tune the orchestra'. He first sat on the bench for matchday twenty-eight of the 1982–83 league season, a 1-1 home draw with Real Betis.

'Where is Rojo?' Menotti asked when he arrived in Barcelona.

'At Barcelona Athletic [Barcelona's B team],' he was told.

'I am referring to the second-best player at the under-20s World Cup in Japan.'

'Yes, yes, that's the one.'

Menotti could not believe it and quipped at the time, 'If Maradona had been born in Barcelona, he would still be kicking the ball with the B-team.'

Menotti was a well-read and broad-minded man and his speeches were hypnotic. 'He is the man with the big words,' affirms journalist Lluis Canut. 'He said that the club had "historic emergencies" that pushed it into making hasty and erroneous decisions. He said we had to define where we want to go and not look back. We never thought in those terms and were left with our mouths hanging open.'

Diego had a deep respect for Menotti, even though he certainly couldn't forget 1978. He offered to help the manager, now that he had recovered from his infection. The coach asked him for one thing: 'Diego, if you want to help me, you have to be the first one to arrive and the last one to leave the training sessions. If I get that, you will see that we are going to build something big with this team.' And Maradona, who would spend hours talking to Menotti about football, did just that.

'In one of the first sessions, Menotti brought the whole team together in the middle of the pitch,' recalls Signorini, a privileged witness to training. 'I see him talking to Diego. Diego goes off with the ball and starts aiming for the crossbar. All the rest stayed in the centre. Later I heard Menotti saying to the boys, "We've got to organise a strategy, but we have to let Diego be free. We can't condition him or put any ideas in his head."'

Barcelona went from playing a longer-passing game to a shorter, more technical one, adopting, in the process, new methodologies of preparation. There was a lot of one-touch and ball-passing, and a lot of Diego. Schuster had a free role around three-quarters of the pitch, dropping deep to help out. Maradona played as a withdrawn striker who tried to combine with Schuster. Marcos Alonso and Carrasco worked to open spaces across the pitch, while Victor and *Perico* Alonso covered the hard yards for the team.

Fans, more than anyone, felt the 'historic urgencies' at Barcelona after so few recent successes, and soon became impatient with the new football proposal. What they were seeing was a style of football similar to what Johan Cruyff and later Pep Guardiola would elevate to the highest level. But perhaps it had a deficiency at its heart, as Cruyff himself identified years later. The Dutch coach analysed that the team couldn't play well because Barcelona had signed the best long-range passer, Schuster, always looking for a pass into space, and the best short-game player, Maradona, who always wanted the ball at his feet.

That was not the only disconnect. The club management had got wind of Diego and Menotti's late nights and called the coach to explain why he held training at five in the afternoon, instead of the morning like every other team. It was a typically conservative Catalan mistrust of those supposedly ignoring a tough work ethic. Menotti was prepared: 'What time are the games played? At five in the afternoon, right? Well, that's the time when you have to train.'

'That particular urban legend is a lie,' explained Gaspart on Barça TV. 'Menotti was not out every night. He lived in my building. He was on the first floor and I was on the fourth. I'm not saying that he didn't enjoy the nightlife. But you only had to watch Carrasco and Marcos, Schuster and *Perico*. They did the running of ten Real Madrid players! It was a hardworking team.'

Maradona wanted to maintain certain on-field privileges he had tacitly obtained during his career. Aged twenty-two, he felt like a *caudillo*, a type of all-encompassing leader, a concept he'd learned in Argentina that allowed him to stand up to club management when he believed there was an injustice.

At the end of Maradona's first season at Barcelona, and four days before the Copa del Rey final between Barcelona and Real Madrid, German football legend Paul Breitner invited Diego and Bernd Schuster to his tribute match in Munich. The directors refused them permission to travel. 'If Madrid won't send Santillana, then you're not going either!' shouted a hysterical Nuñez, who was aware the club retained players' passports for team's trips. Maradona had said to Schuster, 'Never forget that a contract does not buy a life.'

Despite Maradona's insistence for days, the president would not hand the passports to them. One day Diego turned up at the club offices and waited for Núñez in the trophy room, along with Schuster and Barça vice-president Casaus. 'The president is not here,' he was told. 'So Nuñez doesn't want to show his face? I'm going to wait for five minutes . . . If I don't get my passport, all these trophies, these divine trophies, especially the ones that are made of glass, I will throw them to the floor, one by one,' said Diego as he admitted in his *Yo Soy El Diego*. 'Let me know when we start,' responded Schuster. Diego took the biggest one, the Teresa Herrera (an annual pre-season tournament in La Coruña) . . . 'No, Diego,' begged Casaus. Too late: Maradona threw it to the ground. 'It made such a noise . . .' Diego remembered with amusement. The club gave him his passport but managed to get the Spanish football federation to stop him travelling to Germany.

The team won neither the league nor the Cup Winners' Cup that season, but Barcelona did claim the Copa del Rey with a 2-1 victory against Alfredo di Stefano's Real Madrid, thanks to a ninetieth-minute winner from Marcos Alonso. The forward remembers the tackles in the game, especially against Maradona, as 'terrifying': 'Today we would have ended up five against five, the rest sent off.' The first half's opening goal saw Schuster's long ball into space picked up by Maradona, who cut inside the area and spotted the run of Victor who converted – the combination of styles worked this time. Madrid equalised in the second half, and with the match about to end, players would typically be risk-averse. Not Diego: he spotted winger Julio Alberto open down the left and chipped a precise forty-metre pass to his touchline. Alberto beat his man and sent a beautiful looping cross to the far post where a diving Alonso headed across the goal for the winner.

Three weeks later, Maradona had his hands on his second trophy, this time the Copa de la Liga, the League Cup. Again, Barcelona faced Real Madrid, and again they triumphed, this time 4-3 over two legs. Diego scored a magnificent goal in the opening 2-2 draw at the Bernabéu. Put through on goal, he dribbled up to, then rounded, the keeper. Madrid defender Juan José was coming back to cover the goal, and Maradona could have scored immediately. Instead, he brought the ball back from the very limits of the byline, waited for Juan José to run past him, shimmied to the centre of the goal and prodded it home. 'Why did you take so long to score?' asked a delighted but anxious Gaspart.

'Goals must be scored at the right time,' answered Diego.

The following pre-season, the differences between club management and Maradona became more pronounced. At the end of August, hours before a friendly match in the Parc Lescure Stadium in Bordeaux against FC Nantes, the fourth in six days, Maradona, backed up by Schuster, demanded a bigger share of the money the club was getting for the game. They had recently found out that the players would only get 11,000 pesetas for another friendly when the club coffers had earned 11 million net. Casaus, who knew the club would lose eight million pesetas if the Argentine did not play at least an hour, accepted their demands and paid the other fifteen players an extra three million pesetas. The game was played even though the excess of games made Maradona suffer from sciatica.

The team seemed, little by little, to be settling into a playing style closer to what Maradona enjoyed, using all the pitch, taking a lot of touches and generating plentiful attacks. They genuinely believed that if they kept improving it could help them win their first league title since 1974. The fourth game of the season saw Barcelona take on reigning champions Athletic Bilbao at home.

One hour into the game, Maradona tried to calm Basque centre back Andoni Goikoetxea, who had just been on the end of an ugly tackle from Bernd Schuster. Two years previously, Goikoetxea had seriously injured the German, putting him on the sidelines for a year. Maradona set the scene: 'I remember that I had already had an argument with Goikoetxea because he wanted to nobble Schuster again, and I said to him, "Leave it, you've already done him wrong once, you know what he's like, the German is not a bad guy."

'And in that play when I'm talking to him, I see a teammate

dropping it from his chest to his foot, and it goes long. When I go to control the ball, I feel a blow, as if someone had broken a plank of wood.'

Goiko, studs up and with no chance of getting the ball, fifty metres from goal, had taken the Argentinian's ankle from behind.

'I was ten or twelve metres away and I heard the crunch perfectly,' says Lobo Carrasco. The stadium fell silent. Barcelona centre-back Migueli ran to Diego and asked him how he was. 'He broke me, Miguel, he broke me!'

'I wanted to lift my left foot and I couldn't. In Argentina, when they show this bit of play, my mother always cries.'

The referee interpreted it as ill-fortune rather than violent play – despite the ball being four metres away at the point of contact – and the rules did not have a tackle from behind as a straight red. Goiko was given a yellow.

On his arrival at the dressing room with the stricken Maradona, the Barcelona physio called the club doctor, González Ario. With their help, Diego got into the shower. The dressing room was full within two minutes and everyone was on the verge of crying. 'I'm going to the hospital to prepare the operating room,' said the doctor, who performed surgery on Maradona that very night. 'I want to play again, do what you want with me,' said a distressed Diego before an operation that lasted a couple of hours.

Javier Clemente, the coach of Athletic Bilbao, continued to stoke the on- and off-field tensions in his ideological battle with Menotti, Clemente's aggressive philosophy clashing with Menotti's poetic vision. After the game Clemente declared, 'Let's see, he might even play next week.'

Menotti responded with an admonition: 'Someone will have to die for something to change in this game [so that we protect players].'

'I remember the corridor where his room was,' says the journalist Pepe Gutiérrez. 'I went there when the game was over. There were a lot of people: Claudia, Diego's family, his father, his brother Lalo . . . There were a lot of Diego's friends, including his brother-in-law, *El Morsa*. He and others wanted to break Goikoetxea's legs. They decided to get a baseball bat, go to his hotel.'

Someone phoned and warned Javier Clemente, who was staying with the team at the Princesa Sofia hotel in Barcelona. The car park had a lift that went up to the lobby. 'That entrance is not guarded, Javi. Put security in the car park.'

'A mix of common sense and the club's security stopped them,' recalls Gutiérrez.

'I left the clinic with all the newspapers being very definite about the injury, saying that I would never come back,' Diego explained a decade later on TV3. 'I remember crying with my wife. And Claudia told me that if I didn't play again, she loved me as a man, not a footballer. I told her that she could continue to love the man and the footballer because I would come back.' So, another mountain to climb for Diego.

Fernando Signorini went to see him the next day in the house in Pedralbes. The recovery process was led by Dr Rubén Dario Oliva, an Argentine doctor living in Milan. He had led the Argentina national medical team at the 1978 World Cup. 'One day,' Signorini remembers, 'without warning, Oliva said to me, "Well, tomorrow I'm going back to Milan, so you're in charge. Make him go out for a walk, climb the stairs plus do all the things you normally do."'

Maradona suffered irreparable damage to his ankle that resulted in a significant reduction in mobility. He had to adapt. 'He started to practise a new way to support his foot, even turning his hip more to enable him to get closer to the ball,' explains Signorini.

The last phase of the recovery took place in Buenos Aires. Instead of a stretcher, Diego preferred to work on the pitch. There was talk of six months' recuperation, but within three and a half he was ready to return, even though the continual pain meant he was taking a lot of painkillers.

A debate sparked about the need to protect footballers. Goikoetxea was given an eighteen-match ban, but he only had to serve six. 'Who is going to reduce my injury?' asked a frustrated Diego in *Don Balón* magazine. 'It was painful for Diego, the way the serious injury was dealt with,' recalls Guillermo Blanco. 'At first there was an outcry, but little by little the punishment was reduced, like trimming the branches from a tree before it is cut down. Maradona went from victim to assassin.'

It was more than an ankle that broke in Diego. Blanco continues, 'He realised that some of the press was not with him. He was judged by economics: he cost so much, he's yielded so much. And this produced a reaction against him from certain parts of society, that was very difficult for Diego to bear. He could no longer be silent, and there was an unavoidable clash.' Diego reacted, as Blanco describes, 'like an erupting volcano'. The emotional rollercoaster ride descended to ever deeper troughs of depression than usual, often followed by higher peaks of optimism, a recurrent trait of his adult personality.

'I was really looking forward to playing in Spain, but they are making me lose my desire. I'm sure of one thing, nobody else is going to use Maradona,' he told a journalist at *Don Balón*, with an air of resignation he'd not used before. 'I thought that because of what happened to me, the fact I'm Maradona and known the world over, authorities would take advantage of this chance to put an end to the violence once and for all. But I don't think they will.'

On 8 January 1984, Diego played at Camp Nou again. By then he had started six months' work with kinesiology to improve his ankle, as he could only move it up and down with no lateral or circular movement. He wore specially designed boots with the highest heel possible. That evening he scored two goals against Sevilla in a winning 3-1 return.

At the end of that month, Maradona faced table-topping Athletic Bilbao once more, and again he scored twice, this time in a 2-1 win. He could scarcely believe what he thought he heard on the pitch: 'I will never be able to forgive Goikoetxea. He encouraged his teammates to rough me up. He told me he couldn't do it because I had all the press in my favour, that's why it was the others who were hunting me down.'

Goikoetxea never felt much guilt, putting it down to just one of those things that happen on a pitch. Maradona eventually forgave him, although not entirely. 'When he played for Sevilla, Diego came to Bilbao for a game,' explained Goikoetxea years later on the Spanish radio station Onda Cero. 'We spent some time chatting at the Hotel Villa Bilbao on Gran Vía, half an hour having a coffee, talking about our families, even remembering those moments. Well, he had fully recovered from the injury. In fact, after three months, he was already playing again, wasn't he?' The centre-back kept the boots in a glass case from the day he injured Maradona – he'd worn the same ones and scored in a European Cup tie against Lech Poznań a few days later. 'I experienced the worst and the best of football within only four days, that's why I kept them.'

The Barcelona team had suffered without its biggest star. By the time of Maradona's January return, they were four points behind Athletic Bilbao and three behind Real Madrid. In March, Diego recorded the anti-drug commercial for the Catalan government, by which time his relationship with the club and Spanish football was crumbling.

'Players' careers have several stages, like a marriage,' according to the former vice-president of Barcelona, Joan Gaspart, when talking about Maradona. 'When you are in love, you get married. Contract signed. Over the years, there are problems, and that love is lost. We're talking about clubs, footballers, fans. Some players have said to me, "Look, Juan, I have to leave, because when I go out on the street, they don't ask for my autograph any more." And when he arrives at his new destination, there are thousands of people waiting for him at the airport. At Barcelona, we felt that Maradona's credit, the love, had already been used up.'

The first leg of the quarter-final of the Cup Winners' Cup tie against Manchester United in March 1984 was held at Camp Nou, and Barcelona won 2-0. Maradona had been suffering back problems before the game but wanted to play. 'In the twenty-four hours before the match he was given eleven shots of cortisone or anti-inflammatory drugs,' says Pepe Gutiérrez. 'He didn't play well, and he was severely criticised.' The injections made him dizzy, and he was booed while being replaced before the end of the match. An irate Maradona marched straight to the dressing room.

His star continued to rise around the world, however. It grated on

Barcelona that they didn't get so much as a crumb from the extra-ordinary income Maradona produced from image rights, something they tried – unsuccessfully – to change. 'The Catalans are very special. It's like I'm stealing their money,' said Maradona after a match at Camp Nou in which some fans accused him of being a mercenary.

They were eliminated from the Cup Winners' Cup after a Bryan Robson-inspired Manchester United turned the 2-0 defeat at Camp Nou into a 3-0 win at Old Trafford with a brace from the English midfielder. There was not enough time to turn the league around, and Barcelona finished third, one point behind both Real and Athletic Club, with Goikoetxea's team crowned as champions for a second consecutive year.

The Copa del Rey final, Barcelona against Clemente's Athletic, became one of the most shameful episodes in Spanish football. It took place at the Bernabéu Stadium with Spain's Royal Family present. Clemente kept turning the heat up on a game both teams were desperate to win, labelling Maradona 'an idiot through and through' in the press. Maradona asked him to say it to his face.

'We went out to beat them and crush them and score five goals,' recalls Barcelona left-back Julio Alberto, confirming that Clemente was getting the rival manager worked up. The game moved quickly to where Clemente felt his team would be more comfortable – physical clashes and tension suited his less technical group. Athletic played on the limit of the rules, breaking the flow of the game continuously and squeezing out a 1-0 victory with a goal from Endika.

At the death, Maradona wriggled into the box and fell to the floor, claiming a penalty that wasn't given. Some pushing and shoving ensued, along with some spicy verbals. The referee blew the final whistle. Two years of goading and frustration had created a tinder-box that needed the tiniest of sparks to catch fire. The pitch turned into a bare-knuckled boxing den. 'When there is a colleague who is in trouble, and you see that he is being attacked, you try to calm things down, or you defend him,' says the Barcelona player Paco Clos.

'Part of Diego's famous group of friends tried to get onto the pitch,' recalls Barcelona winger Lobo Carrasco. 'The police used their truncheons to beat them back and stopped them joining the players' battle. Thank goodness for that.' Menotti showed his astonishment at the press conference: 'I have never seen anything like that. If what we saw today was a game, football is dead.'

The referee's report didn't mention the post-match incidents. The Spanish football federation's competition committee, however, imposed a three-month ban (eighteen games, reduced to seven on appeal) on Maradona, Clos, Migueli, Goikoetxea, Sarabia and De Andrés. No one ever complied with the sanctions.

'There came a time when I was no longer going to training at Barcelona. I preferred to stay at home waiting to see if anyone wanted me,' Maradona said. Gaspart, despite feeling that the relationship had run its course, suggested to Nuñez he could mend the bond and tried to persuade the player to stay at the club. Maradona had only been there for two of the six years in his contract, and the vice-president offered him a five-season renewal.

'No, I don't feel comfortable,' Diego replied.

Players from Barcelona's city rivals, RCD Espanyol, spent months rehearsing a play, *La Venganza de Don Mendo* ('Don Mendo's Revenge'). It was a group-bonding exercise to raise funds for charity and to be broadcast on the Catalan station TV3. Diego was invited to join in, and typically he didn't hesitate. He played the Muslim Ali Fafez, and those two minutes on stage became his last public act as a Barcelona player.

Ali Fafez announced himself to the audience this way: 'Christians, cursed race, though I pretend to be your friend, sell you red slippers and cordovan shoes, I despise and abhor you!'

# 17
# GOODBYE BARCELONA, HELLO NAPOLI

Joan Gaspart, the Catalan businessman who ran the HUSA hotel chain and was vice-president to Nuñez, had been present at the successful second attempt to sign Diego Armando Maradona for Barcelona in Buenos Aires. Two years later, Gaspart had to conceal his instincts and was a linchpin in Maradona's sale to Napoli.

'Three months after Goikoetxea's injury, we were in Madrid picking up an award the *Pueblo* newspaper had given Diego. The King was there,' recalled Jorge Cyterszpiler. 'It was a beautiful party. That evening Diego said to me, "Jorge, I can't take it any more. Every time I go on to the pitch, I get this feeling that something is going to happen to me. I beg you, please, let's get out." I got a shock, as forty-eight hours earlier Juan Gaspart had offered us a new contract, twice as much money for twice as long, for eight years.'

'Diego and Jorge were sitting at King Juan Carlos and Queen Sofía's table,' Signorini recalls about that evening. 'Five pieces of silverware on one side and five on the other. They bring them plates, and Diego doesn't touch anything. Sofía notices and begins to eat, so Diego copies whatever she was grabbing. And then he says to me, "I just want to eat a *choripán*! [a typical Argentine chorizo sandwich]"'

He was feeling out of place. His rejection of a new contract confirmed Núñez's suspicion that the end was near.

'Coincidentally' more negative stories filled local papers. The Spanish Footballers' Association organised a friendly in Vigo; a newspaper claimed Maradona charged four million pesetas (€25,000) to appear. *El Pelusa* usually gave his time to charitable causes freely and had done so that time too. 'Someone is trying to harm me,' he told

*Mundo Deportivo* in the September of his second and final season at Barcelona. *Interviu* and *Sport* later published derogatory quotes about Catalonia attributed to Maradona while he was in New York playing some friendly matches. 'They made them up,' thinks Pepe Gutiérrez. '*Sport* was close to the club hierarchy. Gaspart had a direct influence – he was a shareholder.'

Barcelona let it slip that the club was aware of Maradona's apparent waywardness. 'Núñez had received a police report pertaining to the start of his drug addiction,' affirms *El País* journalist Ramón Besa.

Then there were the famous *Morenos* ('the tanned'), another weathervane of the mood at FC Barcelona. 'We called them that because they spent hours in the sun watching training sessions,' explains journalist Pepe Gutiérrez. 'They were older people, aged forty or upward, loyal to the club, and it included a female washroom attendant with a club salary. They met near the offices and waited for the journalists, to put pressure on them. Sometimes we had to run away, even get protected by the police! One of the *Morenos* had a high position in the Central Hispanic Bank. They started out being pro-Maradona, but the club paid for their travel, their bus to the stadium, they gave them tickets and had a sort of office or storeroom for their flares and drums. Coinciding with the club's interest in selling Diego, they started to go after Maradona. They even kicked his car!'

'I never really understood the board,' Diego explained to Alfredo Relaño in *El País* years later. 'It was fine that [the president] felt he was the most important person in the club, but I couldn't help feeling he disliked the fact people enjoyed my game and not his desk job. He manages a huge press pack in Barcelona. I just got more and more unhappy.'

The exit was being prepared by Cyterszpiler. He was busy not only plotting Diego's immediate future at a new club but also looking much further down the track. *El Flaco* Menotti once said to Maradona, 'Diego, you have to prepare yourself for an afterwards. You're like Jesse James, the fastest gunman in the West. One day he walks into a saloon in Arizona, and there is a painting with a crooked frame. While he is fixing the frame, a guy comes in and shoots him. And the same thing will happen to you if you don't pre-pare yourself. Your gun is the ball, so get ready for when you don't have it any more.'

Cyterszpiler had secured several advertising contracts. The problem was income didn't keep up with expenditure. They had an office close to Camp Nou and employed an accountant, secretary and a cook. Maradona, as well as the BMW that he had brought from Argentina and the Golf that the club had given him, bought a Mercedes 500 and a convertible Talbot Samba. He paid for those that travelled with him to games or to Buenos Aires. In one of the many trips he made during his stay in Catalonia, he went to Paris to watch the French Open tennis tournament at Roland Garros and six people stayed in the luxurious Concorde Lafayette hotel where they asked for a Mercedes with chauffeur. Cameras were hired to record Maradona's every movement. Reality TV shows about foot-ball players was a concept that did not yet exist, and there was no market for the content. House investments in Buenos Aires were just about breaking even, and other investments failed. Maradona Producciones, footing the bill for everything, was in debt and sorely needed to get back on track.

'I was aware of some of Jorge's mistakes, and of the financial dif-ficulties they were having. I asked Diego if he didn't think at some point he should get some professional advice,' explains journalist Fabián Ortiz, whose partner at the time, Vilma, was the office secre-tary. 'He told me, "Jorge is my brother, and anyone who speaks ill of Jorge speaks ill of me." And I thought, "I'll never tell you anything else again." That was the kind of relationship they had. Diego trusted Jorge blindly . . . until he stopped trusting him.'

'He paid for everything when friends and family filled the house,' confirms Gaspart. 'The flights, the food. I remember one day Diego said to me, "Look, Juan, if I leave, which is what I want, I'll rent a small apartment. When this entourage I have tell me they want to come, I'll tell them to find a hotel." One of the reasons he had to leave Barcelona was that this court of his was ruining him.' The vice-president often reminded him, '"Diego, this can't carry on, it's unacceptable." Since I couldn't convince Diego, I talked to Jorge

Cyterszpiler. "Juan, you are right, but what do you want me to do? They are part of the furniture."'

'Jorge did everything he could to make the breakthrough happen. It was the only way he could keep the ship afloat,' explains Fabián Ortiz. 'They were close to bankruptcy, saddled with debts, and Jorge tried to hide it from Diego while doing everything in his power to secure a move. He first contacted Juventus, a team that offered Diego the chance of winning titles.' The Italian press also linked him with Udinese, with Zico making the journey in the opposite direction to Camp Nou. But the Italian clubs were scared off by the figures being touted. Barcelona preferred to sell Diego to a more modest team like Napoli, who were fighting to avoid relegation at the time.

Núñez, affronted by Maradona's criticism of him, had started a dossier on his star player and prepared fines for his behaviour. 'If I am fined two and a half million pesetas,' Diego told his teammates, 'we will still be owed half a million from the Bordeaux trip that we never got.' The club did not pay the figure agreed with Casaus for those friendlies in France in pre-season.

The opening gambit with Napoli was the innocent request by the Italians for a summer friendly. 'Yes, but Maradona can't play, he's sick,' replied a Barcelona fearful that an injury might disrupt any transfers. Napoli president Corrado Ferlaino called Cyterszpiler. 'Nothing wrong with him,' Jorge confirmed, who also updated Ferlaino on the footballer's strained living situation. 'What if we go for a transfer?' The idea grew in Ferlaino's head, but it did not seem an easy move. 'One day I was told yes, the next, no,' recalls the president. Cyterszpiler told Maradona, who asked his agent to negotiate a salary in case the clubs agreed a deal. Fiorentina and Inter were also sniffing around, but never with as much intent as Napoli.

'They talk a lot but maybe they don't have a penny. Let them bring a bank guarantee,' Núñez told Josep María Minguella, who got involved and communicated Napoli's interest. Minguella continues the story: 'Surprisingly, this "small club" brought a guarantee of ten million US dollars. Someone powerful was behind it. It wasn't Ferlaino's money – he wasn't exactly a multi-millionaire.' The guarantee arrived three weeks before the Italian transfer market for foreign players closed on 30 June.

'Next step: I want to talk to Núñez.' Corrado Ferlaino's request was made to Jorge Cyterszpiler via Napoli's general director Antonio Juliano, a former Italy international. 'Don't worry, I'll get Núñez on the phone,' Jorge said and proceeded to organise a meeting with Minguella in his office the next morning. 'We bought some giant chocolate bars, and Jorge was eating them, bang, bang, bang, he was so nervous,' remembers his secretary Fernando García. 'Minguella arrived, but he didn't know the full picture. So . . . Antonio Juliano calls. "Ciao, Juliano, how are you? Good, good . . . yes, yes . . . Ah, Ferlaino is there. Good. Núñez is here too, yes, I'll put him on."' Jorge covers the phone and says to Minguella, "You're Núñez, talk to Ferlaino." Minguella's eyes flashed wide open. "Hello . . . how are you, President?" And Ferlaino, "Ciao, Núñez," and so on. They spoke a little, they said two or three stupid things to each other. The phone went back to Jorge, Ferlaino gave it back to Juliano, and on we went.'

Antonio Juliano and Napoli director Dino Celentano came to Barcelona armed with an offer of $7 million. It was just a bit less than Maradona had cost Barcelona. Barcelona rejected the approach. The deadline was two weeks away.

'There were no termination clauses in his contract, so Napoli had to negotiate,' Gaspart surmises. The FC Barcelona chairman, who thought the Argentine's departure would free up considerable room in the wage structure, called an extraordinary board meeting to make a final decision on Maradona's future. Nicolau Casaus, whom Diego considered an adopted father, understood that Maradona had to leave, that they had reached the end of the road. But Joan Gaspart was one of four directors who voted against the sale. 'So, president Núñez, a very intelligent man, decided that I should be the one to negotiate with Napoli. "Since you don't want him to go, you'll be the toughest,"' remembers Gaspart.

'I have been told, by many with whom I have negotiated,' he continues, 'that they would rather have all their teeth pulled than sit down with me again. I'm a hardcore culé. When I conduct club negotiations, I am much harder than I am with my own businesses.'

'During those tense days, there was a meeting at Maradona's house in the evening,' recalls Guillermo Blanco. 'Diego had had a few too many drinks. He was crying and hugging one of his great friends from Argentinos, Osvaldo Dalla Buona, who was playing at Sabadell. Dalla Buona told Diego, "Don't worry, if this is over, we'll go back and play like we did in La Paternal." He liked to recreate that impossible dream.'

We are in mid-June. Just after the board meeting, Gaspart declared to the media that Maradona was not for sale; that way Barcelona regained the initiative in negotiations. When Maradona found out, he went straight to Núñez's offices with Cyterszpiler. 'It was not an elegant visit,' Gaspart recalls. Diego (or someone; nobody wants to confirm) kicked in the office door, but Núñez wouldn't receive the two Argentinians. 'The secretary told me he wouldn't see me and closed the office doors,' Maradona said that day. 'I cannot respect a man who has no respect for me.'

Menotti was also parting company with Barcelona, affected by his mother's recent death and preferring the refuge of his family to a long-distance lifestyle. At Menotti's farewell dinner, Maradona tried to change his coach's mind: 'Diego told me that if I stayed at Barcelona, he would not go to Napoli. I told him I was going. He was very hesitant about leaving.' Even though Napoli had made an 'irrefutable' offer, Menotti says the doubt was not whether Diego wished to leave, but where to go, and whether Napoli was the right place.

The uncertainty forced Antonio Juliano and Napoli to give up and change target. On the morning of Saturday 30 June, the day the market closed, the Italian director was preparing to travel to Valladolid. The intention was to sign Hugo Sánchez, Atlético Madrid's prolific marksman who was playing there in the second leg of the Copa de La Liga. Minguella, still acting as the bridge between Barcelona and Napoli, made what he calls two crucial 'mistakes' around Maradona's transfer, a move he never wished for. The first was to go to the Hotel Princesa Sofia to say goodbye and to apologise to Antonio Juliano for the unsuccessful negotiations.

'Twenty minutes after we arrived,' Minguella remembers, 'the hotel manager comes to tell me that Señor Gaspart wants to talk to me. He had called my home, and my wife had told him where I was. I pick up the phone – that was the second mistake on my part. He asks me if Napoli's people are still around and if things could be revived. I tell him that they are a bit vexed and that Juliano is leaving right now. "If you want, bring him to eat at Llavaneras," the village where Gaspart's house was. We travelled straightaway.'

Diego quickly came to an agreement with Barcelona. As it was his desire to leave, it was simple – the remaining four years of his contract would not need to be paid in full. The talks with Juliano advanced well and the Napoli director, conscious of the looming transfer deadline, asked for the contracts to be signed.

'And then I said, "No,"' recalls Joan Gaspart. '"If the president of Napoli wants Maradona, he has to come to Barcelona."'

Juliano couldn't believe it, and neither could Ferlaino when he heard. It was the afternoon on the last day of the transfer window. '"Your president is a millionaire, I'm sure he has a plane,"' said Gaspart. '"Let him board his jet and come to Barcelona. I'll wait for him in my office." Negotiations are not the same when you send a representative along. Napoli had agreed on a deal with Diego and thought it was in the bag. Not yet.'

Gaspart claimed he would meet Ferlaino halfway; the meeting would be at his HUSA airport office and not the one in the city.

'Who will pay for the fuel?' a fulminating Ferlaino barked on arrival at Barcelona in the evening.

'Well, you'll pay for it yourself.'

'You've forced me to come.'

'But you want something I don't want to sell.'

The meeting lasted several hours. Every time Ferlaino took a deep breath and said, 'That's everything?' Gaspart replied, 'No, no. You came with a private jet, so there is no concrete finishing time. There's no hurry.'

Midnight was approaching. 'I have to get back to Naples.' However hard Ferlaino pushed, Gaspart knew he could not return to Italy without Diego.

In the final minutes of 30 June 1984, deadline day for the registration of foreign players in Italy, Maradona became a Napoli player for the sum of $7.5 million, $200,000 more than he'd cost. Gaspart had managed to increase the original Napoli offer.

'He's leaving, much to my regret,' an apparently resigned Núñez said to the journalists, but he had already got the media and fans onside: it was the best thing for the club.

'Footballers always say they leave because of the president. It's the easiest thing to say,' Josep Lluís Núñez told TV3. 'We said that if the 1.3 billion pesetas [$7.5 million] weren't paid, then there would be no transfer. Terry Venables had just come in as manager, and he told us any player who didn't want to play for Barcelona should not be kept.'

'We went from having many meetings at Jorge's house to suddenly getting ready to go,' recalls Néstor Barrone. 'We ate and had a few drinks together that last night at the Pedralbes house. There was no speech, but there was a lot of nostalgia. No one knew what was going to happen. A lot of people turned up, many guys that Diego, out of loyalty, would let in. He would look at the doorman and say, "Let him in, he's a friend of so-and-so." Diego's wine cellar had a beautiful bottle of champagne and some Iberica hams that he'd been given. I remember at the pool we ate some ham and there were toasts. Like the motorsport drivers on the podium, we soaked each other with champagne. It was a symbolic moment. Many of us felt, very intimately, there was going to be a deep absence.'

The media's hounding and chastisement of the clan was at fever pitch. 'Those of us who stayed in Barcelona, without Maradona . . . was the guy who booked you a table in his restaurant going to look at you like before? The guy from bars, from the posh places? Not any more,' Néstor Barrone reflects. 'Diego left in the morning. We went on the next plane and arrived just in time for his presentation. Two of the group stayed with Jorge in Naples. I went back to Barcelona. I did a bit of everything after that. I was assistant manager in the Mexican Olympic football team, I had a beach bar, I restored furniture. I look back at those times, and . . . well, I never thought I belonged to that world.'

Diego scored thirty-eight goals across two seasons for Barcelona, winning three cups: a Copa del Rey, Copa de La Liga and a Spanish

Supercopa. It seemed a small hoard considering the expectations created. 'Amazingly, Diego is not a mega-important part of the history of Barcelona,' concludes journalist Emilio Pérez de Rozas. 'Hans Krankl, the Austrian striker, or [Allan] Simonsen are eternally valued at the club, but Maradona is not. Can you believe that? It may be that part of the unfavourable perception of Diego comes from the clan.'

Alberto Pérez, the manager of Argentinos Juniors, met Núñez shortly after Maradona's transfer to Napoli. 'You were right, Alberto,' he told him. 'He did not adapt.'

Maradona was on his way to a city that would soon remind him of Buenos Aires, and a club that would be built to suit him. On the plane, about to take off from Barcelona, Diego offered his Catalan epitaph: 'They made me want to leave. Some directors doubted Maradona, so I'm leaving.' He gave Barcelona his all and helped them earn money, 'so I leave with my head held high'. Later he would admit that departing entailed 'leaving my house, my friends, to go a little against my wife, who was the one who had made the house a home . . . it was not easy. But when one makes a decision . . .'

Claudia Villafañe understood the complex nature of and need for the departure, but was heartbroken to leave the little world she had created. Her last night was a long one in Barcelona: 'I am convinced it all started there . . . My house was full of people . . . it was a party that never ended.

'I never asked him about that night, perhaps for fear that he would admit it.

'So I kept what happened buried for a long time. I am introverted in character. . . I don't know if it took me a week, a month or a year to think properly about it. And soon after, in Naples, his sleeping problems became more and more frequent. At that point, he already knew that I knew, even though we had not talked about it.'

# 18

# CORRADO FERLAINO AND THE STADIO SAN PAOLO

While the negotiations between Barcelona and Napoli were stalled, Jorge Cyterszpiler decided to visit the town to get a feel for it and cross paths with the relevant people. The Napoli director Dino Celentano suggested he should make good use of his scouting mission to the city and meet Gennaro Montuori, a prominent leader of the club's Ultras. 'I would meet you tomorrow, but it's my son's baptism,' Montuori told Jorge, who was invited to the ceremony. In a separate room away from the service, Jorge appealed to Montuori: 'Diego wants Napoli, but we need your support. You'll have to ramp things up.'

The plan was to apply pressure through public adulation of Maradona, raising people's expectations and creating fertile conditions for the transfer. By placing some pawns, Cyterszpiler bought himself time to create a more in-depth strategy. 'He jokingly told us to drop a bomb in Barcelona,' explained Montuori in *El País*. 'We said that this was more a Camorra thing; we were the Ultras of peace. Maradona had to come for love.'

Montuori and a few of his friends gathered in front of Ferlaino's residence in the prestigious Piazza dei Martiri. Cars flooded the square, flares were lit, and chants started: 'Diegooooo, Diegoooo.' News reached Maradona of a fan chaining himself to the stadium to ensure the transfer went ahead, and others going on hunger strike amid rumours negotiations could be broken off.

'Napoli was not a great team, but Maradona never knew,' said Corrado Ferlaino, club president from 1969 to 2000, in Jovica Nonkovic's documentary, *Maradona Confidencial*. Naples was the third largest Italian city in terms of population. The club was founded in 1926 but had never won a Scudetto, the league title. 'We forgot to tell Diego that we'd missed relegation by a point the previous season. I only told him that the fans of Napoli were waiting for him with open arms and that Naples would be his second home.'

The negotiations were dragging on, the weeks of June passing rapidly. Generations of families from grandparents to grandchildren were hooked to television channels hoping for reliable gossip. The chatter between balconies, in bars and on the street was all about the deal. Napoli's fans, the *tifosi*, saved money and offered to boost the club's transfer kitty. 'Our directors moved to Catalonia for a month,' remembered Ferlaino, this time for the *AS* newspaper. 'In the end, Barcelona sent their conditions to us in writing. They were tough; we surprised them and accepted. They changed their minds and told us that they wanted to keep Diego but, thanks to the document, there was no turning back.'

With just hours to go before the Italian market for foreign players closed, Napoli was drafting the agreement they'd made with Diego, but they still didn't have the green light from Barcelona. Ferlaino stopped off in Milan before travelling to meet Joan Gaspart in an office at El Prat airport. He handed in an envelope at the Italian league offices with the documents of the potential transfer, so then a phone call from Barcelona would be enough to register the player for Serie A. Without the knowledge of the league, the envelope was empty.

On the night of 29 June 1984, Joan Gaspart and Corrado Ferlaino reached an agreement for the sale of Maradona from Barcelona to Napoli for the equivalent of $7.5 million. The media heralded the news that night, even though the official announcement was not made public until the next day. Napoli's president, after confirming the transfer with the league by phone, returned to his Barcelona hotel for the night, went to the bar and ordered a whisky on the rocks. The bartender struck up a conversation.

'Are you a Neapolitan?'

'Yes.'

'Ah. Today we sold Maradona to Napoli for a lot of money. He's fat, he'll play for a year, and then he won't play any more.' The whisky turned in Ferlaino's stomach. He returned early the next morning to Milan, somehow managing to swap the empty envelope with Maradona's and Barcelona's agreements.

'Intellectuals criticised me, saying that Naples was a poor city and that it was an obscene expense. But it was my money, and I wanted to spend it that way,' said Ferlaino. Most of the $7.5 million the footballer cost came from advances from banks, and payments to Barcelona were staggered over three years. Naples was undoubtedly a city with many issues: a shortage of work and the escalating violence from the Camorra, the Neapolitan mafia. But there was a noticeable change after the arrival of Maradona. To start with, income from ticket sales increased dramatically for the 1984–85 season, and within a year, according to Ferlaino, the transfer was settled.

It was undoubtedly a personal success for the president. Corrado Ferlaino was the son of a southern Italian family and the grandson of a judge killed by the Calabrian mafia. An engineer and lover of high speeds, in the early 1960s he competed in touring races around Europe with his own cars. It was to everyone's surprise when, at the end of that decade, he became the president of the club at the age of thirty-seven. From the moment of his coronation, he endured a love-hate relationship with the fans, as his determined and robust temperament caused repeated flare-ups. But he had the courage to part with idolised players like Dino Zoff and take risks to hire expensive talent such as Giuseppe Savoldi or Ruud Krol, a key member of the Netherlands' Total Football team.

Ferlaino first tried to sign Maradona in 1978, shortly after the player made his debut in Argentina's first division. He was successful at the second attempt, but credit for the transfer from Barcelona must be shared between Ferlaino, who learned about Diego's woes in Catalonia from Cyterszpiler, and Antonio Juliano's wife.

Juliano, a Napoli legend and part of the club's sporting management team, was preparing to attend a meeting in the summer of 1984 to discuss the forthcoming transfer strategy. The night before, his wife said to him, 'If you are looking for the best football player, you have to buy Maradona.'

'What do you say? Shall I go and get him?' a smiling Juliano asked the directors.

'Go and get him,' replied the president, who was not scared of thinking outside the box.

Maradona arrived at what was the most powerful league in Europe. Juventus had Michel Platini and Polish attacking midfielder Zbigniew Boniek. At Inter, there was Karl-Heinz Rummenigge, and Roma had the Brazilians Falcao and Toninho Cerezo on their books. The Dane Preben Elkjaer and the German Hans-Peter Briegel were at Verona. The Brazilian Zico was at Udinese. The roll call continues. At Fiorentina, Daniel Passarella and Socrates. Michael Laudrup with Lazio. Napoli had another Argentinian world champion, Daniel Bertoni, and also two veteran internationals, the Brazilian José Dirceu and the Dutchman Krol. These two were in their thirties, and they left the club as Diego arrived that summer of 1984.

'In Naples, I expect peace and respect,' said Maradona before leaving Barcelona. 'For me, Naples was something Italian, like pizza is Italian, and that was it,' he said later. On 4 July, Diego set foot for the first time into an empty San Paolo, a stadium in need of love and some paint. To look at a stadium without a crowd can be dismal, but Diego, walking around the run-down arena, felt he was returning to his roots. In the changing rooms, he gazed contentedly at Guillermo Blanco and Jorge Cyterszpiler: 'This reminds me of Argentinos Juniors.'

Ferlaino whisked Diego to the nearby island of Capri and to his yacht moored in the marina. The next day, a helicopter returned them to Naples. Maradona left his things in his suite at the luxurious Hotel Royal. Pepe Gutiérrez, the sole journalist to fly from Barcelona with the footballer, found him sitting on his bed, practising Italian. Someone had written on a piece of paper: '*Napolitani, sono molto contento . . .*' He was laughing at his own accent. Pepe passed Diego the phone, and from his bed he connected to a live broadcast on Spain's Antena 3 Radio.

A three-car police escort ushered the vehicle carrying Maradona through the streets of Napoli to his official unveiling. More than

70,000 tickets had been sold, so the stadium was close to full capacity. Diego asked for children to enter for free.

Fernando Signorini was also heading to the San Paolo stadium in another car along with Don Diego. The streets became narrower and narrower as they entered the old town, with rubbish piled up on the pavement, flaky paint peeling from the facades of buildings. 'What a hole we're in, this is worse than Buenos Aires!' Don Diego thought out loud. 'Where have you brought my son?'

'José Alberti was in the car with us,' Signorini recalls. 'He is a dear friend from Argentina and he had been in Naples for many years. He turned around, looked at Don Diego, and said, "Don Diego, you are right. But if you stay here for a year, you will never want to leave."'

Now in the dressing rooms, Diego was wearing light blue trousers and a white Puma T-shirt. On the way to the pitch, he entered a long tunnel before reaching the stairs where a ray of light illuminated the corridor. Maradona paused before a small niche within which was a *Madonnina*, a statue of the Virgin Mary. It would not be the last time he would pray to her. Now surrounded by photographers, he gave Claudia a kiss and Jorge a hug. Diego climbed the stairs and sensed the wave of joy rippling around the stadium, a response to movement detected in the tunnel. Dozens more photographers were waiting for him at the edge of the pitch, battling over every available blade of grass. Maradona stopped halfway up the stairs.

'Neapolitans have an innate passion,' explains Néstor Barrone. 'The idiosyncrasies of Argentine football are similar to those of a Neapolitan. Argentinians have a mix of Spanish and Neapolitan, a hint of arrogance from the French and something stately from the English. All these form part of an Argentinian, a strange and heady mixture. In particular, a Neapolitan has a lot in common with someone from Buenos Aires: streetwise, noisy, *colectivo* buses, and enthusiastic, even mad, about football. Neapolitans felt eternally grateful, for they could not believe that a southern club obtained a gift normally granted to the powerful northern ones.'

Maradona was about to feel, as never before, his powers of drawing a crowd, and his sensations pushed to the extreme. His legs, heavy as cement as he climbed up the stairs, began to lighten as he started to sense the expectation of Naples welcoming him; he was away from home in a strange place, and for that the impact was more profound and abiding. Naples was ready to venerate Diego as its new saint, and Diego craved that devotion.

He took another step and now nothing could stop him, not even a fan offering him a club scarf. As his silhouette converged into his outline, the stadium erupted. Standing on a carpet in Napoli's colours, he raised his arms.

*'Buona sera Napolitani, sono molto felice di essere con voi.'* ('Good evening, Neapolitans. I'm very happy to be here with you all.') He passed the test and the crowd went wild. The foreigner felt more and more at home as the noise from the stands escalated.

With a smile that never waned, surrounded by uniformed and plainclothes policemen, Diego approached the stand and threw kisses to the fans.

The press conference was held in the gymnasium. More than thirty television channels and twice as many journalists were granted access. Maradona shared the narrative of how he saw his life: 'I would like to become the idol of the poor kids of Naples, because they are like I was when I lived in Buenos Aires.'

French journalist Allain Chaillou asked Maradona if he was aware part of his transfer had been paid by the Camorra. Maradona pretended not to understand the question. Corrado Ferlaino interrupted the press conference, raising his voice to deny any relationship with the Mafia: 'Naples is an honest city, and so are its people. I demand an apology.' Two club employees invited the journalist to leave the room.

'When it was over I rushed to the airport,' recalls Pepe Gutiérrez, 'and I paid the taxi driver with a signed photo of Maradona. He didn't charge me the fare and immediately put the photo under the windscreen wipers.' Diego was on his way to the airport too, to spend a few days in Buenos Aires, and confided in Claudia that Naples had just welcomed him as if they thought they could be champions. That was the target and the adventure.

*El Gráfico* drew Argentina's attention to the outpouring of devotion only a few days later. The headline read 'See Maradona, and die,' paraphrasing Goethe's famous phrase about the beauty of Naples. But it wasn't front-page news. No one could imagine what was about to happen and that an encounter well beyond sport had just started.

Diego's first training session for Napoli was in the unprepossessing sports complex of Soccavo, with facilities comparable to an Argentine second-tier team. He spotted kitman Tomasso Starace preparing a coffee. 'One for me,' he asked Starace in what soon became a ritual accompanied by Diego's music selection. Very often it would be Rocco Granata's hit, 'Marina', and the players would sing along. *'Marina, Marina, Marina . . . ti voglio il piú presto sposar'* ('I want to marry you at once'). Then he would change and warm up a bit. Generally alone, until the others arrived.

Maradona's arrival coincided with another newcomer, defender Ciro Ferrara, who would spend a decade at Napoli. From the beginning, Diego 'transmitted this kind of joy, of happiness', Ferrara recalls today. 'We played football and had fun, and he counteracted the stress of competition by making jokes. And he would give us confidence. He would say, "Don't worry, Ciro, do your thing, and pass the ball to me."' Argentinian José Alberti had played for Napoli and knew his way around the club and the city. To him fell the task of looking after Maradona, acting as guide and translator.

On 19 August, Maradona made his debut against River Plate, and 80,000 spectators filled San Paolo. But the season was not living up to expectations. There were just four victories in the first fifteen matches, including heavy losses to Verona (3-1) and Torino (3-0).

Maradona had to endure the acceptance of violent play within Italian football. 'Italian football was played at a different rhythm, rougher,' he said in Asif Kapadia's documentary, *Diego Maradona*. 'I sped up my timing to get into play. If I went one way, abandoning my technique, so that I could run faster, I would have been useless. And if I could not survive only with my technique, surely that would not have been enough. I had to find a balance, which wasn't easy.'

Solutions to Napoli's mediocrity were not forthcoming, and the players didn't seem to see Diego either. He was often playing too deep, seemingly lost on the pitch, hands on hips. Doubts crept into Maradona's thinking. 'He used to get hold of five balls in the first half, eight in the second and so it seemed impossible for him. Napoli were a terrible team then,' remembers Signorini. One day, in the car on the way home, the fitness coach let rip to Diego: 'Italian football is becoming unbearably boring for me. Everyone is worried about defending, and with the ball they make me laugh. To top it all off, the only one who usually has fun, yourself, seems to have been transformed into an obedient and tactically disciplined player.'

Maradona was irked. 'And what do you want me to do? I only get the ball every time a bishop dies. Do you think this is easy?'

*El Profe* offered some advice: 'The best way to show solidarity with your teammates is to be selfish. Don't pass the ball to anyone, dribble past everyone and then pass to someone so that they can score a goal. If you don't have fun, no one has fun. This is a beautiful city, and I want to stay here many years.'

Napoli's manager, Rino Marchesi, couldn't get the balance right. 'A team meeting was held with Italo Allodi, a director at Napoli,' Signorini recalls. 'In front of the whole squad, Allodi asked, "Why don't you pass the ball to Diego?" One of the players replied that it was because he was always marked. And Allodi said, "Ah, if we wait for Maradona to be unmarked on the pitch, that will never happen then." That day Maradona demanded a change. "No, no. Pass it to me anyway and I will find the way."'

Diego, Claudia and the those present during that first year in Napoli – Cyterszpiler, often Diego's parents, brothers, friends – lived part of that season in the best hotel in the city, the Royal Continental. One day Ferlaino, after going over the hotel bills, called Cyterszpiler: 'This is intolerable, Jorge.' So after returning from Buenos Aires from their Christmas holidays, they left the Royal to move to a house in the Posillipo neighbourhood, which brought some stability. Claudia, though, stayed in Buenos Aires a little longer and Diego embarked upon a very public romance with Heather Parisi, a dancer and TV personality he had met in December.

*

Napoli's results took a remarkable upturn after the break, and the second half of the season, which was almost wholly free from defeats, included an emphatic 4-0 win over Lazio in the first great exhibition by the Argentinian.

In that game he had pushed closer to the opposition box and was more involved, at ease and essential to the play. He tried to score with his hand – he did it successfully, but it was chalked off. He crossed the ball in from an overhead kick. His opener came thanks to some opportunism, lashing home after latching on to a misdirected header intended for the goalkeeper. That one was dedicated to Lazio's coach, Paolo Carosi, who had expressed doubts about the footballer's value before the game. His second was an outrageous and precise chip, like a flaming arrow, from fully thirty yards over a backpedalling goalkeeper. The hat-trick came after a failed attempt to score from a corner. A second corner swung in like a southpaw's haymaker delivering a knock-out blow, the goalkeeper ending up hanging in the goal's netting like a busted-flush boxer.

Maradona celebrated by leaping up and down by the corner flag with his feet together. The crowd was united in joy, a thousand-headed moving monster bellowing 'Diegoooo'.

When Maradona saw Signorini, he told him, *'Blind man*, we're going to be here for many years.'

# 19
# FROM CYTERSZPILER
# TO CÓPPOLA

In Maradona's first match at Verona, local fans had unfurled an ironic banner: 'Welcome to Italy', an explicit declaration that the south of Italy was not considered part of the same country. Southerners were united by a particular outlook on life and the misfortunes they had suffered, such as the earthquake of 1980 or the demise of the Bank of Naples, once one of the wealthiest financial institutions in Italy. Diego had gone from being a 'spic' in Barcelona, the *sudaca*, to a *terrone* (a derogatory term that means 'from the land') in Naples, looked down on by the industrial north.

Maradona used a television programme, *La domenica sportiva*, to air a grievance never before uttered by a footballer: 'There is a racism problem in Italian football, but not against black people. There is racism against the Neapolitans, and that is a disgrace.' As a banner at his home San Paolo stadium stated, Maradona was already '*Uno di noi*' – one of us. The world, via visiting journalists, started to realise that he had found a new and honourable cause, connecting emotionally with Napoli's fans in an us-against-the-rest-of-the-country battle.

But first the football had to be sorted out. 'I'd been promised an extraordinary team,' Diego Armando Maradona told me. 'Nine games in and we had one point. I was ashamed to call home and tell my mother, "We lost again." I met Ferlaino and asked him if he wasn't embarrassed to have 80,000 people turn up every Sunday only for the team to lose . . . It was a formality for the northerners to come to Naples, win and leave. And that hurt me a lot.'

It wasn't quite as bad as Diego memory paints it – Napoli had 7 points, and not one, after 9 games, 1 win and 4 draws. And Napoli drew 0-0 at home to Milan and also Juve, and only lost away 2-1 and 2-0 respectively. But that first season, despite Diego's fourteen goals, Napoli ended eighth out of sixteen teams, ten points behind Verona, and eleven points above the relegation zone.

'And Ferlaino said to me, "Well, pick some players." So I said, "Renica, Crippa, De Napoli, Careca, this player and so on . . ." The public got behind us. When we went out on the pitch, you could see the entrance corridors, but when the match started the stadium looked uniform, no gaps. Full. We must have been playing with more than 100,000 people. But not only with Inter, Juve or Milan. Against Cremonese too, against Avellino. Some teams were amazed, we were playing the Copa Italia in the heat, in the middle of the pre-season, and there were at least 50,000 people there.'

Alessandro Renica arrived during Diego's second season at Napoli and his other recommendations followed soon after. Ferlaino dismissed coach Rino Marchesi and installed Ottavio Bianchi as head of the team. If Maradona infused a winning mentality, Bianchi doggedly integrated a work ethic, determination and pragmatism to Napoli's play. He wanted a formula for a competitive team without, in his own words, 'too much fantasy or too many fancy moves'.

'If football is the most beautiful sport in the world, it's because individual qualities serve a collective,' Bianchi told *Goal.com*. 'We had the best player in the world and a generation ready to make sacrifices every day.' Managing Diego, insisted Bianchi, was easier than doing it with someone who thought he was Maradona. 'And I have met many of them,' he added. Diego, for instance, never criticised a teammate for making a mistake, something that is all too common today.

Marco Tardelli, who spent a decade in the Juventus midfield from 1975–85, soon realised that it was going to be tricky to stop an ever-evolving and improving player: 'It was exhausting because you started thinking about him the day before. So, when you finally faced him, he had already won because you were psychologically destroyed. I played against Maradona many times, and I was very hard on him on the field, but he never complained, he never said a thing.'

*

Napoli's aim for the 1985–86 season was to improve and finish in the top half of the table, establishing solid foundations before thinking about winning titles. Maradona had already provided flashes of what could be built upon. In a historic game against the mighty Juventus that took place on 3 November 1985, Napoli had won an indirect free-kick, close to the box and a little to the right of centre. The wily Juventus defence had only backed off five or six yards, instead of the regulatory ten. Eraldo Pecci and Maradona were standing next to the ball: 'There was no angle, but Diego told me to tap it to him as he was going to try anyway. I told him he was crazy.'

'Don't worry, just give it to me.' Pecci nudged the ball to Maradona, who, left-footed, flicked the ball over the wall and curled it into the top-right corner of the net following a seemingly impossible trajectory. That 1-0 win was Napoli's first victory over *La Vecchia Signora*, The Old Lady, in seventeen years, and the reason why everyone in the city believed they were closer than ever to glory. Napoli were to finish that season in third place.

Maradona's footballing life was improving, but life in Naples could be oppressive. During his stay in the hotel, he felt like a prisoner. Daily, dozens of people (or 'millions', in a typically exaggerated Neapolitan description) would gather until 1am outside the hotel and sing 'Diegooooo!' 'People climbed twenty-metre streetlights to get a glimpse of Diego,' says journalist Carlo Alvino. 'Finally, he found himself a residence. But when he would leave, the police would send out orders to protect him. "OK, Diego is going to go this way, let's keep an eye on him."' Cars and motorbikes followed him everywhere; people wanted to see him, touch him, dry his sweat, anything to be close to their hero.

Peculiar classified ads started to appear in local newspapers: 'Wanted: disabled people with wheelchairs'. The club looked into it. The disabled seating area was closer to play, and anyone granted access entered for free, along with a companion.

Maradona was Naples personified: cheeky, small, witty, tortuous, gloomy, confusing. For the first time since Buenos Aires, he saw children playing in the streets. Some squares had football pitches with worn-out paint and goals, eternally watched over by an ancient church, weary of the action like some retired granddad. Tournaments and kickabouts were played at any hour. At dusk the plazas were filled with locals hanging out and drinking beer. The city had yet to paint its dozens of murals dedicated to him.

Diego would occasionally escape to an oasis of calm. 'My mother was the nanny, the cook and Diego's Neapolitan "mamma" for seven years,' says Massimo Vignati, son of Saverio Vignati, caretaker of Napoli's San Paolo stadium for thirty years. 'My mother used to make Neapolitan sauce, the typical *pomodorino* [tomato sauce]. Diego would dip bread in the sauce, and my mother would chastise him, "What are you doing? That's not how you eat." I would buy him *mortadella* [Italian sausage], the Neapolitan *Frisella* [whole grain bread]. Diego is like a brother to me. We are eleven brothers, and he said, "I am number twelve."'

Guillermo Blanco looked after the journalists who came from Spain, England, France; the world was intrigued by Maradona's latest career development: 'I didn't have to remind Diego about his appointments with the journalists. Everything was working fine. I think it was one of the best times of Diego's life.'

Maradona used the structures available to him to multiply the heartfelt gestures and generosity of spirit that came to him naturally. He understood that even if there was a price to pay, it complemented his role as a footballer – the game did not end at the final whistle. 'My father asked for the registry for Italian football players,' said daughter Dalma in her book, *God's Daughter*. 'It didn't matter what club you played for, if you were registered as a professional footballer in Italy you would receive a seasonal card from Diego Maradona at the end of the year.'

In 1985, a friendly match was organised at the Atalanta stadium in Bergamo, with funds raised going to an association of children with blood disorders. Significant football figures were invited: Rummenigge, Platini and the Brazilian Dirceu. Maradona was omitted. He had been in the United States to finalise a deal with Coca-Cola, and it was not certain he would get to the game on time.

Matchday was approaching, and several players dropped out. Daniele Martinelli, a leather businessman who knew Cyterszpiler, received a request from the organisers three days before the friendly. 'There were no mobiles in those days, so I called Claudia in Naples first. She called Jorge Cyterszpiler, and Jorge then called me,' recalls Martinelli, who asked if Maradona could save the day and appear even for a few minutes.

Diego and Jorge were still in the United States and were due to fly from New York to Rome and, the day of the game, from Rome to Naples. 'Give me a few hours,' said Jorge. 'I'll talk to Diego and let you know.' After five hours, Daniele's phone went again. 'From Rome, we're flying to Milan now, the closest airport to the ground, no? Diego's boots are arriving from Naples, bring them to us.'

Diego's participation was announced hours before the game. Everyone knew any delay in his travel arrangements would jeopardise his involvement, but that didn't stop the game becoming a 28,000 sell-out. The flight left the US in the afternoon and arrived in Rome on the morning of matchday. Martinelli waited in a car in Milan airport's non-parking zone. 'I have to pick up Maradona,' he told the security guard, who turned a blind eye.

Two parents of sick children who represented the association were also waiting, at the tunnel entrance to the stadium's pitch. The boots arrived just in time in Bergamo. The teams were also ready; one of them included Diego's brother Lalo in their line-up. But there was no sign of the star. The organisers fretted over what to do. The referee suggested a half-hour delay. The crowd were impatient, but no one moved from their seats.

And then Maradona arrived. In the tunnel, both sets of parents jumped on him and hugged him. They kissed him. They cried. Dirceu told him, 'The stadium is full because of you, Diego. Thank you.'

'He was tired,' says Martinelli. 'But he ran like it was an opening league fixture.'

There are numerous examples of Maradona's altruism. A teammate, midfielder Pietro Puzone, asked Diego if he would play in a friendly to raise money for emergency surgery for a boy with a disease in his palate. The match was to be played at the Comunale di Acerra, a poor suburb some fifteen kilometres from Naples, Puzone's home town. Ferlaino feared injury to his prize asset and thought he could stop him playing by insisting he had no insurance for the game. Diego spent the equivalent of €20,000 on insurance. He was going to play, no matter what the president thought.

The town's club was called Acerrana and that day they played a team that included Maradona, Lalo and Puzone himself. The stadium had doubled its capacity to 12,000, the pitch was boggy, the teams warmed up in the car park, and they played an illegal 12 v 12 to avoid any interventions from the football federation. Some five million lire was raised, Diego scored two goals and the boy underwent a successful operation in France. Heaven and hell often meet in the same lifetime and Puzone has now returned to Acerra, a prisoner to his post-football addictions. He is living on the streets.

*El Pelusa* had manoeuvred around the anxieties of Ferlaino and the rules of the federation, which started to feel irked about Maradona, as he would challenge everything he felt needed to be challenged. He complained about the advantages European players had over South Americans when it came to national team games. There was no universal international calendar at the time and South Americans were allowed no time to rest, or their games coincided with league matches. The federation, backed by UEFA and FIFA, threatened to suspend him for his moaning. Ferlaino secretly suggested to the Napoli team to avoid public support of any of Maradona's defiant positions. When Diego found out about it, enraged, he briefly resigned the team captaincy he had been handed by veteran defender Giuseppe Bruscolotti.

These sudden mood swings became more evident and difficult to control. Something was not right. Behind the veil of happiness described by Guillermo Blanco, who was an intrinsic part of the Argentine group that followed Diego in his first years in Naples, a painful break-up was being concealed. Diego admitted its source in *Yo Soy El Diego*: 'Cyterszpiler had done so badly with the numbers that we had nothing. Yes, broke. Financially broke. When I arrived at Napoli, I had zero, nothing, and was in debt.'

Diego's relationship with money at the time was peculiar. He had his wage, and used the money from advertising to 'live well, buy the cars I want, and give my family what they deserve. This is my happiness.' But that lifestyle was expensive and Jorge Cyterszpiler never said 'No', or 'We don't have enough'. He zealously protected Diego from the world while studiously avoiding taking on board any advice about business from more experienced people.

'When the TV series *Knight Rider* was on, Diego said, "I would like to have that car." It was a Pontiac Firebird,' recalls Fernando García, Cyterszpiler's secretary. 'Jorge bought the car in the USA, had it shipped, and the boat journey cost more than the car. Expenses increased, but Jorge never said no. It was more of a love relationship than one of manager to player. He borrowed money to maintain Maradona's habits.'

Cyterszpiler went in over his head, working with businesses that were too big for his station or with others he didn't know how to exploit properly. In the mid-1980s, Maradona's exclusive worldwide contract with Coca-Cola was worth $100,000 a year, which is what a confectionery company would pay a star for a national campaign. When Jorge was offered 40 million pesetas (over US$200,000 at the time) for a doughnut advert in Spain, he turned it down. Only later did he realise the price was well above the market rate. Diego discovered all this further down the track.

A bingo hall in Paraguay, the first of a planned chain, saw Cyterszpiler invest a rumoured half a million US dollars. 'The gambling world was dominated by certain mafias. They were connected to the political power of Paraguay, the dictator and Mafioso Alfredo Stroessner,' explains Fabián Ortiz. 'They put Jorge in a very tight squeeze. They held him captive, and he had to call Josep María Minguella to pull some strings and get him out of there. He called in tears, he was petrified, thinking they were going to kill him. The amount of money he left behind was astonishing.'

As other people started warning Diego about the limited business sense of his friend, an atmosphere of mistrust grew between them. Disagreements and a seemingly inevitable dissolution followed. 'The relationship breaks up because Jorge understands that Diego is already in another world and he, in some way, is also guilty of having taken him there,' said Guillermo Blanco. 'It's not that Jorge wanted to outgrow Diego by earning more for himself. What happened was that Diego's life was no longer the closed life of Fiorito, or Boca, or Barcelona; it was already a much more complex one. And Jorge did not know how to be part of it.'

By then, in the chaos of Naples, Maradona had found his perfect companion: the great hedonist Guillermo Cóppola. Although they knew each other from the Boca era, it became a closer relationship towards the end of the qualifying rounds for the 1986 World Cup in Mexico.

A spark was about to blow everything up for the two childhood friends. The $1 million Cyterszpiler received as his commission for Maradona's transfer to Napoli went into paying off debts. When Maradona asked Jorge where that money had gone, Jorge listed the holes that had been plugged. 'Ah, so you robbed me,' Diego said.

'I stole from you?' replied Jorge. That was enough, Cyterszpiler thought. After sorting out some stuff, Jorge told Diego that he was quitting: 'You think I stole from you, right. So I'm giving you all my share.' Jorge departed for Mexico with only US$300 in his pocket.

'I travelled back to Buenos Aires,' says Fernando Garcia. 'Jorge, who had some flats in the city, told me to go and find somewhere for us to live. He went to Mexico for three months, staying at the house of Eduardo Cremasco, the former Estudiantes footballer, until he returned to Buenos Aires to grieve for his separation from Diego.'

'I will tell you something I never said before,' says an emotional Blanco. 'Diego was no longer the same, and he no longer looked at Jorge in the same way. Life was taking Diego in other directions. Jorge, who had no money beyond the commissions from working with him, was now for El Pelusa the "lame one", the "fat one". Diego's new agent, Cóppola, was on the other hand a playboy from the jet-set, someone who had left more than 300 clients to be Maradona's sole representative. From then on, Diego had the best cars, the best women, he went where he wanted. A part of Diego was heading the way he ended up.'

Maradona Producciones ceased to exist. Cameraman Juan Carlos Laburu decided to stay in Naples, opened a pizzeria and still lives there, doing well. Even though his old empire was breaking up, Diego recognised the two things he couldn't leave behind – the realism of Fernando Signorini, and the glue that was Claudia. Everything else was going to be new.

'He failed me during a difficult period and I was told to report him, but I never wanted to,' said Maradona of Cyterszpiler, that smart kid who had foreseen Diego's future before the player could. A non-aggression pact and an unspoken confidentiality clause had been established, although Maradona broke the agreement in his book when he talked about being insolvent before arriving at Napoli. Cyterszpiler never explained in public what had caused the rift between them.

'On the first day of his new professional partnership with Cóppola, Diego arrived home at six or seven in the morning,' concludes Blanco. 'A whole new story was about to begin.'

# 20
# GUILLERMO CÓPPOLA

During the separation from Cyterszpiler, Diego looked for an experienced agent to help him make the transition. He asked Josep María Minguella to move to Italy with him. 'I can help you,' he answered, 'but I'm not going to Naples.' However, Minguella did do Diego a couple of favours, selling the house in Pedralbes and depositing a $100,000 emergency fund into an account under Maradona's name from his own pocket, in case he was ever in trouble.

'In his second year in Italy, he took me to dinner outside Naples, to a spectacular restaurant on some cliffs with sea views,' Minguella recalls. 'And he says to me, "Tell the president that if he gets me the same house I had, I'll go back to Barcelona." I told Núñez, but Núñez had already lost interest.'

The search for an agent continued. Carlos Randazzo, a former Boca and River player, met Maradona in Buenos Aires. He made a telling contribution, as he explained to Borinsky in *El Gráfico*: 'One day, [Diego] said to me, "Why didn't you ever tell me that Jorge [Cyterszpiler] was pilfering from me?" And I answered, "I don't really think Jorge ever stole from you." Jorge would throw money around, spend it sometimes not too wisely, but he wouldn't steal from him. And I added, "Get Guillermo Cóppola, you know him, you seemed to click, he's a friendly and capable chap."'

Diego asked Randazzo for a favour: 'Take this folder, tell him to start with this.' It was a house in Esquina, Corrientes province, northern Argentina. Cóppola was to shift it somehow, which is where his story as Diego's agent starts.

It was around that time someone told me Diego wanted to talk to me. Diego was interested to know what I was like and how I handled myself. A meeting was organised in his room at Ezeiza sporting city, where the Argentina national side trains. He told me he had some little things that he would like me to oversee. He was timid. Jorge Cyterszpiler was still working with him, and I told him there was no way I was going to get involved if that situation wasn't resolved. 'No, no, that's mine to sort out.' Perfect. When he finally asked me for exclusive representation, it was an important decision for me. But Diego was Diego. The next day I quit the bank where I worked, left behind many other players I represented, and went to Naples.

.I had two seats in the VIP box in the grandstand at San Paolo. I always had a room booked at the Paraiso hotel. From my room, you could see Mount Vesuvius, the gulf, the port. It was perfect. But walking down the street was practically impossible. So I always moved around by moped. In the morning, I would do the banking, take care of our personal things, go to see Diego's training sessions. One day a ball went off the pitch, and I stopped and kicked it back. And Diego says, 'Guillermo, the ball, don't touch it. I don't go to your desk to touch your papers.' The laughs! If Diego wasn't training in the afternoon, we would usually eat on the island of Capri. If Diego trained, I would have lunch at the Sacristia restaurant, where I had a permanent table. Like the Camorra bosses.

Milan, Prince Savoy Hotel, at the award ceremony of the Oscars of sport [*Oscar Mondiale dello Sport*], March 1987. The previous winner handed the sceptre to the new king. There was [Alain] Prost, who gave it to [Ayrton] Senna. [Björn] Borg to [Boris] Becker. And Pelé to Maradona. We had to go down at 18:53 for a photoshoot with Pelé and Maradona before going on stage. We were on the eighth floor, and Pelé was on the ninth floor. At 18:45 I say, 'Dieguito, how are you?'

And Diego says to me, 'This guy, Pelé, I didn't sleep all night because of him. You don't know, he hurt me once, those things he said about me in '86, I'm sure he did it on purpose, this piece of trash . . .'

And I said, 'Well, today he's giving you the Oscar, asshole. Look, we'll head down in five.'

'Fine.' I had the intuition there was going to be a problem. So, I go down, then back up. 'Dieguito, are we ready? Pelé is already on his way down . . .'

'Ah, he hasn't come down yet?'

'No, he's on his way down.'

'Until he comes down, I won't go down.'

So I'm going up to the ninth floor. I grabbed Pelé. 'Hey, we have to go down.'

'When Diego goes down, I'll come down.'

I go down to the eighth floor. 'Dieguito, I just talked to him, and they're coming down.'

'Well, when they're down, we'll go down.' At that moment I wanted to say, 'Everyone go to hell, Pelé, Maradona, the Oscars.'

I said, 'Diego, we're five minutes late. There are a hundred people on the whole programme, and the only ones who are late are us.' But nothing.

I call [Pelé] on the phone and say to Pelé's brother, 'Marcelo, get in the lift, come down, we will be waiting for your lift, and the four of us will go down at the same time.' The four of us are in the same lift. Seven minutes or eight minutes late. Well, giant photo, the press, they were crowding us around. Pelé, row one. Us, row two.

'And why is he in row one?' Diego asks.

'Asshole, because he has to go up before you to give you the prize.'

The award is announced. Diego takes the prize, Pelé gives it to him. Maradona speaks: 'I am proud, grateful and happy to receive this award, but football has only one king, and that king is Pelé.' And he gives him back the Oscar.

'Diego, what the hell are you doing?' I wondered. Pelé didn't know what to do. He had to give it back to Diego again! Diego got a standing ovation.

When he sat down, Diego told me, 'As soon as I took the

Oscar I saw that it had my name on it. Was he going to keep it? It was impossible for him.'

Diego was in demand everywhere. In 1987, at a Red Cross party, the most glamorous man in Monte Carlo was going, Prince Rainier III of Monaco, Caroline and her husband. The table was full, and Prince Albert, who was on our table, at one point gets up and says, 'You guys stay, I have things to do tomorrow.'

That leaves Diego and me with two or three girls. Diego tells me, 'Ask for the bill, to make ourselves look good.' We were staying at the Hotel de Paris Monte-Carlo, 4,500 dollars a night at the exchange rate. And then Diego says to me, 'Why did you ask?'

'Why did I ask? You told me to ask for the bill.' We only had 500 dollars in our pockets, not enough to pay it all. Just a moment . . . we had a car at our disposal, even though the Palace was three minutes away. I tell you what I will do, I'll go to the hotel and I'll bring money. When I get back, the girls were still there. Five grand, with five hundred in tips! That is what we had to pay. Ouch! Perfect.

Years go by, Punta del Este, a heavy night, Diego and I had been out all night. We had rented a house in Punta Piedra, we arrive from the nightclub, walking around the beach on the way to the house, Diego looks up and says to me, 'Look, there is a party, let's go.' It was five o'clock in the morning! There was a barbecue, and who was there? Prince Albert. Diego, I don't know why, had a plastic carrot hanging from his neck. We went upstairs, barbecue, party with models, businessmen . . . Diego crosses paths with Prince Albert, and says to him, 'I'm not leaving here until you pay me the five grand you owe me.'

'Five grand?'

'Yes, five grand.' Diego spoke to him in perfect Italian. 'You left us that day.' In the end, he ended up giving us the money. Ten years had passed or more!

# 21
# CARLOS SALVADOR BILARDO

The Argentine dictatorship had left a calamitous economic and spiritual debt, symbolised by the forty-day Falklands War following the Argentine invasion in April 1982. But in December 1983, after seven years of civic-military dictatorship, Raúl Alfonsín became the first democratically elected president of the Republic of Argentina. He began to rebuild the country as a modern democracy and over the next five and a half years led a nation that, especially at the beginning of his term of office, bloomed with optimism. The delicate, bright flowers of democracy opened up a nationwide sense that peaceful, determined actions could solve social and economic problems. A programme of mass literacy was implemented, censorship was eliminated and attempts were made to reconcile power with citizenship.

However, Alfonsín found himself in a dire situation: the country owed $42 billion to the IMF, seven times more than before the military's 1976 *coup d'état*. All the missing people, the disappeared, were an open wound that was far from healing. Alfonsín's election campaign had promised there would be no impunity for the military junta's crimes, a pledge he was unable to keep.

Every new branch of the emerging democracy served only to accentuate the polarised visions of its future. Politicians and social and cultural leaders drew imaginary lines between themselves. Discussions raged and ended in populist demagogy, dividing Argentinians like the Andes. Perhaps this is the natural state for a country which enjoys long, inconclusive debate. Is Carlos Gardel or Julio Sosa the best tango singer? Are you Boca or River? Or does Jorge Luis Borges

or Julio Cortázar carry more literary merit? Maradona eagerly sim-
plified the world along similarly clear lines; you were with him, or
against him. There was no middle ground.

After the 1982 World Cup failure, the president of the AFA, Julio
Grondona, under pressure from the prestigious weekly magazine
*El Gráfico*, lost confidence in a worn-out César Luis Menotti. The
federation, sensing fresh currents breezing through the streets of
Argentina, exploited the timing of the imminent national elections to replace Menotti with Carlos Bilardo at the end of 1982. A
very Argentinian duality was born into the national team's psyche.
Menotti had coached Huracán into an attractive collective, and that
work brought him the national job. For him, football had its 'other
side', the coaches trained and influenced by the Italian *catenaccio*,
a defensive mindset eschewing risk. 'One of the few guys from *the
other side* that I'd never have coffee with would be Bilardo,' Menotti
said. The ideological discussion about football still continues between them and their loyal following.

'The greatest manager I ever had was Menotti,' Diego Maradona
told Diego Borinsky in *El Gráfico*. 'Tactically, Bilardo is ten times
better than Menotti, but he had you on the pitch for a long time to
get it. *El Flaco* broke it down and explained it in a simple engaging
way, so you quickly understood.' In the national side, Menotti set up
a team with Maradona as the soloist. Bilardo decided to put the team
under the absolute command of his number 10.

Shortly after taking over, the new manager travelled to Barcelona
to talk to Diego. 'You're going to play here, they're going to mark you,
you're going to play here, and here,' etc., etc. Aware of the considerable amount of information he had imparted, Bilardo apologised:
'I know you didn't understand anything, but in time you will see,
it's easy. And I'll tell you one thing, you're going to be the captain
of the team.' The new coach had to raise his team like a phoenix
from the flames after the disappointment of the 1982 World Cup,
and he chose a sledgehammer strike of the anvil as the source of the
spark. 'It was not easy to take the captaincy from Passarella, *la puta*,
a world champion,' Bilardo explained in *El Gráfico*. 'But I saw Diego
as the ideal leader.' Maradona would be above everyone else. In a

way, it was a one-trick strategy; performances greatly depended on Maradona's individual contribution.

Argentina's first game with Bilardo at the helm was a friendly against Chile in May 1983, and the team exhibited the early signs of his extreme pragmatism and rigour. It is claimed midfielders were forbidden celebrating goals to save energy. He was not the usual sort of manager. 'He called [Oscar] Ruggeri one day and told him to come to his house with his playing kit on,' explained fellow international Claudio Caniggia in *Jot Down* magazine. 'Bilardo made him go down to a plaza in front of the house where some young boys were playing football. There was a nine-year-old in goal. "Boot it at him!" Bilardo shouted. He wanted to see, in that strange way, if he was fearful of being tackled and shooting after having just recovered from an injury.'

Bilardo would record training sessions, unusual for the time. 'He made me watch a video of myself, with my hands on my hips,' remembered Caniggia. 'He told me I shouldn't put myself in that position because I looked tired. . . If I touched my hair, he said I would lose focus.' Every individual talk with players had two witnesses present, so nobody could twist the coach's words further down the line.

Maradona became devoted to the national team and asked teammates for the same dedication in return. As the world football calendar in that era was not synchronised like modern football, and federations would not agree on schedules in advance, it was common to hold qualifying matches, like those for the '86 World Cup, in the middle of league seasons, and for European clubs to oppose their Latin American players travelling to games. But it was impossible to stop Diego.

In 1985, the Italian federation reminded him he was forbidden to travel and threatened him with suspension. 'Not even [Italy] President [Sandro] Pertini can stop me from travelling. He can't stop the planes leaving Rome,' he said. 'Maradona defies the League,' screamed the Italian press. He ended up playing five matches in fifteen days; three in Italy with Napoli and two with the national side in Argentina.

'The Aerolíneas Argentina flight left, as always, at ten o'clock at night,' Maradona explained in his autobiography. 'The game with Juve must have ended at seven o'clock in the evening, and I had two hundred and fifty kilometres to cover, from Naples to Fiumicino airport . . . with all the Sunday traffic stacked up against us.' A few days later, on the way back from the Argentina game, he arrived back in Naples: 'I ate something and went to sleep. I think I woke up a minute before the game started.' It was against Hellas Verona and Diego scored two goals after travelling some 80,000km in those two weeks.

To distance his team from the old regime and create a new one, Bilardo wanted to strengthen ties with Argentine teams. He wanted to give opportunities to their players in games held predominantly in South America. He already knew what Diego brought and, to make sure that he did not waste unnecessary energy, despite the star's protestations, he left him out for an unusually long time – nearly three years – while establishing a 4-4-2 as the base to best harness his number 10's potential. Bilardo did change to 3-5-2 during a critical World Cup game, but that would come later. But one thing worked against the new regime: the coach spoke so quickly, and players found it difficult to understand his instructions at times. 'It was basic Chinese for some,' was how World Cup-winning centre-back José Luis 'Tata' Brown put it.

Whatever the words, the demands were the highest. 'Do you know what it was like to train with Bilardo? Double shifts,' recalled full-back Julio Olarticoechea in *El Gráfico*. 'I would arrive home and feel shot, physically and mentally. . . videos and more videos.'

A refreshed Maradona returned in mid-1985, but inside and outside the camp, the stage was set for an inevitable conflict. Menotti's ageing, World Cup-winning gladiatorial veterans against the up-starts, the new generation with a different interpretation of the game.

Ex-captain Passarella was naturally cautious. He had a good relationship with the powers-that-be, and argued for a continuous respect of rule and hierarchy. He believed Maradona ran too many unnecessary risks using any resource to appeal to referees and rivals in noisy confrontations. But deep down, it was just that Maradona's was a football philosophy that didn't represent him. On the other hand, Diego came into his element when facing institutional power, using the authority handed over to him as captain. The rebel with an armband.

In Argentina's opening qualifier for Mexico 86 against Venezuela, cracks could not be papered over within the side. On arrival in Caracas, Bilardo told his captain he was considering playing *Tata* Brown in defence. A rattled Passarella made a fuss but kept his cool. He went on to score the second goal in a 3-2 win in Venezuela, sandwiched by a Maradona brace, and played a vital role in the crucial last game, against Peru.

It had been a topsy-turvy World Cup qualification campaign and they made it into Mexico 86 just ten minutes before the end of that final match. They were losing 2-1 at home to Peru when the visitors cleared a corner, and the ball was launched back into the box. Passarella was still up from the corner, ignoring Bilardo's instructions to get back in defence. He chested the floated ball into his path, ghosted past a defender and shot from the right-hand corner of the six-yard box. The ball hit the far post, and Gareca bundled the bobbling ball home to secure the top qualifying spot with a 2-2 draw.

There were logical misgivings about the team. The *Clarín* newspaper doubted Bilardo from the start and continued to do so on the way to Mexico City, as did a section of supporters who didn't see their Argentine football spirit reflected in the play. Passarella himself acknowledged, 'If we don't improve, we won't go very far in the World Cup.' They were not innocent criticisms.

'The media is powerful, they bring down presidents. How could they not bring me down?' admitted the coach in private. In fact, the government, following president Alfonsín's instructions, attempted to remove Bilardo before the Mexico tournament. A waiter who knew the coach overheard a table of politicians mention Bilardo's name, and along with a colleague, deciphered the conversation: they were plotting Bilardo's dismissal. The manager was told and confided in AFA president Grondona, who gave him his backing.

After the Peru game, Maradona had to play his last few rounds of the league with Napoli. He was suffering knee pain from a torn cartilage and the consequent accumulation of fluid, which he had to have extracted regularly. But that never put in doubt his leadership in the eyes of the manager.

*El Gráfico* organised a cover-photo session with a smiling Passarella and Maradona posing in Mexican sombreros, barely concealing the tension between the two. The team was also dividing along old territorial lines. Team Bilardo featured Pumpido, Brown, Ruggeri, Garré, Giusti, Burruchaga and Maradona. The Menotti followers, Valdano, Passarella, Borghi and Tapia were joined at first by Batista and Olarticoechea, but they later switched sides.

Fernando Signorini shared his thoughts with Diego about how the group's leadership and tense dynamics could play out in a tournament that was going to be contested at altitude and in hot temperatures, reducing the effectiveness of rough man-marking. 'This is your World Cup,' he said. 'Well, it's either your World Cup or Platini's.' Something spicy had to be added to the pot for Diego to react against.

Diego encouraged Signorini to read, listen and speak with physiologists, biomechanics and traumatologists to fully optimise his preparations to be with Maradona at the World Cup as his personal fitness coach. Fernando Signorini peppered a physiologist with questions during a meeting. 'Don't ask him so much stuff,' Diego rebuked him. 'Can't you see? The doctor will think that you don't know anything.' At that moment, Signorini realised Maradona saw asking a question as a sign of weakness, which he couldn't afford to do.

It was discovered that the treasured number 10, athletically, was like a cat. 'He was capable of periods of very high intensity, but of short duration,' explains Signorini. 'Afterwards he needed a good period of rest to recover his energy. He couldn't just run around, he had to select his moments. So we upped this type of training, with a lot of power, back and forth, working all the muscles in an integrated way. And in the exercises I used to challenged him – one day we were competing against France, the next day against Germany.'

Internally, a belief that the impossible could happen was being fostered within the group, despite the fact there remained one puzzle to be solved: its harmony. Would the inevitable confrontation help?

'There were several meetings,' said Bilardo in *La Nación*. 'In Colombia and also in Mexico. A manager has to provoke them sometimes. You can't let players meet without knowing about it yourself. If they've called a meeting, you can't leave them alone for more than fifteen or twenty minutes. In that space of time, things will have already been said. And you have to have your informants. If not, they'll trample all over you.'

'We went to play a game in Barranquilla, Colombia,' explains Jorge Valdano. The night before the game there was a meeting that clarified a lot of things. Things we needed to confront and say, face to face.'

That clash was one of the most important disputes in Argentine football history. 'The meeting in Barranquilla was terrible, very hard, but it was wise to do it,' Jorge Burruchaga told *La Nación*. 'We were on the verge of killing each other. I have never experienced a situation like it since. But it was good for us, we all had to talk.'

After a tumultuous encounter, the two warring factions that were dividing the squad decided to 'be smart' and work for the common good for a month. 'We have to come out world champions, and then we'll see,' Maradona said to his teammates.

But even though it set the tone for their relationship, it was a very fragile peace treaty. In fact, it still needed clarification of who was the boss in the Maradona–Passarella confrontation. That particular conflict was resolved in Mexico City.

The Argentina national team based itself in the grounds of Club América in the Mexican capital. On one occasion, Passarella entered Maradona's room without knocking. Allegedly he caught Diego and some other players by surprise and Diego was snorting cocaine, information Passarella shared with his closest allies. Diego arrived fifteen minutes late for a meeting soon after. Passarella reproached him, insisting a captain mustn't ever be late and hinting that even if Diego did not drop other unsavoury behaviours, poor timekeeping mustn't be tolerated. Maradona confronted Passarella in front of everyone, as *El Pelusa* explained in his book.

'Are you finished? Well, then let's talk about you now,' said

Maradona, grabbing the bull by the horns. 'All right, it is true I take cocaine. But let me tell you something. On this occasion, I was not taking anything. And you're accusing other kids that have got nothing to do with it. You are a dirty grass!'

There was a $2,000 phone bill that no one was taking responsibility for. Diego revealed that the number belonged to Passarella's house in Italy. 'You're a piece of shit,' Valdano shouted at the former captain. A definitive line had been crossed.

That friendly in Barranquilla against Junior FC had ended 0-0, but the team made a good impression, as the hero of the night was the rival goalkeeper. 'But three days before the first game, Bilardo set up a friendly against the Club América youth team,' Jorge Valdano remembers. 'In the first half, we were losing 3-0!' It was difficult to have faith in that side, but at least it seemed the hierarchy was now sorted.

Fernando Signorini had one lingering doubt, so he went to the small room Maradona and Pedro Pasculli were sharing. Argentina's number 10 was tucked up in bed, reading a magazine with the television on.

'*Profe*, how are you doing?' said Pasculli. Signorini winked at him. Maradona said nothing, nor did he look up.

'Fantastic, Pedro! I noticed . . .' Signorini lowered his voice, and Diego started to pay attention. 'I notice the press say it's going to be a mediocre World Cup. No one is going to be a star.'

'Why don't you leave me in peace to read?' Maradona shouted.

'OK, see you later!' And *El Profe* left the room.

Bilardo had organised press interviews for the week. A few days later, Signorini went down to have breakfast with the staff and saw newspapers scattered on the table. A Mexican newspaper carried the headline 'Maradona Opens Fire: This Will Be My World Cup'.

# 22

# THE 1986 WORLD CUP IN MEXICO: THE SUPERSTITIONS

'You are the genetic sum of the best of Argentine football, and perhaps the world. If you concentrate and believe in yourself, the miracle of a World Cup win can be transformed into reality.' Fernando Signorini told Maradona that several times in different wrappings during the last few days before the tournament.

'He was the figurehead of the down-at-heel, of the boys whose only entertainment was Diego scoring a goal on Sunday,' *El Profe* explains. 'It's not just about playing football, no, no, no, and he was aware of that and happy about it.' Others may shy away from such a challenge; this twenty-five-year-old merely asked for directions to Mount Olympus to confront the gods. Perhaps without knowing it, he had been preparing for this tournament all his life.

From childhood, we are praised for being obedient. As children we believe people will only recognise us, and indeed want to acknowledge us, if we are compliant. In short, we do what we are told. We grow up and discover what we really yearn for, and we learn that those who obey end up wherever their boss tells them. Those who disobey will walk their own path, draw their own boundaries and go where they wish. Maradona learned very early on to say no. He was fifteen years old when he became not only the head of his family but the master of his own destiny. His struggle and survival relied on his rebellious nature, to not do what he was told.

The Latin culture, with its strong Judaeo-Christian influence, is based on the strength of community and sharing, a moral diktat contrary to the demands of human survival: that the one who is selfish and rebels for his own cause, survives best. That is exactly how Maradona's evolution took place, while he was dealing with the unexpected complications of continued success. Those who triumph say some kind of personal harm is inevitable, and it is a challenge not to feel isolated once you reach the top. There is no vaccine for success, no guidebook for coping, no strategy for the changes experienced. You are forever under the gaze of others, from your parents to friends, fans and journalists. No longer can you behave as before, your actions anaesthetised and conditioned to your observer's expectations.

You may not wish to change. You may believe you can return to your roots with some trifling gesture, but this is to combat the truth that transformation is inevitable. Fame and success bring as many disadvantages as advantages, and both must be accepted and tolerated. Entry cannot be refused to one or the other, and all are building blocks of ourselves. Maradona's personality was rebellious, egotistical and mature before his time. He learned to cope with growing up on display in a showcase, ogled by the world's covetous eyes. On the pitch and in the dressing room, he knew what was good for him and what was not, who helped and who didn't. Deep down, he knew something was not fully right, but he couldn't identify what it was.

At the Mexico World Cup, Diego felt at the peak of his physical power coupled with a champion's mindset, despite the insidious advance of his addiction. Argentina had been waiting for decades for a redeemer, and that national desire is indispensable to understand what happened during the tournament and thereafter. 'We need myths, we need people we can idealise, who are capable of doing what we can't, who can make our dreams come true,' Signorini concludes. 'Afterwards we can destroy them.'

'We played a friendly against Platini's France four months before the World Cup, lost two-nil, and I've never seen Diego play so badly,' recalled Jorge Valdano in conversation with journalist Ezequiel Fernandez Moores in 2013, part of a series of talks titled *Fútbol Pasión*. 'Diego was doing a kind of pre-season with Fernando Signorini . . . but I was apprehensive that day.'

'Maradona was an excellent player before that World Cup, but he still wasn't the father-figure in his homeland,' added Fernandez Moores. 'But in Mexico, Diego would speak to about 300 journalists, standing alone behind a fence, responding as if he were Barack Obama.'

The group, built around Maradona's needs, had no doubts about their route to victory. Defender Julio *'Vasco'* Olarticoechea shared players' fears at the time 'I used to get up to go to the bathroom and try to make as little noise as possible. It would cross my mind: "I hope he doesn't wake up, he may not be able to sleep and it'll be my fault if he plays badly tomorrow."'

Looking back, the Mexico World Cup had poor infrastructure and basic, almost insufficient, resources for the teams. But the Argentinians thrived in this more amateur atmosphere that was akin to their hometown neighbourhood teams. Even the old, yellow team bus that took them to games and to training was a little tight on space and outdated, but suited them perfectly.

Argentina was the first team to use the new Club América's facilities and residential quarters, located near the Azteca Stadium. There was one public telephone, and one television in the dining room, upon whose table was a selection of Mexican newspapers and that week's copy of *El Gráfico*. 'We had to put the lampshades on, not all the rooms were finished,' recalled Maradona, who claimed the same expenses from the Argentine federation as everyone else: $25 a day.

About a hundred metres from the players' quarters, a shed divided into four rooms was built for the team. Here, four of the players would stay in even more basic conditions. 'When you agreed to go to the shed,' admitted Jorge Valdano, 'you are actually saying that you are willing to do everything, to live in bad conditions, to do things on the pitch that you didn't like. That need to share everything, I think, favoured the group, which became more and more homogeneous. It's the biggest transformation miracle I've experienced in my sporting career.'

'There was one thing, I don't know how to say it . . . it was all very amateurish,' explained Diego in his book, *Mi Mundial, Mi Verdad* ('My World Cup, My Truth', subtitled 'Touched By God: How We

Won the Mexico 86 World Cup'). Evidently it was fun, but at the same time, the players complained about things, including the clothes. In the official team photo before the start of the World Cup, members of the coaching staff and even Bilardo are wearing different brands of kit.

Conditions were generally challenging for the players: high pollution levels at 2,000 metres of altitude coupled with noon kick-offs in subtropical temperatures. A new synthetic ball was being used. It was difficult to control, especially in third-rate stadiums with dry, threadbare pitches.

There were protests about the setting, with Maradona and Valdano the most vocal, focusing mainly on the schedules. 'It was June, it was tremendously hot and the games were played at 12 noon,' said Valdano. 'It would kill the entertainment. We said it innocently, without thinking there would be such a violent reaction from FIFA.'

Any doubt footballers had about their role in the hierarchical order of football were banished: the president of FIFA, João Havelange, came to tell the players to shut up and play. 'I didn't want to ruin the television business for them, that's up to them,' continued Diego. 'What I was asking was they consult us, the players, the real owners of the show because without us they are nothing.' It was the first confrontation between the star and FIFA. 'We spoke up for the good of the game. They spoke for the good of business,' Valdano recalled.

Life was monotonous in Club América's training facilities. 'In World Cups, you hardly have to train,' explained Bilardo in *El Gráfico*. 'The boys arrive dead after their club season. We stitched them up for the first game, then looked after them. I was "simulating" training sessions. If you don't do some kind of training sessions, the journalists break your balls.' With little to be done, Maradona, to the annoyance of Nery Pumpido and the other goalkeepers, would spend up to an hour practising strikes on goal.

The team purposely drank *mate* at the same time. In Argentine culture, *mate* and superstition are integral components of any group. Pre-game routines seemingly influence invisible powers and give security to footballers in a sport where chance, coincidences and accidents are relevant. 'We had a million different routines,' *Tata*

Brown told Borinsky in *El Gráfico*. And as the opener against South Korea approached, the superstitious rites accumulated.

It went something like this. The squad organised a barbecue the day before the game, the meat brought from Buenos Aires by two Aerolíneas Argentinas pilots. Full-back Néstor Clausen had bought a camera and started using it that day, recording *Vasco* Olarticoechea asking people questions as if he were a journalist. At five o'clock, Bilardo phoned his wife in Buenos Aires.

Some squad members went to a shopping centre and ate hamburgers and were caught by team doctor, Dr Raúl Madero. 'You're irresponsible,' he admonished them. 'It's all right, Raúl,' Bilardo said when the doctor related the news.

The opening day had finally arrived. At breakfast, Brown bumped into Bilardo. 'Hello, Brown, how are you?'

'Good,' he replied.

The coach continued walking. Suddenly he stopped: 'Ah, Brown, you're playing today, OK?' Nobody had informed Brown that Passarella was not available.

What had happened to the former captain of the national team, and world champion? The diagnosis was clear, the origin of the problem a little less. Passarella and his friends had been saying for years there was a conspiracy to remove him before that World Cup from the leadership and the squad, but they never provided any evidence.

As soon as the team arrived in Mexico, Dr Madero instructed the players not to drink tap water, not even to brush their teeth. It could contain damaging bacteria because of the earthquake that had devastated the capital the year before. All precautions were taken – the waiters opened bottled water at the tables, *mate* water was boiled. But a week before the start of the tournament, Passarella felt unwell and was suffering from diarrhoea: Montezuma's Revenge. He took charcoal tablets and medication but found it difficult to return to normal.

'Passarella smoked and drank whisky at night, and thought that ice cubes wouldn't harm him,' Dr Madero told *El Gráfico*. Passarella trained as usual two days before the match against South Korea and was announced as a starter. The next day he relapsed and had to be hospitalised, missing the first two matches. He lost seven kilos.

On 2 June 1986, on the way to the Olympic Stadium, every footballer sat where he wanted in the ramshackle bus. Attacking midfielder Carlos Tapia shaved shortly after arriving at the stadium. It was another day of suffocating heat. Maradona made the figure of a body on the ground with some boots, a shirt and socks; no one was allowed to walk over it.

With the massages done, the public phone in the changing room rang. Brown answered it. There was no one on the line. Diego approached the centre-back as he started to tie his boots, and said, 'Come on, if you play well, I'll play well. Come on, you're the best, we're going to kill these bastards.'

Maradona was the first to enter the pitch, jumping onto it. Brown's heart was bursting out of his chest. Carlos Salvador Bilardo gave Burruchaga, the last player to take the field, a pat on the back. The coach shouted again, 'Give everything, eh!' and went to sit by himself at one end of the team bench. The substitutes and the coaching staff sat where they liked. Midfielder Ricardo Giusti left a sweet in the middle of the pitch.

Argentina faced South Korea first followed by Italy then Bulgaria; two teams qualified for the next round. From the kick-off, the game plan was clear: simple passes in midfield then give the ball to Maradona as the grand solution. Bilardo had shown the team numerous videos of how South Korea played, but on the pitch, according to several players, they were unable to tell their opponents apart. Diego was fouled ten times, sometimes violently. The referee, Spaniard Victoriano Sánchez Arminio, produced just two yellow cards all game, provoking protests from Diego after the match.

Two goals from forward Valdano and one from Ruggeri, each assisted by Maradona, reflected Argentina's superiority in a 3-1 victory. The two points were much appreciated. 'We weren't sure about beating South Korea,' Valdano recalled to Diego Borinsky in *El Gráfico*. 'In fact, I shouted almost as loudly for the first goal as I did for the goal in the World Cup final, it was such a relief.'

The forward had a confrontation with Diego during the match: 'After scoring two goals, I kept shouting for the ball, as was my habit.

I was unmarked for long periods, and I shouted so whoever had the ball knew where I was. At one point, Diego said to me, "You want every ball," or something like that. We footballers have that macho, fighter thing. We went for about ten days without talking to each other.'

'How did you reconcile?' asked Diego Borinsky.

'Maradona always played home. I had to go to his room.'

Argentina's next match was against Italy at the Cuauhtémoc stadium in the city of Puebla, two hours away from their base. The day before the game, a barbecue was organised. Aerolineas pilots were again asked to bring the meat. *Mate* was drunk at the same time. Bilardo's wife picked up the phone in Buenos Aires at 5pm, seven in the evening local time. Olarticoechea did his video report. The fugitives ate hamburgers again.

This time everyone sat in the same seat on the dilapidated bus. Carlos Tapia shaved in the stadium even though he didn't need to. Maradona designed his invisible little man on the ground. The telephone in the dressing room rang. 'Hello,' said Brown. Silence. 'Ah, well, go to hell,' and he hung up.

Maradona jumped onto the pitch, first out. Bilardo was first to the bench, and the substitutes sat in the same places as they did against South Korea. Ricardo Giusti went to the centre of the pitch to drop his sweet.

Diego expected – and received – man-marking; midfielder Salvatore Bagni was his shadow. A few minutes after kick-off, Italy took the lead with a penalty. Argentina slowed down the game, accelerating only in the final third when Maradona would dribble or attempt a pass. Around the half-hour mark, Valdano chipped the ball to the left of the box, over the head of a now turned and struggling defender. Diego had run past his man, watched the ball bounce invitingly, then steered the ball home from a tight angle.

Gooooooal! Goalkeeper Giovanni Galli was motionless, apparently unable to anticipate so feathered a finish. 'Giovanni later joined Napoli, and I asked him about that goal,' explained Signorini. 'He told me, "When Diego jumped to strike the ball, I thought he was going to blast it, hard. And then I . . ." Giovanni had made himself rigid to block the ball. Because the shot was so subtle, he tried to change his posture, couldn't, and he had to watch it go past.'

'Your friend would have been an exceptional fighter pilot,' Dr Dal Monte told Fernando Signorini months later while they were studying Maradona's biomechanics, impressed by what that goal showed – the footballer's peripheral vision, similar to a wide-angle camera.

The match itself was dull with few scoring chances. 'The spectators, who were mainly Mexican or neutral, were shouting, "Play, play, play,"' recalls journalist Sergio Levinsky, who was at the game. 'Argentina passed it, Ruggeri to Brown, Brown to Ruggeri, Ruggeri to Brown, Cuciuffo to Brown.' The scoreboard never threatened to move from 1-1, the final score.

Things were going well and Carlos Bilardo was now the guru of a sect, as Ricardo Giusti once put it, and a sect that was on its own divine path. Nobody asked to change the rickety bus. The day before the game against Bulgaria, there was a barbecue. Bilardo's punctual call. Tapias shaved again in the Olympic Stadium. In the changing room, the phone didn't ring. The players looked at Bilardo. Nothing. Bilardo said, 'Well, come on, let's warm up.' The phone rang. Brown ran to answer it. Nobody was at the other end.

'The Bulgarians were looking at us with fear. Especially in the tunnel before we went out on the pitch and when we started to fuck about with *Tata* Brown and a few others,' said Maradona in his autobiography. 'What did I do? I got on his back, like a piggyback, and was shouting like a gorilla, then I got off and started hitting my chest. All of a sudden, all of us were screaming at each other like crazy. "Come on, fuckers!" The Bulgarians looked like someone from hell had just appeared.'

The Bulgarians put up little resistance and were easily overcome 2-0, the win lifting Argentina top of their group. Uruguay awaited in the last sixteen, a River Plate *clásico* not seen at the World Cup for fifty-six years. The previous meeting had been in the very first World Cup final in 1930, and Uruguay had won.

Circumstances forced changes as the tournament progressed; Brown continued as a starter ahead of a struggling Passarella, while fellow defender Oscar Garré's yellow cards total meant Olarticoechea was called upon. Midfielder Héctor Enrique wasn't in the original line-ups, but with his performances on the training ground he forced his way into the starting eleven. Clear-the-air meetings continued, dealing with tough subjects, soothed somewhat as confidence grew with the positive results. 'It's those group transformations, almost miraculous, that took place in the space of a month, the purification of the atmosphere, which were bringing the triumphs,' explains Jorge Valdano. 'We reached the final [knockout] phase of the championship as a real team.'

Before the game against Uruguay, the hamburger crew ate a hamburger, the rest had a barbecue, the phone calls were made and received, a sweet put in the centre . . . 'The rituals made me uncomfortable,' Valdano admits today, a man more inclined to read books than to seduce fate. 'I am very respectful of personal ones, but I am bothered by collective ones. At the end of the championship, we had so many it was like a play that had been performed a thousand times.'

Maradona spoke of winning the *clásico* for 'the honour of our homeland'. Argentina knew their South American neighbours and rivals very well, both offering similar characteristics: tough in defence and a practical game plan. Diego had a sensational match. He moved freely across the pitch, offering himself constantly. If he went to the wings, the game passed through him there; he tracked back to recover possession; he tried to prise chances from plays that appeared clamped shut. It was his finest game for the national team up to that point, 'but it won't be better than the next one,' Pasculli, scorer of the only goal, said at the following press conference. Argentina deserved more than the 1-0 scoreline suggested. Next up was a quarter-final against England. Maradona had already amassed four assists and a goal.

Passarella had returned to training before the match against Bulgaria, but he had torn a muscle in his left leg, his first muscle injury in ten years. Dr Madero confirmed that the legendary centre-back had intensified his training without permission, diametrically opposed to the player's version that he broke down after being forced to train. Either way, Passarella left and went to Acapulco with his family. Maradona couldn't forgive him; as he wrote in his book: 'In '86, we were breaking our souls while he was sunbathing in Acapulco.'

Passarella appeared at the stadium to watch the victory over Uruguay and declared to the media he would be fit for the quarter-finals. On the eve of the match against England, he felt ill again. He ended up in Español hospital with a colon ulcer, losing weight and attached to drips. There were hardly any visitors. Maradona didn't go to see him.

Back at Club América's ground, training remained light. 'Do nothing, sit down or go for a swim,' Bilardo told them. The heat forced them to spend hours in the pool. Six days passed between the Uruguay and England matches. 'Do you know what it's like to spend six days farting about, scratching your balls?' said Diego, who decided to train alone to fight the boredom. 'Bilardo knew there were people who didn't sleep much, and at night he walked around with little sandwiches on a tray.'

In the run-up to the match, Néstor Clausen and *Vasco* Olarticoechea filmed some women sewing. Burruchaga's commentary said, 'It's the day before the match, at six o'clock in the evening, the women are still sewing our shirts. If we become world champions, they'll have to make a monument to us all. A day before the big game, and we don't even have numbers on our shirts!'

Argentina had to play in their second kit, the dark blue one they had worn against Uruguay. Bilardo told his AFA technical assistant, Rubén Moschella, he wanted a different type of shirt because the heat made them heavy and unbearable. 'Bilardo wanted to show us how to make a lighter, more refreshing open-necked shirt, so he started to make some terrible cuts with some scissors,' recalled Moschella. 'I call the representative of Le Coq Sportif, and he tells me that unfortunately he doesn't have any blue open-necked shirts, and he can't make them with so little time. In desperation, I decided to trawl the whole of Mexico City.' Kitman Roberto *Tito* Benrós went with him. 'We ran from one side of the city to the other with a backpack.'

The pair found two options, one similar to the existing second kit and the other in a brighter blue. 'No! No, not those!' said Bilardo upon seeing the latter ones. There remained forty-eight hours before the England game. 'That's when Diego strolled in,' remembered Moschella, 'and he says, "What a nice shirt this one is, Carlos," pointing to the bright blue one. "With this one, we'll beat the English." Carlos looks at it, I crossed my fingers and he said, "OK, let's go with this one."'

The issues of the AFA badge and numbers remained to be solved. The son of Club América's president knew a shop that sold fabrics to make numbers. 'They only had three colours, blue, red and yellow, and none of them worked for us,' kitman Tito remembers. 'Suddenly, a silver-grey fabric appeared, and we decided to try it out.' They were American football numbers. Another member of Club América had the old coat of arms of the Argentine federation. And right there, in an improvised workshop, kitmen and Club América employees embroidered numbers and badges onto the new shirts during the twenty-four hours before the England match.

The next day Argentina participated in a game that is still being played today.

# 23
# ENGLAND–ARGENTINA. FIRST HALF

In 1986, Argentina's democratic spring, led by President Raúl Alfonsín, brought hope to the streets. Argentina, chest out, was facing the world proudly and confidently. 'It's just football, full stop,' Maradona said to the cameras when asked about the England match, but he did not really mean it. Four years earlier, the Falklands conflict had resulted in the death of 649 Argentinians and 255 Britons in combat, most of them under twenty years of age; more than 2,400 people were wounded. Veterans' associations state that between 300 and 500 former soldiers, from both sides, committed suicide in the years that followed.

The national team had been used and lied to in 1982 by Argentine authorities, but in 1986 the picture was much clearer. Rather than what the dictatorship had claimed, it was clear that the defeat could not be placed squarely at the door of the USA, following the line of the military junta that they had not provided the help which had been promised. The then US president, Ronald Reagan, loyal to his historic European ally, had demanded that Argentina seek a diplomatic solution. Without the help of USA, the ill-equipped and ill-prepared Argentine army stood little chance of victory. When they returned home, the junta made sure their stories, faces and futures were put in a box and the key thrown away. Now the details were beginning to emerge.

'I remembered '82 well,' Maradona wrote in his autobiography two decades later. 'When we arrived in Spain, we saw all those Argentine kids scattered around the Malvinas, the massacre, legs and arms, while the military sons of bitches told us that we were winning the war.'

After the conflict, a narrative of rivalry between both countries had been created and it was transposed to football, often described in warlike terms. 'In my time as a player there was already rivalry with the English,' Carlos Bilardo told *El País* in 2006. 'At school, they taught us about the English invasions [in 1806–7] and what happened when they passed through the streets – we threw boiling oil at them.'

During England and Paraguay's last-sixteen tie, some English fans sang, 'Bring on the Argentines, we want another war.' 'We distanced ourselves from the ruckus the Argentinians wanted to cause, they would have had us all going on the pitch with a machine-gun,' recalled Diego. 'England were only our football rivals on the day . . . I just wanted to nutmeg them, flick the ball over their heads and lead them a merry dance.'

England striker Gary Lineker explains that he and his teammates were not oblivious to the game's wider significance: 'It was a massive game, quarter-finals of the World Cup! But yes, it did seem to be on another level. I remember the questions at the press conferences were always a little more pointed than usual.'

Some ex-soldiers sent telegrams to the national team, urging them to recreate the performance of the Exocet missiles that sank the British destroyer, HMS *Sheffield*. Six of the Argentina side that played against England were born in 1962, the year of birth of recruits chosen by lottery to fight in the Falklands, which included a footballer.

'We all declared before the game that football had nothing to do with the Malvinas war . . . Bullshit!' insisted Maradona in *El Nacional*. 'But we chose to keep ourselves distant, calm.'

England, despite having a proven goalscorer in Gary Lineker, box-to-box midfield leader in Bryan Robson and powerful centre-back in Terry Butcher, had lost the opening match to Portugal and drawn with Morocco, matches considered easily winnable. Successive 3-0 victories over Poland and Paraguay restored optimism, aided by Lineker's five goals in two games.

Bobby Robson sought to use the same media strategy as Bilardo's boys. When asked about the Argentine threat and the 'added dimension' of the game, the England manager replied emphatically, 'Don't waste time on questions like that. Don't ask me anything regarding the diplomatic situation or the political situation. We're here to play football.'

'He was always a measured individual,' Gary Lineker tells me when we review the game. 'By this stage, the most important thing was our physical condition. We'd played two [of the three group] games in Monterrey, in the heat of the day, forty-three degrees! I thought I might die at some stage. And then we went to Mexico City [to play Paraguay then Argentina] where suddenly we were at altitude. I thought, "How am I going to survive this?"'

The English had stopped pushing themselves in training and Bobby Robson understood that his job was to create a relaxed atmosphere and accentuate the positives. They were about to face the man who was, according to Lineker, 'by far the best player at the moment. Zico, Careca, Butragueño, there were good players, but Maradona was on another level. We players admired him.'

'We talked among ourselves about Diego', Lineker explains. 'How do we deal with Maradona? He moves around so much. We'd always played 4-4-2. And whenever he came to get the ball, the nearest person would go to him.' Terry Fenwick, a no-nonsense central defender with a record number of yellow cards in a World Cup, was picked for the starting eleven, but there was never any intention to man-mark Maradona – the English players felt the tactic didn't suit them. Otherwise, the team was as expected, with winger John Barnes on the bench.

Argentina had just beaten Uruguay with a single goal by Pedro Pasculli in what had been their best display. One day before the England match, Bilardo asked Maradona to leave the room: he wanted to talk to Pedro Pasculli alone. Bilardo was going to leave Pasculli out of the starting line-up; Diego would later console a sobbing Pedro. *El Negro* Enrique and *Vasco* Olarticoechea came in, Olarticoechea making his first appearance because of Oscar Garré's suspension. Bilardo introduced a novel 3-5-2 formation. Maradona and Valdano would play up front as strikers, and they would drop deep to connect with the midfield.

It was Argentina's first match at the Azteca Stadium, five minutes away from their lodgings, and it would be their fourth played in the intense midday heat. The bus was scheduled to leave at 9.30am, but the players were there half-an-hour early, with an almost military punctuality.

Once in the stadium, the Argentinians went through their rituals, and the English theirs. 'I used to have a hot bath before a game,' Gary Lineker explains. 'Despite the heat, I did it in Mexico, too, in a small pool. Just filled it up and stood there and did some stretching exercises. Just to get loosened off. Then I went out to warm up. I never shot at goal during warm-ups, just in case I used one of my goals up!'

In a room close to the changing rooms, some players exchanged greetings. Osvaldo Ardiles chatted briefly with Tottenham teammate Glenn Hoddle, and Maradona came by to say hello. Forty-five minutes before the match, Bobby Robson spoke to Fenwick about Argentina's number 10: 'Don't worry, Terry, he's little, fat and he's only got one foot.'

'We went through the usual in the dressing room,' Maradona recalled in *Mi Mundial, Mi Verdad*. 'All we talked about was we were going to play a football match, we had lost a war, yes, but not because of us or the boys we were going to face.' Nearly 115,000 spectators filled the stadium, but in the tunnel Maradona could hear only the sound of football boots on the metal floor. Nobody was talking.

And suddenly, Diego's voice could be heard in the Argentine line, parallel to the English one: 'Come on, come on, these sons of bitches . . . come on, this lot killed our neighbours, our relatives, these sons of . . .'

The grass was in a bad state, the roots seeming to come out of the ground. During the warm-up, both teams realised you'd have to step hard to be able to run, demanding extra effort. The heat was stifling, an advantage for the Latin Americans, as was the altitude. Argentina had been staying in Mexico City (England in Monterrey, 1,000 metres less high) and had already played two games in the nation's capital, helping them acclimatise.

'Then you get to the centre of the pitch, and they play the national anthem,' *Tata* Brown recalled with emotion. 'And I'm telling you the truth, it was like I put a knife between my teeth. I wanted to see if I could get revenge by winning a match. I left my normal life behind. And we all thought the same thing. We never talked about the problem of Las Malvinas, but we all transformed.'

Maradona played the first half through the centre, slightly to the left. He only went right a couple of times, where he would do more damage in the second half. During those first 45 minutes, Diego made two runs that could have unpicked a defence in what was a tight game. After eight minutes, he collected the ball up on the left, dropped two English players and was about to attack the box but instead drew a foul which earned Fenwick a yellow card. Tunisian referee Ali Bennaceur was marking his territory, nipping in the bud any dirty play against Maradona. 'It was a problem for me,' Fenwick recalled. 'I had to live with the danger of being sent off.'

Only Italy had man-marked Diego in the '82 World Cup, so every English player had to be alert to any of his runs. From the opening whistle, Maradona was moving quite freely among the English players, who were playing hard but fair. He was as sharp as he had ever been, and with the most minimal of touches he would gain a precious advantage on his rivals, who had to resort to fouling him because they were arriving half a second late.

Possession belonged to Argentina, but the game was played at a plodding pace. The three centre-backs, with Ruggeri and Cucciuffo as defenders and *Tata* Brown in a sweeper role, were solid. Giusti and *Vasco* were patrolling the flanks, and Maradona kept dropping deep trying to create chances, but without risking a pass that could leave his team exposed.

Half-time.

'The surface isn't helping us,' thought Maradona. Terry Butcher wasn't happy either: 'The first half was awful. Neither team really played.' Gary Lineker barely touched the ball. The Tunisian referee picked up the ball and headed for the dressing-room tunnel. He smiled at his linesmen, especially the Bulgarian Bogdan Dotchev, with whom he could communicate only via looks and gestures. They had already refereed the Paraguay–Belgium group game together, with the roles reversed. That game was level at 2-2 draw when, in the 87th minute, the linesman Bennaceur was better positioned than referee Dotchev to flag a Belgian goal as offside, much to Dotchev's relief and gratitude.

Before the World Cup, FIFA specifically instructed referees to put absolute confidence in the assistant closest to the action, if in any doubt. The Tunisian Bennaceur's smile to the Bulgarian was also a relief: the match was being controlled, and they hadn't missed much. There was a hint of an off-the-ball elbow from Butcher on Maradona on the edge of the box. Still, Bennaceur told the English centre-half he considered it accidental.

Bennaceur was accompanied to the dressing room by FIFA escorts, who had chaperoned him and every other referee ever since their arrival in Mexico, including travel between hotels and stadiums. Before locking himself in with the linesmen, the head of stadium security spoke to Bennaceur via an interpreter: 'When it's time to blow for the end of the match, do it when you're near the pitch markings close to the tunnel. I have twenty-five agents available to protect you.'

The referee closed his changing-room door at the same time as the English closed theirs. 'We're doing OK – more of the same. Chances will come . . .' Lineker remembers Bobby Robson and some of the other players repeating the phrases, albeit he usually disengaged during the half-time interval. After the break, the team prepared to leave, and the battle cry was heard: 'CAGED TIGERS!!' It was Terry Butcher. 'It terrified me!' says Lineker, laughing now.

In the Argentina dressing room, Maradona asked for more effort: '"Come on, lads, not a step back. Not a step back!" I felt that we were dawdling a little bit, and I didn't like it one bit . . . Bilardo, nothing. He didn't say a word. Or maybe one short comment: "Diego is right."'

# 24

# ENGLAND–ARGENTINA. SECOND HALF

Six runs that Maradona makes with the ball define the match. Two had happened in the first half and the remaining four will forever mark Maradona's career. In the first period, he patrolled the left. Intuition told him there would be more openings from the right of the Argentine attack, so after the break he moved mostly on the centre-right area.

Five minutes after the resumption. Argentina wins the ball back and moves it from right to left. It reaches *Vasco* Olarticoechea, the wing-back on that side, who gives the ball to Maradona. The number 10 sprints forward with the ball, driving diagonally towards the centre of the crowded English midfield. He skips one half-hearted challenge and bears down on the penalty area 'D'. The goal is in his sights, but it's congested, and his teammates are all marked.

Burruchaga, as he would for three of the six drives that Diego made throughout the game, takes a diagonal run from right to left in front of the number 10. He offers himself as a decoy, teasing the defence out of position. Maradona accelerates, leaving one defender behind and cutting two Englishmen from the game. Still with the ball, he looks for a blue shirt, someone to anticipate a way through that at that moment doesn't exist, a quick one-two. Shilton observes the play developing and takes a step forward.

Burruchaga and Olarticoechea are free to Diego's left. Maradona goes right, and sends a short, ten-foot pass to Jorge Valdano, on the edge of the D. The message is clear: he wants the ball back. A good ball through and he's one-on-one with the goalkeeper. Shilton spots Maradona running into the area and recognises the ploy.

Valdano loses control of the ball, and it bounces up and over his shoulder. Midfielder Steve Hodge is covering, anticipates and has a half-second to choose his next move as the ball loops up into the area. Butcher slows down, waiting and expecting Hodge to clear the danger. Hodge, who has a trusty left foot, stretches and volleys the ball with the outside of his left boot back to Shilton to catch – deliberate back-passes to goalkeepers were still permitted at the time. The connection is good, and Hodge sends the ball high, making Shilton's claim easier.

Shilton doesn't realise it's a back pass and doesn't foresee it, losing a vital half-second in the race to the ball. Still, he thinks he'll be first to the ever-rising ball. Maradona impulsively jumps, crucially before Shilton does. Hodge is surprised to see Maradona bearing down on the goalkeeper. 'Why is he there?' he asks himself.

'I'll never reach it, please come down, come down,' Diego says to himself. He has an idea. 'What if . . .'

Standing at 5ft6in, Maradona has no choice but to jump for the ball and stretches his arm to provide leverage for his jump. He is in the air, his muscular legs have helped him climb high, and he pulls them into his body, like a frog, to gain extra ascendency. His upper body is stretched out; he doesn't know if he'll get there before Shilton, but he's gambling on it. 'If they catch me, they catch me,' he thinks. The goalkeeper still has the advantage and starts to lift himself, too, both arms raised.

Shilton, eyes on the ball, thinks that Maradona has more impetus and is going to collide with him. So he changes his mind and decides to fist the ball, making sure he'll be the first one to make contact. He just has to clear it. Peter Reid turns around and ignores the play because he thinks everything is under control. That ball is Shilton's.

In the air, Maradona shapes his body as if about to head the ball. A fist thrusts out. Shilton closes his eyes while he tries to connect with the ball. Referee Bennaceur sees Shilton's hand which appears to cover Diego's. What is about to happen is almost impossible to perceive from the referee's position. 'If I just do this . . .' thinks Maradona. His objective cannot be reached by fair means, so mischief makes the decision for him.

Maradona punches the ball. Shilton has lost sight of it as it tumbles towards the goal.

Bobby Robson has seen Diego's arm bend and also his closed fist hitting the ball. Steve Hodge is five yards away, and he sees the ball go into the goal, and he thinks, 'Jesus, have I made a mistake there?'

Valdano believes Diego can't possibly have headed the ball. Glenn Hoddle sees the handball and turns towards the referee, convinced Bennaceur will call for a foul.

The ball bounces once before slowly entering the middle of Shilton's unguarded net. Maradona lands before the ball goes in, turns and looks at the referee before starting to celebrate. He jumps up and raises both arms to the sky, then runs away as quickly as possible from the scene of the crime. 'Argentina Gooooooal, Die-goool! Diego Armando Maradona,' Víctor Hugo Morales shouts to the country on Radio Argentina.

Hodge is surprised that the ball went in so gently. A header would have generated more power, but Hodge doesn't really know what happened. He sees Shilton protesting. The linesman, the Bulgarian Bogdan Dotchev, sees the referee give the goal. The rules at the time state that the assistant can give his opinion only at the referee's request. Bennaceur has not hesitated, but while he is returning to the centre-circle, harangued by English players, he looks at Dotchev, who had a better angle than his. Their gazes meet for a second. He has complete confidence in his assistant, who owed him one from the previous match. Bennaceur doesn't change his mind or decision. The goal stands.

Maradona runs to the sidelines, furtively glancing at Bennaceur, who is walking to the centre of the field. The linesman Dotchev heads upfield, too, keeping his head bowed. Terry Fenwick, the defender closest to Maradona during the move, objects furiously with Shilton for company, the goalkeeper convinced of foul play from his teammate's reaction. Hodge raises his hand, appealing for offside. Gary Lineker considers the reaction of Shilton, Butcher and Fenwick, who has run towards the referee, and guesses something is afoot. 'With the hand,' he thinks. Bobby Robson keeps looking at the leaping and celebrating Maradona. He can't believe it. The substitutes' bench all saw the handball, and all cry foul.

'For me, he jumped and hit it with his hand to score,' Víctor Hugo Morales continues telling listeners in Argentina, 'sending the ball over Shilton. The linesman didn't see it, the referee glimpsed it, while the English were delivering all kinds of justified protests.'

*Checho* Batista approaches Maradona, slowly, as if he thinks he is not going to claim the goal. 'But you scored with your hand!' he says. 'Shut your mouth, asshole, and hug me!' Maradona yells. If his teammates doubt the goal's validity, the referee may chalk it off. He orders them to come closer, but only Valdano and Burruchaga do, neither looking back in case the referee sees their doubt-ridden faces.

*El Gráfico* journalist José Luis Barrios looks down and writes, 'Diego, handball, ruled out'. Next to him, a journalist elbows him hard – it would hurt him for three days. 'He gave it!'

'He's given the goal,' says Glenn Hoddle, whose stomach is churning – he knows that the referee won't change his mind. Bilardo looks at his defence, making sure they are well placed to react if the goal doesn't count and the opponent counter-attacks.

For the first time in history, people at home can watch television replays from three different angles. Almost all of them arrive at the same conclusion.

'The goal was with the hand, I can shout it with all my soul, but I have to tell you what I think,' continues Víctor Hugo Morales' commentary. 'Argentina is winning one-nil, and God forgive me for what I am about to say. Against England, one-nil, with a handball goal . . . Well, what do you want me to say?'

Maradona wants to speed up the restart. He looks at the grandstand area where Don Diego and Coco, his father-in-law, are. He sends them a message with a closed fist, and they reply with the same gesture.

Fenwick tries to talk to the non-English-speaking referee. Lineker looks at the linesman and is convinced that the Bulgarian, with a guilty look on his face, has seen everything but doesn't dare tell the referee. Shilton realises that there is no turning back. He feels cheated, betrayed.

Víctor Hugo asks Ricardo Scioscia, his co-commentator, if the goal was handball: 'No, Víctor Hugo, it was with the head.'

Lineker tries one last time: 'Referee, it was handball.' Bennaceur replies, 'Please play.' The English accept the verdict, their protests nowhere near as vehement if it had happened the other way around. Resigned, with nothing to be done, forgetting that pressuring the referee could have brought future benefits, England resume play just thirty-five seconds after the goal.

Víctor Hugo, following a few minutes of anguish, sees enough repetitions on a nearby monitor to calm down. 'We lied to ourselves by saying that we should not mix football with patriotism and politics,' the Uruguayan journalist recalls today. In 1986, he played the role of a triumphant Argentinian. 'That day, Argentina was about to win the game equipped this time with equal arms.' The story of Maradona's second goal would give Víctor Hugo universal fame. Still, he is most proud of his 'Well, what do you want me to say?' commentary, despite the political connotations. 'It was the spontaneity of the moment,' he says.

'It's like stealing from a thief, it's like I stole a thief's wallet,' Diego repeated many times after the game. 'I have a hundred years of forgiveness.'

'If you watch that from behind the goal,' Glenn Hoddle says as he follows the game again thirty years later for an ITV documentary, *The Hand of God: 30 Years On,* he has done that before because . . . watch his head. Don't watch his arm, watch his head. As he does it, he flicks his head.'

Valdano adds to the supposition: 'In training, we practised corners. Out there Maradona scored an incredible header, and I saw someone laughing, and I said, "What are you laughing at?" "He put it in with his hand!" He would jump and make the same movement with his hand as with his head. I was on the other side to his hand, and I couldn't see the dexterity. He trained at everything.'

Maradona scored many goals with his hand. Once, in the same Parque Saavedra of his first trial, his rivals saw it and they all appealed to the referee, who gave the goal anyway. 'You want to get to the ball, and your hand goes off by itself,' said *El Pelusa* more than once. When he was playing for Argentinos, another referee ruled out a handball goal against Vélez and advised him not to do it any more. Diego thanked him for the advice but replied he couldn't promise anything. Diego liked to imagine that referee celebrating his first goal against the English in Mexico.

'I'll tell you about one against Zico,' Maradona said to me in a public interview we did in Amman in Jordan. 'It's the ninety-fourth minute, and I'm at the near post. I'm one metre sixty-five, and I cannot beat anyone to a header, I was surrounded by people who were one metre ninety. Two Udinese defenders jump up to clear, the ball falls to me and, bop [makes a gesture with his hand], I tucked it in. Goal. Referee . . . goal. Zico comes up to me and says, "Diego, please, you know it was a handball, we need the points." "And so do we," I tell him. And he says, "Please, come clean. Otherwise, you are not honest." So I say, "I am Diego Dishonest Maradona. Delighted to meet you." Obviously, this is about whether the referee or the linesman sees you.'

This survival instinct is the *Viveza Criolla*, the sharp intelligence of the Creole that is mythologised in José Hernández's Argentine literary classic, *Martín Fierro* (1872). Martín Fierro is a gaucho from the pampas whose survival on his ranch depends on resisting the police, army and state. They come to recruit him for the war, but he refuses conscription, deserts his home and loses everything. Fierro later encounters the gaucho Vizcacha, a cynical thief, who teaches Fierro that cheating, tricks and setting traps are the ways to achieve what you desire.

This *Viveza Criolla* engenders imitation; it's amusing and brings short-term benefits. Small acts of foul play are an intrinsic part of Latino football. They are considered indispensable because they supposedly help you win. Throwing the ball high and far away after a foul to buy time to organise defences, pinching a few yards with free-kicks, claiming every throw-in, play-acting and more are all 'fair game'.

But the reality of those gestures is its anti-social effects. Cheating pollutes respect for others, breaks the social contract and the rules of communal systems. On and off the pitch, authority is compromised, and distrust permeates everything and everybody. The thief thinks everyone thinks as he does, creating for himself an elaborate and unhealthy world, inhabited by the profoundly suspicious who trade in deceit and duplicity.

'I would like to see the English, or Europeans in general, viewing football as the only way to be happy,' asserts Víctor Hugo who sees it differently. 'I'd like to see them live as complicated a life as Latin Americans, with tremendously humble origins like all the players and most of the fans. They have not been given many chances. When you have half a chance, you want to take it. That creates a mighty pressure to win, and not to disappoint. It explains a lot of things.'

Back to the Azteca Stadium. Maradona has grown several centimetres with his goal. The pressure is on England, and a feeling of grave injustice, still felt today, is taking hold of Shilton and the English players.

Nine minutes into the second half, just three and a half minutes after the first goal, and the ball is in the middle of the Argentine half. Glenn Hoddle attempts a short pass and it's intercepted by Ruggeri. Batista fouls the English midfielder, but Bennaceur fails to see it.

Ruggeri passes to Enrique, who gives the ball to Maradona. It is a tricky ball to deal with; Maradona has his back to England's goal, in his own half. Losing possession could compromise the Argentine defence that is readying to attack. Striker Peter Beardsley and midfielder Peter Reid are close by.

'He plays it to Diego. There's Maradona; he's marked by two. Maradona steps on the ball,' reports Víctor Hugo in the commentary box.

Maradona avoids Beardsley's half-lunge while first controlling the ball. Bennaceur thinks about blowing for a foul but allows play to continue. Diego steps on and drags the ball back and away from Reid. The latter is left two metres behind Maradona, who has spun and whose third touch has him rampaging towards the England goal.

Steve Hodge spots Butcher and Fenwick in the channel where Diego's run will lead, out to the right wing. Hodge feels things are under control, and Diego is still a long way from danger.

Peter Reid tracks Maradona but always remains two metres behind. Bennaceur follows the play, too, looking at Diego. After the first goal he doesn't want to miss anything. Despite the plus forty-degree temperature, the referee feels good physically. He practised athletics in Tunisia for many years, and FIFA had appointed a Polish trainer, a specialist in altitude training, to condition the match officials in readiness for the tournament.

The English midfield is open, and Maradona reaches cruising speed on the right-hand side. Reid, still behind the play, provides cover should Diego stop or pass. Terry Butcher sees Reid to his right and opens his body to invite Maradona to head towards the touchline. The move is too obvious, too early. Maradona, with a simple dummy and a subtle touch, moves to the right of Butcher's outstretched leg and cuts further into the exposed English central belly. He sprints to within a few yards of the edge of the box.

Burruchaga contemplates crossing again in front of Diego, to drag a defender out of position, but he sees that Diego is cramped for space on the attacking right and there is no room for the run. He accompanies play, available for the rest of the attack in case a one-two is needed, or to finish a final pass. If only Burruchaga had a camera to record what was undoubtedly the best view in the house.

Butcher keeps tracking back, running after Maradona, who is close to getting into the box. Diego feels Butcher breathing down his neck, but knows his acceleration has bought him a second while he solves more immediate problems in front of him.

Maradona does not have great speed. Fast-paced, incisive dribbles require tricks, deceptions, twists, turns and feints to succeed, which is how Maradona beats his rivals.

Bennaceur enjoys what he is seeing. 'Many things were happening, I was happy not to have intervened earlier,' he explained years later.

Fenwick is on a yellow card and marking Jorge Valdano. He decides to abandon his man and step up to stop Maradona crashing into the box. He tries to block the number 10 and has to decide: foul or not. An obstruction is the only way to stop Diego, leading to a certain second yellow and expulsion. He stretches out an arm, but it brushes the rushing Maradona's stomach and no more. 'They're rocking me like a baby,' Diego thinks. Nothing and nobody will stop him at this pace and power. He feels indestructible.

Diego feints left, but sees a motorway of space to Fenwick's right and accelerates into the open highway. He jumps Fenwick's belated attempt to trip him. Bennaceur has seen Fenwick's foul. 'Advantage, advantage,' he shouts and play continues.

Lineker watches from the other half, turning disbelief to admiration. 'In this pitch, with this grass . . .' he thinks.

Maradona is inside the area. He sees Burruchaga and Valdano to his left, unmarked, asking for the ball and in position to receive it. But no matter what he says later to Valdano in the shower, the ball is going to no one. 'No way am I passing the ball!' he thinks. 'It's like I'd brought it all the way from my own home!' Valdano is transfixed and follows the play, as much a fan as a teammate. This play is the sum of Maradona's talent, dominating the ball, tricks, the changes of direction and rhythm.

'The genius of world football starts from the right and leaves a third man behind and makes to play for Burruchaga! Always Maradona,' booms Víctor Hugo. Maradona looks up briefly at Valdano, another deception. He is left with goalkeeper Peter Shilton to beat.

The right-back Gary Stevens forgets the unmarked Valdano and moves to cover Shilton's right, on the edge of the six-yard box. The insignificance of his decision is reinforced by Maradona's next trick. A few chosen players are blessed with a speed of thought that produces dozens of options to overcome hindrances encountered on the way to the goal. Diego considers placing the ball inside the far post. But he quickly negates that option and Stevens' run in the process. He sees more possibilities of scoring somewhere else.

Maradona had been in a similar position against England at Wembley six years earlier when he stabbed the ball just wide of Ray Clemence's far post. *El Turco* was about seven at the time and spoke to his elder brother after the game: 'You idiot! You should have feinted, brought him out and put it down the right. The keeper was already diving.' Maradona replied, 'You son of a bitch! It is so easy when you watch it on TV!'

Shilton rushes out to meet Maradona, not noticing Stevens to his right. All the calculations have been made; Maradona has decided from the several paths open to him. No need to dummy, just push the ball forward.

With his left foot, he moves the ball a little to the right. Shilton deposits himself on the ground, in an almost sitting position, with his hands covering first his face then pushing him up to try to re- cover lost ground. With that subtle touch of the ball, the goalkeeper is left behind. 'I felt sorry for the defenders,' Bennaceur would later admit.

Terry Butcher has thought a thousand times about what he should have done; he should have possibly fouled Maradona earlier, outside the area. He does all he can now; he's right behind Diego and has only one option. He drops to the ground and stretches his left leg to try and take out the ball, or the man. Or both.

After beating Shilton, Maradona is preparing to score, he can do it even with his right. He feels the physical contact of Butcher, who cannot see the ball and knows that, by going on the floor, he runs the risk of scoring an own goal. As the Argentine starts to fall under the defender's tackle, blocking any chance of Butcher stealing the ball, a last-minute solution is still needed. Butcher clears out Mara- dona's right ankle – the pain will come later – and the referee has the whistle between his lips. It's a penalty, but Bennaceur doesn't blow. The ball rolls in front of Diego's left foot.

He hits it 'with three toes'.

'Genius! Genius! Genius! Ta-ta-ta-ta-ta-ta! ¡Gooooooalll! ¡Gooooooalll! I want to cry! Jesus Christ! Long live football! ¡Golaazo! Diegooooo! Maradooona! I have to cry, forgive me! Maradona, a memorable run, the best play of all time, a cosmic little kite. What planet did you come from? To leave so many English in the ditches on the way, to make the country unite, shouting for Argentina!'

Little kite?

Ten seconds have passed since Maradona received the ball from Enrique.

Maradona springs up and runs to the corner flag, leading crazy celebrations with the Azteca Stadium. He never choreographed them. Passion takes over; he always meant to be as natural as possible on the pitch. And, in his eyes, every goal deserved the same emotion you would dedicate to the last one you ever scored. But, of course, that one even a bit more. He embraces Salvatore Carmando, his masseur at Napoli and the national team, and the rest of the team is coming over.

'Argentina two, England zero. Diego, Die-gooo, Diego Armando Maradona! Thank you, God, for football, for Maradona, for these tears, for this ... Argentina two, England zero,' continues Víctor Hugo.

Víctor explains the kite reference. 'Menotti had said that Diego was a little "*barrilete*", which means kite but also short and stocky, which was what he meant, and I used the sentence often on the league games. Almost every time Diego made a play I'd say, jokingly, "There's the little *barrilete*."'

'Oh! You have to say that's magnificent,' narrates Barry Davies on the BBC. 'There is no debate about that goal. That was just pure football genius.' Martin Tyler, on ITV, classified it straight away as one of the best goals in the history of the World Cup.

Diego covered almost fifty-five metres in eleven seconds, a poor athletic performance. Usain Bolt ran twice the distance in less time. 'If we asked the five Englishmen he dribbled past to cover the same distance and shoot, Diego's time would see him come last,' says Fernando Signorini. 'Deception is the key.'

Maradona defined it as 'the goal of dreams. We always dream of scoring the best goal in history. And in the World Cup, incredible.'

'The world belonged to him,' wrote Jorge Valdano in *El País*. 'He was running and knew instantly ... that he had crossed over to the other side, to those who get to know what glory tastes like. We adored and envied him in equal measure because he had just done what we, asleep or awake, had all dreamed of.'

Valdano, who had been free in the centre, admits he was a little upset by not getting the ball and said to himself that Diego could 'celebrate and shout alone' then kicked the ball away. Resignedly, he went to embrace his teammate. Maradona was kneeling and Valdano wanted to lift him up, 'to embrace him as an equal'. But it did not work. In fact, Valdano thought, they were never again going to be equal in the eyes of anyone.

Momentarily, Lineker believes the game is over. Then, something else: 'My God! What a goal that was! I should applaud. And he did it against these players . . .'

John Barnes replaces Trevor Steven after seventy-four minutes, the winger offering more width. Barnes changes the game from the left with his dribbling and crosses. From a standing start on the edge of the box, he manages to beat two Argentina defenders. He chips a perfect cross from the byline to Lineker, who heads home his sixth tournament goal, enough to earn him the Golden Boot. It's 2-1, with ten minutes to play.

The Argentina team wastes a minute before kicking off again, then immediately attack. Diego picks up the ball just inside the England half and wriggles through three players. He plays two one-twos, releasing Tapia into the penalty area. After a tussle with a defender, Tapia smacks a powerful right-footed strike against Shilton's right post and the ball flies across the goal-line to safety.

As the match is drawing to a close, something happens that could have changed the history of Diego Armando Maradona, John Barnes, Gary Lineker, Bobby Robson, Steve Hodges and Terry Butcher; in fact, all those on the pitch. It is a reminder of how football's heroes-and-villains' narratives are built on quicksand. Not everyone remembers this particular and final grain of sand that fell through the hourglass, but it is as important as the rest.

In the eighty-seventh minute, one of the new substitutes, winger Chris Waddle, loses the ball and Maradona makes a break on the right. He drives forward but far too slowly, allowing Hodge to recover with a side tackle and push the ball to Hoddle, who gives the ball to Beardsley. The Liverpool player sends a raking pass to John Barnes, who is hugging the left touchline. Enrique backs off, Barnes takes him on again and beats him easily, sending another precise left-footed cross from the byline.

The ball floats parallel to the goal-line, over the redundant and stranded goalkeeper Pumpido. Lineker attacks the far post. Olarticoechea remembers the first goal and that Barnes crosses as soon as he can, so his instinct makes him look for Lineker. Where is he?

Lineker is at the far post, about to head the ball in; he thinks he's going to score, two metres from goal.

'Ah, I see where he is,' thinks Olarticoechea, now running in the direction of Lineker.

The striker has a clear header, one foot from the goal. It will be a goal, won't it?

Suddenly, Olarticoechea appears between the ball and the goal. He has launched himself without following the path of the ball, trying to disrupt play while covering space but really praying for a small miracle.

Lineker nods the ball homewards. Barry Davies and Martin Tyler announce a goal. Olarticoechea makes a minor, but sufficient, flick with his head while flying in the air. His head connects with the ball but he doesn't know if it has gone in or not. Both players end up inside the goal, confused about what has happened. Lineker smacks his knee against the post. The ball, somehow, goes out for a corner.

'I would have lived in bitterness all my days,' says Olarticoechea, when contemplating scoring an own goal.

Bennaceur smiles. He admitted in 2018 to the BBC, 'I would have liked a draw and the uncertainty of extra time' between Maradona-Argentina and an improving England. In any case he felt privileged to have been part of that spectacle.

The referee adds one minute to the regulation forty-five. He blows the whistle and immediately television cameras, fans, players and coaching staff surround Diego Armando Maradona.

# 25
# ENGLAND–ARGENTINA. THIRD HALF

After speaking to Britain's ITV, Steve Hodge met Maradona face-to-face in the tunnel by the changing rooms. He tapped Diego on the back and pointed to his shirt. Could he swap it? Hodge gave him his white 18 shirt in exchange for the blue 10. Later, he declared he wouldn't have dared if he'd known about the handball. Shilton and his colleagues have often said publicly they would never have asked for it.

Maradona and *El Negro* Enrique met at the doping station. 'Everybody is congratulating you, but I gave you the pass!' Enrique joked with him. 'I put you clean through!' Terry Butcher was also taking a drug test. He looked at Diego and pointed at his head and his hand, and asked in English, 'How did you do it?'

'Maradona pointed to his hand,' Butcher, surprisingly, said to the media. 'It was probably the best thing he ever did because I would have killed him if he hadn't.'

Maradona was buried under an avalanche of kisses upon entering the Argentinian changing room, kisses of love and admiration. Everyone wanted to touch the genius, to thank him and venerate him.

Jorge Valdano admits that at the time he did not expect the passionate fervour the game generated. Perhaps nobody did. Now Argentina constantly references it, searching to reconfirm it has a special place in the world, rather than the one it often inhabits, one of doubts about political leadership and of regular financial crises. Moreover, looking back at the goals, both seem to represent Argentina, magnifying Maradona's importance.

'We are like that,' Valdano says in Christian Rémoli's documentary *1986: La Historia Detrás De La Copa* ('The Story Behind the Cup'). 'A *potrero* [which, as well as describing a piece of waste ground to play football, also means the streetwise chancer, an admired character of Argentine culture] doesn't applaud honesty, he applauds the daring and the mischievous. He applauds the one who knows how to take advantage, to bend the rules. And also he applauds virtuosity, those who dare to do things differently. Diego covered everything with those two goals.'

People searching for heroes, as Signorini says, now had, with Maradona, 'plenty of cloth to cut from'.

In the showers, Maradona told Valdano and Burruchaga that in the build-up to his solo goal, after leaving Reid behind, he could see two blue shirts running level with him. 'But Jorge, you were ahead of me and, unlike Burru, you were asking for the ball. Do you know how that works for me? You helped by distracting the defenders—' An incensed Valdano turned off his shower and also cut off Maradona.

'Woah, stop, stop, stop . . .' Valdano was agog.

Diego was thanking him for his parallel run because that way Fenwick had to mark him instead of going to Maradona: 'That's why I always had the ball close to my foot, to make him hesitate. He had to think, "Is he going to give it to him, or is he going to keep going?"'

It was not so much the decoy role he played that bothered Valdano, there was something else: 'Fuck you and your sister, you're humiliating me. You can't possibly have seen all that, it's not possible.'

Of course, Maradona saw it all and was ready for whatever the defender decided. Fenwick eventually left Valdano and failed to foul Diego, but if he had succeeded, Maradona was ready to offload the ball to his unmarked teammate, leaving him one-on-one against Shilton. At the same time, Diego was confident he would not need to pass to anyone, aware he was creating a dream goal sequence. 'The number of ideas processed and discarded in those ten seconds . . .' wrote Valdano in *El País*. There is something miraculous when all the decisions taken in such a short space of time are the right ones.

Gary Lineker had walked despondently into the tunnel and then the changing rooms; it was a defeat, but they had been so close to turning it around. He heard angry voices directing their rage at the referee, the linesman and, yes, Diego for the first goal. 'I don't get angry, so I was just disappointed,' Lineker tells me. And in pain – he had tweaked his medial ligaments when he hit the post with the last chance, and realised he probably wouldn't have made the semi-finals anyway.

Years later, Maradona met Lineker in Buenos Aires for a BBC programme, an encounter Diego recounts in his autobiography: 'The first thing he asked me was, "Did you do it with your hand or with the hand of God?" I remember he told me such a move in England was considered to be cheating and the person that did it a cheat. I told him, for me, it was mischief. And the one who did it was mischievous. We had a good chat, footballer to footballer.'

One of the Argentinian kitmen brought in some shirts to give the England players in case they wanted to swap. Midfielder Ray Wilkins, who hardly ever swore, went ballistic. The kitman left immediately. 'A lot of England fans will never forgive Maradona for what he did,' Chris Waddle says now. 'But if Gary Lineker had done it at the other end, he'd still be being hailed as a hero.'

In the documentary *1986: La Historia Detrás De La Copa*, the journalist Ezequiel Fernandez Moores asked, 'Michael Owen's dive in France 98. Did we say that, here in Argentina, Owen was representing the pirates, English villainy, the greed of Francis Drake and company? No, we didn't say that here. We consider mischief to be a natural part of football. Football is a game of rogues. If someone doesn't understand that, they don't understand this game.'

Shilton believed every other player would have apologised for the handball. For that reason, the goalkeeper refused Diego Maradona's request to appear alongside him on a television programme several years ago. Later on it was Maradona who declined to meet Shilton – he rejected the only condition of the meeting: to genuinely apologise. 'We've been approached several times to put it to bed,' Peter Shilton admitted at the time. 'But he won't apologise, and I won't shake hands with him or acknowledge him. I always say he's the greatest player in history, but I don't respect him as a sportsman and I never will.'

'I won a court case against an English newspaper. They ran a story called "Maradona, the repentant", which had never crossed my mind,' wrote Diego in his autobiography. 'Neither when it happened, nor 30 years later, not until my last breath or before I die. Shilton was angry. He said: "I am not going to invite Maradona to my benefit game." Ha! Who wants to go to a farewell game for a goalkeeper?'

Steve Hodge walked into England's changing room holding Maradona's shirt. 'I wish I'd got the shirt myself, to be honest,' Lineker says. Nobody said anything to Hodge, who stuffed the top into his bag. The shirt spent sixteen years in the attic of Hodge's house in Nottingham. It remains imbued with Maradona's DNA; it was never washed. When Hodge discovered a Pelé shirt from the 1970 World Cup was sold at auction for £157,000 he tried to insure Maradona's, but nobody would do it because its value was unknown. So, Hodge handed it over to the now-defunct Football Museum in Preston. Today it is housed at the National Football Museum in Manchester, next to one of Franz Beckenbauer's from the 1974 World Cup. The shirt is valued at an estimated £300,000, and it is displayed in what the museum called the 'Steve Hodge Collection'.

Don Diego was present at the Azteca Stadium. He had not cried at Diego's debut with Argentinos Juniors; with the England game, something opened the sluices. 'Son, you scored a really great goal today,' he said while still in the stadium. It may have been a rare out-burst of praise for his son, but it would not be his last. He had kept quiet until then, as he saw his son conquer the world. Many others threw compliments in his direction, but his role was simply to support and offer total devotion. Now, as he was growing older, he felt more relaxed demonstrating his excitement at his son's talent. Ten years after beating England, Maradona recalled in *El Gráfico* that receiving public parental approval meant he finally became aware of the symbolism of what had happened.

The match went into extra time – the part with the media. In the dressing room, Bilardo asked Diego about the controversial goal: 'No, Carlos, it wasn't with the hand.' And the coach believed him. When asked by journalists, Bilardo's answer was clear: 'Noo! Why with the hand?' Bobby Robson was unambiguous: 'Maradona handled the ball into the goal, didn't he? Didn't he?' his rhetorical question spat out in frustration.

Maradona, already showered, was emphatic about his first goal: 'I swear on my life, I jumped with Shilton, but I hit it with my head. You could see the goalkeeper's fist, and that's why there's confusion. But it was a header, no doubt. I even had a bump on my forehead.' When later he was reminded of his words, Maradona used to laugh; he didn't want referees to go against him in upcoming games, or so he used to say. It could also be said that it can be hard to recognise deceit. It was not Diego who first spoke about a hand of God – it was Néstor Ferrero, the Argentine editor of the Italian news agency ANSA. He commented, 'Well, it must have been the hand of God, then.' Maradona responded, 'Must have been.'

Diego explained the goal differently many years later, crystallising the moment into legend: 'I was thinking about all the kids who died [in the Falklands War], all of them, that's when I realised that it was God's hand that made me score. Not that I was God or that my hand was God's. That the hand of God, thinking about all the young men who had been killed in Las Malvinas, was the one that scored that goal.' That is how he told it in his book. Now imagine the same words by him if England had won the game. It doesn't work, does it? (Incidentally, the next day only the Argentine newspaper *Crónica* reported the first goal was scored by '*La mano de Dios* [the hand of God]').

Football, whose only purpose is to entertain, showed that on a symbolic level, in certain parts of the world, a victory could in some way compensate for a lost war. The repercussions of a match can be gigantic. As Jorge Valdano once said, 'As an experience, it goes beyond a mere social game; it implies feelings of adhesion and of shared identity, and even plays a role as an intermediary between parents and children, something increasingly difficult to find elsewhere.'

The match referees continued to debate the goal in their hotel. Ali Bennaceur called the FIFA interpreter so he could talk to his Bulgarian assistant. 'Are you sure it wasn't Maradona's hand?' he asked. Bogdan Dotchev's answer left no room for doubt, according to Bennaceur himself: 'He said no, that he was convinced that the goal was totally legal.' When the Tunisian saw the goal on television shortly afterwards, he realised there was a problem. Two days later, Dotchev had changed his story. He told a member of the refereeing commission that he had seen Maradona's hand, but that he didn't disallow it because the referee had already deemed the goal valid.

Bennaceur received a 9.5 out of 10 rating from his supervisor for his arbitration. 'The English praised my performance, but also said, "the Bulgarian should be dropped (laughs),"' he told *El Gráfico* years later. In fact, the match has served as a case study in refereeing academies – the Tunisian had followed, to the letter, directives given in pre-World Cup training. But none of the refereeing team officiated in any further Mexico 86 – or any other – World Cup games.

Twenty-nine years later, Maradona and Bennaceur met again. It was in Tunisia, Maradona taking advantage of a trip for a publicity event. Bennaceur invited him to a typical Tunisian meal at his home. Maradona, accompanied by a translator, surprised him by arriving early and giving him an Argentina shirt, signed, 'For Ali, my eternal friend.'

Maradona spent a couple of hours chatting animatedly with the retired official about that day in Mexico City. As he left, Bennaceur gave him a photo he had hanging in his dining room of the two team captains, Maradona and Shilton, posing together before the start of the game.

Signorini, in the stadium, thought the goal had been a header. When he saw the replay on television and also found out English bookmakers were paying out on 1-1 as the correct result, he went to talk to Diego.

'It's a dishonest goal, a shitty goal,' Signorini said. 'Cheating is as crap in sport as it is in life.'

'Well, lap it up. Look, I picked their pocket.'

'Yes? What if Lineker had scored that goal? If you'd wanted, you could have said it was with your hand and later you could have scored another goal. You're in prime condition to do that and much more. Do you need to cheat to win?'

If we accept the hand was spontaneous, what followed wasn't.

From the first spark of Maradona's celebration, a bonfire of parallel stories and justifications grew. 'He turns around and who is he looking at? The referee,' Signorini tells me in Buenos Aires. 'If he'd stopped in his tracks, come back and said it was with his hand, it would have saved a lot of work for teachers, coaches, philosophers and physical trainers around the world. "Maradona says no to cheating." That would have been much better, even if Argentina lost.'

Signorini rebels against the role deception plays in Latin culture: 'It must be eradicated. That is what we have to fight against. I despise it because it is a weakness of character. Sport has to serve for something else. When Diego decided to do things well, no one can match him. And when he decided to do them badly [laughs], the same.'

Privately Maradona reflected on cheating, too, but as Signorini adds, 'He had his reasons for not letting his audience down.' Admission of weakness at that moment in the Azteca – when he looked down on the world from high, when he saw us applaud genius, when his magic and our submission to it came together – could jeopardise the idea that emerged then: that Maradona and football are the same and, like the game, Diego is eternal.

Is anyone brave enough to put the brakes on that alluring and absorbing ride for him?

# 26

# THE SEMI-FINAL AGAINST BELGIUM AND THE FINAL AGAINST WEST GERMANY

'None of them likes football,' Maradona commented to Valdano at the end of a training session during the 1986 World Cup. He was referring to the journalists who were about to talk to some national team representatives. Diego laid a bet to confirm his suspicions. He kicked a ball with his usual precision to within a few metres of the press pack. If they passed it back with their feet, Valdano would win the bet. A reporter grabbed the ball with his hands and tossed it back, throw-in style. 'Poor guy. He was embarrassed to kick it back because you're here, Diego,' Jorge Valdano said, looking to justify the journalists. In an article for *El País*, the forward added, 'Diego was, as always, quick to retort: "If I am at a party at the president's house in a dinner jacket and a muddy ball comes to me, I chest it and pass it back, as God commands."' Cebollitas coach Francis Cornejo would have been happy hearing those words that he had predicted years earlier.

Maradona exhibited an abundance of street arrogance at the Mexico World Cup, mixed with extraordinary powers of intimidation and the ability to perform dozens of actions that only he could do as regularly and effectively as he showed that summer. Back-heels (including airborne ones), nutmegs, close-quarter dribbles in cramped spaces or running at speed in open areas, wall passes (including with the chest), expert control, crossing, long balls on a sixpence over fifty metres, laser-beam short passes, changes of speed and directions, stealing the ball, tackling, precise free-kicks, flicks, stepovers, shooting and assists. Maradona floated around football fields, demonstrating his talent and superiority, a soloist who had complete dominion over the ball. He played in a perfectly calibrated Argentina team, which Valdano referred to as a team that, finally, 'had all the screws perfectly adjusted', with a lucid plan.

In the semi-final, Argentina met Belgium, the surprise package of the tournament. The Belgians had just eliminated Spain on penalties. They counted midfield maestro Enzo Scifo and star goalkeeper Jean-Marie Pfaff among their ranks. Argentina stuck with the same eleven and also the same system they started against England and were not going to abandon in Mexico, 3-5-2, another of Bilardo's moments of inspiration: three central defenders, two wingers (Olarticoechea on the left and Héctor Enrique on the right), two holding midfielders (Ricardo Giusti and Sergio Batista, closer to the central defenders) and Jorge Burruchaga, who played in and around the two forwards, Maradona and Valdano.

Victory over England made the Argentinians feel indestructible and liberated their play. From the first minute, they took more risks. Diego led the attacks, going through his trick book, but it was not enough to earn the lead after the first forty-five minutes. In fact, Argentina were a poor imitation of themselves when the ball wasn't played through their star. Maradona came out for the second half determined to have even more influence. What happened next is among those select passages of World Cup history.

Five minutes after the restart, Jorge Burruchaga carried the ball and decided to surprise the Belgian defence. In previous games Burruchaga had acted as Maradona's foil, and their understanding and relationship grew during the tournament. Burruchaga was a fast, intelligent player who used space well, and his precise passing made him ideal for one-twos. This time, he served *El Pelusa* a feathered through-ball from the centre-right of the pitch, bouncing invitingly towards the lateral line of the six-yard box and catching the Belgians flat-footed. Diego sprinted ahead of two covering defenders towards the onrushing goalkeeper, Jean-Marie Pfaff. With his first touch, Maradona used the outside of his left boot to lift the ball over the keeper for the opener.

Diego showed surgical precision every time he took a decision, no matter where he was on the pitch. Every time the ball arrived at his feet, the crowd held their collective breath. What would the little master do? What had he seen, anticipated, that they hadn't? Keep an eye on him or you will miss something.

Maradona picked the ball up some forty yards from the Belgian goal, in a central position. The defence, inexplicably, had backed off. Diego accelerated forwards, eliminating three approaching opponents from the play. The last man, like Butcher against England, showed Diego the channel on the right. Maradona dropped his shoulder and went to his left, slicing through to leave Belgium's goal at his mercy. Before the goalkeeper had decided whether to rush or stay put, the number 10 stroked home his side's second goal with the outside of his left boot, the ball flying past a bemused Pfaff's ear.

It had taken Maradona twelve minutes to solve the semi-final puzzle, which would end up 2-0.

Maradona was channelling his powers at their peak in that second half, having a 'Napoleonic influence' on proceedings, according to Valdano, perhaps the best demonstration of one footballer's capability to influence proceedings in World Cup history. 'In that match, I was decisive, I even beat myself,' Maradona wrote in his book about the Mexico tournament. He touched the ball ninety-eight times, the most he had had in the tournament, in which he had already scored five of his team's eleven goals.

Argentina had reached their third World Cup final, their second in the last eight years. On 29 June they would face West Germany, defeated finalists against Italy in 1982. It was a fitting confrontation, involving two era-defining teams. Maradona and company were where they thought they belonged.

'Look at the video we shot the day before the final with the camera we had bought,' says Burruchaga for a documentary about Mexico 86, *The Story Behind the Cup*. 'We were less than fourteen hours away from playing in a World Cup final, and we're not really conscious of it. To give you an idea, you have to remember that back then there were no mobiles, we were ringing people from coin-operated booths. We had no conception of what we were going to experience or where we were heading. That's why all our answers were so calm and natural.'

The world was not aware yet, but it would realise as time passed that Maradona in that World Cup was giving one of the most complete performances ever seen in a team sport.

World Cup final day. The rituals start; everything had to be in its practised order before arriving at the stadium and while there. Bilardo encouraged the good luck rites in order to make sure, as he kept repeating, that 'if the ball hits our post, it does not go in'. The coach asked Brown for some toothpaste. Maradona bathed, shaved and met up with Valdano. Bilardo gave his twenty-minute talk after lunch. He told Valdano about Hans-Peter Briegel, a West German defender with an engine like a locomotive. Team helper Pachamé was last to board the bus. Fitness coach Echevarría asked, as always, if everyone was there, and if they were all sitting in the same place.

Aboard the bus, three songs had to be played in their entirety before arriving at the nearby Azteca Stadium. The playlist was 'Total Eclipse of the Heart' by Bonnie Tyler, 'Eye of the Tiger' by Survivor (the theme of *Rocky III*) and 'Gigante Chiquito' by Sergio Denis. The journey was going well too, and the driver was told to slow down so all three songs would finish.

The great Lothar Matthäus was tasked with handling Maradona, which he did with enormous effect in the first half. The Argentinian was repeatedly caught with fouls and appeared only sporadically. In the twenty-third minute, Argentina had a free-kick deep in West Germany's half, close to the corner flag, and Matthäus was booked. Burruchaga stepped up to place the resulting dead ball onto *Tata* Brown's head for the opener.

Brown plied his trade as a substitute for Deportivo Español. Many doubted him, but Bilardo backed him and had been repaid; Brown hadn't come just to carry everyone else's bags, as people said. A few minutes after scoring, he injured his shoulder. He told the doctor that if he took him off, he would kill him. Brown made a hole in his shirt, hooked his finger inside and hung his arm, like a sling, to alleviate the pain he clearly felt throughout the rest of the game.

Argentina sat back, absorbing attacks. Maradona dropped deeper, mimicking his role at Napoli. This ruffled the West German markers and opened up space for the runs of Burruchaga and Valdano.

Diego had learned that every sector of the field, in every match, demanded a different style of play. As César Luis Menotti declared at the time, 'I was surprised because I saw him being generous, I saw him thinking. He wasn't looking to take on his marker or make it personal. In the centre of the park he would do one-touch football and assisted often, working with the humility of a great.'

Ten minutes after the restart, a West Germany corner came to nought and Argentina launched a rapid counter-attack, an end-to-end move elegantly finished by Valdano. At 2-0, the final was very much in Argentina's favour. But West Germany pulled one back through Karl-Heinz Rummenigge, who poked home a flick-on from a corner. They equalised in the eighty-third minute when Rudy Vöeller headed home from four yards after another corner had been headed back across goal. Bilardo, who had worked hard on set-pieces, could not believe it.

Olarticoechea smashed the ball into the netting from within the goal. A draw was an injustice, he felt, they'd controlled the match until that moment. 'If you talk to all my teammates, you'll see nobody thought we were going to lose it. I thought the same thing,' he admitted years later to journalist Diego Borinsky.

Seven minutes remained of normal time.

In the eighty-fifth minute, a bouncing ball landed in a busy centre-circle. Maradona headed it to his right, looking for a headed one-two. It duly came back towards him. Two West Germans closed down his space, and two defenders were blocking forward plays. Burruchaga had spotted Hans-Peter Briegel hanging around in his own half, so gambled on a diagonal run to the Argentine right. While this was happening, Maradona let the ball bounce twice and across him, opened his body and threaded an inch-perfect, left-footed pass through to meet Burruchaga's run. The locomotive Briegel pumped all his pistons but couldn't cover enough ground to stop Burruchaga's third touch, a striker's finish into the bottom corner.

'He gave me the best pass of my career, the way only he can. I drew strength from I don't know where to run those last metres,' recalls the striker.

It was the number 10's quietest match of the World Cup, but his decision-making at the vital moment brought the World Cup to Argentina. It was his fifth assist, which coupled with five goals, meant involvement in ten of the team's fourteen tournament goals. He also took half the team's total shots on goal.

'Now I believe,' Burruchaga said to Valdano as he returned to his half. A tense five minutes followed, and the final whistle sounded – Argentina were once again world champions.

Maradona dropped to his knees. He couldn't remember who he hugged as the pitch was invaded. He embraced Bilardo at some point – in fact, he embraced everyone who offered him open arms. This was the answer to all the insults, all the invective he had received – victory, served with a cold dish of revenge. 'I went onto the pitch,' Signori tells me, 'and he hugged me very hard, and said, "Look at those sons of bitches."' Victory drew a line that separated those who were with him from those who were against him. Pelé, for example, had said that it was Maradona's last chance to show that he was the best in the world, that others (Platini, Zico, Rummenigge) were ahead of him. Maradona remembered Pelé at that moment.

FIFA president João Havelange handed the FIFA World Cup Trophy to the President of Mexico, Miguel de la Madrid, to present it to Argentina team captain Maradona. Diego shook Havelange's hand perfunctorily, and without looking him in the eye, an avenging smirk on his face. 'I didn't care who gave it to me, I only cared that they gave it to me. I held it like you hold a child. First, I picked it up, and then I pressed it, like this, against my chest. Yes, like a son,' wrote Maradona in his book. Conrado Storani, the Argentine government representative, tried to talk to Diego, but he ignored him.

As he returned to the pitch, World Cup in hand, a fan lifted Maradona off the ground and put him on his shoulders. 'I thought they were going to pass me over their heads,' Maradona said. 'I came face-to-face with this big lad, and I looked at him as if to say, "Lift me up." He put his head between my legs and up I went.' Between them, they had unknowingly composed one of the most emblematic photos of Diego's life.

The footballer remembered steering the fan from his mid-air throne by digging his heels into his sides. Diego didn't know who the fan was until almost three decades later when he was introduced to him. Roberto Cejas was a guest on Maradona's television programme *De Zurda* and told him how he had travelled to Mexico with friends and without tickets.

Back in the dressing room, everyone was jumping, kissing, hugging and singing. Bilardo was in a corner, doubled over, a tortured poet unable to face the flaws in his verse. West Germany had scored two goals from set-pieces, and he couldn't stand it: 'I was saying to myself, "No way, no way," and they said, "Carlos, we are world champions." And I said, "But . . . how can they score two goals like those?"'

In Naples, everyone was either in front of a TV or watching one of the giant screens set up across the city. Everything Diego did, every goal, assist or trick, was celebrated with Neapolitan gusto. At the final whistle, Napoli became an enclave of Argentina, awash with flags, enjoying a victory they felt was as much theirs.

The Argentina touring party had a small tribute they wished to perform. Diego Maradona described it to *El Gráfico*: 'When we arrived at Club América sports centre, our home, a place of arguments, rituals, discussions and challenges, all the players took each other by the hand, and we did a lap of honour, around the training ground; the lights were not on. All together, close, as one. Just remembering it gives me goosebumps. It was an intimate celebration.'

Today, Jorge Valdano acknowledges that they never found another way to celebrate the title, and they never enjoyed it together again. 'He's right, it's true,' admitted Olarticoechea to Diego Borinsky. 'The directors carry some of the blame. They never organised anything, but then again, none of us thought to say, "Hey! Let's do something, all of us together." We all lacked the right attitude.' For Argentina, the World Cup in Mexico was an ephemeral, once-in-a-lifetime alignment of stars and human enterprise.

Since that private celebration on that dark pitch, this garlanded generation of footballers fought more often than not. Backbiting

comments reported from afar were ignored then festered and mag-
nified, straining relationships. Diego much later called the team 'the
little bitches from '86'.

The party flew that same night from Mexico City to Buenos Aires
on a regular scheduled flight. The federation directors were in first
class, while the team travelled tourist class. Maradona asked everyone to sing a chant against the 'pancakes' (those that run away from
difficult situations), referring to journalists that had criticised them
and were now celebrating the win.

Magazines and newspapers across the world splashed Maradona
on their front covers, including those who usually ignored football.
L'Equipé, Guerin Sportivo, Time and Paris Match led with photos of
the diminutive genius. Special supplements, T-shirts, flags and merchandise of all kinds were produced to meet the massive demand.

Maradona had created a masterpiece on the world's grandest
stage, and the world constructed a myth worthy of the work. Everyone had their contemporary hero. Heroes protect us from our base
fears and bring a sense of hope. They satisfy society's irrational urge
to make mortals immortal.

'It made him an immediate hero,' Valdano said. 'He could have
returned to Argentina on a white horse, like San Martín did [patron
saint of Bueons Aires]. People would have applauded him, would
have acclaimed him, not just as a footballer, but as a political or military or social reference. He transcended his footballing role.'

A successful relationship between an idol and those that project
their desires onto them depends on the one who is worshipped fulfilling and accepting the role. The idol must continually meet expectations, and should entreaties fail, idolatry soon converts into great
hostility. This is the razor edge upon which our icons walk.

'When I stepped on to the balcony of the Casa Rosada, with the
World Cup in my hands, I felt like Juan Domingo Perón when he
was addressing the people,' explained Diego. He was never as happy
again as he was then, nor did he feel so in harmony with what he was
doing.

And what is more, Diego Armando Maradona enjoyed at that
moment, more than ever, what he was becoming.

# Part IV

# DIEGO ARMANDO MARADONA

# 27
# CRISTIANA SINAGRA AND THE FIRST SCUDETTO

Naples returned Maradona to his roots. Once more he was the boy from the neighbourhood, formed by the dirty brickwork of narrow streets infused with the briny sea air, resonating with the city's constant noise. His family were with him for long periods, Claudia too, which helped him create something of home. She returned to Buenos Aires in December 1985, however, tired of his mess and neglect. During this impasse, Diego met Cristiana Sinagra, the sister of Lalo's girlfriend.

While love runs fickle, other truths remained constant at Napoli. Any victory over a rich northern rival was celebrated by the entire south of Italy. Aspiration for a cause fuelled Diego, who readily invited himself into people's hearts, 'forever and without needing surgery', as Guillermo Blanco once described it. As he swept away the established order in Serie A, Maradona became something of a populist leader.

Political scientist María Esperanza Casullo described those types of leaders in her book, *Why Populism Works*: 'They talk about themselves, about their childhoods, their values, their families; they weave the public, the private and the biographical in one and a thousand ways. The representational bond between followers and leader is based on loyalty which, by its own strength, transforms the leader into a symbol.' People follow the leader, and he valiantly comes to the people's rescue. Napoli and Diego had a perfect understanding. Meanwhile, he felt he was playing for honour as he had for Cebollitas.

On the pitch, Maradona was learning how to unpick a variety of defensive strategies while avoiding the hard knocks from the Italian defenders. He trained hard, and it changed his anatomy. Diego had arrived from Barcelona with severely reduced left-ankle mobility, with only lateral movement and barely any rotation. While this would not improve, he learned new ways to support his foot through new leg and hip movements, a long, complicated and laborious solution that required many hours of studying and training with Fernando Signorini, and plenty of sacrifices.

Maradona always played, but was not always in perfect condition. His body was often abused with painkillers so that he could be sent out. 'Punctures that made me cry. A ten-centimetre needle stuck in near my groin,' he recalled in *Yo Soy El Diego*. Napoli's coach Bianchi gradually came to accept Diego would train just three days a week with a ball, on top of any specific exercises he required.

Naples welcomed back a happy World Cup champion, a man who had found his place in the world. He enjoyed leading battered Napoli into battle, to away grounds where opposition fans draped banners beseeching an active volcano to smite him. 'Vesuvius – go after them', was seen in a few rival stands. Juventus owner Gianni Agnelli boasted arrogantly they had passed on signing Maradona because they were 'not so poor they had to dream about him', when in fact he had tried to do so on several occasions. This may explain why, after his winning free-kick defenestrated the mighty Juventus, Maradona declared, 'I represent a part of Italy that doesn't count for anything.'

'After the World Cup everything got bigger,' explained Guillermo Cóppola in the documentary about Diego's life, *El Representante de Dios* ('God's Agent'). 'We travelled by private plane, we got calls from judges, politicians, players, actors and cabaret actresses. They opened nightclubs for us. We went to La Finestrella restaurant a lot. We were given exclusive tables, where [the famous Italian singers] Eros Ramazzotti, Franco Califano, Zucchero, Pepino di Capri all dined.'

Napoli sold 40,000 season tickets after Argentina's World Cup success. President Ferlaino was about to be surprised: 'I thought, "He'll ask to double his contract." Instead, Maradona came back and simply said, "I'm a Napoli player again." And I said to him, "I want to give you a personal gift. What would you like?" And he said, "Whatever you want, President." I gave him a Ferrari.'

Wherever Diego went, he was always surrounded by people, all kinds of people. Rival teams would take Diego to dinner then they'd spend the evening together in nightclubs. Cars piled up in his garage, Porsches and Lamborghinis whose speed was useless in a city with hundreds of traffic lights. 'I'm allowed to drive through the red lights,' he explained to Jon Smith, the English agent who looked after his business interests for a while.

Every gesture by Diego appeared to have great value. Guillermo Blanco and Signorini were driving behind him once and a car overturned nearby. Maradona ran over to help the stunned occupants. One of them recognised Diego and shouted his name. 'Everyone woke up immediately like they'd been resuscitated,' recalls Blanco.

What Napoli needed next was to win their elusive first title. Following last season's third place, the sixty-year wait seemed close to ending. Centre-back Ciro Ferrara and defensive midfielder Salvatore Bagni were signed to bolster the defence, alongside Italian international winger Fernando Di Napoli and forwards Andrea Carnevale and Bruno Giordano, attackers who would complement Diego's play.

The team started with a 1-0 win at Brescia, thanks to a first-half goal from Maradona. Expectations soared. But before the second round of fixtures . . .

In September 1986, on the eve of the Udinese game, Diego was training at Soccavo, Napoli's training ground. Around two o'clock in the afternoon, Carlos d'Aquila, the first Argentine basketball player to play in Europe, called Fernando Signorini: 'Enrico Tuccillo is at my house. He is Cristiana Sinagra's lawyer, and he wants to talk to Diego.' The Italian television channel RAI was about to broadcast an interview with the young woman. Tuccillo wanted to know if Maradona accepted that the child his client, Cristiana, had just given birth to was his. Cristiana and Maradona had had a relationship from December to April of that year. 'Wait,' said a surprised Signorini. 'I'm going to call a taxi.'

The taxi scooped up Maradona and took him and Signorini to Carlos d'Aquila's house. On arrival, the basketball player, his wife and the lawyer Tuccillo were waiting for them. Diego was incredulous, confused; he felt like he'd been disembowelled.

'Diego, you are a champion at football and in life . . .' the lawyer started.

Fernando glanced at Maradona. He saw the lawyer was, as they say in Argentina, *twisting the snake* – twisting the knife. Diego was shrinking in stature, his head drooping, adopting the body language of the defeated. The lawyer continued his speech.

'A newscast is about to air an interview with Cristiana in which she tells everything. If you accept the child is yours, and we reach an agreement, if you commit yourself to take care of him, nothing will be broadcast.'

It was not a long meeting. Clearly Maradona was not accepting anything that was not part of the script he was so proudly writing. Much less about what he considered then a mistake. When he learned of Cristiana's pregnancy, he asked her to have an abortion. 'She should have,' he repeated hundreds of times in his head from that day.

'First, go home at once,' Signorini recommended. 'The interview is about to start, and Claudia is at home.'

From room 509 of the Sanatrix clinic in Naples, Sinagra, a twenty-two-year-old woman, later described as an 'unemployed accountant' by the newspapers, told Massimo Milone, a journalist from RAI, that the baby she had given birth to that same morning was the result of her relationship with the Argentine footballer. He would go by the name of Diego Armando Jr.

In a state of shock, Maradona and Claudia watched the news together at home. Diego sought the support of his people, phoning Guillermo Cóppola so he would return from Buenos Aires. Napoli put their lawyers at the player's service. The city itself rode the aftershocks.

The story erupted on to the front page of *Corriere della Sera* the next day. Enrico Tuccillo explained, 'Neapolitans will understand, I am convinced they will place more value on a baby than on idolatry, on life than a backheel, however elegant it may be. People will be on our side, because for us, children come first.' Tuccillo made it clear the relationship had lasted four months, and they were not looking to exploit Maradona economically – only that he would take responsibility.

Maradona had a disastrous match against Udinese, which ended in a 1-1 draw. Some fans rebuked him, waving dummies and holding a banner aloft: 'Maradona, go and take care of the baby'. Diego would only make any statements about football after the match: 'Everything I have to say will be before the judge. It will be what the truth and my conscience dictate.' Cóppola landed in Italy to dozens of waiting journalists. 'May RAI say farewell to Diego for ever,' he said. 'He'll not talk to them again.' Rumours abounded that Diego was planning to leave the club.

*Gente* magazine reported that RAI had paid the girl $8,000. Her father, hairdresser Alfredo Sinagra, made sure that no photographer took pictures of his grandson at the hospital. A Napoli fan was at its entrance and warned, 'If you see her, tell her if Maradona leaves Naples, she will have to deal with me.' Dozens of fans called the clinic to insult and threaten the new mother. The Mayor of Naples condemned the Sinagra family for having made such a fuss about the incident and not thinking about 'all the negative consequences that could result from it. I'm sure, though, Maradona will not tire of Naples so quickly.'

The media had taken sides. The woman, as always with Maradona and in countless stories since, was either secondary or guilty. Nobody, far less a woman, could take on the best player in the world, the greatest asset to Italian football. Journalists close to the footballer had known about the relationship for months, but had kept quiet or hidden what they knew.

Three days later, there was a meeting in a civil lawyer's office. Present were Maradona's attorney Vicenzo Siniscalchi, Diego's sister María and her husband Gabriel *'El Morsa'* Espósito, Claudia, Cóppola, Signorini and Diego himself. His lawyer immediately stated it's a 'wonderful idea' to question who the father is, just as Maradona wanted to do. *'A questa ragazza la sputanamo per tutta la Italia,'* said Siniscalchi – 'We'll spit on this girl all over Italy'. He was ready to save Diego, whatever the truth might be. The civil lawyer, whose name is not recorded, tried to convince the group otherwise: 'In among all this, there is an innocent creature, and the truth is only equal to itself.' Signorini never forgot those words.

Journalist Bruno Passarelli was the first to get a statement from Maradona. 'Report from an anxious man,' was the headline in *El Gráfico*. 'I wonder if this is the price I have to pay for those hours of joy in Mexico. I don't understand how the girl could have done such a thing, using Maradona to publicise herself. Someone capable of such a thing, of such diabolical extortion, can only be sick, very sick. They can call me a womaniser, a good-for-nothing or whatever, but I don't want them to invent a child for me.'

The baby was registered as Diego Armando on 1 October, the same day Napoli were eliminated from the UEFA Cup by Toulouse on penalties. Maradona missed his spot-kick. 'It's the worst moment of my life,' he later told reporters. 'I'm sick and feel bad, bad. Anyone who hates me is definitely enjoying it. Whoever loves me, don't worry, because I will win in the end, no matter how difficult the battle.'

Alfredo Sinagra asked for 'understanding and humanity. We are fighting so the child cannot reproach us one day for not having done anything for him.' Cristiana – the media's so-called 'liar' and 'puerile' villain – spoke to the Italian version of *Gente* three months after her son's birth. 'I didn't like Diego at first, but I fell in love . . . He felt the same emotions as me . . . He dedicated all his goals to me.' She admitted she had received death threats and was stuck at home with her baby, entrapped like a prisoner. She kept dreaming that Diego would phone her as he was accustomed to doing, as soon as he awoke or immediately after training. She said she could not believe that so kind and generous a man could alter so much.

The birth of Diego Jr. is a fundamental turning point in Maradona's story. He never suspected that a woman, tied to whatever role Diego designated her, could bring him to his knees. He was not prepared for a plot twist that contradicted his sense of reality. From here on in, the braggadocio dissipated, his eyes lost their shine, his mood transformed, and he became careless about his personal affairs.

And cocaine was no longer just a distraction.

'You need people that are keen to help you, not those that have no intention of doing so,' Fernando Signorini told Diego.

'No, don't worry, it's every now and then, I can handle it, I can control it . . .'

'He had broken his ankle,' Signorini explained. 'But he was recovering. The problem was how to fight against cocaine, it was obscuring his reality, and he knew it.'

Cristiana Sinagra never accepted money offered to her for an abortion, for her silence or to not acknowledge Diego's paternity. And Claudia? Maradona's long-term girlfriend, pregnant with their first daughter Dalma, had spent the broadcast of Cristiana's interview on TV in silence and shaking her head. Diego denied everything, and she believed him. Much further down the line, when Claudia became aware of what had really happened, she repeatedly insisted that if Diego was still asked to acknowledge his son, he should do so. In April, Dalma was born, followed two years later by their second child Giannina, new arrivals that further undermined Diego's equilibrium as he was disappearing from the centre of his woman's world.

In 1992, after three refusals to do a DNA test, the Italian justice system ordered Diego to give his son his surname and Cristiana the equivalent of around €3,000 per month. Still, he continued to deny everything . . . for thirty years. His only children, he repeated, were 'Dalma and Gianinna, because they were conceived with love'. Around that time, a mutual friend put Claudia and Cristiana in contact by phone, to talk about Diego Jr.'s food allowance.

In April 1996, Claudia discovered Maradona had had a fourth child, Jana, as a result of his relationship with Valeria Sabalain, a waitress whom he had met in a restaurant. Diego once again denied everything. The infidelities were more than numerous, but Claudia was satisfied that he always came home. Then, one day in 1998, Diego didn't return. He went to Cuba and fell in love with Adonay Frutos, then Judith, then Eileene during which time he had three more children from two different mothers. Later, he would have relationships with Verónica Ojeda and Rocio Oliva. To his dying day, he acknowledged five children from four women – Diego Fernando is the other, Verónica Ojeda's son – and there have been six more paternity suits. All the while, he lived without giving explanations, eternally free and by his own rules. That is to say, irresponsibly.

In May 2003, Diego Jr., who at the time played in the youth academy at Napoli, travelled 150km intending to meet his father for the first time at a charity golf tournament in the Fiuggi Hotel and Spa complex. He slipped onto the course after asking security to let him study the greens, as he was about to take golf lessons. He was wearing a cap and sunglasses. 'This is your son, Diego,' he muttered when he got close, but Maradona moved to sit on the buggy with the intention of running away. 'This is going to be the last time you will have to meet me,' Diego Jr. shouted. The buggy stopped.

The pair spoke for over forty minutes. Diego Jr. heard him say, 'I know that you are my son.' The final embrace, mixed with tears, lasted years for the son – three, in fact, which was the time that elapsed before Maradona would hug him again, this time in Buenos Aires. Diego knew his son was appearing on a television programme and tracked him down. Their story was told on air. That's how Gianinna, watching the programme at home, heard the bombshell, and said she would have liked her father to call her and say, 'Look, daughter, I lied to you all these years.'

In July 2017, at a prestigious restaurant in Naples, Cristiana Sinagra and Diego Jr. shared a table with Maradona. Cristiana told Diego she had forgiven him, that they had both always known the truth. Diego admitted he loved his son. When Diego Jr. announced years later that he was about to become a father, Maradona used Instagram to declare, 'I am going to enjoy my grandson, in the way I didn't with Diego.'

Because of the eruptions in his private life, that 1986–87 season started off haphazardly for the player. The Napoli squad decided to show support for their star. Giuseppe Bruscolotti, club captain, handed the armband to the Argentinian. Maradona was moved to tears. 'Thank you, Peppe, you've given me something that I will never forget . . . as a captain, I will bring the title,' he said.

Maradona ordered that the club doors be open to fans during training more often, wanting to reinforce the link with them and, as a team spokesman, he agreed to hold a weekly press conference. On the pitch, coach Ottavio Bianchi created a solid block around which Maradona could weave his magic. The results gradually improved, including a 3-1 win over Juventus at the Stadio Comunale in Turin. It was a clear statement of intent. In that November 1986, Diego had already recovered his grit and strength after Cristiana had announced the birth of their son on television.

Maradona's trips to Buenos Aires to see Dalma, his newborn daughter, coincided with Napoli dropping five points in the last third of the season. Complaints were raised by some at the club, aimed at Diego. With four games remaining, Napoli faced Silvio Berlusconi's Milan at home. The future president of Italy was presiding over his first season at the club. The 2-1 victory, with a goal by Diego, meant the destiny of the title was in Napoli's own hands, with Platini's Juventus lagging behind. Diego had scored only ten goals, but he had played in every game except one. After an away 1-1 draw at Como, celebrations were prepared for the penultimate match, home against Fiorentina, where a draw would seal the title.

That weekend, balconies were decorated with flags, giant plastic dolls dressed in Napoli colours filled the streets, everyone wore the blue club shirts, and hotels were full to capacity. Television sets were set up in strategic locations in bars and shops. At night, the streets rang with the song, 'O mama mama mama / Sai perché mi batte il corazón / Ho visto Maradona / Innamorato sono' ('Oh mother, mother / how my heart beats / I've seen Maradona / and now I'm in love'). A very Neapolitan circus was in town. The stadium's stands were decorated with emblems and flags on the day of the match, with 90,000 fans filling it. Don Diego couldn't miss it, nor Hugo or Lalo.

'When I think of that day,' his teammate Ciro Ferrara remembers, 'our coach arriving at the ground . . . we couldn't drive along the usual road, not even with police help. Cars were parked next to each other, two or three deep. Kids and adults on top of them to see Diego. It was absolutely crazy.' Salvatore Carnando, the physio, has a vivid memory of that day: 'Women, young and not so young, had their boobs out, painted in blue alongside the Napoli crest. They were saying, "Look at us, Maradona, thank you for what you have done for us.'"

Napoli scored first. Fiorentina equalised, and a 1-1 draw brought the necessary point and ignited what Maradona described as 'the biggest party I have ever experienced in my whole life!' On 10 May 1987, six decades after its foundation, Napoli occupied top spot and could not be shifted. The fans had fulfilled their dream, invading the pitch and kick-starting the first of many days of celebrations. Maradona participated in them the only way he knew, crying, bellowing and hugging people, walking around the pitch and sharing in the exultation, arms raised. 'This is my home,' he repeated.

In the changing rooms, naked players were jumping around like men possessed, singing, '*Ho visto Maradona, ey mamá, innamorato sono.*' ('I saw Maradona, mum, and I'm in love'). Maradona joined in, topless but with the captain's armband still on. 'We created this Napoli from nothing!' he shouted, while someone started a new song.

A million people, swathed in blue, invaded streets full of communal happiness and companionship, without a single serious incident. A lot of people didn't turn up at work the next morning. Schools were opened, but attendance wasn't obligatory. Someone sprayed '*Che vi siete persi*' ('What you just missed!') on Poggioreale Cemetery's wall. Banners hung in the streets declared '*Scusate il ritardo*' ('Sorry about the delay') or '*I figli del sole strappano lo scudetto ai figli del fredo*' ('The children of the sun [in the sunny south] pluck the Scudetto from the children of the [northern] cold').

Front pages of the national newspapers finally spoke positively about Naples, and with good reason. The city had changed for ever. The sporting hero had completed the adventure, despite the odds and against doom-laden predictions. Naples gave two fingers to those who said, 'You can't handle anything, you don't have an industrious mentality.' What had been considered to be defects were transformed into virtues. Maradona confirmed, albeit ephemerally and via the conduit of football, that the south was the north's equal.

In that ecstatic city, Diego Armando Maradona could be, do or say whatever he wanted.

There was time for more joy. On 7 June, three goals defeated

Atalanta in the first leg of the Copa Italia. It was followed six days later by a 1-0 away win, securing a handsome aggregate victory. In the process, Napoli became the first team from the south to do the league and cup double, and one of just three in the history of Italian football.

In his book *Maradona al Desnudo* ('Maradona Undressed'), journalist Bruno Passarelli, then correspondent in Italy for *El Gráfico*, noted the following about Napoli's successful season: 'Because of the euphoria, few realised that Maradona's league form was far from that which had dazzled at the Mexico 86 World Cup.'

After spending a few days with his family in a hotel in Granada in Spain, Maradona received an unexpected invitation. The Cuban government was offering him a beach holiday at Varadero, followed by a meeting in Havana with Commandante Fidel Castro. They went, but there was no sign of Castro. Two days before returning to Italy, an emissary informed Diego, 'The Commandante has requested your presence.' The family waited patiently for the Cuban leader in one of his official residences. Surprisingly, as midnight approached, a bus took them to the Plaza de la Revolución. Once inside the austere government house in the square, they were greeted by the imposing figure of a smiling Fidel. It was a captivating five-hour audience. 'Is there a secret to scoring penalties?' asked Castro. 'Before I shoot, I look at the goalkeeper,' confessed Diego. The Commandante jotted it down in his notebook.

As the sun rose, Castro said his goodbyes and gave his cap to Diego. 'The bus was moving off,' recalls Fernando Signorini who was present. 'Castro came to the window, looking worried and asked again. "So, before I take the penalty, I must look at the goalkeeper, right?" as if that was the most important advice he had been given in a long while.'

# 28
# ALL MARADONA IS IN NAPOLI

Before the first Scudetto win, Diego wanted to celebrate his sister María's birthday with the family. A filmset-style logistical operation, with Guillermo Cóppola as director, was required. A friendly restaurant owner was told an ungodly arrival time, so its regular service would stop at 10pm. Around half-past ten, the restaurant's blinds were closed, and all the lights turned off. The Maradona family would wander into the oasis of calm around 11pm. 'You can't go anywhere with this son of mine,' Doña Tota was heard saying again.

After the title win, the pace increased. 'The city was out of control,' Cóppola remembers. 'People were obsessed. They were crazy about Diego. Everyone was dying just to be near him. Everyone.'

Football entered a new phase during the eighties. World Cups had an ever-increasing budget and a much wider audience. Against this background, Diego Armando Maradona emerged as the first global star. His origins, success and magical ability fascinated all the more because he invited people to share his life. More than 500 hours of filming (at home, in pyjamas, playing with his daughters, in restaurants, training, walking, singing, in bed, at parties) were, for instance, the basis of Asif Kapadia's award-winning documentary *Diego Maradona*.

Sociologists Fernando Segura and Sergio Levinsky studied the growth of football and listed its various guises:

Football can be 'a total social cause' (Ignacio Ramonet), 'a summary of the human condition' (François Brune), and 'the revealer of all passions' (Christian Bromberger). It can be 'the glory of cheats' (Eduardo Galeano), 'a unique sport' (Phillipe Baudillon), and 'a secular religion' (Manuel Vázquez Montalbán). There are even those who wonder if it is 'a sport or a ritual' (Marc Augé).

Maradona paraded in them all.

'Players from the opposing team started asking him to swap shirts after the game,' remembered Dalma Maradona in her book. 'He said yes to everyone. He used it as a strategy sometimes, promising his shirt to the strongest on the other side, talking to them and making them follow him around the pitch. It left his teammates free from their markers!'

'We were flying once, sitting at the back, travelling discreetly,' says Guillermo Blanco. 'Suddenly we hit a lot of turbulence, and the plane began to move as if it were disintegrating. The passengers were close to panicking, then a guy stood up and shouted, "Don't worry, friends. Nothing can happen to us. God is travelling on the plane!" The passengers broke into applause, turning their heads towards Diego.'

Naples lost itself with Maradona in the way sailors yielded to the city's mythological founder, the siren Parthenope. Maradona's semi-divine stature was turning into what Signorini described as 'asphyxiating, clinging affection'.

A nurse who had carried out a blood-test on Maradona took a tube with the player's plasma to the city's cathedral, where lie the bones of St Gennaro, the city's patron saint. Three times a year, thousands of people crowd the cathedral to see if a reliquary containing Gennaro's dried blood will liquefy. The nurse placed Maradona's tube next to the saint's, to see if it would do likewise.

Maradona went to training sessions at Soccavo under the watchful eye of three police officers on motorbikes. They would also accompany him to and from meetings at the Hotel Royal and to matches at San Paolo. Dozens of Vespas buzzed around the escort, worshipping Maradona every moment he was present in the public domain. Claudia had no choice but to buy the clothes her man chose while he was hidden in his car, or alternatively invite fashion designers and tailors to their house.

Meanwhile, Cóppola knew that everything had a potential commercial return. He charged $250,000 a month for a TV show on RAI and signed a $5 million contract with Hitoshi for sportswear bearing the footballer's name. He branded and sold school supplies, *alfajores* (two chocolate-covered biscuits filled with *dulce de leche*, an Argentine speciality), soft drinks and more.

The twenty-seven-year-old Maradona had stepped on to a waltzer ride of fame and was pinned into its spinning car. He developed a routine to cope. On Sunday he played a game and then took cocaine and enjoyed the nightlife until Wednesday morning. From then until Saturday night, he cleaned himself up, sweated it out and played again, before heading back to the fairground.

Clearly that drug was not taken to upgrade his game. One day, Signorini, tired of excuses about sore ankles and feet and dubious food, went to pick Maradona up. The player told him he didn't want to go to training.

'Again?' said Signorini. 'What do you want me to say now?'

'Say that I couldn't sleep because Dalma was—'

'No, no, no,' *El Profe* cut in. 'Don't be such a son of a bitch! Leave Dalma out of this!'

'Don't yell at me. I've already fought with my old man, and I don't know why. I'm not going to fight with you.'

'Do you know why you're not going to fight with me? Because in your present condition, the slap I'll give you will turn you into an acrobat' – an expression stolen from Maradona's own sharp and inventive lexicon – 'so go on. Take a shower, and we'll be off.'

Two minutes later there was another man in front of Signorini, ready for training. This pantomime played out dozens of times, but once on the pitch, the problems disappeared. Away from the playing field, the man who had the world at his feet was required to behave appropriately. 'He looked for an artificial way to live up to the demands,' says Signorini.

How did Maradona fall so rapidly into the never-ending cycle of the rewards and punishments of drugs? The player explained it all to journalist Gabriela Cociffi in *Gente* magazine years later, in a series of interviews and conversations. It didn't make for easy reading as Diego explained what it feels like to live in a metaphorical fishbowl and be the fish that forgets to breathe.

Maradona has admitted to first taking drugs in 1982. In other interviews, he has identified Spain, two years later, as the starting point, aged twenty-four. However, when he became that age he was at Napoli. In his book, he repeats he started his drug-use in Barcelona. In Asif Kapadia's documentary, he mentions a discotheque.

Yet everything points to his first dabble with drugs taking place at the leaving party at his Barcelona home, the night he signed for Napoli. Claudia and Fernando Signorini went to pick him up at El Prat airport, where the contract had been signed at the last minute, and they returned together to the Pedralbes house to celebrate. Signorini didn't know the majority of the crowd. With the party getting into full swing, most of the twenty people present jumped into the swimming pool, which was turning pink after several bottles of champagne were emptied into it. *El Profe* went home – it was not his type of party – and the festivities continued until the early hours.

Someone – Diego never said in front of a camera who – offered the footballer cocaine. The fictionalised series of his life produced by Amazon adds a disturbing fact, allegedly approved by Maradona himself: his former father-in-law, Roque Nicolás Villafañe, *Coco*, Claudia's father, was the one who introduced him to the drug. According to their daughter Dalma, Diego denied to Claudia that he had agreed to tell this peculiar version of the story, although even Claudia also seems to think that he consumed cocaine for the first time on that last evening in the Catalan city.

Diego felt alive. His initial emotion was of a shockwave, of wanting to 'take the world by storm. And in subsequent experiences, the feeling was similar. Everything was so beautiful, so clear, and everything was so funny.' Every time he took cocaine, he won a title or a cup – so what does anything else matter? After the highs came tremendous loneliness, fear and self-doubt. To remove himself from that state, he had to rediscover the feeling of being alive, over and over again.

Maradona became a regular bathroom ghoul, haunting them not only in his own house but in restaurants and bars. He even partook in the Papal Palace during a private audience with Pope John Paul II, granted to Napoli in 1985. Often the light would be turned off and, in the dark, Diego would powder his nose a little. His fear of his wife or Dalma catching him led to him putting latches on the toilet doors at home. At four o'clock one morning, his daughter knocked on the bathroom door.

'Dad! Can I come in?'

Maradona hadn't taken anything, but he was about to. He didn't want to answer. He flushed the cocaine down the toilet.

'Yes, darling, yes, yes!' Maradona opened the door and sat his little girl down on his lap.

'What's the matter, Dad? Why are you here, can't you sleep?'

'No, love, I can't sleep.'

Diego would simply get his hit later, even though the initial euphoria was diminishing as time passed by. 'There is no more joy, no more fun, no more nothing. On the contrary, after that comes crying, anguish and anxiety,' he told Gabriela Cociffi. He wondered why he had started. His solution was to sleep and forget everything the next morning. He didn't mention his habit to anyone, because he thought they would forsake or abandon him, and they wouldn't understand him. He admitted that he could not discuss drugs with his father – it was work and football only.

Maradona also lied to anyone who discovered his vice. 'I can handle it,' he would say, not being fully sure he could. Fernando Signorini even told him that he didn't need a physical trainer because he was no longer a player and should look for people who knew how to help him overcome his addiction. 'But no, he always said he could beat it,' Signorini recalls. Maradona was consuming alcohol to reinforce the effects of the cocaine and prolong the high, but the combination can be lethal as the potential damage to the heart and liver can be greater than with either taken individually.

Eventually, he did open up to two friends: his supplier was one, and Guillermo Cóppola the other, a fellow drug user and his travel companion on the journey to the darker side of life. Maradona also turned to a psychologist who advised him to stop seeing Cóppola. Maradona knew that this wouldn't solve anything, as Cóppola was a willing and necessary partner.

'If he asked for frogs, mussels and Provençal [wine] in the middle of the desert, I had to get them,' explains Cóppola. The duo would frequent the Posillipo and other nightclubs, arriving in the early hours of the morning. They would request female company for their hotel rooms and usually stayed at the Paradiso hotel. With the first sounds of the morning filling the streets, the night was over.

Claudia Villafañe tired of the predatory girls who, in pairs or threesomes, walked within view of the family home, waiting for a gesture from Diego. The constant turmoil tested her mettle. She even approached him when she noticed something was wrong, but Diego rebuffed her: 'What's wrong with you? Why do you do it? Why do you lock yourself in? Why don't you sleep?' People would drop by the house at two in the morning with deliveries. Claudia persisted: 'Why did so-and-so come, and why did so-and-so call in?' Maradona found many reasons to take drugs, among them a real and powerful one. Dalma's birth had displaced him, and he felt Claudia didn't pay him enough attention any more.

On occasions Diego would lock himself in the bedroom and not open the door to Claudia or anyone else for hours. Alone, he became introspective and thought about his old neighbourhood, his father, his mother and who he really was, and what he had become. Maradona wanted to recover the idealised beliefs, values and ways of living from his childhood, but such reflections were often accompanied by more cocaine, as if he was mourning a lost country.

Claudia sometimes left him alone all day. At others she would knock at the door, just to let him know she was there; more often than not she would curse him to the devil. But she loved him and didn't want to leave him. Maradona pleaded for the girls to be left out of the matter, despite that never crossing Claudia's mind. Why would it?

'Diego, what's wrong with you?' she would ask. 'We'll talk tomorrow,' was often the answer. That tomorrow could see Diego distant, impulsive and sometimes violent. Claudia would be reduced to tears, his bad moods affecting those next in line, Dalma and then Gianinna, who could not escape the unfolding drama.

Diego would occasionally be clean for a month or two, often coinciding with the season's run-in when results were needed. It wound Claudia up when he was invited to a party. He didn't want it said his wife wouldn't allow him out, so sometimes he would sneak out. But Claudia couldn't keep him under lock and key. All she could do was leave him to it or pull a face at those who wanted no good for her man. It all had a duck-egg fragility.

Claudia never forbade Diego anything, nor did he ask permission for anything. It was left to her to handle this so-called freedom that endlessly returned Diego to his own hell, and eventually to self-incarceration in some room in the house. Claudia would let time pass and then 'go into the room. He would be lying there, in the dark. He was very ashamed of me seeing him like that,' she explained to *Gente* magazine.

'I would get close to him, keeping the light off so Diego wouldn't be embarrassed, and I would sit on the bed and touch his hand. And I would ask him, "How have you come to this, for God's sake, Diego? There must be something inside that's led you here, you have to look deep inside yourself."' It took him a long time to admit the deep-rooted cause. Cocaine – and the associated nightlife that so enthralled him and focused even more attention on him – was the antidote to insecurity.

'He doped at dismal parties, to forget or to be forgotten. He was surrounded by his glory and couldn't live without the fame that didn't allow him a life,' says Signorini. 'He played better than anyone else despite the cocaine, and not because of it.'

Maradona said many times there have always been drugs in football, something others admit after retiring. Diego never used cocaine to improve his game: it's a drug to cloud judgement and builds unscalable walls. 'There were plenty of times after I'd taken a line that I tried to control a ball but couldn't,' Diego told me. 'Do you know the player I would have been if I hadn't taken drugs,' he often speculated.

'Everything he lived through was disproportionate, and so were the solutions he sought,' according to Jorge Valdano. 'We accelerated the growth of the myth and, ergo, the disease. We generated the disease together, but only he suffered from it.'

'I was a drug addict, I am a drug addict, and I am going to be a drug addict for ever in the eyes of the world,' Maradona proclaimed in the 1996 interview with Gabriela Cociffi in *Gente*. 'And that is because a drug addict never gets forgiven. The drug addict is discriminated against, the drug addict is a son of a bitch. Parents don't want him, neither does society. The drug addict is not wanted by anyone. And if you are famous, you are doubly punished. They say they want to help you and then they batter you. A drug addict must be seen as a victim, as a sick person. Give him a hand, but don't expose all his weakness and suffering.'

Lalo Zanoni revealed in his book *Vivir en Los Medios* ('Maradona Off the Record') that Dalma kept two copies of *Gente* with that revealing interview with her father on her bedside table for many years. She wanted to read them to her sister Gianinna when she was old enough to understand, which she eventually did. One day in 2002, Gianinna threw herself into bed with her mother, and they read the interview together, and she asked her mother for a blow-by-blow account of what it had all been like.

According to the Argentine sociologist Juan José Sebreli, Maradona saw himself as a left-wing protestor, critical of authority, rebellious with or without a cause, yet his choice of drug went against that image: 'Cocaine is a drug used by executives, [his] actions, the outbursts, the fights, the aggressive behaviour were the typical outbursts of a spoiled brat, a rich and extravagant man. Or a young man who does what he wants because he has money and because nobody will oppose him.' But that, of course, was the drug of choice of his privileged, moneyed circle of friends.

Maradona's adventures in Naples were secretly recorded, something he always suspected. Antonino Restino pursued Diego for eighteen months, starting in January 1988, and spilt the beans in 2019 in the book *El Espía de Dios* ('Spying on God'). Napoli president Corrado Ferlaino and director Luciano Moggi attached Restino to the assignment, content to listen to his reports and have knowledge of rather than do anything about the drug addiction. Shockingly,

Ferlaino became angry only when he learned that Maradona trained alone with Signorini away from the group, not a done thing at the time.

The relationship between the two – what the president called 'my bitter love' – was broken by the end of the Argentinian's stint at Napoli. Ferlaino acknowledged that other young footballers were also taking drugs at the time, and in 2003 revealed to the newspaper *Il Mattino* how Diego passed drug tests: 'From Sunday night to Wednesday, Diego was free to do whatever he wanted. On Thursday, he had to be clean.'

There is more. Moggi and Salvatore Carmando, the masseur with whom Diego hugged after scoring his wonder goal against England, would offer a small bottle with someone else's urine, which would be poured into Diego's analysis. These cover-ups were more frequent after Napoli won their first Scudetto.

The night was Maradona's stage and refuge. The fashionable places he frequented with Cóppola were also haunts of the Camorra mafia, the same syndicate he was asked about at his first press conference in July 1984.

The Camorra was the lifeblood that drove the city, and contact with them was inevitable. 'In Naples, the boundary between a good and a bad life is very subtle,' says Rino Cesarano, a journalist at the *Corriere Dello Sport*. 'You can go to a bar for a coffee, and there's a great chance you'll meet one of them. If you don't have a strong will, you risk getting lost. Especially if you are important.'

The Camorra had had a presence in the city since the seventeenth century. They used violence to control areas the state had abandoned for decades. Naples had been neglected by the rest of Italy; it was in decline, especially after the 6.9 magnitude earthquake in nearby Irpinia in 1980, which had left more than two thousand dead, almost eight thousand injured and a quarter of a million people homeless. It provided a breeding ground for an alternative economy. In the mid-eighties, a turf war between thirty clans resulted in hundreds of deaths every year, ultimately leading to the removal of the Cutolos family from the seat of power in Naples. They were replaced by the

Giuliano family, a more entrepreneurial clan who made money via control of public works, tobacco smuggling and drug trafficking.

Football was modernising, thanks to an influx of television money. The new clan muscled in and took over the city's lucrative street betting (*Totonero*), competing with the official state bookies (*Totocalcio*), netting them €60 million a year. The Camorra, never far away from any business, approached Napoli and vice versa. 'Ferlaino became rich thanks to the real estate business, Camorra territory,' explained Maurizio Valenzi, the former mayor of Naples. 'He built without permission, like the Camorra. They threatened him by flying one of their planes over the San Paolo stadium and killed his uncle, clear signs they inhabited the same world.'

The Giuliano family ran all the businesses that operated in and around the San Paolo stadium, from unofficial merchandising to ticket resales. Jorge Cyterszpiler knew of this during his exploratory visit to Naples, before Maradona's transfer. In Asif Kapadia's documentary, the player claims he never cared that Neapolitans made a living from his image. The team's victories fed the black market and were responsible for doubling the production of flags, T-shirts and other products, all manufactured in illegal sewing workshops.

It was easy for the Camorra to access Napoli's dressing room using tried and trusted methods: parties, high-class prostitutes, money and cocaine. Management and playing staff alike were seen heading to the gang's luxurious headquarters located in the humble Forcella neighbourhood.

Francesco Maglione, a lawyer from the Giuliano clan, told *El País* newspaper, 'Maradona, as soon as he arrived, asked who the most powerful person in the city was. He was not asking about the mayor, but a Mafia capo.' Logically, the Giulianos wanted to meet Diego too. 'They are the Camorra, and Cyterszpiler and Diego had to meet them; they are who they are. And they thought, "Let's tell Maradona to come because he's Maradona!"' says Cyterszpiler's assistant, Fernando García.

Carmine Giuliano, a high-up member of the clan and a Napoli fan, got in touch with Gennaro *'Palummella'* Montuori, the leader of the Ultras faction in Naples and a friend of Diego's, to invite the player to the Forcella residence, the headquarters of the family. There are pictures of the meeting, with Maradona in a shell-shaped bathtub between Carmine and his brother Guglielmo Giuliano, a snapshot kept for years by the police.

Diego felt less suffocated in town with the Giulianos. He used to refer to that first period of the relationship as the 'golden age'. Once a week he would open a bar or nightclub being run by a Camorra man, or attend a family wedding and be given a gold watch for his troubles.

In that period there was something that bothered Maradona – not being able to give his daughters the education he wished because of this disordered existence in a Naples that, in his eyes, presented too many dangers for children. One day, Diego told Carmine that he had read in *La Gazzetta Dello Sport* that if he didn't return to Naples after the 1987 Copa América, a real possibility, the Mafia would take revenge on his daughters. Carmine told him, 'Rest assured, Dalma and Giannina will not be touched by anyone. This is my word, and the word of the whole Giuliano family.'

As in the movies, Diego had arrived at the 'your problem is my problem' moment. When you trust the Camorra, you become their property. He was closest to Carmine – they played indoor football together, and he soon became Maradona's principal drug supplier.

Over time, Diego would discover the extent of the Mafia's reach. On one occasion he was told not to leave the hotel or, better still, take his time over dinner. The next day he learned that there had been a fight, a blood feud, with lives lost. 'I don't associate with bad people,' the footballer responded confusedly when asked at the time. 'I don't know who is bad and who is good. I didn't go around asking for their ID or passport or to have my picture taken. They asked me, and then the photos were in the newspapers and turns out they were Camorra. But I didn't know that. I have never, ever asked anything from the Camorra.'

Their relationship flourished, and so did the group's business confidence. Luigi Giuliano, Carmine's nephew became a police informant years later and admitted they fixed football matches. Diego remembered a defeat to Milan in the 1987–88 season after which, visibly upset, he stated, 'Never in a one-off race can a Fiat 500 beat a Ferrari.' Almost all of Naples and Neapolitans around the world had staked a fortune on Napoli to win the title, via the Camorra's unofficial *Totonero* betting system. A Scudetto for Maradona's team could have bankrupted the family. Those bad results for the local side saved them.

No one could prove anything, but that season one of Maradona's cars was destroyed. There were robberies at some players' houses. In the 1990s, Mafia turncoat Pietro Pugliese told a court and judge about alleged match-fixing, yet Diego's teammate Ciro Ferrara responds emphatically every time he is asked about it: 'It's a stupid claim that doesn't deserve any comment.'

All in all, Maradona was living in a golden cage. Bernard Tapie, the controversial owner of Olympique de Marseille, asked him a few times to leave Napoli, a proposition that became much more attractive from 1988 onwards. Michel Hidalgo, Marseille's football director, and agent Michel Basilevitch met Diego for dinner at the La Sacristia restaurant, and the player was practically convinced to change pastures. A gentleman approached their table when Diego had gone and, with a subtle gesture, revealed a holstered gun. He told them they were not welcome in the city, and that he was non-transferable. Real Madrid, with Ramón Mendoza as president, also tried and the Camorra sent the same message. Maradona did reach an agreement with Berlusconi's Milan, too, but it had to be rescinded due to public pressure.

It was a miracle Maradona survived in Naples.

'One day we were going to training,' explains Signorini, 'and we had to stop at a traffic light. People turned and saw him, and they came over, some even pushing their noses against the windows. Diego had a moment of angst, hit the windscreen, and it cracked.'

There was always someone hanging around outside the door to Diego's house in Via Scipione Capece, number 5. From time to time, he would come out to say hello and occasionally an angry Dalma shouted at them to go home.

Fernando Garcia says, 'The day Maradona went to the dentist in Pozzuoli, a little town near Naples, and people saw him go in, about seven thousand people gathered around the dentist's practice, or so it felt. It was like all of Pozzuoli was in that block. The police came, they climbed over the people there, and Diego had to leave via the back entrance of the building.'

Diego became, in a positive sense, an authentic Neapolitan rascal, doing good for others by pushing norms to the limit. He would talk directly with fans and with the Ultra leader, Palummella. He would party, drink and dance with supporters, often standing on tables, bellowing out songs. Maradona was godfather to Palummella's daughter. The Ultra's son was named Diego Armando, and hundreds of Neapolitan children born between 1986 and 1990 were named Diego, too.

He surrounded himself with working-class people, the only ones with whom he felt entirely at ease. Saverio Vignati was caretaker at San Paolo stadium for three decades, and his wife, Lucia Rispoli, was the cook and housekeeper at Maradona's house in Naples. 'She used to make him Neapolitan food,' he recalls. 'Pasta with potatoes and provolone cheese, and huge quantities of fruit salad. She always brought him a sandwich with mortadella slices [a type of Italian sausage] before games.' Sometimes, Maradona would arrive unannounced and incognito at Vignati's house in the humble Secondigliano district for a Neapolitan dinner. Saverio and Lucia's daughter was the nanny to the player's two daughters.

'Naples may be very beautiful, but it has many flaws,' Maradona once explained. 'And this "Maradona is more than my mum," or "more than God," I just don't understand. The Neapolitans could have a much nicer city if they tidied it up a bit. But the Neapolitans are how they are. Maradona is not going to come from 20,000km away to correct these mistakes. All I have to do is accept how it is and, from Sunday to Sunday, give them the maximum happiness possible.'

# 29

# FROM THE SECOND SCUDETTO TO THE 1990 WORLD CUP

Coffins were burned to ashes in Naples during the title celebrations, bearing inscriptions such as 'May 1987, the day the other Italy was defeated,' and 'The birth of a new empire'. A new era was dawning for the club and indeed for Maradona. The potential energy of his life was transformed into a kinetic frenzy, a rock crashing down a hillside. He orbited the extremities of love and hate, generosity and narcissism, liberally sprinkled with cocaine. Neither he nor anyone else knew we had probably already seen his best football.

The British press published a story in 1987 that Leeds United, favourites to be promoted to the then first division, wanted to sign Maradona. 'Their managing director, Bill Fotherby, joined me at lunch,' explains Jon Smith, Maradona's UK commercial agent at the time, in his book *The Deal*:

'Think he'd sign for Leeds?' [Fotherby asked].

I was taken aback. 'Er ... probably not. The weather isn't quite as good as Naples for starters.'

'Yeah, but if we paid him a lot of money? And we arranged a big house, spared no expense, that sort of thing, what about then?'

'I don't really know. Maybe.' I thought no more of it. But from that one answer, they [Leeds United's sources] leaked story after story to the press about how Maradona was weighing up a move to Leeds.

Tottenham offered $15 million for Diego's signature; Milan tried as well, and these press revelations were not accidental. Maradona's Napoli contract had two years left to run, and Guillermo Cóppola was busy negotiating a new deal with his Italian club.

Silvio Berlusconi had bought AC Milan in 1986, and coach Arrigo Sacchi inherited a team that included Ruud Gullit and Marco Van Basten. During a Milan–Napoli game, Cóppola was invited to Berlusconi's box and suggested they talk about Diego. A week later, Cóppola agreed terms with two of Berlusconi's assistants, but Napoli was still to be convinced.

'And what about you?' Berlusconi asked Cóppola, and continued, 'You, Diego's friend, are more important than Maradona. Do you know Milan? What do you like about Milan? Piazza San Babila, for example. We'll give you a flat in Piazza San Babila worth up to a million dollars. What cars do you like? Choose one up to a quarter of a million. You dress well, fifty thousand a month on clothes. Happy? There will be VIP seating in the stadium, women, fame . . .' Cóppola needed no more convincing, nor Maradona. Milan would double Napoli's contract, and Diego felt a change of scenery would help a new beginning and the abandonment of vices.

Claudia wasn't so sure: 'We don't really have to leave here.' She felt change had to take place in Diego, and would not necessarily happen by moving.

The morning after the Milan meeting, there was quadruple the usual dozen journalists jostling for position at Napoli's Soccavo training ground. Canal 5, an Italian TV channel owned by Berlusconi, had announced the Milan agreement with Maradona.

'What's going on?' Diego was asked at the press conference he organised in which he had Cóppola seated beside him.

'Guillermo went to discuss a personal contract of mine. Do I have to tell you what I do outside Naples? I wish they did want me in Milan. The fact is Mr Berlusconi is interested in giving me a contract for a book about my time in Naples.' Maradona dodged like nobody else in pressure situations, coolly defusing this potential bomb. But the smoking fuse forced Napoli to act, and a new deal was signed. It would keep the player where he was until 1993 with the then-largest contract in football history – $12 million a year.

The 1987–88 season had just started, and the Italian press was surprised by a sudden absence. Maradona was injured, a muscle issue of some kind. The player was not seen for twenty days. When he returned at the end of September, he was thinner, had cut his hair and looked a new man – detoxified.

That year, Napoli fielded Serie A's most feared attacking triumvirate: Maradona, Bruno Giordano and Brazilian Antônio de Oliveira 'Careca', one of the stars of the 1986 World Cup. They were baptised with the first two letters of their names – Ma-Gi-Ca (magic). Careca came to Napoli for Diego: 'I had another offer at that time from Real Madrid, but I chose Napoli because my dream was to play with Maradona.' They scored thirty-six of their team's fifty-five goals that season.

Napoli's start was resounding. Milan hadn't quite got off the ground, and Juventus – without Michel Platini but with striker Ian Rush from Liverpool – didn't have much consistency either.

With five matches remaining in the championship, Napoli led the standings by four points, having only lost twice all season. It was two points for a win then, and the league appeared to be sewn up. As already mentioned, the Camorra feared financial ruin if Napoli retained the title, with thousands of underground bets backing the champions. A strange sequence of results followed: of the five matches left to play, Napoli drew one and lost four, including a crucial home defeat to AC Milan in their antepenultimate game, helping Milan win the league.

'I never thought I'd be accused. I was ready to leave Napoli if people thought there was a player who had sold out,' Maradona explained years later in his autobiography. He was the team's top scorer that season with fifteen goals. Justifying himself, he said, 'I don't accept it today, and I didn't accept it then. That's why I stayed in Naples after the championship finished because I wanted to show my face.' Nobody could ever prove any wrongdoing.

The campaign that had started with a clean-up job, ended with one of those paradoxes Maradona preferred not to think much about. In the summer of 1988 Maradona played alongside Pelé in Michel Platini's farewell game and had his picture taken alongside the Frenchman, both wearing an anti-drug-campaign T-shirt.

President Ferlaino decided to freshen up the squad and renewed Bianchi's contract, even though the coach and Maradona's relationship was wearing thin, with the player increasingly absent from training. Diego took Bianchi's continuation as an affront and another opportunity to fight with authority via the media. Ferlaino had to bite his tongue a lot during that period.

The following season (1988–89) could well have been Maradona's final one in Napoli's colours. The team performed robustly, battling on three fronts for honours and achieving a club first. From the start, they fought for the league with Inter, who had been bolstered by newcomers Andreas Brehme and Lothar Matthäus, and were runners-up in the Coppa Italia, losing the final to Sampdoria. The tournament that was to bring Napoli joy was the UEFA Cup, their first-ever European success.

Injuries were beginning to take their toll on Maradona. Before the first leg of the UEFA Cup semi-finals against Bayern Munich, Diego had to be treated by Dr Rubén Dario Oliva, the Argentina national team doctor, and played the game in difficulty. Napoli won the first leg 2-0 at home, with Maradona setting up both goals for Careca and Carnevale. He was then rested against Milan in the league and only played a few minutes against Fiorentina before the return leg in West Germany.

The Opus hit 'Live Is Life' was booming through the Olympia-stadion's speakers. Maradona, bootlaces untied, incorporated the music into his warm-up routine, flicking the ball from foot to head to shoulders then to the knees, with the occasional hip shimmy thrown in. The rest of the team was going through their standard stretching routine. Maradona, knowing he was the centre of attention and hoping for an intimidating reaction from the rival team, was enjoying himself and gave posterity one of the most iconic football moments of the eighties. German broadcaster ZDF wasn't live during Diego's twelve-minute routine, but Belgian producer Frank

Raes recognised the value of the moment and requested a copy of the footage, which can easily be accessed now.

The game ended 2-2 for a 4-2 aggregate win that propelled Napoli into their first European final. Diego set up both goals, the first by pinching the ball and setting up Careca, and the second a counter-attack, again feeding Careca to seal the team's safe passage.

Back in Naples, Maradona commemorated the team's success at La Stagnata restaurant, the joy spilling out onto the streets where invited guests danced and sang, with Diego as their conductor. 'Who do you think you are? The owner of Naples?' an old woman, who'd been disturbed by the noise, shouted from her balcony. Diego's riposte was to sing the fans' chant from the Sao Paolo '*I am . . . Maradoooo, Maradoooo.*' The lady quickly forgot her bad mood, blowing Diego kisses, joining in the song and applauding. 'I don't know if they should love me so much,' said Diego to his friends afterwards.

Bernard Tapie, president of Olympique de Marseille, knew of the star's disenchantment and reignited his interest in the world's best player; Diego responded with interest. One of the club's directors travelled to Naples and Maradona, ready to flee once more, asked for one thing – peace of mind. 'A house, the sea and a pool, OK?' he said to the director, after promising, in the third person, that Diego himself would try to convince Corrado Ferlaino to let him go. Marseille offered to double Maradona's new $12 million annual salary, provide private security and a residence in the city's most exclusive area on the Mediterranean coast.

Ferlaino, who despite everything wanted him to stay longer, asked UEFA and the Italian federation for help to alleviate the pressure on him. He knew he held a winning card. At that time, footballers could not transfer between clubs without prior permission from their present employers. But he hid his real intentions so Maradona would give everything on the pitch – Maradona believed he could count on the president's word to let him go. Just in case Diego got his wish, the way out had to be prepared from the club's point of view – the Neapolitan newspaper *Il Mattino*, of which Ferlaino was a shareholder, continually published criticism of the footballer's wanton life, speculating that hip and back injuries were simply down to his excesses.

Ferlaino played lip-service to all parties, but Maradona had his own microphone and voice. The Neapolitan TV channel Canal 10 had him for two years on a programme called 'Superstar, Supersport 10'. From these surroundings, Diego announced Claudia's pregnancy and that his wife wanted to have the baby in Argentina. He gave voice to his dream of returning to Boca if they wished to have him and if 'I can earn my place'. But Boca could not pay European wages and Ferlaino, holding his trump card, didn't want Maradona to go anywhere.

The first leg of the UEFA Cup final against Stuttgart was in Naples. Maradona, not fully fit and a bit overweight as training continued to be an irregular occurrence, took free-kicks and corners, assisted teammates and generally tried to direct play without running excessively. The West Germans took the lead thanks to a howler by goalkeeper Giuliani. A hard shot from distance by Gaudino was spilt by him, and it looped into the net to give the visitors a one-goal advantage at half-time.

In the second half, Maradona was inside Stuttgart's penalty area, controlled the ball with his chest and rifled a volley against defender Schäfer's hand. The Napoli captain scored the resulting penalty, sending Immel the wrong way with a feint. Three minutes from the end, the ball broke to Maradona on the right side of Stuttgart's area. With a deft clip, he left his marker on the floor, attacked the byline and poked a cross in with his 'bad' right foot. Careca stumbled after controlling the ball but managed to get his shot away from inside the six-yard box to make it a 2-1 victory for Napoli.

Four days later, Napoli played Bologna away in the league. Twenty-four hours before kick-off, Maradona was reportedly injured again, this time his back. On matchday he declared he felt fine and would fly to Bologna in a private plane. Ferlaino forbade it. But Maradona had to put his side across and used his Canal 10 programme to plead the veracity of his injury: 'If the president doesn't believe me but believes the press, I cannot continue here.' Maradona was betting the house: how dare the president not let the best player in the history of the club play?

*

The day before the UEFA Cup final second leg, Maradona was in his Stuttgart hotel while Claudia was in labour in Buenos Aires, giving birth to their second daughter, Gianinna Dinorah.

The second leg was a rollercoaster game at the Neckarstadion. Napoli opened the scoring through a scruffy Alemão effort, then Jürgen Klinsmann, who had missed the first game, put Stuttgart level with a header from a corner. Towards the end of the first half, Maradona took a corner that was cleared back out to him. He then headed the ball immediately into the centre for Ciro Ferrara to volley Napoli's second goal from close range. The Italian team's third came seventeen minutes after the restart in a counter led by Maradona. He was put through, but his lack of pace saw him caught by the last defender. Maradona checked his run and waited, then delivered a perfectly weighted ball to Careca, who lifted the ball over the on-rushing keeper and into the net. Two defensive errors – an awful own goal followed by an even worse lofted back-pass that Stuttgart striker Olaf Schmäler headed in – led to a tense 3-3 scoreline. With an aggregate result of 5-4 to Napoli, Diego lifted the only European title of his career.

During the celebrations, Ferlaino whispered unwelcome news in Maradona's ear: a few more days off than the rest of the team, but no transfer. 'Until '93, we're together, right?' Diego couldn't credit what he'd heard. 'It is not the time to talk about it, president,' was Maradona's response. But Ferlaino insisted now in front of the media, 'Maradona will stay in Naples as long as I want him to stay in Naples.' The doors were being closed by the 'gaoler', a description the former Napoli chairman now uses for himself.

The lavish, six-year contract Diego signed in 1987 was turning into a gilded cage. Maradona found it hard to accept the direction his sporting life was taking, but there was little he could do, unless . . . Careca and Diego publicly criticised Ottavio Bianchi for his de-fensive tactics. Ferlaino wanted to stamp out any insurrection and used the coach as a shield against Maradona's anger. Eventually, Bianchi's attempts to staunch the flow of almost daily controversies instigated by his best players ended in his own dismissal – almost every big crisis has got at least one victim. The more diplomatic

Albertino Bigon replaced Bianchi with the clear intention of keeping the star happy. All the while, the press continued to detail Diego's latest nocturnal Neapolitan lapses.

There was no escape route to Marseille or Boca. 'We can only see him in pictures, and even those are out of our reach,' admitted the Boca president, Antonio Alegre. Football seemed to lose its lustre for Diego, and training became work, not play. It was getting harder and harder to drag him out of bed; Claudia spent hours sitting on the other side of the locked bathroom door at night. She offered her support in silence, while Diego, barricaded in his dark, self-constructed cell, cried and took more cocaine.

'He was surrounded by good players, yes. But let's not forget Maradona gave away 30 per cent of what he could have given,' Argentine international Claudio Caniggia told *Jot Down* magazine. 'He trained whenever he wanted and we know what else was going on. He was the best in history, no doubt about it, and we never got to see the full extent of his talent.'

This hero's self-destructive triumphs increasingly showed his bipolar perception of life, scaling celestial heights only to descend to infernal underworlds of despair. His family was often in Argentina. He would join them on occasion, sometimes with club approval and often not, and his sense of isolation was increasing. 'No matter how much you surround yourself with people, you are alone,' Fernando Signorini told Argentine journalist Jorge Lanata in his TV programme *Malditos*. 'He once said, "I was kicked up there, I was put on top of a mountain, but nobody told me what to do or how to do it." Sometimes you could see a kind of sadness and disenchantment in his face.'

Injuries kept Diego out of the next three games, and gallstones stopped him playing against Ascoli. In the seventeenth minute of the final home league match against Pisa, Maradona asked to be substituted when he felt a muscle pull. The supporters whistled, insulted Cóppola, Claudia, even Dalma, and everyone sitting in the VIP box. Maradona did not play the last league game at Como either, a 1-0 win, and Napoli finished a distant second, eleven points behind the triumphant Inter.

*

On 16 August 1989, with Maradona ending his holiday in Buenos Aires and due to return to Naples, Cóppola faxed the club. Diego was to check-in at the Villa Eden clinic in the alpine city of Merano in Italy to detox. He would join pre-season training twelve days later, on the twenty-eighth. Ferlaino refused the petition, so Diego went fishing with his father in Esquina with explicit orders to Cóppola not to be disturbed – by anyone. Flights were cancelled. Napoli threatened to rip up his contract, not let him play for any other team, and even refuse him permission to play in the 1990 World Cup. Fans, encouraged by a rabid press gunning for the Argentinian, felt every announcement like a fresh stab in the back.

As many believed in that summer of 1989 that Maradona had no intention of returning to Napoli, local papers published threatening words from fans and polls that always pointed the finger of blame in the direction of the player. On 23 August, Cóppola issued a statement to the media explaining why Diego and his people didn't want to return to Naples. In *Yo Soy El Diego*, Maradona explained that in it 'we gave details of the attacks we had suffered, like a steel ball thrown through the front windscreen, robberies that were never investigated, like when they took the 1986 Ballon d'Or from my home. We were telling the world there was a conspiracy against my family.'

The city had been named as an accomplice to the supposed terror in which Diego lived. The Camorra didn't take the affront well, either. Before the world, Maradona's megaphone declared Naples once again a city of crime. Suddenly, photos of Maradona with Camorra leaders, taken in the first years in Napoli, appeared in the press. Do they look like the enemies? newspapers provokingly asked. A 'Summer Farce' is how *Gazzetta Dello Sport* dubbed it.

The media reacted as was the norm then. The rebellion of a footballer was uncommon. Clubs usually handled team messages and were mostly perceived to be in the right. The substance, however, was little discussed. He wanted to escape. Trying to take advantage of it all, Marseille countered with a juicy offer to tempt Napoli and Maradona, which was rejected once more.

Serie A kicked off on 27 August 1989, without Diego, who was still fishing with his father. On 2 September, *El Pelusa* made his way to Ezeiza airport in Buenos Aires but refused to board because he didn't have a first-class seat. That morning, he promised to return to Italy the following day and to resolve any issues with the club. By the afternoon, he announced he wanted to retire from football. At a police station in Naples, a member of the Giuliano family reported Maradona for cocaine abuse.

On 4 September, a more placid Maradona landed at Fiumicino airport near Rome and requested a meeting with Ferlaino. The president reduced his star player's privileges, including the choice of day of training, and four days later Diego was back with the squad. Maradona did extra work with Signorini in the afternoons to regain his form; he lost weight and knocked cocaine on the head. The newspapers gushed about the Argentine's positive attitude. When he took the field at the San Paolo in the second half of the fifth game of the season, in which his team were trailing by two goals to nil against Fiorentina, he was cheered by a relieved and happy fanbase. Football doffed its cap in gratitude, too. The two-goal deficit was turned around and became a 3-2 Napoli win, thanks to a swash-buckling Maradona performance – he even missed a penalty. Such eye-opening spikes in form defined the rest of his career.

Two weeks later Napoli beat Arrigo Sacchi's Milan 3-0, the first two scored by Carnevale and both set up by Diego, with the third goal scored by *El Pelusa*. He went one-on-one with the goalkeeper, dummied his shot, then chipped the ball over the stranded stopper, who was sprawled on the floor after buying Diego's feint. Napoli topped Serie A.

Following the birth of his second daughter, Diego felt there was one massive matter still pending in his life. Years back, when they were still living in Buenos Aires, Maradona asked Claudia for her hand in marriage. They were sitting in a parked car behind the Navy Mechanics School in the Argentine capital, with only a bottle of cider to hand. 'I've only got this, my love,' said Diego, drawing the cider from his bag, then the engagement ring.

The wedding had to wait. On 7 November of the stormy year of 1989, two days after another Napoli league victory, Diego and Claudia celebrated the most lavish wedding in living memory in Buenos Aires.

In addition to family and friends, players from Cebollitas, Argentinos Juniors, Boca, Napoli, Argentinian footballers in Serie A, directors, showbiz people and many more were among the guests. Some 250 people flew in a private plane from Italy to a ceremony with more than 1,100 guests, with many more invited who didn't attend. Fidel Castro couldn't, for reasons of protocol and security. Jorge Cyterszpiler was not invited. Former midfielder Massimo Mauro described recently in *Corriere Dello Sport* the unforgettable revelry. 'Diego transformed it into a party for his friends,' he recalled. 'He wanted to make them happy, to make them feel at home. When I arrived, a blonde girl with blue eyes opened the hotel room and said to me, "I am at your disposal for three days."'

The bride and groom passed first through the Civil Registry office. After being declared husband and wife by a Justice of the Peace, they went to change at their hotel. A few hours later, Maradona entered the Basilica of the Holy Sacrament church on the arm of Doña Tota, with Claudia Villafañe on the arm of her father, Coco.

Claudia and Diego rode in a convertible Rolls-Royce, 1937 model, to Luna Park for the reception, driven by Giorgio, a doorman at the New York City nightclub.

It was 3am when the couple went on stage to cut their cake. There were a hundred white ribbons hanging from it, one for every single woman at the party to pull, concealing a gold ring for each, except for one, a diamond ring that was picked by Cali, the youngest of Diego's five sisters. The festivities lasted until around 8am, and the couple scooted away in a Mercedes-Benz, with a decoy Mercedes hired to throw the press off the scent. The couple honeymooned in Capri with their two daughters and a group of friends, all led by the organiser of the whole event, Cóppola.

Argentina was in the midst of a financial crisis, racked by unemployment and rising inflation. The country had not been impoverished by Maradona, but was it the right time for such an ostentatious display? Bold marketing and advertising operations before and after the wedding, including the selling of TV rights and photoshoots, paid for most of it, but that didn't stop the sniping. Maradona had an answer for the critics. 'They are afraid of throwing themselves at those on top. They prefer to attack a football player,' he said. 'They fixate on my party, but not at all the other economic parties that destroyed the country.'

The Napoli team continued to be the backbone of the city's social life. One fan shouted *'Ti amo più che ai miei figli'* at Maradona as he drove around Naples – 'I love you more than my children'. But not everyone was happy. Careca remembers it being a season of ups and downs, conflicts with the press and even with the fans. 'They always want us to win, and there are times when you just can't,' explained the Brazilian striker. 'But we were a very level-headed group.' That year AC Milan and Napoli battled for the league until the last matchday.

Years later, Ferlaino explained on ESPN how all 'details' were taken care of during the 1989–90 campaign. 'The Verona–Milan game was important. I had a good relationship with the man who appointed referees, [Cesare] Gussoni. Milan had a very friendly little ref, [Tullio] Lanese, who was nicknamed "The Milanese". We, on the other hand, were closer to Rosario Lo Bello.' The championship race was now entering its definitive moments, so every aspect was crucial. In the penultimate round, Milan travelled to Verona, and Ferlaino's friend Lo Bello was the appointed referee. The match had everything: verbal confrontations, fury and three red cards for Milan. Sacchi's team lost 2-1 to an eighty-ninth-minute Verona winner. Napoli also beat Bologna 4-2 away from home, with one goal from Diego, his sixteenth of the season, the team's top scorer. They had one hand on the club's second Scudetto.

Napoli's last league match was at home to Lazio. It was standing room only at a rowdy San Paolo stadium, hundreds of flags flying in the wind, song after song blasting out and fans blinded by flare smoke. The home players took to the field with their offspring, led by Diego and Claudia with Dalma and Gianinna in their arms. Victory would guarantee the title. After just seven minutes, Maradona's left foot delivered a free-kick on to centre-back Marco Baroni's head for the only goal of the game.

At the final whistle, the pitch was a rabble of journalists, fans, club members all crying, laughing and hugging each other. Men, women and children of all ages shared their joy with the celebrating players. Signorini took to the field with Dalma on his shoulders.

In the dressing room, an unbridled and truly united celebration unfolded, directors and TV camera operators sharing the moment amid laughter and cheers. There was, of course, plenty of singing, 'Ho visto Maradona / Ho visto Maradona . . .'

Diego, parading in front of the cameras, grabbed a microphone and improvised an interview with Napoli's president. 'Are you happy?' he asked. When Ferlaino replied they could have won the two previous leagues, Diego quipped, 'Mamma mia, we have to let others win, or it will become very boring. You are a great president.' He turned around and returned to the group jamboree.

In the mid-1990s, Neapolitan judges investigating drug trafficking were cross-examining Italian footballer Massimo Crippa. He detailed how the Napoli squad carried on the title-winning party. They relocated to a ship captained by Cóppola that was anchored off Vesuvius. A jet ski came to deliver two packages. Crippa told the judges that Cóppola had shouted, 'The cocaine has arrived!'

Quartieri Spagnoli is a central neighbourhood in Naples with humble housing and is the former stomping grounds of pickpockets, smugglers and other criminals. Its people are unassuming and modest but also trapped by their deprivation. As the summer of 1990 dawned, one of its squares commenced a decorative mural in Maradona's honour, a three-storey painting of Diego with other photos and drawings recreating his years at Napoli and his victory at the 1986 World Cup.

It is said that Maradona, alone, drove to the piazza one night, and spent five minutes looking at himself in the enormous mirror.

# 30
# THE 1990 WORLD CUP IN ITALY

'One day in Naples, Bilardo rings my doorbell at nine o'clock at night,' Maradona recalled about his Napoli years on Argentine channel TyC Sports. It was the evening after the team had beaten Como. As Diego was having some drinks with teammates, Claudia came up to him to tell him Bilardo was downstairs. 'They all went stiff as boards, on high alert, and tiptoed like naughty kids to my bedroom,' Maradona explained with a cheeky grin. The footballers left one by one avoiding the manager. 'Bilardo said to me, "I'm not taking Caniggia to the World Cup." I said, "It's OK, you have lost two forwards straightaway." And while he was adjusting his tie, all nervous, he said to me, "He's not taking care of himself." And I say, "Stop being stupid!"'

Argentina's World Cup defence in Italy would be under Carlos Bilardo again, the same coach as in Mexico. Caniggia was eventually called up to a squad that hadn't been refreshed and depended more on reputation than football ability. Argentina had won only seven of their thirty-four matches since 1986, and not even the Argentine press named them among the favourites. What they had was the absolute certainty of Maradona's leadership which could affect his teammates, opponents and the referee.

Maradona stopped taking cocaine for a while and got himself into shape. The 1990 World Cup offered him the chance to continue being hailed as the best, by playing well over a possible seven games. His biggest concern was his delicate and much scrutinised left ankle, which had swollen up like a tennis ball during the Italian league campaign. He could hardly put his boots on at training, spending the day in flip-flops in an attempt to protect what was probably the most photographed ankle in the world. Rubén Moschella, Bilardo's assistant from the Argentine federation, told Lalo Zanoni in *Maradona Off the Record* that 90 per cent of the squad were in the treatment room before the tournament started. Diego's ankle was always swollen, and on the eve of a match he was given a hot-cold treatment, a sort of tar-like paste, in addition to the medication he received. But as soon as he started playing, it would swell again.

'Guillermo Blanco also informed Zanoni that when Diego was playing for Napoli he had to go back to Barcelona to have the screws removed from his ankle. On one occasion the head of a screw broke off and they couldn't remove it: it was there forever afterwards. Before Argentina's opening Group B match against Cameroon, Diego also lost the nail from his right big toe.

Diego was never in perfect physical condition, but made it clear he would be playing every second of the tournament. He was equally daring in the game played out at press conferences too. For those who followed him closely, his black and white definition of the world was growing sharper; you were simply for him or against him. 'I'd rather be unfriendly than keep quiet about things,' he said. Diego spoke out in the name of his truth, some of which, two decades later, seemed more like premonitions.

João Havelange, FIFA president from 1974 to 1998, had inherited an almost amateur organisation and turned it into a slick multinational one, although often things were done and undone on a whim and on the sly. Along the way, he and other prominent members at FIFA became rich through bribes reaching into the millions, maintaining close relations with and giving favourable treatment to dictatorships like Argentina's. Havelange was the perfect villain, and justifiable target, for Maradona's tempestuous theatre.

Diego, ignoring the good relationship between his federation and FIFA, saw ghosts and defended his proclamations that the World Cup draw had been a farce, one that was prejudiced against Argentina. FIFA threatened to sanction Diego, who ended up apologising for the last time. A few days before the curtain-raiser against Cameroon in Milan, he pulled out his verbal knives again, this time to protect all footballers, who often had to play in extremely hot conditions. 'Why should we play a game at three o'clock in the afternoon in 70 degrees heat, we are the ones who have to go out there. Give Havelange a pair of boots, give [Sepp] Blatter [FIFA secretary-general] a pair of shorts. You know how ridiculous they'd look out .there.' Interestingly, Argentina did not have to play at 3pm, the most-feared kick-off time, all tournament.

Impotent in the first game, they lost 1-0 to Cameroon, conceding in the second half to a team down to ten men that would be reduced to nine players before the final whistle. Drums of courage were beaten to rally the Argentinian cause, a country that thrived on epic drama. It is perhaps why Argentinians talk about this World Cup as much as they do about winning it in 1986.

'The next day, when we went to lunch, I looked at everyone's faces,' Carlos Bilardo told Diego Borinsky in *El Gráfico*. 'I'd read a book about a German who had lost a battle, so he went and cut his hair, spruced himself up and dressed nicely. I did the same, perfume, everything. I went [to the press conference] with Diego, walking past everyone, saying hello, how are you and so on until I got to the centre. Afterwards, Maradona said to me, "That's the first time in my life nobody stopped me." "That's right, they were all looking at me."'

Bilardo had put all the responsibility squarely on his own shoulders. His next line-up against the USSR, who'd also lost their first game, was riddled with uncertainty and five new faces. Number one goalkeeper Pumpido was injured early on and Sergio Goycochea, later to play a vital role in the tournament, made his World Cup debut. The match is important for two critical reasons. At 0-0 in the first half, a Soviet corner was met with a powerful header that travelled towards Argentina's unguarded net. Maradona, with a deliberate movement of his arm, stopped the ball going in. The referee, metres away, waved away Soviet appeals for the clear handball, and Argentina went on to win 2-0. The Hand of God had intervened once more, but nobody talks about the sequel, perhaps in order not to ruin the original.

A final 1-1 draw with Romania left Argentina as the best of the four third-placed finishers. They joined the top two from the six groups in the last 16. It brought them up against Brazil, a team containing Taffarel, Careca, Valdo, Dunga and Alemão (Romário and Bebeto stayed on the bench), and one that had just won their group. 'Maradona was playing at about twenty per cent, but it doesn't even occur to him to desert,' wrote Aldo Proietto in *El Gráfico*. His left ankle wouldn't support him. 'Give it to me, doctor,' Diego said before the match in Turin. The doctor handed *El Pelusa* a syringe of anti-inflammatory drugs. Maradona hammered the needle into his ankle. Within a few minutes of the game starting, Maradona's friend Alemão had already given that famous left ankle a couple of welcoming kicks.

The Brazilians were dominating the game, which was played in intense late-afternoon heat. On the stroke of half-time, a strong tackle from Ricardo Rocha left Argentina midfielder Pedro Troglio requiring treatment. The medical team came onto the pitch and brought water bottles with different branding to those the Argentinians were drinking. Brazil's wing back Branco drank from one supplied by Argentina's physio Miguel di Lorenzo. Branco soon began to feel nauseous and dizzy, a possible side-effect of the intense heat. Or possibly the result of Bilardo's instructions to Miguel di Lorenzo to mix a Rohypnol sleeping pill into the water.

'Some of our team went to drink water. Julio Olarticoechea almost drank some. I shouted, "No, *Vasco*! No!"' said Maradona on TyC Sports some twenty-five years later. 'I said to Valdo [Branco], "Go on, Valdo, drink it. It's so hot." Branco drank it all, then he was falling over at free-kicks, and his vision was blurred. Someone had put a tranquilliser in the water bottle, and everything went wrong for them!' said a smiling Maradona on the programme. FIFA didn't investigate, despite the Brazilian confederation's protests. Once more, the Argentine public, aided by Maradona's cheeky explanation about events, collectively transformed what was cheating into an action worthy of praise from their clever *criollo*.

In the eighty-first minute, Diego picked up the ball in the centre-circle just inside his own half, with Caniggia his only teammate ahead. He beat one Brazilian and started one of his trademark rolling runs. 'They all came with me,' Maradona recalled in the same programme. 'I kept dribbling, and I could only see Caniggia. I risked a pass with my right foot, and it worked perfectly. I think it was the best pass of my life.' Caniggia rounded the keeper and scored. There was still time for Brazil's captain Ricardo Gomes to be sent off for a professional foul before his team was eliminated by that single goal.

The quarter-final brought about a dull scoreless draw against Yugoslavia. After thirty minutes of extra time failed to break the stalemate, the tie was decided on a penalty shoot-out, in which Maradona and Troglio missed their spot-kicks. Goycochea saved two of the Yugoslav's failed three attempts, including one from the outstanding Dragan Stojković, and the holders were through.

The semi-final would see Argentina take on Italy in Naples, the city where Maradona was still a club player. *La Gazzetta Dello Sport*, sensing something, led their pre-match coverage with the headline 'Maradona Is the Devil'.

'The best player in the world became the most hated,' wrote Lalo Zanoni on Argentina news website *Infobae*. 'For me, that is the key match in Diego's career. Not the most important, nor the most magnificent (his play rated 7 or 8 points), nor the most famous match. But it was the game where he used all his intelligence and all his extra football nous. The high-profile beast that he is, he managed to split Italy a few days before the game.'

'I will divide Italy today,' Maradona said to his teammates when he found out Italy were the opponents and before making an appeal to the Neapolitan people. 'After so much racism, it is only now that [the Italians] readily remember that Naples is part of Italy. For 364 days of the year they talk of the southerners, the *terroni*, that stink, the sinister and damaged people. Infamous attacks,' said Maradona in a *Corriere Dello Sport* article headlined 'Naples Loves Me'.

'His statements to the media caught the public and our squad off guard,' acknowledged Italian midfielder Aldo Serena, who was on the bench for that game. 'The crowd was not like the one we had in Rome for the quarter-final. It was divided.'

'The day Argentina played Italy, I was in the back seat of the bus on the way to the San Paolo stadium,' recalls Signorini. 'I look back. About fifteen metres away were the police motorbikes, but in front of them was an Enduro motorbike with large handlebars. It was Carmine Giuliano.' Diego's relationship with the Camorra had changed since Diego and Cóppola had hinted that the Camorra were behind incidents making their lives more complicated. But Carmine wanted to be close to the action.

The game played out in a tense atmosphere, with Maradona being insulted and whistled at constantly. Argentina continued their defensive strategy, essentially waiting for Maradona and Caniggia to whip up some magic. Italy scored first after seventeen minutes through Salvatore 'Toto' Schillaci, who went on to win the Golden Boot as top goalscorer and Golden Ball as the player of the tournament. The tackles from both sides were often on the fringe of what was allowed, and frequently unlawful.

Argentina drew level in the second half, Caniggia heading home a looping cross from the left. Ricardo Giusti was given his marching orders for a second yellow card during extra time, but ten-man Argentina held out for penalties. Maradona, who had a very quiet game, was among the first four Argentina penalty takers, who all scored. Goycochea saved the last two Italian penalties, giving his team a 4-3 shoot-out win. Italy was out of their home World Cup. That night in Naples, the streets were filled with 'Maradona, figlio di putana' insults ('Maradona, son of a bitch') mixed with a few reticent 'Maradoooo' calls.

Diego had three years left to run on his contract in Italy. 'I don't want to be an enemy, I ask you to understand me,' he proclaimed, having just invoked a nationally emotive clash that would soon transform into revenge. Asked by journalist Diego Borinsky which had given him more pleasure, the defeat of England in '86 or eliminating Italy in '90, Maradona didn't think too long before retorting, 'Italy, for all the connotations it had.' Even though the majority of these were tremendously negative.

The Italy game served to ratify his status as the best footballer on the planet, appearing when needed in a crucial match. It was also the beginning of the end, his farewell, according to Lalo Zanoni, who wrote that Maradona did it 'in a big way, in his own way. Knocking out Italy, with the FIFA leaders watching on in disbelief from their box as this swarthy little upstart from Villa Fiorito rewrote history.'

West Germany would again be Argentina's rival in the final, this time in Rome.

Maradona and many more have given their versions about what happened next in Italy, denouncing FIFA and claiming the organisation was plotting to stop Argentina from winning. Havelange, Blatter and Julio Grondona, the Argentine federation president, were all implicated, leaders – Maradona would claim – of a corrupt organisation.

For Diego, it all became clear on the eve of the final, after Argentina's training session at Rome's Stadio Olimpico. While Diego was in the shower, Grondona approached him. This is how Maradona tells it in his autobiography:

'It's all done, Diego. We've reached the final.'

'What? What are you talking about, Julio?'

'That this is it, we did what we could. Look where we've got. And you're run ragged. We're done.'

'Bollocks to that! We've got a final tomorrow, and we want to win it. Don't tell me you've sold the final? Eh?'

Years later, Maradona furnished Borinsky with more details: 'It had all been set up. We'd fucked up [Antonio] Matarrese [member of the World Cup Organising Committee] and Italy. The final had been shaken on, and it was to be Italy–Germany. The whole business was ready, we'd fucked up 180 million dollars for the World Cup organisers, we'd destroyed FIFA's flag, their megaphone, fucked up the celebrations, television rights. We'd made it a total disaster. And of course, we had to pay.'

The final symbolised the definitive break between an angry Maradona, who was railing against the world, and Italian football. It also ruptured relations between the player and football's big shots. Diego's relationship with the public was about to change for ever, morphing from an extraordinary footballer, a redeemer and a winner, to that of an indestructible myth, a tireless fighter for just causes. If the England match wrote his place in history, the

Maradona raises his glass as he sits with Guillermo Cóppola during a dinner at an Argentine restaurant in Mexico City. Maradona travelled to Mexico to watch Boca Juniors' second-leg Copa Libertadores semi-final against America, but was delayed and did not arrive in time to see his team's match.

22 October 1988. Maradona playing with his daughter Dalma after a training session at Centro Paradiso, Soccavo, Naples. The smile . . .

17 October 1986. Maradona in action during a training session at Centro Paradiso, Soccavo, Naples. Training was not his thing, and for many years he would only train when he felt mentally and physically ready.

10 May 1987. Napoli won their first Scudetto after drawing 1-1 with Fiorentina in the penultimate round of the league. The previous twelve months were the peak of his happiness – and also the beginning of the end.

7 November 1989. Maradona kisses Claudia Villafañe during their wedding at Luna Park Stadium, Buenos Aires, Argentina. It was a huge party in her honour, but it was not what Claudia had wanted. Amongst Diego's women, she was always the one he cherished most.

1992–93. Maradona during a Spanish League match between Sevilla FC and Espanyol. He was not in top-professional shape, but his touch was still unmatched.

1996. Maradona and Claudio Caniggia famously celebrate the first Boca Juniors goal against River Plate in the Torneo Clausura.

1999. Maradona on holiday with his family in Punta del Este, Uruguay.
Diego was photographed all the time.

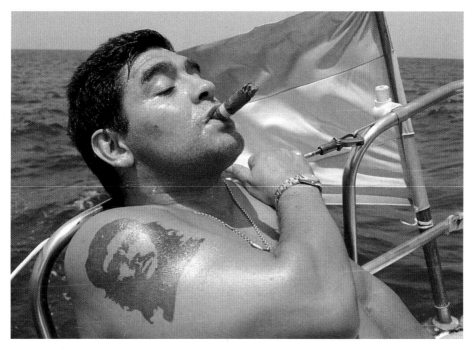

April 2000. Maradona smokes a Cohiba cigar as he sails in waters off Havana,
Cuba, during his rehabilitation programme to try to conquer his cocaine addiction.
The tattoo is of Che Guevara. He identified with him, and his rebellious nature.

10 November 2001. Diego Maradona is overcome with emotion during an event in his honour at 'La Bombonera', stadium of Boca Juniors – and left us with a memorable sentence.

27 October 2005. Maradona in Cuba to record his special interview with Castro for *La Noche del 10* ('Number Ten's Night'), his weekly programme broadcast in Buenos Aires. He had lost 30 kilos after being close to dying.

March 2009. Maradona, then coach of the Argentina national team, speaks with Lionel Messi during a training session in Ezeiza, Buenos Aires, before Argentina meet Venezuela for their FIFA World Cup South Africa 2010 qualifier. His coaching did not equal the standard of his playing.

14 June 2012. Diego embraces his father before the start of Copa Libertadores first leg semi-final between Boca Juniors and Universidad de Chile. The quiet Don Diego left a huge vacuum when he died in 2015.

8 January 2021. Supporters of Napoli burn flares during the inauguration of the mural painting by street artist Jorit Agoch in Quarto, close to Naples. Diego Armando Maradona is a god in Argentina, and a very different one in Naples.

1990 World Cup gave him legendary status. The Napoleonic leader again.

The final in Italy's capital saw a solid West Germany team playing a decimated Argentina; Caniggia, Giusti and Olarticoechea were all out of the starting squad. Maradona had added a muscle injury to his gammy ankle and sheared toenail. As the Argentine anthem started up, the German and Italian fans started whistling. Maradona, full of combustible fury, waited for the camera to focus on him before roaring two unmistakable 'Sons of bitches!', his answering shot replete with indignation.

At the toss of the coin, referee Edgardo Codesal – a Uruguayan by birth but Mexican by nationality – addressed Maradona: 'Diego, take it easy. Don't lose your head, demonstrate what kind of player you are. You have 90 minutes to show it, and get this thorn out of your side.' But the wrath was buried deep. 'No, no. These sons of bitches . . .' Maradona snarled. Codesal, recalling that day in an interview for the Uruguayan radio programme *Tirando Paredes*, said to Maradona, 'Don't you want to understand that I, at least, have some sympathy for you? Will you be calm? Let's toss the coin and let whatever happens be what God wants.'

A quiet first half didn't improve much after the break until the sixty-fifth minute. Pedro Monzón – who had replaced the injured Oscar Ruggeri at half-time – flew in late on Jürgen Klinsmann, raising his studs into the West German's shin, long after the ball had gone. He was shown a straight red card, the first player to receive his marching orders in a World Cup final. Referee Codesal continued, 'And right there, Maradona. He comes and says to me, "We already knew we'd be robbed. FIFA sent you to steal the match from us, so we wouldn't win." I had grounds to send him off!'

With five minutes of normal time to play, Rudi Völler ran into the Argentina penalty area after receiving a slide-rule pass from Lothar Matthäus. Argentina's Roberto Sensini was tracking Völler but got caught on the wrong side and slightly behind the run. The referee, behind the play, didn't have a great view as the defender clumsily tried to take the ball with his right foot, going across the attacker. Sensini's awkward starting position resulted in a jumble of arms and legs, with both players tumbling to the turf. Argentina, whose own penalty claim had been waved away minutes before, had given away a spot-kick. Years later, Andreas Brehme and Matthäus admitted in interviews the contact wasn't enough for a penalty.

The referee addressed an incensed Maradona: 'Listen, this a World Cup final, you are the best player in the world, calm down and play football.' Diego's protests could easily have resulted in his own dismissal, especially as this was his second dressing-down. 'He gives the penalty and then later he gets a job as the boss of the referees in Mexico,' Maradona wrote in his book. Codesal responded thirty years later on Uruguayan radio: 'He's one of the worst people I have ever met in my life.'

Brehme stroked the resulting penalty to his left and into the bottom-right of Goycochea's net, the goalkeeper being unable to repeat his penalty-shoot-out heroics. Monzón didn't hold the distinction of being the only man to be sent off in a World Cup final for long. Striker Gustavo Dezotti got a straight red card for grabbing Jürgen Kohler by the neck near the West German corner flag, then slamming him into the ground, swiftly joining Monzón on the long walk down the tunnel to the changing rooms. Maradona's persistent protests were finally punished with a yellow.

When the referee blew for the end of the match, a weeping Diego repeated his mantra, 'Sons of bitches, sons of bitches.' His rebellion would no longer be silenced or diplomatic; there was to be no hiding and no negotiating positions. He ignored Havelange after receiving his runner-up medal, a very public and spiteful gesture. 'I was hoping that this black hand of power would not be so strong, but . . .' he told the press shortly afterwards. FIFA was 'a mafia' thereafter.

Maradona sobbed all night. 'I felt that we had been unfairly treated, and Havelange had made us pay,' he explained in El Gráfico. 'We have different origins. A relationship is impossible, no matter how much he says he loves me like a son.' The accusations against football's leaders came regularly. 'I would call João Havelange's website ladrón.com [robber.com],' he fumed. 'The AFA needs a hand-grenade under it and made anew.'

As a child, Maradona never accepted defeat. And as as an adult, he kept pushing at boundaries by continually claiming injustices, whether real or imagined. 'He defended his class status, he stood up to oppressors and perversity,' insists Signorini. A character was cast, then baptised, in that final. It came from Maradona himself and also from 'that part of journalism or the system that exploits you, that plays you'.

'The media continued to squeeze and tighten around Diego. His guard got higher and higher, and he became more and more forceful in his statements,' his former physical trainer says today. 'They weren't studied declarations but came from his ancestral culture, perhaps from his grandparents or from Don Diego. Maradona was ruthless with power, which was ruthless with him.'

Power reacts to challenges and those that rebel, always ready to shatter any opposition. 'Because I left Villa Fiorito, I cannot speak?' asked Diego in *Yo Soy El Diego*. 'I am the voice of the voiceless . . . I had a fight with the Pope. I argued with him because I went to the Vatican and saw the golden ceilings. And then I heard the Pope say that the Church cared about poor kids. Well, sell the roof, beast. Do something! What is the Banco Ambrosiano for? To sell drugs and smuggle weapons?'

'They tried to buy me several times,' said Diego in his other book, *My World Cup, My Truth*. '[In 1993] they gave me a medal for being the best player in history, and then they locked me in a room with Havelange. Blatter was there, too. And they said to me, "Dieguito, we want you to be part of the FIFA family."' Maradona rejected the proposal and tried to create instead a Footballers' Union. ('Footballers cannot be passive in the face of all that is happening in the game,' he told the media.) He had a meeting in Paris with some players, including Eric Cantona, but never drummed up enough support. To Diego, 'this factory is doing better and better because its workers accept everything'.

Diego was fascinated by power, and that is why he became, declaration by declaration and fight by fight, a power himself.

# 31
# THE END AT NAPOLI

French TV channel Télé Monte Carlo (TMC) travelled to Naples to interview Maradona at the beginning of the 1990–91 season. Diego wanted to record himself with the lights off. And he said in Italian, 'So much has been said this week about my dark side that we cannot fail to present that dark side to the viewers of Télé Monte Carlo. This is my dark side. See you soon.' His life of contrasts was so public that it formed part of his own jokes. All the while he was laughing at himself, he could ignore his rapidly advancing downfall.

In 1990, Maradona was a drug addict with no control over his behaviour, turning his back on potential solutions and hunting new enemies instead. Cocaine and sciatica meant no day passed without pain or pressing needs. He found no succour in the league win or in the runner-up spot in the World Cup; nor did the pre-season 5-1 win over Juventus in the Italian Super Cup give him the positive mindset he needed to reset his relationship with the club. Maradona severed ties with Guillermo Cóppola a few months after the final against West Germany.

After the World Cup, every trip from Buenos Aires back to Naples was torture for Maradona. He didn't want to, and perhaps couldn't, play football any more. The hate was being turned on his associates, too. 'One day I went to the bank with my motorbike, and someone threw a stone at me,' recalls Cóppola, scared by the turn of events. It was not just fans reacting to new stories about Diego wanting away but something darker, he thought. Maradona cancelled marketing film shoots at the last minute, would ignore commercial obligations, and there were lawsuits. The player needed protection and felt his old friend was not offering that. The wear and tear of the relationship took them to breaking point and, on Cóppola's birthday, as he will never forget, 'we went our separate ways'.

The agent needed time and space to confront his own demons, quitting cocaine that same year. Maradona looked for a different support mechanism from Cóppola, employing Marcos Franchi, a business administration graduate and Cóppola's lieutenant. Franchi did what needed to be done: manage. He used doses of reality to try to turn Maradona's listing – and rapidly sinking – ship around. 'You can't be a player living like an ex-player,' he once told Diego.

In November 1990, Napoli travelled to Moscow for a last-16 European Cup tie against Spartak Moscow at a snowy Central Lenin Stadium, since renamed the Luzhniki. Maradona was enthusiastic about his first trip to the Soviet Union, then failed to show up at the airport. The club asked Ciro Ferrara and two other teammates to pick Maradona up at home. 'He's sleeping,' Claudia told them. He had actually locked himself in his room, hiding under the sheets and refusing to talk to anyone.

'Many people reproached us for in some way being accomplices to the situation,' explained Ferrara in an ESPN documentary. 'I was very young. I didn't have the personality to stand in front of Maradona and say, "What the hell are you doing?"' The squad waited two and a half hours at the airport for him, but eventually left without the Argentinian.

Luciano Moggi, Napoli's general manager, signalled that this behaviour was the beginning of the end. 'It's been a key day in Maradona and Napoli's relationship,' said Ferlaino while confirming the club was about to drop their star. 'He is the club's employee and not the other way around.'

The next day Maradona paid $30,000 to rent a private jet and flew to Moscow with Claudia and his new agent, Franchi. He said he was going as a fan and not a player. 'Haven't they said they are going to punish me, and I can't play?' On arrival, Maradona went to Red Square, where the Soviet police initially forbade him entrance. In the end, after he had been recognised, he took a private tour around Lenin's mausoleum and arrived at the hotel where the squad was staying, at three in the morning. He asked Moggi to allow him to play.

Some sixty-five minutes into the goalless game, Maradona replaced Gianfranco Zola in attack. It remained without score through to extra time and Napoli were eliminated 5-3 on penalties in what proved to be Maradona's last European match for the Italian club.

In December 1990, Luciano Moggi petitioned Antonio Matarrese, the president of the Federcalcio (Italian Football Federation), for help with Maradona. The recalcitrant player wasn't training, and Moggi feared Maradona wouldn't return to Italy after taking his usual Christmas break in Argentina. The Federcalcio competition committee fined Diego $70,000 for his absences, and Napoli sued the footballer for damaging the club's image with his errant behaviour.

Franchi announced his client would 'leave elite football by July 1991 at the latest', and that a return to Boca was 'very close'. Although he had two and a half years left on his contract at Napoli, Franchi said, 'Diego can't give any more' to football, and offered to pay off the rest of this contract. Maradona did return to Italy in early 1991, and soon discovered he was treading on quicksand.

Moggi and Ferlaino had decided they had to get rid of Diego before he unduly affected the club's prestige. They were not the only ones pushing him towards the door. The Camorra hadn't forgiven Maradona for publicly bad-mouthing the city and turning his nose up at what he had previously inhaled with gusto.

These were difficult times for the Neapolitan mafia. The state had been breathing down its neck ever since the launch of Operation China in November 1990, the investigation by the Carabinieri of Camorra links with cocaine trafficking. Maradona's penchant for prostitutes drew him into the web of the criminal group's illegal activities and conversations were recorded which implicated him: the cops had wiretaps on the hookers. In one he is asking for 'two women' and in another one an anonymous voice admits he is sending him women and 'roba', street argot for cocaine.

Maradona's personal gates of hell yawned wider. The newspapers filled pages with statements from various characters from Napoli's less salubrious nocturnal haunts. Five prostitutes declared that Maradona had given them cocaine before having sex. He was, without trial, found guilty of all charges by the press. The hysteria not only affected him, but his family, too.

On 17 February 1991, Maradona went to court to testify, charged with the 'use and distribution of cocaine'. He talked to the media beforehand – 'I have never been so calm' – admitting he was attending voluntarily on the advice of his wife and daughters. He said his family had also suggested 'giving up football and going back to my homeland'. In the witness box, Maradona's testimony lasted three hours. His lawyers recommended that he acknowledge his sexual adventures, about which he gave many details, but that he reject the accusation of use and distribution of cocaine, which carried an eight-to twenty-year prison sentence. He was given a criminal record, but his sentence – fourteen months in prison and a four-million-lira fine for possession of cocaine – was suspended without punishment.

Maradona's analysis was clear and succinct: it was a vendetta. By FIFA, who felt threatened by his accusations. By the Italian football federation – which was tightening its anti-doping controls – because of the World Cup. By Napoli, who would no longer hide his excesses. By the Camorra, who no longer needed their fallen angel. By Silvio Berlusconi's media outlets, which published and broadcast his miseries. The shelter provided until then by the same press, the same judges and the same club had simply disappeared.

'There was already a campaign by the powers-that-be, in this case Napoli, to get rid of this lemon which no longer had any juice,' Fernando Signorini explained to Jorge Lanata on his TV programme *Malditos*. 'All the world knew Diego took drugs. Not just Napoli, the world football authorities knew about it. But he was still performing. He kept filling up stadiums, he kept serving. When the problem, his problem, the tremendous thing that happened to him through addiction, when it became unbearable, they threw him away like a cigarette butt. He was no longer of any use.'

It is relatively easy to manipulate public opinion, even against the greatest of idols. *La Repubblica* published a poll that indicated Maradona was the most hated person in Italy, ahead of Saddam Hussein, the repressive dictator of Iraq. The country was living out a character assassination.

The background noise stopped slightly after the court case, but the rot had set in. Maradona continued to train at Napoli, although he and the club had already decided to go their separate ways. A week before a Napoli–Bari match played on 17 March 1991, Ferlaino reminded Maradona that if he stopped taking cocaine before Thursday the 14th, it would not show up on the anti-doping test. Maradona no longer controlled times and dates, nor did he care: 'I have not consumed anything.'

'Are you fit?' Moggi asked before the game.

'Everything's fine,' the player replied.

The president of the Italian federation, Luciano Nizzola, called Ferlaino after the Bari game. 'It's positive,' he said. According to the Napoli version, Ferlaino asked Nizzola what could be done. 'Nothing now,' was the reply. Diego found out while he was at home, and began to tremble and weep, then asked for his lawyer, Vicenzo Siniscalchi. When his legal representative arrived, Maradona was sound asleep under a blanket. Upon waking, he said, 'We've lost everything. Forgive me.' But that brief sense of guilt did not last long. He began listing the betrayals and deceptions he had suffered by those that in the past called themselves friends.

Had Maradona been caught? Or was it more a cry for help? 'I tested positive almost on purpose – yes, on purpose. I wanted it,' he later admitted years later to journalist Daniel Arcucci. 'Testing positive for drugs at that time saved me,' he told Gabriela Cociffi six years later for *Gente* magazine. 'I didn't get high [at the Bari game], I got high before, but I knew I could get caught at any time. I was pushing the limits. Drugs were everywhere. It was pretty much offered to me on a plate.'

'It was my fault, I'm not going to blame anyone,' Maradona said to Diego Borinsky almost two decades after that positive test. 'Now, let me make something else clear. All those who say they didn't take drugs with me? They were all taking them. I won't name names because I'm not some security guard or snitch, but if they say something to me I'll respond.' As it often was with Maradona, the blame had to be shared.

Eight months after the 1990 World Cup, and despite doubts put forward about the keeping and transportation of the test-tubes by the prestigious anti-doping doctor Manfred Donicke, doubts that were ignored by the authorities, the Disciplinary Commission of the Italian League barred him for fifteen months till 30 June 1992, a ban extended world-wide by FIFA. 'After my doping, [Claudio] Caniggia was also caught and punished, but after that ... no one else,' Diego explained in Emir Kusturica's documentary. 'In Italian football, nobody took even a Paracetamol, except for Maradona and Caniggia.'

In *Mi Mundial, Mi Verdad*, written more than a decade after his drug ban, Maradona makes a contemporary and accurate observation about the absurdity of punishing drug addicts, pointing out that out on the streets an addict gets treatment, not punishment. In other words, if he's no good for football, at least he is good for life, and that you have to get the person back if you cannot retrieve the footballer.

Diego Maradona, a player who, despite being a playmaker, was Napoli's top scorer until 2017 with 115 goals in 259 games (including thirty goals from free-kicks). The man who had brought a winning mentality to the team – two league titles, one Italian Cup, one Super Cup and one UEFA Cup – was about to leave the club by the back door. Napoli, for their part, finished eighth that 1990–91 season and abruptly ceased to be competitive once Maradona sailed away. They were relegated to Serie B twice and went bankrupt, to be rescued in 2007 by Aurelio de Laurentiis, a member of the famous family of film producers.

On the evening of 31 March 1991, friends and journalists closest to Diego all received a call summoning them. Maradona welcomed them at the door of his mansion in Posillipo wearing a tracksuit and a pair of slippers adorned with stuffed dogs. He wanted to say good-bye. Italian journalist Vittorio de Asmundis asked him directly the deep, hidden reasons for his departure:

'You are escaping like a thief.'

'They are forcing me to escape.'

'Who? Ferlaino? [Napoli's vice-president Gianni] Punzo? And who is behind them? [Ferrari chairman, Luca di] Montezemolo, [president of the Italian League, Antonio] Matarrese, [Paolo] Casarin [who designated referees for Serie A]?'

In his autobiography Maradona accused Ferlaino and Matarrese of being behind the events: 'They made me pay because I was a foreigner and because I prevented Italy from being in the World Cup final.' He left the country with four unresolved court cases: the Sinagra 'case'; accusations by the informant Pietro Pugliese, former *camorrista*, that he had been involved in drug-trafficking; Napoli's denunciation of him for breach of contract; and the still-unresolved cocaine-and-prostitute case.

He got into the car that was taking him to the airport, leaving his parting words hanging in the air, unheard but poignant: 'I don't run away.' Without a game at San Paolo to enable the mourning of an end of an era, it indeed appeared Diego was doing just that, a far cry from the ecstatic welcome he'd received from 70,000 fans just seven summers before.

Not everyone arrived in time to hug him and say goodbye. The Vignati family, the Neapolitan mother and cook who had adopted Diego, found the door closed. But he left clear instructions on what to do with his possessions – they were to be shared among those who served his domestic needs, as explained by Sergio Levinsky in *Infobae*. 'The Honda 750 for Ignacio, the koala for Ciro, the electrician, a car for Felice, the Seat Ibiza will be handed to Gianni, a Rolex for Federico and all that was in the kitchen for Lucia . . .'

The Neapolitans felt betrayed by this 'cursed footballer' who had abandoned them. He was great as a footballer but failed as a human being, according to the word on the streets. It took several years of sporting and political frustration for Maradona to reclaim his place as an honorary citizen of the city. 'I've seen Maradona play,' is a typical sticker seen plastered on Naples' cars and motorbikes today, and his image decorates walls in neighbourhoods that remain neglected.

Fernando Signorini and Marcos Franchi were already planning the next moves, despite Maradona's claim to be in control of the situation and his addiction. They wanted him to consult three specialists: a psychiatrist, a psychologist and an internal medicine specialist. Addiction specialists ridiculed the selection as 'like giving a mint to a cancer patient', and recommended shock treatment instead. Signorini and Franchi sought Diego's acceptance to attend a rehabilitation centre in Colorado Springs, where film star Elizabeth Taylor had been treated. He refused, preferring to go home and be with his family. Psychologists eventually convinced him to go to Buenos Aires and isolate from the world for a while. This plunged him into depression, and he continued to take cocaine.

'I remember that when he started his treatment in Buenos Aires in April 1991, in the flat he had on Avenida Libertador, Claudia called me,' Signorini explains. 'I had stayed in Naples to sort everything out for Diego – his car, clothes, furniture, jewellery. I had to assemble all the containers, and depending on what Claudia told me, throw things away, give them to assistants or send them to Argentina. Claudia told me the therapists wanted to see me, as Diego had talked about me a lot.'

Signorini went to Maradona's Buenos Aires flat. Dr Julio Villena Aragón was leading the treatment in Argentina. He asked the trainer to talk about Maradona in front of the player. 'All addicts want you to be, as they say, one of them,' continues Signorini. 'That day with Dr Villena Aragón, Diego had said that he was afraid of me. But it wasn't physical fear. He was afraid that I wouldn't respond to him. Actually, he was testing me all the time and I knew it. He needed someone firm, someone he could trust, someone he couldn't bend.' Maradona's physical trainer needed to be the strict father-figure Diego never had.

A month after returning to Buenos Aires, Maradona was arrested along with two others around three o'clock in the afternoon in a flat on Calle Franklin y Rojas, in the Caballito neighbourhood. It was reported he was charged for possessing thirty grams of cocaine. The bust was part of a 'covert' surveillance operation that somehow attracted the attention of reporters, who appeared with cameras and microphones at the building's entrance at the time of the arrest.

'It's a lie that I was found using drugs, a lie,' he told Gabriela Cociffi. 'I didn't realise they were raiding the flat. I was so fast asleep that they had to pull my legs to wake me up. When I woke up, I even shouted, "Claudia!" because I didn't know where I was. I had also taken sleeping pills, I'll confess to that. I was in a bad way.'

Maradona entered the Federal Police anti-drug department crying and was held for more than twenty-four hours. He was released after posting $20,000 bail and returned home, sporting dark circles under his eyes and an unkempt beard of several days.

# 32
# SEVILLA FC

According to the agreement that Marcos Franchi had reached with the Argentine justice system, Diego would not have a criminal record for cocaine possession and use, but he would have to undergo regular court reviews. The judge Amelia Berraz decided not to start legal proceedings; instead, she ordered him to start rehab treatment and to visit the court regularly to confirm his improvement. For nine years, Maradona had pined for his home country, to unwind among the familiar. On arrival, his living nightmare haunted his every step.

'There has been a black hand moving things behind the scenes in Argentina for a long time,' Maradona told journalist Gonzalo Bonadeo in his first interview after his release. 'And now Maradona is the target. Everyone is worried about Maradona, but they don't want to know how Diego is doing. What I did was bad, but compared to what is happening in this country, it's nothing.' A chaotic mix of issues governed his thought processes.

'Maybe because of the pressure I was under and the stress I suffered, I forgot to love myself,' Maradona said on Italy's RAI TV. 'At the end, in Italy, I was like Ayrton Senna, racing a Formula 1 car that never stopped. Now I'm pootling along quietly with my family in a Fiat 500. My life will be very different without professional football, but I've not yet decided what I will do next. But if you ask me today, I will not be back on a pitch again.'

The best player in the world was in the middle of his fifteen-month ban. It sounds bizarre now that it was accepted as though a criminal had been caught, when in fact a drug addict was being punished. His sanction was over on 1 July 1992 and Naples requested his reinstatement for pre-season training. In reality, the club wanted a transfer fee for a player who still had a year left on his contract. Maradona rebuffed a return to Italy, the country 'guilty of everything that happened to me', and daydreamed of signing for a club that would let him play and prepare him for the 1994 World Cup. Marcos Franchi asked Catalan agent Josep María Minguella for a helping hand.

Minguella informed Napoli president Corrado Ferlaino that Maradona was worthless because he wasn't playing. Still, if an affordable price was touted, 'I'll make you some money,' Minguella purred. Ferlaino imposed one condition: that Maradona did not go to another Italian club.

In the summer of 1992, Carlos Bilardo was signed up as coach for the Spanish club Sevilla. Minguella called him. 'But we don't have a single peso,' replied the Argentine. 'I suggested playing friendlies to pay both Napoli and the player,' Minguella told me.

Bilardo accepted Maradona's condition of only training three times a week, while playing his own part in securing the deal. During pre-season, he stated, 'If Diego doesn't come, I'll take my suitcase and go back to Buenos Aires.' The future president of Sevilla and lawyer, José Maria del Nido, negotiated the details of Maradona's contract and admits now that the signing was one of the most complicated of his career, with payments to foreign-based companies creating a tangle of legal issues.

'Bilardo gave a team talk at the hotel where we were staying when it seemed Maradona was going to sign,' explains Sevilla goalkeeper, Juan Carlos Unzué. 'There was a picture on the wall. The manager split the picture into two separate sections and pointing at the top part said, "Here we are, the team and the coaching staff. On the other side of this line, there's Diego. He goes his own way, with different rules and schedules. It's exceptional, but I'm sure he won't let you down. He won't disappoint you."' The reaction was as expected. 'We were living a kind of dream, a legend was coming,' said Monchi, Sevilla's reserve goalkeeper. The three captains, Manolo Jiménez, Rafa Paz and Juan Carlos Unzué, agreed to hand over the captaincy to the newcomer.

Negotiations had dragged on for eighty-six days and were still not concluded when Maradona, about to turn thirty-two, travelled to Seville to force a conclusion. He crossed himself before getting on the plane in Buenos Aires and again once inside it. He hardly slept during the long trip. He spent the night talking to his entourage of Don Diego, Claudia, mother-in-law Ana María Elía, his psychologist Carlos Navedo, agent Marcos Franchi, and a selection of Spanish and Argentine journalists. Diego was returning to football, and his enthusiasm was contagious; he wanted to build another championship-winning team. Upon landing, Franchi announced to the waiting journalists Maradona intended to start training with Sevilla the following Monday, 14 September 1992. Despite still being contractually bound to Napoli, that's precisely what Maradona did.

'When he arrived, we were all at a hotel on the outskirts of Seville,' recalls Unzué. 'I will never forget it. Everyone was in a large room, and he just appeared. He had long hair, was a bit overweight, but . . . he was Maradona, damn it. The coach wanted to get him out of Argentina and put him back into a football environment, a dressing room, so that he could recover and find himself again.'

FIFA wanted to see the player take to the pitch at the 1994 USA World Cup to make it more attractive, and pressurised the two clubs to reach an agreement. On 22 September at the FIFA Players' Status Committee in Zurich, the fee was fiercely debated by the club presidents, Napoli's Ferlaino and Luis Cuervas of Sevilla.

While the final figure was being thrashed out, Maradona went house hunting and visited several villas. Hours passed, and the day stretched as the final fee decision was delayed. Diego, trailed by a pack of international journalists, went to the gym to train, asking them periodically, 'Do we know anything?' In private, Maradona asserted he would retire if he couldn't play for Sevilla. After training, he sat down to eat with his relatives at the hotel. It was almost three o'clock in the afternoon when Franchi received the anticipated call.

The Italians would receive a total of 750 million pesetas ($7.9 million) for Maradona. Sevilla would make an initial payment of 300 million pesetas, followed by four interest-free payments every six months. Minguella sold the friendly rights to several television channels, including Spain's Telecinco, the property of AC Milan owner Silvio Berlusconi, who curiously enough became the transfer's biggest sponsor. If everything went well, Sevilla would not end up out of pocket. In fact, according to Minguella, it would almost be free to the club.

More than 150 journalists from across the world attended Maradona's unveiling ceremony at a hotel in Seville's city centre. Maradona gushed that 'returning to a football pitch is like walking again'. He thanked Ferlaino for giving him his freedom and suggested they should sit down together one day to reminisce about everything they'd been through, a meeting that never took place.

Maradona's Sevilla debut was against Bayern Munich. His first official match was against the same opponent he had faced in his final Barcelona match, Athletic Club de Bilbao. He continued to push himself in training, as he had done for a couple of months, and when Fernando Signorini arrived in November, the man who best knew Diego's limits moulded his pupil into a more powerful form. 'He was trying to train hard, [but also] testing other things that weren't related to football,' Signorini explained in *The Robinson Report* on Canal Plus. 'I could see it was too stressful for him, still being in the eye of the storm.'

Sevilla played friendly matches in Argentina – twice against Boca – Switzerland and Turkey, where 3,000 people greeted his flight. His new teammates were discovering the draw of their new star player. While they returned to their hotel to relax, Maradona had to meet the powers-that-be and receive honours and awards. The one place he could not go, which Telecinco wanted, was Italy: Maradona owed $4 million to a Treasury very eager for him to pay up.

Maradona spent a period living in the Andalusí Park hotel before settling in Simón Verde, a town near Seville. There, he rented the house of Seville's prime bullfighter, Juan Antonio Ruiz Román, 'Spartacus'. The large, brightly coloured house was adorned with bullfighting memorabilia, bullheads and posters, as well as surrounded by spacious patios. 'Impressive,' Maradona wrote in his autobiography. 'The gift I was most grateful for was the peace that the Andalusians gave me.'

Many people spent some time living in that house; his wife and two daughters, his parents, in-laws and Franchi. Staff lived on-site, too – maids, a driver and a couple that ran the house. Maradona's thirty-second birthday party was held there, with a surprise guest. Argentine singer Fabiana Cantilo flew in from Miami, announcing her arrival by singing in the courtyard. 'It was like Diego had seen Madonna,' Monchi says. 'He had to change his shirt several times, because he was soaked in sweat from singing and dancing so much.'

Journalist Enrique Romero described that oasis of tranquillity for *El Gráfico* in May 1993. 'He's changed, he's someone else; Diego Armando Maradona is unrecognisable. He is calm. He trains. He plays. He doesn't go out much. He has fun with his daughters. He always arrives home before ten o'clock at night. A miracle? "Seville is magic," says Diego. His family, his colleagues, the locals and his psychologist performed this miracle.'

'Diego made himself lovable. He was noble and treated us all equally, from the kitman to the veteran players,' says Juan Carlos Unzué. 'He was always looking out for his teammates, defending them against the management and leading the team's demands. He didn't ask for things for himself but for the group. During his first few days at Andalusí Park, he would leave his sports cars for team-mates to try out on the motorway at Huelva.'

The squad, just like Argentinos Juniors many moons before, were delighted to be travelling the world. But when Maradona found out that they were not being paid for the friendlies, he demanded they receive $10,000 per person each game. 'In the league, most of the trips were not on chartered flights, like they are now,' continues Unzué. 'We often stayed in the city where matches were played. Normally we would sneak away, but with Diego we couldn't. Sometimes we would get together in a room, all sixteen of us. He would talk about his experiences and tell us, "I'm sharing all this with you because I'm fond of you and I don't want you to make the same mistakes that I did."'

A callow Diego Simeone looked at Maradona with admiration. Davor Šuker, another rising star from Croatia, was learning his trade from the Argentine. 'Davor,' Diego said to him, 'don't look back, just run ahead, and I'll get the ball to you.' Striker Nacho Conte said, 'I was getting passes and I was thinking, "What am I going to do? I didn't even expect to get the ball."' Maradona won extra seconds with his knowledge of the flight of the ball and the control he applied to it. And he needed that time, as he had lost pace.

'You couldn't guess anything, you would never know where he was going to shoot, not until the last moment,' says goalkeeper Unzué. Monchi adds more: 'He had a small foot, his kicking was clean, the ball moved a lot and dipped very quickly. A goalkeeper has to use his intuition, but Maradona's technique looked the same, whichever side of the ball he ended up hitting.'

Maradona had Gianni Versace clothes brought in from Milan and gifted them to colleagues. 'We went to Barcelona to play against Espanyol,' Monchi remembers. 'We went for a walk in the morning on Las Ramblas. I was wearing a fake Rolex that I bought in Ibiza. "Why didn't you buy a real one?" he asked me. "Man, I don't really earn that much, you know?" Four months later he invited me to his house for dinner. He gave me a bag, and inside was a Cartier watch!'

With Maradona on the teamsheet, Sevilla had a record 38,000 season-ticket sales. National sports newspapers sold more copies with him on the cover than with any other player from Barcelona or Madrid. 'It was so difficult for Maradona,' surmises Unzué. 'I remember there being fifty television cameras in the training complex, and three thousand people just to watch him train! And Sevilla was on all the news programmes across the world.' Dozens of kids wanted autographs at the end of training sessions. 'We had to wait for him whenever we went for lunch together,' remembers Unzué. 'In Seville, some people are a bit cheeky. Once someone touched his hair, something he couldn't stand. He turned around and snapped, "What are you doing?" And that was the only clip they showed on the news.'

'He spent a lot of time locked up at home, and when he needed to get out he went to Málaga, to Jerez,' his teammate Pepe Prieto told website A la contra. 'We had team dinners every three weeks, and he always came. They would close the restaurant for us.' Diego told Signorini that 'he felt like another gipsy', seeing himself reflected – the marginalised, the punished, the partygoer – within the ethnic group that lived in some neighbourhoods of the city.

'You dream of reaching the top, of being the best in the world, but it comes at a price, and we saw that with Diego Armando,' Rafa Paz explained to ESPN.com. 'You need huge mental strength to deal with that. We tried to help, and we even had strategies to do so, but he had tendencies he couldn't control.'

Maradona was still receiving steroids, anti-inflammatory drugs and painkillers, allowed at the time for his fragile ankle. 'They usually injected you if you were in pain,' says Unzué. 'We didn't know what they gave us. He had to play with injections, from Sunday to Sunday. We are a generation for whom complaining was forbidden. They took away the pain, but we didn't think about the origin of the pain.'

Maradona scored and starred in a league game against Sporting Gijon. He would come alive with short-term projects, losing five kilos before a pre-Christmas home game against Real Madrid at the Ramón Sánchez Pizjuán stadium. It was his best match in the Sevilla shirt, a 2-0 victory illuminated with several of his trademark wonder passes. 'It was the first game in which he dared to face up to his rivals,' Unzué remembers. 'Until then, it was "Give me the ball, and I'll distribute it." He had not been in good physical condition.' Before 1992 drew to a close, Maradona was hinting at renewing his Sevilla contract.

Maradona's body continued to pain him, from his knees to his back. He spent a lot of time on the recovery table, and was frequently absent from morning training sessions. Fewer journalists came to the sports complex. Maradona still had to travel back to Argentina to comply with his judicial rehabilitation agreement, and after one of those trips – and especially after the Madrid match – he was even less visible. Bilardo believes the decline came even earlier. 'I think he "went" when he started to get lower-back pain,' he told *ABC* years later. 'Those fifteen, twenty days when he stopped because of it. He found it hard to get started up again. It was after the match against Oviedo [in November].'

Expectations were not being met and a watershed moment passed: a 2-0 defeat against Logroñés on 21 February 1993. Maradona and Diego Simeone had been called up by the national team to play two friendly matches that coincided with the Logroñés match. Against the club's wishes, Diego chartered a plane to fly to Argentina after the match. His anger towards Cuervas and del Nido, who did not want to let him go, was tremendous. From that moment on, his sciatic pain became more severe, and his motivation dwindled. Maradona gained weight and sought any manner of excuse to miss more training sessions, even matches.

Sevilla opened disciplinary proceedings against the two Argentinians. The club paid Maradona the $1,350,000 stipulated in his contract till that point, but examined how to avoid paying the fourth and final instalment of his salary due in May, based on the understanding that his time at the club was over. The directors informed the media that the failed Maradona deal would cost the club more than 200 million pesetas, as payments for friendlies were reduced.

'The feeling we got from the squad was that the club had decided Maradona didn't represent the future, and his time was over,' Pepe Prieto told the *A la contra* website. 'Economically, it was a big hit. They tried to renegotiate and change conditions in the contract. Maradona felt the club didn't trust him, and the relationship deteriorated.'

In a game against Cádiz, Maradona overheard the opposition bench insult him a few times during the game and reacted after the final whistle. Police officers had to restrain him. La Liga suspended Maradona for two games. The player told the media there was mafia outside Italy too.

The club hired an agency to investigate the footballer's private life, building up a dossier for future legal battles. Staff were aware of the surveillance. 'They were very sloppy,' Prieto confirmed with *A la contra* website. 'The detective was chasing him on a scooter while Maradona was in a Porsche.'

Manuel Aguilar was dedicated to reporting exclusively on Maradona at the time. He told *A la contra*: 'Del Nido showed Maradona a briefcase which had a videotape in it. He told the player he had to forgo some of the money owed by Sevilla. If he didn't, the tape would go public.' Journalist José Manuel García recounted something similar. 'Sevilla blackmailed Maradona, using detectives and documents, so as not to pay him the million and a half dollars they owed him.' It was already known Maradona used cocaine, and giving up more than a million or whatever figure it was suggests some great embarrassment. Just what had the detective found out? What was on the tape? Or was it all a perfect bluff?

By the end of May, Telecinco wanted to sever its ties with Maradona – he repeatedly broke agreements with no-shows on programmes, drastically reducing Sevilla's income.

'When he was at crisis point, he shut himself away and slept it off,' admits Pepe Prieto, 'using anti-anxiety drugs to be as relaxed as possible. And when he woke up, he would go and train. One day he got caught speeding by the police.' A training session in May had been changed from the usual training complex to the Ramón Sánchez Pizjuán stadium; Maradona tanked his Porsche at 120km per hour (75mph) through the Seville city centre.

On 23 May, Madrid's Bernabéu stadium filled in anticipation of seeing Maradona. The following day's newspapers were scathing about an 'absent' performance that was 'pitiful'. By 12 June 1993, Maradona's Sevilla adventure was over. In the team's penultimate league game against Burgos at home, Diego took a half-time painkilling injection to play the second half. Coach Bilardo substituted his star player seven minutes after the restart. Maradona threw away the captain's armband and didn't even shake hands with Pineda, who was replacing him. 'Son of a bitch!' Diego shouted at Bilardo, who was ignoring his player. Maradona went straight to the changing rooms.

Bilardo saw Maradona's reaction that night on television. He went straight to Diego's house, but he had fled to Madrid. On Monday the 14th, the club's board of directors informed the press they were considering rescinding Maradona's contract because of his lifestyle, backed up by their detective's dossier.

The manager fretted and hardly slept until the footballer's return three days later. In the dressing room, Maradona apologised to Pineda. A rueful Bilardo paid another visit to the footballer's residence in the afternoon. 'I took three big needles to carry on, and you subbed me anyway,' Maradona spat out, as told in his book *Yo Soy El Diego*. 'Then he came at me and pushed me. I lost it. I punched him.

Bam! I threw him to the floor, he dropped, pinned to the floor. And when I was going to hit him again . . . I couldn't, I couldn't. Claudia came, Marcos came, they grabbed hold of him. Diego kept shouting: 'Never again for Sevilla, never again. I want to quit football rather than play again. We're leaving.'

Sevilla finished seventh and missed out on European qualification. They ripped up Maradona's contract, citing non-compliance, and persuaded disgruntled fans, their expectations crushed, to side with them. Maradona had played thirty official matches – the club didn't collect data from the friendly games at that time – some twenty-six in La Liga and four in the Copa del Rey, scoring seven goals in total. It would take another year for the two parties to reach a financial agreement. Sevilla withdrew their claim for damages, and the player forfeited his final salary payment.

In the afternoon of 23 June 1993, Diego Armando Maradona left Seville, ten kilos overweight and wearing sunglasses to hide the despondency his eyes couldn't disguise. He knew irredeemably he was no longer fit to play for the elite.

# 33
# NEWELL'S OLD BOYS AND THE ROAD TO WORLD CUP USA 94

Newell's Old Boys coach Jorge 'El Indio' Solari suddenly switched training to the unusual time of 6pm. It was also rare for him to be making the three-hour trip from Rosario to Buenos Aires so often. The experienced players felt that something was up and wanted an explanation.

'Lads, what would you think if we signed Maradona?' asked Solari. After leaving Sevilla two months earlier, Diego was listening to offers. 'Maradona at Newell's? Impossible!' The person vocally expressing his doubts was the team's starting centre-back, Mauricio Pochettino.

'It could be a possibility,' El Indio responded. 'What would you think?'

'We'd die of excitement!'

The idea of recruiting Diego had first occurred to Ricardo 'El Gringo' Giusti, a former teammate of his who worked as an agent, while watching a Newell's match: 'They need a boost and I know just the guy.'

Thanks to journeys to Buenos Aires and never-ending conversations between Diego and El Indio, and Diego and El Gringo, the offer became simply irresistible.

Around that time, along with agent Marcos Franchi and Claudia, Maradona witnessed Argentina being crushed 5-0 by a Colombia side containing the great Carlos Valderrama and Faustino Asprilla at El Monumental, Buenos Aires, nine months before the 1994 USA

World Cup. The result saw the fans clamour for Diego's return, and a call from the Julio Grondona, the AFA president, soon followed.

The national team had survived in his absence by winning the Copa América in 1991 and 1993, under the stewardship of Alfio Basile, with new stars Gabriel Batistuta and Diego Simeone, yet qualifying for the World Cup had become a struggle.

Franchi recalls Grondona saying to him, 'We need him, he has to come back, he has to get fit, no matter what. If he needs help . . .'

A week later, Diego accepted the offer from Newell's. His salary was going to be 40 per cent higher than the top earner and he would receive a percentage of the revenue from friendlies, especially the lucrative ones at the end of the campaign. Maradona asked for something else – a gift for the rest of the squad, whose bonuses were doubled.

Seven days after that, he had a meeting with national coach Basile in Ezeiza and his return to the national team was announced.

He wanted to see, feel, be cheered by a packed-out stadium once again.

*El Gringo* Giusti gave Diego's phone number to some of the other players in the squad, including Pochettino: 'Should I phone him? How do I address him? Diego, Maradona or what?' He was about to call the guy who was endlessly controlling a ball in a poster hanging above his bed, and who had watched over him sleeping every night in his first flat in Rosario.

'Yes, Diego, it's Mauricio Pochettino. I'm going to be your teammate.'

'*Poche!* How are you doing, *Poche*? I'm very grateful to you for phoning me, I'll soon be heading over there . . .' Pochettino could not string a sentence together, dumbstruck.

The airport was heaving upon his arrival. Hundreds of fans headed there to get a glimpse of Diego, Claudia, Don Diego, Gianinna and Dalma. He signed on 9 September and was unveiled to 40,000 people on Monday the 13th. Even the odd Rosario Central flag could be seen in an unlikely showing of respect from rival supporters. The players looked at one another, mesmerised by Diego's aura: 'No way is Maradona here with us.'

There was no gym at Newell's, so the club made use of the facilities on nearby Mendoza Street. Diego was diligent in his training, working hard to build up strength in the morning and then joining the squad in the afternoon. He would often watch matches on TV with the team. Once, a player attempted an overly ambitious shot and Pochettino shouted out, 'Look at that guy! He thinks he's Maradona?' Mauricio, suddenly realising what he had just said, turned quickly to him waiting for a reaction. Maradona exploded with laughter.

His Newell's debut was in a friendly against Emelec of Ecuador in October. El Coloso was filled to the rafters and there was a special little fan in attendance – none other than a six-year-old Leo Messi who was even asked to do (and did) keepy-uppies on the pitch. Maradona scored a goal with his right foot that was celebrated as if it were the first or last. Friends and supporters of all ages jumped onto the grass, and the photographers ran after him. Many players asked for his shirt after the game, but that was already reserved for Fidel Castro.

When he wasn't with the team, Maradona barely had a social life. It calmed him down, but also intimidated him not to have people around him. He would butt into conversations with random people at the bar in the hotel where he was staying.

One day at the training ground, Carlos Haro, who worked for the club in ticket sales, went to the toilet in the dressing room and found him showering with his head raised and eyes shut. Diego noticed his presence.

'What's happening, *gordo*?'

'Nothing, Diego. Erm ... How does it feel there, on your own, without anyone harassing you?'

'I'd happily live in the shower for ever.'

That eternal battle ...

For the first time in two years and seven months, Diego got called up by Argentina for the World Cup play-off against Australia, a step either to reliving success or to total failure.

The World Cup organisers had used real celebrities to grab the attention of US soccer fans (Bill Clinton, Rod Stewart, Stevie Wonder,

Faye Dunaway) and yet a survey suggested that 90 per cent of the population didn't know that the World Cup was going to be held on home soil. Only Diego Maradona was recognisable in such an 'exotic' sport. The major sponsors and FIFA needed him.

Maradona led his countrymen forward and helped seal qualification. Incidentally, there were no doping tests during the play-off tie.

Julio Zamora, a regular under Basile who had missed out on the squad for the Australia fixture, received a call from Diego: 'Mate, I just got a cheque from the AFA for qualifying for the World Cup. Half of it is yours.'

During training, you could often hear calls of 'Diego, Diego' from behind the fences by an elderly lady. 'Peek over to see what's going on,' Maradona asked one of the assistant coaches. 'She wants to speak to you.' Diego duly obliged. A few days later, he arrived with a folded rectangular piece of paper. 'Give it to her. Don't let anyone find out,' he told an assistant. 'What have you given the old woman?' The assistant couldn't stop himself and looked at it. It was a cheque for $8,500. It had happened before and it would happen again.

Although he did not get injured, Diego was finding it harder and harder to recover from physical efforts. His legs weren't responding in the way that he wanted, and he had gone five matches without scoring. On 26 January 1994 he faced the Vasco de Gama team from Brazil and was then supposed to feature in another friendly in Mar del Plata, but it had to be cancelled and ticket refunds were issued. Diego had disappeared.

Soon afterwards, it was communicated that after five official games and two friendlies the contract would be rescinded 'by mutual consent'. Maradona claimed that it was the president's fault and that he wanted to return: 'I apologise to the Newell's fans for not meeting your expectations.'

But there remained a short-term goal in place. Diego called Fernando Signorini to help him reach the World Cup, but the fitness coach refused: 'What for? You've already played in three!' Maradona came out with a whole host of reasons, including that it would be the first time that Dalma and Gianinna would see him play in one. He said to Signorini, 'You choose the location.'

Maradona weighed 104 kilos (16st 5lbs) three months before the World Cup. He boarded an outdated light aircraft to where Fernando Signorini had set up a field, 40km from Santa Rosa in the province of La Pampa. 'Here?' the player asked.

'I've brought you to Fiorito. We're going to be alone here with no distractions, which is what you need. If you want to get back to the top, as it says in the lyrics to the "El Choclo" tango, you have to leave "the sordid bog and look for heaven".'

Daniel Cerrini, a bodybuilding coach introduced by Cóppola to the group, was also involved in the training camp, which consisted of three daily sessions. He was taking care of Diego's diet and made him take a large number of pills, which Signorini grew suspicious of: 'I said to him, "No, not that way. Diego, you'll get there with nourishing food, none of these strange things."' But Maradona took them.

'We stayed there for twelve marvellous days,' 'recalls Signorini'. 'It may well have been the best time of my life. He put his nose to the grindstone and I remember that he had stopped taking cocaine of his own volition. He left it in Buenos Aires and didn't bring even half a milligram with him.'

Signorini heard a noise one night and went to see what it was. Diego was at his door, staring at him intently. He gestured with his head and neck to tell Signorini to follow him. 'And I understood, so I quickly put on my shoes, wrapped myself up warmly and off we went. He was having withdrawal symptoms. We ran them off, up and down, another sprint, another lap. "Ahhhh! I'm better now." It had passed. Remembering that makes me emotional because only Diego and I know what a huge effort he put into defeating that bloody cocaine and make Dalma and Gianinna happy. It was a gesture of love towards them and the ball. In a way, the World Cup was incidental.'

After those days of total dedication, which included playing in a friendly against Morocco, the group headed to another base in Norberto de la Riestra in Buenos Aires province, before joining up with Basile's national team. The squad had some sensational players: Redondo, Ruggeri, Simeone, Batistuta, Ortega . . . An elaborate and jumbled tour covering Chile, Ecuador, Israel and Croatia was organised, although it didn't yield good results and led to doubts about the side's credentials. Maradona threatened to go back to Buenos Aires on two occasions.

Caniggia explained the situation on lanzalaboladeportes.com: 'It all started with a flight to New York. We were World Cup winners in 1986 and runners-up in 1990, and yet before the 1994 World Cup kicked off they stuck us on a thirteen-hour flight in economy class. Two of us were here, another two further back, all with people we didn't know. Maradona was sitting with three tourists. I was in a row of three with a man in the middle who I didn't know. Batistuta was also with two strangers.' There were twenty-two players scattered among 250 people. Diego was getting irritated. Basile went over to him and said, 'There's space in business class,' and Maradona answered, 'I'll stay here with all my teammates.'

After finally arriving in New York the team couldn't find anywhere to train. The coaching staff asked the players to take a taxi to a park, which turned out to be waste ground with worn grass, broken glass and stray dogs. Maradona couldn't take it any more. He didn't want to stay and said as much, although it was more of a threat to provoke a reaction from the AFA.

One night, at around 2am, another type of anxiety overcame Maradona, who was pacing around the hotel lobby. The hotel felt like a maze to him, as he shouted out that he wanted to go home and talk to Claudia. Carlos Losauro, a boxing specialist who was covering the World Cup for *La Nación*, called him over to the bar and said, 'Come over here, sit down and stop messing about. Let's talk boxing, come.' Diego obeyed. 'Yes, you're right. Let's talk boxing.' He calmed down.

Nobody wanted anything to go wrong and just in case, the Argentina medical team suggested a surprise doping test to Grondona, which they could pass off as a FIFA requirement for everyone, not just Diego. The president said that it would be a nuisance for the players, and refused to allow it.

In spite of everything, the ups and downs, Diego had developed a feeling of well-being. He had the level of fitness that he wanted under Signorini and trained with Dalma and Gianinna at the gym on the last day. His weight had gone down to 74.5 kilos, which was even lower than in 1986.

'We were so happy, Fernando was so happy,' Maradona recalled. 'I knew that, even though we didn't voice our feelings to each other. We kept looking at each other and thinking, "We got to where we wanted to be." Now the World Cup starts for us.'

# 34
# THE DOPING IN THE 1994 WORLD CUP

On the way to Foxboro Stadium, which has since been demolished and turned into an enormous shopping precinct, the Greek and Argentine fans brought colour to an atmosphere that otherwise could have been closer to an IT conference than a World Cup. Although FIFA used Diego's image in the press to draw in fans from around Massachusetts state, there was no sign of advertisements or photos of him around the stadium.

Maradona had lost weight, and he glided about the pitch with all the nimbleness of former days. He got on the scoresheet alongside hat-trick hero Gabriel Batistuta in a comfortable win over Greece in Argentina's opening game on Tuesday, 21 June. Diego's goal was preceded by intricate interplay between Abel Balbo, Fernando Redondo and Claudio Caniggia. Maradona finished it off by putting the ball where nobody expected with the accuracy of a darts player who can hit the bullseye from the 2.37-metre line.

He had returned, although this would prove to be his last international goal. He had shared his orgasmic celebration with a TV camera, and in so doing had left an image portraying the ecstasy of revenge, which was and still is logically misinterpreted.

Nigeria were the next opponents on the Saturday, once again at Foxboro Stadium. The Super Eagles were a strong side, with plenty of quality. How could they be beaten?

The players of both national teams were waiting in the tunnel for the referee for what seemed an eternity. Diego suddenly started hugging each of his opponents. 'Brother! My friend!' More and more hugs ensued. Maradona even greeted them by name. The Nigerians couldn't believe it. It was behaviour more associated with post-match pleasantries, rather than before a potential qualification decider. Not much was done by chance with Diego with regard to winning a game. It eventually kicked off. Maradona was barely touched by the rivals and Nigeria hardly put up walls for set-pieces.

The Africans opened the scoring, which seemed to fire up Diego, as he chased every ball. Caniggia turned the contest on its head with a brace, the second of which stemmed from a quick free-kick by Maradona that caught the opposition off-guard. That Argentina team, with Simeone, Redondo, Ruggeri, Balbo and Batistuta, had made it through to the next round and become contenders to win the tournament.

An indelible picture was conjured up at the end of the match. Diego left the pitch hand in hand with a blonde nurse. What was she doing there? But Sue Carpenter was not a nurse but one of the four FIFA helpers who were tasked with taking the players to their urine doping tests. She decided to wear white that day. But did she need to approach Maradona in front of everyone? And take him by the hand?

Minutes before the end of the game, Carpenter was in the tunnel talking to Dr Roberto Peidró, part of the Argentina medical team, and she mentioned that her ex-husband was Argentine. When it was discovered that Maradona and defender Sergio Vázquez were going to be tested, Peidró had a suggestion: 'Go and get Maradona. Your ex-husband will recognise you on the television.'

Already on the pitch, a Chilean member of the FIFA press office stepped in between Maradona and Carpenter. 'What's happening with this girl?' asked Diego. 'She's come to escort you,' replied the Chilean. 'OK, let me say hi to Claudia and my people first.' Looking and smiling cheekily towards his wife, Maradona shouted in her direction, 'I'm going to inject this nurse with something myself.' That sent Claudia into fits of laughter.

In the directors' box, the head of the Argentine federation, Julio Grondona, made the sign of the cross and muttered, 'God help us.'

On the early afternoon of the day before the final group game against surprise package Bulgaria, the Argentina squad made a technical stop-over in Baltimore during the American Airlines flight from their base in Boston to Dallas, where they were going to train at the match venue, the Cotton Bowl, that same evening. Coach *Coco* Basile got off the plane for a moment feeling content: things were going according to plan. Then an official came up to him and ensured nobody else was nearby before saying, '*Coco*, there's a positive. We don't know who yet.'

'What are you talking about?' Basile couldn't believe it and feared the worst.

On the plane from Baltimore to Dallas, Basile asked an assistant to bring Sergio Vázquez over to him. 'Did you take anything? Did you do something you shouldn't have done?' he asked him.

'No, nothing.'

Diego immediately realised that something was up, but Basile decided not to talk to him during the journey.

When they landed, the squad was faced with the first of many groups of journalists looking for a reaction. Nobody stopped to talk to them and the players got on the coach to head to the hotel, where reporters were gathered on the stairs of the entrance.

Diego's urine sample, which contained a code but not his name, had been sent off to Los Angeles. He had tested positive for pseudoephedrine, which was a banned substance according to FIFA but is sold over the counter in the United States. Daniel Cerrini, who wasn't trusted by Diego's inner circle, had made a mistake in buying Ripped Fuel, which came in two versions: with or without pseudoephedrine. Either Cerrini didn't see the label (stating 6 per cent ephedrine) or he felt it was an insignificant amount.

FIFA secretary-general Sepp Blatter had informed Grondona, who was already in Dallas. 'Let's do it together,' the AFA boss told the Argentina head coach at the hotel. Basile and Grondona both went to speak to Diego and there were tears. The team coach soon headed to the Cotton Bowl for training where more journalists were lying in wait.

Grondona told Basile that there was a glimmer of hope. During the World Cup in Mexico, the Spaniard Ramón Calderé was tested positive for pseudoephedrine and received only a one-match ban.

'We'll make the same defence,' he said. 'We'll meet at 8.30 in the morning at the FIFA hotel.' Basile did not get any sleep during what he later admitted was the worst night of his life.

Back at the team hotel in Dallas, somebody knocked on the door of Signorini's room. He had not gone to the stadium with the squad.

'Who is it?'

It was Cerrini. 'Have you heard the news?' he asked.

Fernando replied, full of anger, 'What are you doing here? Get on a plane to the end of the world because Don Diego is on the way and if he sees you here, he'll shoot you. Get on a plane to somewhere as far away as you can get!'

During breakfast the next morning, the national team coach received a call and headed to the reception to take it. It was Grondona. 'We're almost ready to go and meet you,' said Basile. The AFA president replied, 'No need.'

FIFA president João Havelange had told Grondona that Maradona was going to be suspended, and the win over Nigeria was going to be overturned, with the national side sent home and disallowed from taking part in the following World Cup. 'No, I don't think we will do that,' said Grondona, who mentioned to the head of FIFA some topics that nobody wanted uncovered: didn't Havelange give Juan Antonio Samaranch, president of the International Olympic Committee (IOC), money to fill some gaps from the Olympic Games in Barcelona? Where did the money go? Did it end up by chance in the pockets of the head of the Brazilian Football Confederation, Ricardo Teixeira? And so on.

After an unpleasant discussion, they reached an agreement that avoided a sizeable punishment for the AFA, but one that left Havelange, who felt part of the sport's aristocracy, content as it would be sold to the world as an exemplary punishment based on the IOC anti-doping rules.

Maradona had to be pulled out of the World Cup squad by the AFA, with his sanction to be determined further down the line, after the completion of the tournament.

Grondona broke the news to Basile over the phone: 'You don't need to come here. Diego is banned from the World Cup. He has to leave the hotel and can't be around our travelling party.' Basile wanted to die, which is how he described his own feelings years later.

Signorini, who had been informed of the suspension, made his way to Diego's room: 'It was all dark and I gave him a shake ... "Come on, Diego, up you get. They've annihilated us." I said "us" to convey that it hadn't only happened to him; it had happened to all of us and it was a way of showing our solidarity. He was pretending to be asleep, as if he could banish the moment. "What's happened?" "It's over, Diego." I headed out and left him alone. I shut the door and heard a thud followed by a cry that encompassed a range of emotions, anger and anguish, all rolled into one.'

In the next few minutes, his agent Franchi, Ruggeri and Signorini went into his room to try to calm him down. 'It's over, *Diegucho* ... That's it, over, go home, it's over, they killed us ...'

In a press conference, FIFA gave details of the suspension and reserved a decision on any further punishment for Maradona until after the World Cup. Havelange said, 'The United States spend $50 billion per year on fighting drug addiction. Do you think we could let a case like this pass?'

Argentina, morale destroyed, lost 2-0 to Bulgaria at the Cotton Bowl. They were knocked out in Los Angeles by Romania in the next round.

In August that year, FIFA eventually announced the punishment: a fifteen-month ban from football for Maradona, domestically and internationally, plus a fine of 20,000 Swiss francs. Daniel Cerrini got the same treatment. The AFA couldn't appeal.

Nowadays, the ephedrine that Diego took would not be considered doping. The doubt remains over why there were no doping tests in the play-offs against Australia. Perhaps FIFA felt it was necessary that Maradona play in the World Cup. Certainly Grondona went a long way to make sure that he did.

As the only travelling party that had a player who was not in line with the regulations, the AFA directors might have expected a punishment from the governing body. Grondona, however, stayed on as FIFA vice-president and president of the organisation's finance committee, despite not speaking a word of English.

Maradona had won a total of ninety-one Argentina caps and scored thirty-four goals. The 1994 World Cup was his last involvement in international football as a player, but certainly not his final dispute with FIFA. The bird was not just punished, rather its wings had been cut off. 'It was very sad,' explained Signorini, 'because he'd made such a monumental effort, including the fact that he left cocaine in Buenos Aires and risked suffering from withdrawal symptoms, which are awful. There was now no real chance of a return to the top again.'

Maradona decided to speak out soon after his dismissal. Argentine journalist Adrián Paenza's described the interview in the podcast *¡Hola! ¿Qué tal, cómo estás?*

When the doping story broke, I arranged with his agent Marcos Franchi to speak to Diego, because the whole country was waiting. It was a very delicate situation. The hotel in Dallas was a tall cylinder with 5,000 journalists outside, or so it seemed. We arrived and when the door opened I could see Diego sitting in the shadows in a Buddha position on a large armchair. When he saw me, he got up, came over to hug me and started crying in a way that made me cry as well, as if someone's son had died. He was saying to me, 'I didn't take drugs, I didn't take drugs.' Grondona then came in and asked me, 'What are you doing here?' Diego replied, 'What does it matter to you? Adrián is my friend and he's staying here. You've already kicked me off; I'm no longer part of the national team.' Marcos Franchi told me to go to his room, a few doors away, and wait there. Diego came in and we did the interview.

MARADONA: It really hurts because they've cut off my legs. They've taken me down during a time when I had the chance to come back from so many things. The day I took drugs, I went and said to the judge, 'Yes, I took drugs. What's the punishment?' I accepted it. It was a very tough two years of going every two or three months, or whenever the judge called me, so that they could give me a rhinoscopy and take a urine sample, but I just don't understand this . . . I thought the justice system would be good, but it looks like they got it wrong with me.

PAENZA: So why did that substance show up, Diego?

MARADONA: I don't know why. Maybe because of an oversight by us, but I swear on my daughters' lives that I didn't take drugs. I think they've kicked me out of football definitively because I don't think there'll be another comeback. I promised my wife that I wasn't going to cry and I promised my daughters, but . . .

# 35

# BOCA JUNIORS AGAIN IN THE SLIDE DOWN

Maradona's fifteen-month ban stretched to September 1995, and although he wasn't allowed to play, he could manage. Former Argentina national goalkeeper Sergio Goycochea was turning out for Deportivo Mandiyú in Corrientes and helped coax Maradona into accepting the managerial role at the club. Once more, Diego was swimming back upstream towards his roots, working for a club close to where his grandmother and father had settled after leaving Santiago del Estero. He knew the area well: he would often go fishing there with Don Diego during his recuperation and refuge phases.

Carlos Fren had been in the same Argentinos Juniors first team as Maradona, and was offered the role of his assistant. 'It's perfect, it will keep you busy, so if you want, we'll go,' Fren said. The duo shared training sessions and ideas about how Diego's footballing blueprint could stave off relegation from the premier division. Their ongoing discussions took place around a barbecue – and also on fishing trips to a lake, which meant the club freezer was soon full of fish. Maradona would stay at the team hotel the day before a game while Fren fine-tuned tactics with the squad. Matchdays saw the sunny side of Diego, the new coach transmitting positive energy and motivation.

Maradona's coaching debut was a 2-1 home defeat by Rosario Central on 9 October 1994, but he had to watch from the stands as he awaited his trainer's licence and authorisation from the Argentine Football Association. A few games later, Deportivo Mandiyú almost beat River Plate in a 2-2 away draw. After a home loss to Independiente, Maradona accused referee Ángel Sánchez of being a mafioso and launched a verbal assault on Independiente's president.

If his team was playing in Buenos Aires, Maradona travelled the day before the game. After all, Buenos Aires was where the action was.

An intense opening two months brought Maradona one victory and six draws from twelve games. Such form compelled the Mandiyú president Roberto Cruz to storm the dressing-room to dish out insults and tactical advice. 'I'm in charge here,' Maradona countered, then handed in his resignation.

Despite leaving Mandiyú on the verge of relegation, the president of Buenos Aires' historic and popular Racing Club, Juan Destéfano, opened negotiations with him. The now thirty-four-year-old Maradona asked Cóppola to return and seal the deal that saw him take over Racing's managerial reins in early 1995. Amid all the activity, Maradona, banned from the pitch, received the Ballon d'Or from France Football in recognition of his playing career.

Fren stepped up to the challenge of being Maradona's number two at Racing too, despite the disparity in remuneration. Mandiyú paid Fren US$15,000 a month, while Racing Club offered 'ten pesos. It was one of those strange deals Maradona used to do, but I just wanted to work,' explained his assistant. However, the waters soon muddied. Diego started to miss training sessions and then matches. 'Diego's routine was totally destroyed even before full retirement, and without the rigour of proper training and devoid of real motivation – apart from having an audience – alcohol became his crutch.

Before a game against San Lorenzo, Fren had to tell Maradona he was an 'embarrassment' to everyone. They had agreed to go out on the pitch in suits. However, Maradona had had a row with Claudia and he didn't have the right clothes. They both gave the team talk, but as they were walking out on to the pitch Fren realised something wasn't right. They locked themselves in the dressing-room and Fren told Maradona some home truths. He started to cry, saying it was beyond his control. The match was lost 2-1 and Maradona disappeared. Fren didn't see him again for two or three weeks.

The Racing Club adventure lasted four months, with two victories in eleven matches. A few days after his departure, Maradona went with Fren to meet the directors of Boca Juniors, the club he dreamed of managing. On the way back, they stopped at the waterfront in front of the airport. Maradona leaned against the barrier where people fish, looking out over the river. He challenged Fren: 'Seeing as you know everything, what's wrong with me?'

'It's obvious what's wrong with you. Half your brain wants to go home to Claudia and the girls, and the other half wants to go and end up like you always do,' Fren replied. Maradona tearfully told Fren he was right, then ended up in a nightclub until the early hours.

'They used Maradona,' said Fren. On 27 December, Fren's birthday, Diego called him at three in the morning from Cóppola's house. He was depressed. The others had gone to Punta del Este and left him at home for three days. Fren went over to find him in a bad state crying because he had fought with Claudia. His assistant took him to Claudia's house. A few days later, Maradona called Fren and thanked him, because he'd spent New Year's Eve with his daughters.

Argentina was led from 1989 to 1999 by President Carlos Saúl Menem of the Peronist Partido Justicialista, ushering in the so-called Menemist era that echoed a period of global hedonism. Menem encouraged state company privatisations and promoted the illogical parity of the US dollar and the Argentine peso. He was spotted driving his sports cars and having his photograph taken with icons as diverse as the Rolling Stones, Bill Clinton and Maradona. That era of extravagant wastefulness would eventually lead the country into debt and social chaos. But before the predictably severe crisis of 2001, Argentine football experienced its own enlightened period, with top internationals in all the major teams. Some were returning from abroad, while younger South American stars showed off their talent at home without European giants picking them off with inflated transfer fees. River Plate, San Lorenzo, Vélez Sarsfield, Racing Club and Independiente all fought Boca for the cherished title.

In 1995, Pelé met Diego in Brazil with the idea of signing him for Pelé's old team, Santos, as soon as the FIFA ban was lifted. It was leaked that an agreement had been reached, maybe to generate publicity for both player and club. But it was yet again a half-baked project, like many others involving Diego.

It was always going to be Boca that drew him back. Not content with announcing his desire to play once more for Boca, Maradona wanted to train them too. The club's management kept Silvio Marzolini as coach, but the league's desire to shine demanded return of its football genius. Several business people pooled resources to pay his salary, allowing Maradona to don the Boca colours as a player once more.

Once again Daniel Cerrini helped him get into shape at Punta del Este. The player made his second Boca debut in a 2-1 friendly win against a South Korea team in Seoul in September 1995, fourteen years after his first appearance in their shirt. Maradona provided an assist before being subbed, a trademark in-swinging corner setting up Boca's opener.

More than 300 journalists from all over the world were in attendance. The media itself was metamorphosing. With more broadcast hours dedicated to football, the press devoured the sweetmeats of Diego's return as he played alongside legends like Carlos Navarro Montoya, Cristian 'Kily' González and Claudio Caniggia, setting up Boca for a mouth-watering title challenge.

But training bored Maradona. He satiated his appetite for confrontation with authority by helping Eric Cantona create the World Footballers' Union (which only lasted two years) and enhanced his prestige by accepting awards such as Oxford University L'Chaim Society's 'Master Inspirer of Oxford Dreamers' diploma.

As the season unfolded, Boca led league challengers Vélez by six points at one time, but a late-season collapse saw the Xeneize finish a distant fifth. 'I did think about becoming the coach on the pitch,' Maradona wrote in his autobiography. 'I didn't think Marzolini would get angry.' Maradona threatened to leave Boca, whose response at the end of the season was to sack Marzolini and to choose a new chairman, the future Argentina president Mauricio Macri.

The ever-expanding football industry grew fearful of the looming possibility of Maradona's retirement. The AFA banned Juan Funes from playing because of his heart problem. Maradona carried the same risk but was allowed to keep playing, despite almost fifteen years' cocaine addiction taking its toll. Some parts of the media asked cocaine not to be included in the list of banned substances, as it did not affect positive performances on the pitch, thus trying to make football subservient to its idol's requirements.

Boca chose Carlos Bilardo to lead them for the 1996–97 season, a move which once again pushed Maradona into making threats to leave. He remembered all too well the pair's clashes at Sevilla. He finally acquiesced, went through another detoxification process and started to get into shape in March 1996. The great midfielder Juan Sebastian Verón joined the club too, hoping to boost Boca's potency.

Maradona was dictating games with his passing, but covered little ground and didn't always play the ninety minutes. He missed a penalty against Newell's Old Boys, then tore his left calf muscle, putting him on the sidelines for a month. By June, Boca's performances continued to drop. In a game against Vélez, referee Javier Castrilli sent off an apoplectic Maradona. Diego shouted at Castrilli, 'Speak to me. Or are you dead?' In his book, *Yo Soy El Diego*, he added, 'If it had been up to me, I would have broken his jaw.'

Castrilli himself thinks the two had contrasting ways of understanding life:

It was all because of a goal Vélez scored. That was the trigger. Boca were winning 1-0 until the incident. My assistant tells me that Boca's goalkeeper, Carlos Navarro Montoya, has carried the ball over the goal-line. I have to give the goal. That was when Boca lost it [they were eventually defeated 5-1] because instead of playing against Vélez they started to play against the referee's decisions. The players were outraged, out of their minds and treating me like a madman.

Then the sendings-off started, and [the] Boca crowd's response was violent, breaking fences and trying to invade the pitch. In the middle of the commotion is Maradona. He is about seven or eight metres away from me, now coming towards me, pointing to what's happening, police throwing tear gas, firefighters throwing cold water over people on what was a freezing cold night, and he was pointing at me. I interpret this as an incitement to violence and send him straight off. As I'm walking towards him, I notice that he has seen the red card, and he turns around and leaves. I show him the card, and I head for the centre-circle. I don't remember if it was a journalist or a policeman who asked me if there were any way to reverse the red card. I told him no – while I'm here in charge, Maradona doesn't play. Just at that moment, when the police had got everything under control, I found myself among a large group of people. In the middle of them, in front of the cameras, was Maradona, who was supposedly coming to ask me for an explanation, even though he knew why he was off. I never made a decision in my life without the player knowing why I was making it.

Like any sport, football educates and shapes people, and is therefore a vehicle for transmitting values. If football, which covers every realm of society, shows people how to achieve objectives outside the law, and that justice is complicit in achieving that objective, and if obtaining these results illegally gives success, power, fame and money, that society becomes corrupt.

A spectacular *Superclásico* win over River Plate (4-1, featuring another penalty miss by Diego) was not enough to draw Boca into the title chase, but it did produce an iconic image: Maradona and Caniggia's full kiss on the lips following a Boca goal. Caniggia accepted the clinch and added that someone had said, 'Let's see if you have the balls.' Caniggia's then wife, Mariana Nanis, said she was 'disgusted'. Maradona responded, 'Claudio is my friend, but if he can't control his girl he doesn't exist for me.' Diego's machismo was mixed with a certain hedonistic ambiguity that at times became overt. It was a challenge to the football world, which was, and remains, full of prejudice. Maradona had already been seen dressing up at discos with big furs and provocative clothing, sometimes dressed as a woman at parties, or sensually moving his backside when he knew he was being filmed. Still, it didn't curtail his use of expressions to denigrate homosexuality.

In Boca's penultimate league match against Estudiantes de la

Plata, with the title already gone, Maradona missed his fifth consecutive penalty. It was August 1996, and he wasn't seen on a football pitch for another eleven months.

'I was, am and always will be a drug addict . . . I don't want the kids to catch it,' Diego said at the time, as part of the Argentine government's *Sun Without Drugs* campaign. He had travelled to a clinic in Switzerland to try to overcome his own cocaine addiction. Two days after his admission, Dr Harutyun Arto Van gave a press conference without Maradona's permission. He 'told everyone everything about me', complained the vexed footballer.

'His basic problem is an existential one,' Arto Van said. 'My work consists of strengthening psychological immunity over ten days, so that he can resist these existential problems. He approaches cocaine when he feels excessively pressured and not because of physical addiction. He feels vulnerable. He is not a happy man, and he considers himself a loser.'

Maradona left the clinic. 'I'm sorry, I couldn't stand the media pressure, everyone wanted to know,' was the doctor's clarifying apology on his behalf. 'I've been living with that pressure for twenty years, and you couldn't stand it for two days.'

That autumn of 1996, Cóppola was arrested because a judge thought that not only had he consumed cocaine, but he was part of a drug cartel. The world was collapsing around a disillusioned Maradona, who watched Boca's matches from a private box. In an interview with TV channel América, he insisted that he wouldn't commit suicide because of his love for his daughters.

In 1997, a mentally stronger Maradona attempted his third reprise at Boca, employing tried and trusted techniques – for example, speaking to journalists to pressurise club leaders in public. In April, he was admitted to hospital after suffering a rise in blood pressure during a television programme. Days later, he was out of breath after dancing *cumbia* on another show. But he kept hammering at Boca's door, and secured a deal that was celebrated throughout all the Argentine media management offices.

Maradona wanted to sign his new contract 'live' in front of the cameras, but Boca ended up holding a press conference. He was thirty-six years old, and it had been eight and a half months since he had played an official match, and at least six seasons since he had trained consistently and professionally. Boca's new coach was Hector Veira, and Diego got into shape with Canada's disgraced former Olympic sprinter, Ben Johnson. Maradona's return to the pitch was the lead story across the press on 9 July when he played against Newell's Old Boys.

Some six weeks later, on 24 August, and after helping to defeat Argentinos Juniors 4-2, Diego returned another positive doping test; traces of cocaine were found in his system. He insisted it was a plot, that he had received calls threatening to place the drug in his tests. The counter-test was also positive, and the inevitable followed: suspension by the AFA, media scandal and personal depression. Don Diego's blood pressure soared alarmingly. 'If this happens to my father again, I'll give up football.'

Judge Claudio Bonadío, who was linked to Argentina President Menem's government, waived prosecution but imposed regular anti-doping tests on *El Pelusa*. The AFA had to lift the suspension. Maradona still felt persecuted by power, even though the same power, as well as the media and fans, had just protected him and looked after him.

Fit enough once more, Maradona returned to the pitch. The romance of football blossomed as he strode down a seemingly flower-strewn and heroic path to glory. Boca was competing for the title, and sporadically Maradona's left foot traced daubs of artistic genius onto the game's green canvas. An injury against Colo Colo in Chile, and he was gone again – his colourful palette locked away in the same dark rooms of old. The dust would not completely settle, nor dull the radiance, as Maradona recovered in time for the *Superclásico* against River. He was again injured and replaced at half-time by rising star Juan Román Riquelme, with Boca winning 2-1. Maradona ran onto the pitch at the final whistle, celebrating in front of the rival River fans. Having taken both the AFA's and Judge Bonadío's anti-doping tests, Maradona went home and opened a bottle of Cristal champagne, singing and celebrating long into the night.

Rumours of a positive test result swirled before they had even been analysed. Diego had been told that a radio station had announced his father's death. He called home in despair. 'He's here with me, son,' Doña Tota said. Maradona met Don Diego a few days later at the player's Buenos Aires residence in Villa Devoto. Doña Tota looked at them from a distance but knew what was being discussed.

The next day, on his thirty-seventh birthday, Maradona announced his retirement from playing football via Argentine radio station La Red.

'I'm leaving. I can't take it any more. And this is definitive. My old man, crying, asked me to do it. My family cannot suffer any more, everything being scrutinised, every wave of a rumour that envelops us. I'm leaving. I can't take it any more.'

After 692 games, 352 goals and 11 major international and club honours, Diego Armando Maradona was no longer a footballer.

Now that he would never misplace a pass, cross, penalty or shot again, his road to deification was clear. It still, however, required a miracle.

# 36

# THE ROAD TO BECOMING A GOD

Carlos Sorín's movie *El Camino de San Diego* ('The Road to San Diego') is set in the spring of 2004. It follows Tati Benítez, a young man obsessed with Maradona who lives in the impoverished province of Misiones, Argentina. In case you can't recognise who the cheap tattoo on his upper arm represents, Tati had the name Diego written underneath it. He can tell you how much Maradona's daughter Giannina weighed when she was born. He wanted to call his first-born daughter Diega, but this feminine version of Diego is a name that doesn't exist in Spanish. Tati wears the same Argentina number 10 shirt to his job every day. For work, he helps a local artist find wood in the local forested areas. He gets caught in a torrential downpour during one forage, the force of the rain bringing a timbó tree crashing down. Using more than a little imagination, Tati can see Diego, arms raised, celebrating a goal within the exposed roots. Nobody else really sees the similarity. After working the wood, it perhaps has something.

In a two-month-old newspaper he reads that a Boca museum is opening and the inauguration day is soon. Perhaps they will exhibit the wooden statue? Or maybe Diego would like to keep it. His friends laugh at the idea. 'Who wants a piece of wood from a kid from Misiones? Maradona talks to kings and to Fidel Castro, not you!' One morning a friend wakes him up. Maradona has gone into intensive care in the Suizo-Argentina hospital in Buenos Aires; he has had severe heart failure and he is fighting for his life. The next forty-eight hours are going to be crucial. Tati runs from his tiny shack, where his four family members live, to watch the only TV in town.

Hundreds of people from all over the country congregate at the doors of the hospital. Some hold banners – 'Diego you will always live, God does not want any competition', or simply 'D10S', a play on words with the Spanish word for God, *Dios*, and the number 10, while others chant his name. Women kneel and say the rosary and some kiss the relics of saints. All of them, including Ultras from Boca and rival River Plate fans, gaze up reverently at the windows, just in case Diego comes out to greet them. Four members of the Church of Maradona, which at that point counted around 20,000 followers, are present, expressing devotion 'to the greatest'.

Tati consults a shaman who confirms he must urgently go to Buenos Aires. He hasn't much money but needs to buy a camera – nobody will believe him if he doesn't have a picture when he hands over his gift to Maradona. He boards a bus for part of the journey and hitchhikes the rest of the way: a truck, an ambulance, then another bus. People wonder what he is carrying. When he shows them, some want to buy it, and others pass on their names so Tati can tell Maradona how much they love him.

The roads get more prominent, and the people he comes across have lighter and healthier skin. It takes Tati more than a day to get close to the capital, and as he approaches it, cars and trucks are blasting their horns. Maradona is out of hospital. In fact, he has gone to play golf. Tati follows his idol's every move on the TV screens at service stations. Helicopters follow Maradona's car to the golf course, radio stations discuss every detail of his illness and miraculous recovery. 'He is immortal, he will bury us all,' someone says.

Tati arrives at the entrance to the golf course while journalists give minute-by-minute updates to their audiences. He shows his wooden statue to a security guard. Another takes it away. A few hours later, 'Diego is about to leave,' someone shouts. Chaos. Ambulances, police and limousines appear out of the blue and separate the crowd: more noise and more chanting. In a second, they are gone.

Tati asks about his gift. It seems it has been taken away. By Diego? It must have been, because they took a few things with them. Tati has to return home without the statue and no proof of it being given to Maradona. Still, he has never felt like this before. He is in awe, strangely fulfilled, sensing that his pilgrimage has brought him close to the presence of a spiritual being.

Diego, a god? How did that happen?

*The Road to San Diego* is perhaps the most emotional of the more than a dozen films about Maradona, and the one that best captures and explains the phenomenon. There are some thirty documentaries about him, hundreds of university studies, and more than fifty books, notwithstanding the billions of media words written and spoken. Everything is chronicled; the tagging, recording and documenting only increasing after Maradona's return to Argentina and his subsequent retirement in October 1997. In those years, newspaper income, the price of publicity in all kinds of media, and television audiences all increased exponentially, and he was a large part of that world. There was more space dedicated to what journalist Juan Pablo Varsky labelled the 'periphery' around Diego – the business, his statements, his worth – than to his decaying football. A new Maradona trend was being created, a process that would be reiterated until the very end.

After accepting that he could no longer play professionally, Maradona's legend grew many heads like Hydra, the monstrous water snake that lived in the depths of Lake Lerna. One head was the little abandoned boy from Villa Fiorito, the next a man who desired to remain relevant to the public. Another was Maradona drowning in legal cases: rumour had it that separation from Claudia was imminent. There was also the nocturnal head whose outings ended in conflict. The public head appeared worldwide, and finally the more private face of unremitting anger. And now one more head was emerging that required his nurturing, one of particular import to his followers – that of the myth of Maradona.

In 1998, three friends from Rosario, Héctor Campomar, Alejandro Verón and Hernán Amez, invented the Church of Maradona. Laced with a fine thread of irony, the trio announced their adoration of Maradona and, after a media request, wrote Ten Commandments: *The ball is never soiled*; *Spread the word of Diego's miracles*; *Call your son Diego*; *Love football above all other things*, and so on. There are sacred dates in its calendar too. Maradona's Easter is on 22 June, the day he scored his famous brace against England in the 1986 World Cup. There are no prayers, no petitions for alms, no temples to worship and no pilgrimages to make. The church is theatre and folklore, there in order to give Maradona thanks for all he has given to the world. The very first Maradonian Christmas (30 October, his birthday) saw the three founding friends and a few others gather for some beers.

This post-modern religious parody stemmed from Diego Armando Maradona's deification, a process with an observable beginning. It does not start with the goals against England, with the 1986 World Cup win or his successes with Napoli. In fact, it started with Maradona's first resurrection, two years after his retirement and confirmed latterly with his second rising.

On 31 December 1999, Maradona travelled by private plane to Punta del Este in Uruguay to celebrate the arrival of the new millennium. Claudia, their two daughters, other relatives and friends like Guillermo Cóppola were part of the procession, all arriving at eleven o'clock at night. At midday on 1 January, in intense heat, they lit a barbecue. 'Diego ended up exhausted,' recalled Cóppola in his life story documentary on Canal Infinito. He consumed two impressive plates of food and slept for twelve hours solid in his private cabin.

On 2 January, Maradona gave an interview to the Uruguayan magazine *Caras*, played for a while with his daughters, then went out to dinner with Cóppola and some friends. He ended up in Las Dunas hotel where Claudia was staying. The next day, Maradona went to a butcher's seeking a hard-to-find delicacy: a cow's udder. They sourced three kilos (7lb) for their unique client. Maradona ate two and a half kilos of it, then retired to his room to rest. The light stayed on all night.

When Cóppola woke up at around seven in the morning, he went to Diego's cabin. Diego was sitting with his head leaning forwards as if he were asleep, in a position like a Buddha. 'Then I go in, talk to him, and he doesn't answer. I see a green liquid coming out of his mouth, which I touch, but he doesn't move.'

Diego recalled the dream he had at the time. 'I dreamed that I had climbed the summit of Aconcagua,' he told Gabriela Cociffi for *Gente* magazine. 'Then I started to fall. I got hooked on to the top of the mountain, on to a rock . . . it saved me. It's a dream for a psychologist, right?'

Diego was in a coma. Cóppola started screaming for a doctor, trying to revive him with ice in a towel. A quarter of an hour passed before a doctor arrived. According to witnesses, Cóppola initially refused to let Maradona be taken to a hospital for fear of the media's reaction, but finally agreed to transfer him in a van.

'Two hours later, this is the medical rundown,' Cóppola explained on Canal Infinito. 'Diego is dead. He isn't reacting – no reflexes. His parents, family, daughters, the press, a deluge, the whole world comes. We're in an adjacent room, and suddenly the door opens, and there's a guy there with tubes all over him. "Guille, Guille, get me a steak with chips and an egg and get me out of here. Where am I?" That's where we made the decision to go to Cuba.'

The official diagnosis from the Uruguayan hospital was that he suffered a 'toxic dilated cardiomyopathy due to cocaine and probably alcohol abuse'. Only 38 per cent of Maradona's heart was functioning correctly. 'The man above gave me another chance,' Maradona told *Gente*'s Gabriela Cociffi, who visited him in hospital in Punta del Este to chronicle his return from the dead. A study by the Mount Sinai School of Medicine revealed that the continued use of cocaine can cause chronic damage to the parts of the brain that regulate self-observation and social behaviour. Those affected find it difficult to recognise and respond to their mistakes. Gabi asked Maradona if he wasn't killing himself with the binges, the drugs, and by doing whatever he wanted: 'The choice to die is mine. It's not the Argentines', nor Jesus Christ's, nor the doctors'. It is mine.'

It sounds like brave words, but Maradona must have been pursued by fear: his medication for at least half-a-dozen conditions included tranquillisers, pills for choking sensations, others for a skin rash, liver pain and a bloated stomach. Cóppola asked Cociffi to include an oblique mention that Diego was in dire need of work: 'He needs to lead, to be in a project.' For the first time, people on the streets were praying for his recovery. About a hundred people held hands and sang his name outside the hospital room. Maradona leaned out of the window, as the Pope does for his benedictions. As he acknowledged the crowd, his pulse quickened, and his doctor recommended rest.

Maradona had to testify before the Uruguayan courts because his blood and urine tests showed traces of cocaine, but he was let off. After several days, he was transferred to his residence in Buenos Aires and then flew to Cuba, where he continued his rehabilitation treatment, thanks to Fidel Castro's sponsorship. It was complex. Diego encouraged the circus and special treatment and felt immortal, making his recuperation near impossible. He needed to *de-Maradonify*, to *un-Diego* himself. Yet neither he nor his entourage was capable of taking the necessary steps.

According to *El País*, during a twenty-minute meeting with Castro, Diego said, '*Commandante*, it was very easy to get into this, but very difficult to get out.' The encounter apparently had 'a therapeutic effect', according to the footballer himself, Maradona considered Castro a 'second father', and his 'source of inspiration'. He already sported a tattoo of Che Guevara on his right forearm and decided to ink Castro's face onto his left calf.

Claudia, who never stopped being 'Claudia Maradona' despite their marriage difficulties, accompanied Diego during those first months in Havana. She helped him get back into shape, talked with the doctors, controlled his diet, answered emails, thanked people for their good wishes and helped out with visitors. 'Once I asked Claudia how Diego had managed to survive,' film director Emir Kusturica said in his documentary about Diego. 'She answered that nobody had ever asked her how she did it.'

Both Claudia's and Diego's parents travelled to Cuba. For the first month there were thirty people there, then a month and a half passed, and there were three left: Cóppola, Claudia and Diego. Three months passed and it was solely Cóppola and Diego. Maradona spent his time listening to music, playing golf and watching a lot of football. He was also preparing his autobiography *Yo Soy El Diego* with Daniel Arcucci, giving media interviews and resting. He would often be found sitting by the front door of his house or by the sea, filling hours with quiet contemplation.

Diego would wake up and fall asleep mouthing the name *Guillermo*. The two enjoyed La Habana. 'I calculate that in Cuba alone I must have been with 700 different women. I didn't do anything else,' Cóppola admitted. Maradona didn't lag far behind his agent. From his affairs on the island, four children were born: Javielito, Lu, Johanna and Harold, from three different mothers, all of whose claims Maradona initially rejected.

Someone suggested a testimonial match for Diego. He insisted it 'not be called a farewell performance'. Enthused by the idea, he returned for a short while to Buenos Aires. Even as a weakened man, he knew the value in fanning the flames of his legend.

Just three years after its inception, the Church of Maradona counted 150 'parishioners' at its 2001 Christmas meeting, on 30 October.

On the same day of the testimonial, on 10 November 2001, Maradona interrupted a television interview he was giving to tell Cóppola he wouldn't play. 'But, Diego, Pelé's there, Platini, everyone. Everybody's there.'

'You told me the stadium would be full and it's empty.'

'Yes, Diego. You're right. It's empty because they haven't opened the doors yet, that's why it's empty.'

Four years after Diego had hung up his boots, and only eleven months after being on the verge of death, Boca Juniors' Bombonera stadium was full. Maradona's Argentina team was coached by legendary manager Marcelo Bielsa. It featured Aimar, Verón, Roberto Ayala and Mauricio Pochettino in the line-up. They faced a star-studded Rest of the World side that included Lothar Matthäus, Davor Šuker, Hristo Stoichkov, René Higuita and Juan Román Riquelme.

After the game, which Argentina won 6-3, including two successful Maradona penalties, Diego addressed the 50,000-strong crowd with the same intimacy of a one-to-one conversation. Wearing his Boca shirt, he spent five minutes thanking everyone involved in the testimonial and picking the most opportune moment to burnish his portrait. He admitted to his mistakes, apologised to football and asked for help. Up in the stands, Claudia and Don Diego wore the Argentina national team shirt. Doña Tota was dressed in black and, unlike her husband, did not applaud her son's every utterance.

'I tried to enjoy playing football and make you all happy. I think I succeeded. This is all too much for one person, too much for one player.'

'I shed several tears,' Jorge Valdano told Diego Borinsky in *El Gráfico*. 'I was moved by his unique way of owning the stage and the spontaneity of the speech. Unforgettable passages like, "This is too much for one person." Above all, the moving recognition of his errors in a country that doesn't do much work in that area.'

'I waited so long for this game,' Maradona continued, 'and it's already over. I hope the love I feel for football will never end, and this party will never end, and that the love that you have for me will never end.'

Diego embraced himself. It was his way of connecting with the audience and keeping an even keel. He couldn't hold on for long.

'I thank you in the name of my daughters, in the name of my mother, in the name of my old man, of Guillermo, and of all the football players in the world.'

Then his voice broke.

'Football is the most beautiful and wholesome sport in the world, let no one be in any doubt. If someone makes a mistake, football shouldn't pay the price for it. I was wrong, and I paid. But—'

The crowd's ovation interrupted him. As so often before, Maradona found the right words at the right time.

'But not the ball. The ball is not soiled.'

A single tear streaked down his cheek as another ovation washed down from the stands.

Pochettino was crying, too: 'How could we not? Our idol was going.'

'Have a good afternoon, and may this love never end, I beg you, please, in the name of my daughters and my family. Thank you. I owe you . . . I owe you a lot. I love you very much. Goodbye.'

He had forgotten to mention Claudia.

*

Two years later, in 2003, Maradona's two great relationships were over. On 7 March, and after fourteen years of marriage, Claudia filed for divorce. Legally, she had to plead a cause, which was stated as 'Abandonment of home since July 1998'.

In Havana, the money was running out. Cóppola started sharing a house with Diego. 'So the relationship became that of a couple,' Cóppola explained on Canal Infinito's documentary. 'We had lunch together, we had dinner together, it was already . . . a marriage!'

The intensity of the unforgettable highs started to diminish because of the relationship's constraints. Cóppola wasn't allowed another confidant or girlfriend or to represent another football player. 'On his forty-third birthday, Diego tells me someone's coming to film a report. I said, "Diego, no cameras." "You want to fuck up my birthday? They're coming." There was music, we had fun, but that night I wasn't the same. I was down, and I wanted to be alone. So I left and went to sleep.

'The next morning, I surveyed my surroundings, and for the first time I thought about going home. In the afternoon we sat down to talk. It was a day I'll never forget. "You're not the same," Diego said to me. "Neither are you," I answered. Nothing else was said. We hugged each other, and both of us started to cry. We cried a lot. "I love you," he said. "I love you too," I replied. I told him I was leaving. He understood. "Go, then," he said.' Cóppola wept like a child all the way to the airport.

They spent years not talking after that goodbye.

Maradona's proximity to his mortality focused a melancholy admiration for a talent that was now sailing towards the horizon. He was regularly in the media lens. 'When my father is driving, and he comes across a car with his name or signature on it, he honks his horn or flashes his lights and gives them the thumbs-up. Imagine!' Dalma Maradona wrote in her book *La Hija de Dios* ('The Daughter of God'). 'I've seen all kinds of reactions throughout my life, like big guys who got out of the car and started crying instantly.'

Maradona went to Rosario to inaugurate the grandstand at

Newell's Old Boys stadium that would bear his name. He met Alejandro Verón from the Church of Maradona. Diego and Alejandro took a photo of themselves together, with the Church card in the shot. It was too much for the church founder; he burst into tears in the dressing-room tunnel. Someone tapped his head. 'Why are you crying?' It was Diego.

'Do you know how many people would like to be in my place?' Alejandro replied. Maradona invited him to the hotel to chew the fat. The Church of Maradona began as an ironic tribute, and now it has more than half a million followers worldwide.

Maradona's celestial image needed more embellishment before he could truly aspire to heaven's tapestry. In 2004, he was still using cocaine. In April, he was admitted to the Suizo-Argentina hospital in Buenos Aires with soaring blood pressure, breathing difficulties and a malfunctioning heart. Once more his time on earth was under threat, and he was placed in an induced coma in an attempt to help him recover. 'It was like I was in black tar and they were throwing hooks to help me, and I was trying to grab them with my hand, but I couldn't get out,' he recounted to Argentina TV channel TyC Sports.

Verónica Ojeda, Diego's partner at the time and mother to their son Dieguito Fernando, was joined at the hospital by Claudia. Outside, hundreds of Argentinians formed prayer chains around the building, arriving from all over the country, as far afield as Tati's Misiones.

Maradona left the clinic without actually having been discharged. At the start of May he was admitted to the same clinic and doctors recommended a rehabilitation centre. Some rejected him but he ended up at Park Psychiatric Clinic in Buenos Aires' Ituzaingó district. Fellow inmates claimed to be Batman or Tarzan. 'But nobody believed me when I said I was Maradona,' he told Daniel Arucci.

By January 2005, Maradona tipped the scales at 120kg (19st). His body could hold no more Diego. As documented in the book *Vivir en los Medios* ('Living in the Media'), the French newspaper *L'Équipe* stated, 'This pure footballing genius was buried a long time ago. What is left are the wretched excesses of a 44-year-old man who is lost in his own myth.' What remained was a walking urn containing only the ashes of Maradona's spirit.

'It was enough that this number 10 proposed a new return, the umpteenth to his name (to football, to Argentina, to life, to his never-ending drama), for this modern-day Lazarus from Villa Fiorito to once again get up and walk,' publicist Luis Hermida wrote in *Clarín*. He continued, 'A couple of personal decisions [he decided to give up cocaine at his daughters' request] and a gastric operation [in March 2005, he travelled to a clinic in Cartagena in Colombia, where 80 per cent of his stomach was removed; he lost more than 30 kilos/4½st] brought forth a miracle: the prodigal son had returned.'

In that same year Boca Juniors celebrated their centenary, and club president Mauricio Macri invited Maradona to a celebratory evening as the special guest. The last year had been brilliant for the club, winning all five honours they had fought for. Macri was working towards Argentina's presidency that electoral year. He wanted Maradona as the link between leaders and players, plus the kudos it would lend his bid to lead the country. Maradona accepted. He travelled to Europe, meeting Ronaldo, Roberto Carlos, Santi Solari, Fernando Redondo, Jorge Valdano and Arrigo Sacchi. He also went to the Cannes Film Festival with film director Emir Kusturica. 'I don't live for nightlife any more. My daughters got me out of an ugly situation, they saved me,' Diego explained at the time.

Quitting cocaine was a miracle. But the unintentional consequence was that other vices took its place, with excessive quantities of alcohol and anxiolytics being consumed with abandon from then on.

In May, Canal 13 announced Maradona would host his own programme, *La Noche del 10* ('Number Ten's Night') for thirteen consecutive Mondays. Media group *Clarín* boasted Canal 13 in their portfolio and splurged, hiring 260 production staff and using fourteen cameras for the show. Maradona interviewed Fidel Castro, Mike Tyson, Pelé and Argentina actor Ricardo Darín. He also invited Leo Messi to play tennis-football against Carlos Tévez and ex-footballer and comedian Rubén Enrique Brieva. The programme burned the other channels' ratings, reaching peaks of 39 per cent national audience share. 'A year and a half ago, I was dead,' he told the audience.

Maradona also interviewed himself. An elegantly dressed Diego fired questions at the more informal Diego, grilling him about his regrets. Listing being away as his daughters were growing up, 'I missed some of the girls' parties.' He added that he would have preferred not to have 'made my old man, my old lady, my brothers, and those who love me suffer'. He admitted to 'using drugs, not sleeping much . . . we took them, and we went on to the pitch. I gave my rivals an advantage.'

'What would he say when death comes?' he asked himself. 'Thank you for letting me play football, because it is the sport that gave me the most joy and freedom. I touched the sky with my hands, thanks to the ball.'

For three months, Maradona invaded people's living rooms, filled newspaper columns, radio hours and web pages, all ably supported by the powerful *Clarín* operation. His almost daily statements made headlines. As Lalo Zanoni observed in *Vivir en Los Medios*, Maradona was the lead story for nearly all news sections one day in early November 2005: in politics, for leading the anti-George Bush march in Mar del Plata and for interviewing Fidel Castro; in culture, for auctioning off ten works by renowned artists; in entertainment, for the latest edition of his programme; and in sports, for meeting with AFA president Julio Grondona about a possible role with the national team, a proposition that was to come to fruition three years later.

'It was as if his return was the last *bondi* bus to Fiorito before everything else exploded, flooded or simply died out. And we all got on board,' Luis Hermida continued in his *Clarín* column. 'We were joyful, happy and exultant [to be part it all]. Overnight, Maradona became a desirable, sought-after brand once more.' Coca-Cola was the only product that was better known in Argentina than Diego Maradona.

But the characteristic spark was missing. The establishment had domesticated the beast while forming this well-balanced marriage of convenience. The successful, saturated coverage of Maradona's shows led to a logical and inevitable excess of praise and lack of criticism from all quarters. 'The media had a divine fascination with Maradona, something not seen before,' Zanoni explained in his book. 'They called the show "God's Night", using exalted phrasing like that to talk about Diego. Almost all Maradona stories carried headlines containing the word "God".'

The 'Hand of God' had been Diego's first brush with divinity, a seed that germinated and would blossom three decades later. *Noticias* magazine discussed the topic after his final TV programme had been broadcast: 'This year [2005], we Argentinians went crazy. His sanctification speaks of a society orphaned from support and control. Why does everyone fear him, and why does no one dare to criticise him?'

In Argentina, like much of Latin America, football is a way to express oneself, serving to build a nation's image and narrative and acting as a barometer of society. The temptation then was to believe that Maradona followed the typical narrative of the mythological hero's deification – just don't look too closely while you do it. Tourist shops in Buenos Aires' San Telmo district sell gourds for *mate*, images of Carlos Gardel and Evita, people dancing the tango, and merchandise plastered with Maradona's face. Photos of football icons represent a country.

Maradona was born in a poor village, a fact he boasted about after gaining success despite never really returning there. He was a child that fell into a rubbish dump and clambered out of the pit unscathed, a skill he used to significant effect throughout his life. Emerging from the village, his achievements were measured against these humble origins while any darker shades were ignored. He didn't fit into well-heeled Barcelona but was a redeemer in Naples, despite mingling with the Camorra mafia.

He interwove folk tales into his own history, elevating them to myths that readily became symbols of Argentina. Maradona, the avenger of social ills, a representative of the humble and a rebel for the young. He was a poster boy for the Left after learning about the Latin American socialists and Communist leaders of the seventies while he was in Naples, although this didn't stop him signing contracts worth millions with multinational companies.

Diego instinctively sensed that fairy tales triumph over reality in our battles of conscience, but those fantastic stories need an audience. One day Daniel Arcucci accompanied him for an hour's walk around Bern in Switzerland. People either didn't recognise the footballer or observed him from afar. 'Diego, you must come and live here, it is the ideal place for you,' the journalist told him. The star retorted, 'Within two days, I would kill myself.'

At the height of his Italian adventure, newspapers like *Gazzetta dello Sport* would be delivered to newsstands in Buenos Aires a few days after publication. Arcucci followed Diego closely, but that was not common. Written accounts of his success with Napoli were relatively unknown in the rest of the world.

Maradona needed television so that he could be Maradona. As if to affirm this view, he found his first glimpse of fame juggling a ball in a 1970s TV interview and talking about his dreams at a time when no football matches were broadcast live. He was the eighties idol, wearing the Napoli shirt or the Argentina one, followed by television audiences from Buenos Aires to Corrientes, from London to Tokyo. In the nineties, he was the football genius who could be followed anywhere, anytime, his ecstatic goal celebration against Greece in the 1994 World Cup coinciding with the explosion of satellite and cable television and catapulting his fame even further. The twenty-first century's digital media provided a platform for the latest generation to watch Maradona's melodrama, keeping him at the forefront of the football conversation and family.

Argentina's media circus was growing. Debates, live reports from training grounds and real-time coverage of anything from a team's plane taking off to an ambulance arriving at someone's house. As the number of opinionated commentators grew, so did the battle to stand out. Points of view became more polarised and accelerated, given the platforms provided by the rise of social networks. Decades after kicking a ball as part of his profession, Maradona remained a worldwide media phenomenon.

Journalists and those that crossed paths with him can testify to his streetwise, witty chat and his charisma. Virtually no one he met felt slighted and he knew how to take advantage of that and his special relationship with the media, who would fall prey to his power to achieve his objectives. He used his authority as he wished, giving free interviews to a kid, or demanding millions for a chat with a global media outlet.

A perfect storm had formed for Maradona's deification: the collapse of the great ideologies in the 1980s and 1990s (Communism, socialism) coupled with the hedonists' rise to the pinnacle of social life, and the appetite for stories of the rich and famous, all that fuelled by social media. As the writer Eduardo Galeano said of Maradona, 'Anyone can recognise a synthesis of human weaknesses in Maradona, or at the very least the masculine ones: womaniser, greedy, drunkard, cheat, liar, braggart, the man without responsibility.' The perfect rebel and a maverick dissenter, who also wore Nike and Versace.

'I like being Diego, *El Pelusa*, Maradona, a son of a bitch, good, normal and ignorant. I like being the way I am,' Maradona said for a Tifosi del Rey video, a musical quintet that adapted a fans' song about Diego. Supporters felt this young millionaire spoke like them and shared their desires. Diego also needed to be one of them, be one among them and, in the process, not be punished every time he dodged the law.

No other footballer has enjoyed such success in popular culture. Films enhanced the legend, while documentaries allowed his extraordinary talent – and mistakes – to remain in the public eye. Music completed his divinity, from a tango by the Quinteto Negro La Boca to Potro Rodrigo's anthem that carries the words: *Y todo el pueblo cantó: Maradó, Maradó, nació la mano de Dios* – and everyone sang: Maradó, Maradó, and the Hand of God was born.

And was he the best in the world? Pelé, Cruyff, Di Stéfano, Messi and Cristiano Ronaldo scored many more goals and were more prolific for more extended periods. But the populist demagogy and megalomania of Argentina, a country that admits to being narcissistic, intense, obsessive and theatrical, allows no possible discussion of the point. Any doubting of Maradona's claim to be the best is taken as an attack on national identity and Maradona's divine aura, this tragic hero who fights back from every adversity slung at him.

Conversely, there comes a feverish criticism of what is considered a failure. Messi was painted as a vanquished man for not winning a World Cup, losing three finals and being cold-blooded. In reality, they are punishing him for not being Maradona.

Referee Javier Castrilli adds for this book a critical footnote to the unending if sterile debate: 'I dare say that all the Argentinians who are against Messi deify Maradona. It is not a coincidence. What aspects of Maradona's personality awaken such a blinding, fanatical devotion, a deification which in turn is used as a tool of antipathy towards a different type of person? Perhaps these people do not want anyone to eclipse their God.'

In 2007, Maradona was admitted to hospital once more, with acute hepatitis due to excessive alcohol consumption. He returned to a psychiatric hospital for treatment for a few months before being appointed Argentina's national coach. His capacity for regeneration was perceived as superhuman. '*El Barbas* [The Old Man] doesn't want me yet,' Diego insisted. Despite the unrestrained familiarity with which Maradona addressed God, he was a believer. To laughter, one day Diego proclaimed, 'There is only one God. He has children and loves some more than others. I am one of those he loves the most, and that is why he gives me so much joy.'

He continued to live a thousand and one lives, seemingly always in and out of health centres. His strength was diminishing every time he confronted new headwinds. Yet, with each fall from his pedestal, his divinity grew. Maradona's razor-sharp mind blunted. He fought legal battles with Claudia and others and admitted to being the father of more children.

His parents died, and without an anchor the madness grew and the ship went adrift, leaving behind the shadow of a talent, the shouting of the choir, the collapse of the body, the victory of vice and, for wanting to live his way, the punishment of the gods.

# EPILOGUE

The shell of Maradona ghosted from Dubai to the USA, from Belarus to La Plata in Argentina and Sinaloa in Mexico. Various sporting projects satisfied the illusion of his relevancy – and his bank account – despite his damaged body's protests. But a brain injury and resultant treatments slowed his speech. His propensity to self-medicate did not adequately address his lung, liver and cardiovascular problems, which did not help. On 30 October 2020, to mark his sixtieth birthday, two of Maradona's assistants took him out of house confinement. He was a person of risk in the middle of the Covid-19 pandemic, and they helped him take a laboured stroll inside the Gimnasia y Esgrima stadium. He was still the team manager, and a Copa de la Liga match was scheduled later that day. The La Plata club continued to promote Diego the icon, regardless of his tired and defeated demeanour. Fans did not know what to think, for it was difficult to watch him literally dragging his feet. He returned home before the match started.

All life's battles weighed heavily on a soul who struggled to achieve normality for even a day. 'I would like to take a holiday from Maradona,' he told his inner circle, who convinced him to go to hospital for what appeared to be anaemia and dehydration. The doctors found a subdural haematoma – a vein in his brain had ruptured – and Maradona went into theatre. His recovery faltered from the beginning; withdrawal from alcohol and sleeping pills left him confused and anxious. He wanted to leave hospital but was kept in for eight days until being moved to a rented house in San Andrés in Buenos Aires, close to his daughters Dalma and Giannina.

His temporary home consisted of two floors and four rooms. The doors, windows and furniture mirrored the house's worn-out tenant.

Diego couldn't climb the stairs, so a room was prepared for him on the ground floor, next to the kitchen, with a television, a chemical toilet and a massage chair.

Maradona's nephew, Jony Espósito, moved in, while his personal doctor, Leopoldo Luque, saw Diego every three days. Several nurses took turns caring for him, his entourage completed by an assistant, a security guard and a cook. Maradona had regular sessions with a kinesiologist, psychologist Carlos Días and psychiatrist Agustina Cosachov, who requested a proper and complete 'medical home internment' that never truly materialised.

Diego took all his medication without protest, but there were no more jokes. People in Cuba, Venezuela and Barcelona prepared plans to move him and save him. Days passed with no news about his condition. Gianinna and Dalma visited, as did his son Dieguito Fernando with Verónica Ojeda, Dieguito's mother. Jana, daughter of Valeria Sabalain, with whom Maradona had stopped all communications once she fell pregnant aged eighteen after meeting him in a nightclub, also dropped in.

After they left, Diego requested no more visitors – he wasn't in the mood and hardly spoke anyway.

One day he fell and hit his head but refused the offer of medical assistance. His blood pressure was through the roof. He cried when he remembered Doña Tota and Chitoro, and he spoke of them often. Neighbours saw him drinking *mate* a couple of times on the internal patio of his house. Eventually, he just stayed in his room.

He had drunk his life away and probably felt satiated.

Nephew Jony said goodnight to Diego at 11 o'clock on the evening of 24 November. The next morning, the cook heard some movement from Diego's room. Perhaps he was taking his pills, so he decided not to disturb him.

At an unknown time on 25 November 2020, all alone, Maradona died.

He was finally released, spared from the effort of being Diego Armando Maradona.

The autopsy stated Maradona died of 'acute heart failure in a patient with dilated cardiomyopathy'. In simple terms, it was a heart attack. There was an inevitability to it, the 'logical suicide' of the 'chronic depressive' of which Dr Alfredo Cahe, his family doctor for two decades, speaks. One of Maradona's assistants had warned Dr Cahe some days before: 'He has done everything in this life.'

Maradona was never going to die at the age of ninety while watching TV at home, so his mythological aura endures. As is all too often the case, his transgressions were accompanied by self-destructive impulses. The autopsy told exactly that same story: there was no trace of alcohol or drugs, but there were psycho-pharmaceuticals to treat his severe depression, anti-psychotics, anti-epileptics and naltrexone to prevent alcohol withdrawal. His heart weighed more than twice that of a healthy one, but he was not on medication for that condition. From the autopsy, the conclusion was that his final death throes lasted six to eight hours; it was inevitable that possible medical negligence would be investigated.

Maradona's coffin, covered with an Argentina flag and a Boca Juniors shirt, was transferred from the autopsy room in San Fernando hospital to Casa Rosada, the Argentina president's residence. It was placed in the Hall of Latin American Patriots, watched over by Dalma and Giannina, Verónica Ojeda, Dieguito Fernando and Jana. Claudia, who organised the funeral, was in attendance too. Teammates from the World Cup-winning squad were present, along with goalkeeper Sergio Goycochea and physio Loco Galíndez, who had worked with him in Barcelona and Napoli. Guillermo Cóppola was there. Diego Jr. had planned to come from Italy after his father's operation, but he tested positive for Covid-19 and couldn't travel. He learned of his father's death from the television. Maradona's last lawyer, Matías Morla, was not invited, nor was his last partner, Rocío Oliva. Both had had very public differences with Claudia and her daughters about the treatment of Maradona, who was at times isolated by Morla and Oliva from his first wife, as well as from Dalma and Giannina.

Improvised altars with T-shirts, photos, flowers and banners – *'Diego lives on in us'* – were set up in emblematic spots across Buenos Aires. There was one at Argentinos Juniors' ground, the Diego

Armando Maradona stadium, and another at Boca. His Devoto neighbourhood address attracted one too. It became known in the nineties after Maradona challenged rival player Julio César Toresani to a fight after a game: 'Segurola y Habana 4310, seventh floor, and let's see if he lasts me 30 seconds.'

More and more people congregated outside Casa Rosada. Images of Diego's life were projected onto a screen on one of its facades. Impromptu stalls popped up around the president's residence, selling hats, *choripénes* (chorizo sandwiches) and beers, creating a football-stadium atmosphere. The chants started up, '*El que no salte es ingles*' ('The one who doesn't jump is English'), and '*Dieeeego, Dieeeego*', more like a rallying cry than a farewell. Some folk were crying, others were hugging each other. The grief was felt all over the country.

The Casa Rosada doors were opened at six o'clock in the morning of 26 November to allow people to view the coffin. At first the queue was orderly and the public – the majority wearing masks to prevent Covid-19 spreading – were sprayed with disinfectant alcohol before entering the funeral chapel. The flowers and wreaths piled up as the line of people waiting to pay their respects grew. It would have required days for everyone to file past the coffin.

The family wanted the wake to end at seven that same evening. Quickly, the atmosphere turned tense as the agreed deadline approached; altercations broke out, and paying respects became a police matter. There were beatings, fights, people jumping perimeter fences and hundreds of people broke into the Casa Rosada. Officers fired rubber bullets and used pepper spray to try to calm an out-of-control situation. The coffin was rushed out. It was all so very Maradona, so very Argentine.

More than a thousand people ensured the hearse's safe passage to the Jardines Bella Vista cemetery, with thousands more saluting and marking its journey. Most Argentine TV channels broadcast the wake, the walk to Bella Vista and the burial, with drones filming above the cemetery.

No more than thirty people were at the graveside. Among them were Diego's brother Lalo (Hugo could not make it from Italy because of the restrictions of the pandemic) and his five sisters. Two of his former partners. His daughters. Guillermo Cóppola was one of the pallbearers, as he had been at Don Diego's funeral. 'The last thing I said to him was that he had failed me because he was the one who was going to take me [to the grave],' he told the Argentine TV show *Verdad Consecuente*. The most poignant moment of silence during the ceremony came before the coffin disappeared from view; the same profound silence Diego had discovered in Cuba while sitting on a rock, gazing out at the Caribbean Sea.

Sixty court cases remained unresolved at the time of death, some with Maradona as a plaintiff, some as a defendant, the charge sheet as varied as it was long. For damages and losses, paternity, fleeing a car accident, gender violence (against Rocío Oliva), sexual harassment, tax evasion in Italy and for shooting at journalists with an air rifle. Add to that seven lawsuits featuring his ex-wife Claudia. Many of these will expire due to statute of limitations.

Leopoldo Luque, Diego's personal doctor for four years, was accused by Dalma and Gianinna of neglecting their father. Luque and other people who looked after him in his last days were investigated when it was decided to check if there was any negligence in Diego's passing. Writer Andrés Burgos used Twitter to declare that 'a hunt for the guilty over Maradona's death has begun, as if his deterioration had only been in his final days, and not because of what he did or didn't do since he was 40. It's like looking at the photo, and not the film.'

Maradona's assets numbered cars, properties, investments, royalties from clothing companies, a football school, the brands of *Diego Maradona*, *Diego* and *El Diez*, plus dozens of gifts, including an amphibious tank. With a total value of around $75 million, the estate is due to be shared among his five recognised children and natural heirs: Dalma, Gianinna, Diego Jr., Dieguito Fernando and Jana. There are other unacknowledged offspring, some of whose paternity processes prevented Diego from being cremated so that his DNA did not disappear. Santiago Lara (aged nineteen) in La Plata, Magalí Gil (twenty-four) in Buenos Aires, and four born in Cuba, aged between nineteen and twenty-one at the time of Diego's death.

The disputes over the inheritance will last for months, perhaps years.

There is also a container with 200 objects of sentimental value. Diego's life, held in a big box.

The whole world bade Maradona farewell, from the Pope to presidents. Pelé said he hoped that 'one day we will be able to play together in heaven'. His memory was honoured in the United Kingdom, perhaps more in Scotland than in England. On the same day it was announced that the UK's economy had suffered its biggest slump in 300 years, it was Maradona who dominated the front pages of the *Guardian* and *The Times*. Peter Shilton was quicker to react than when he came off his line in 1986. He stated – apparently unaware of the irony – that Maradona 'had greatness in him but sadly no sportsmanship'.

I heard about his death as I was covering a Champions League game at Inter Milan for CBS. I decided to head to Naples. As soon as I walked out of the train station on the morning of the 26th, someone approached me trying to sell me some Maradona memorabilia. The rest of the city, in the middle of the pandemic, was quiet. I was driven up the hills to the Spanish Quarter, where the streets are narrower and where you sense, then see, then smell the deprivation.

People had come together next to one of the Maradona murals that cover a whole wall. At the one where I stopped, he is wearing a Napoli shirt. Some young Neapolitans stood around their friend, who was sitting on his scooter. They talked and smoked, face masks dispensed with. They'd never seen Maradona play. 'My dad told me about him, he was someone that made us feel proud,' one told me. He started talking about beating the north, the rich ... and how that evening everyone would put something to remember him by on their balconies – flags, banners, posters, whatever they could find.

Nothing prepared me for what I saw at the ground, which was rechristened that same week as the Diego Armando Maradona stadium. A day after his death, Napoli played a Europa League game against Rijeka behind closed doors, and an initial crowd of 5000 people or so had gathered outside. Two hours before the match, almost 10,000 had congregated, many with cigarettes in their mouths, chanting, all covered in smoke from flares. Men in their twenties and thirties belted out the old songs – '*ho visto Maradona, ho visto Maradona!*' ('I've seen Maradona') – even though they hadn't. Flares went off, flags were waved and a giant 'The King' banner was unfurled in one of the stands.

I had been isolating for much of the previous seven months – the pandemic and writing commitments to blame. The world of smoke and masculine martyrdom asphyxiated me, and I had to move away. Perspective is everything and, from a distance, the picture was magnificent. Without warning, thousands of mostly young men surrounded the ground and lit red flares that illuminated the stadium.

They were not crying; they were claiming him. Even though Maradona never wanted to be held up as an example of anything, those fans saw him as one of them, yet above them. In Naples, he was a different type of god to the one that dazzled in Argentina; a more vengeful and visceral one, certainly less complex, but never forgotten. That was why they were there. They were telling the world that they won't ever let him go.

# ACKNOWLEDGEMENTS

Writing a book is never the task of one single person. I needed advice, support, ideas and so much more, and I got it as always from my team: my assistant Maribel Herruzo who will be able to rest her punished shoulders; the knowledgeable and affectionate Sergio Levinsky; always William Glasswell; the loyal Brent Wilks; the ever-reliable Peter Lockyer; the talented Marc Joss; and the latest addition, the happy Tom Shearman. My mum, my sister Yolanda, my brother Gustavo and his partner, Jana, plus my niece Alba brought me the positive energy that pushed me forward. Luis Miguel García always had an ear ready to listen and discuss things. Mark Wright gave me plenty of details about Maradona's cars, and Paul Ruiz offered his help every time it was requested. I am sorry Peter Bennet will not be able to give me his very detailed feedback any more, but he will not be forgotten. Thank you to Teresa Carvi of Mediapro and Garth Brameld of the BBC who allowed me to take breaks that helped me finish the book. And also Tony Kennedy for suggesting the right music to accompany my trips and the long periods of writing. Alan Samson of Weidenfeld & Nicolson knows how to make a writer comfortable and appreciated, so a huge thanks to you (and so good to work with Lucinda McNeile again). My literary agent David Luxton even had to deal with the shape of the 'G' on the cover, so you can imagine how grateful I am for his role!

The conversations about Maradona have been constant for more than two years, so a list of those that made me think of new angles to this fascinating story would add even more pages to this already lengthy book. Let me mention, though, those that sat down with me to give me information and share their own experiences: Paco Aguilar, Daniel Arcucci, Néstor Barrone, Guillermo Blanco, Gustavo

Berstein, Diego Borinsky, Lluis Canut, Javier Castrilli, Rodolfo Chisleanschi, Nacho Conte, Gerry Cox, Fernando García, Juan Gaspart, Jesús Gómez, Quique Guasch, Pepe Gutiérrez, Gary Lineker, Daniele Martinelli, Josep Mª Minguella, Víctor Hugo Morales, Fabián Ortiz, Alberto Miguel Pérez, César Pérez, Emilio Pérez de Rozas, Mauricio Pochettino, Adrián Remis, Ramón Rodríguez 'Monchi', Fernando Signorini, Santi Solari, Víctor Tujschinaider, Juan Carlos Unzué, Jorge Valdano, Julián Varsavsky, Eugenia Vega, Leandro Zanoni and Claudio Zuth.

# SOURCES

p.xiii, 'It was worth $430,000 . . .'
*Código F,* TyC Sports Channel, Argentina, 17 August 2017

p.4, 'As there are . . . '
José Ignacio Maradona to Germán Carrara. *Detrás de las raíces de un mito. Enganche* magazine (enganche.com.ar)

p.7, 'We used to play . . . '
Gabriella Cociffi. *Diego Armando Maradona: 16 recuerdos increíbles de mi infancia.* Infobae, 30 October 2016

p.7, 'It's not my fault . . .'
*Detrás de escena, con Diego Maradona.* Afa Play interview, 16 October 2019

p.10, 'He's a cry baby . . .'
https://diariohoy.net/el-clasico/la-vida-de-don-diego-desde-corrientes-a-ser-el-papa-mas-famoso-53141

p.17, 'Sometimes I'd be washing . . .'
Doña Tota, *Gente*

p.19, 'Where do you live? . . .'
Diego Borinsky, *El Gráfico,* 21 September 2017

p.22, 'Goyo had a magic . . .'
Francisco Cornejo, *Cebollita Maradona.* Editorial Sudamericana, Buenos Aires, 2001

p.26, 'Here we are . . .'
Based on interview by Diego Borinsky with Goyo Carrizo in *El Gráfico,* 21 September 2017

p.29, 'I started dreaming . . .'
Diego A. Maradona. *El Diego: The Autobiography of the World's Greatest Footballer.* Random House, London 2005

p.35, 'He totally dazzled me . . .'
*'Informe Robinson: los años felices'* on Maradona's early days. Directed by Michael Robinson, for Canal+ Spain, 2016

p.38, 'They were thinking . . .'
Diego A. Maradona. *El Diego: The Autobiography of the World's Greatest Footballer.* Random House, London 2005

p.39, 'Being in the changing rooms . . .'
Detrás de escena, con Diego Maradona. *Afa Play,* interview, 16 October 2019

p.40, 'The entrance of the Maradona boy . . .'
Miguel Ángel Bertolotto, *Clarín,* 21 October 1976

p.48, 'When I was younger . . .'
Diego Barceló, *10 gracias Maradona*, Lantia, 2019.

p. 47, 'He came on for the second . . .'
Segundo César Cheppi, *La Capital*, 15 November 1976

p.47, 'Maradona was acclaimed . . .'
Carlos Ruberto, *Goles*, 16 November 1976

p. 47, 'Expectations about Maradona's performance . . .'
Segundo César Cheppi, *La Capital*, 15 November 1976

p.48, 'We started taking care . . .'
Ricardo Giusti, *El País*, 11 November 2001

p.49, 'We win matches . . .'
*Clarín*, 6 September 1978

p.51, 'Plenty of time . . .'
*Sport CB*, ESPN

p.53, 'Anyone can see . . .'
*Informe Robinson*, Moviestar TV, dir. Michael Robinson, Canal+ Spain, 2016

p.57, 'But what a sacrifice . . .'
Guillermo Blanco, *El Gráfico*, April 1979

p.61, 'It's not for nothing . . .'
Guillermo Blanco, *El Gráfico*, April 1979

p.62, 'One day we scored . . .'
Cristian Grosso and Pablo Lisotto, *La Nación*, 5 September 2019

p.63, 'Do you know . . .'
Diego A. Maradona. *El Diego: The Autobiography of the World's Greatest Footballer*. Random House, London 2005

p.63, 'You've already fulfilled . . .'
Guillermo Blanco, *El fútbol del sol naciente*. Al Arco, 2019

p.64, 'From there, we travelled . . .'
Cristian Grosso and Pablo Lisotto, *La Nación*, 5 September 2019

p.65, 'We all went with long hair . . .'
Rodrigo Tamagni, *Infobae*, 22 September 2019

p.75, 'The house is located . . .'
'Aquest any cent!', TV3, Catalunya, 24 September 1999

p.85, 'Roberto Mouzo . . .'
Diego Borinsky, '100x100', *El Gráfico*, April 2009

p.86, 'After the move . . .'
Diego Borinksy, '100x100', *El Gráfico*, April 2009

p.88, 'The kids rushed past . . .'
Diego A. Maradona. *El Diego: The Autobiography of the World's Greatest Footballer*. Random House, London 2005

p.92, 'The World Cup champion . . .'
Ossie Ardiles, *Daily Mail*, 28 November 2020

p.94, 'Gentile? Good, good . . . in 1982.'
*DIOS: The Story of Diego Armando Maradona.* Pitch International, 2012

p.103, 'Two such different mentalities . . .'
Bernd Schuster's interview, Lluis Canut, *Quan s'apaguen els llums,* TV3, 24 September 2017

p.106, 'Maradona's attitude – and anything . . .'
Leandro Zanoni, *Vivir en los medios: Maradona off the record.* Marea, 2006

p.107, 'My relationship with Maradona . . .'
Bruno Passarelli, *Maradona al desnudo: La caída de un ídolo.* Ediciones B, Barcelona, 1991

p.108, 'It was Thursday . . .'
*Podemos hablar,* Telefé, November 2020

p.115, 'If I had done . . .'
'Aquest any cent!', TV3, 24 September 1999

p.119, 'One day, Diego's father . . .'
Any Ventura, *La Nación,* 24 September 2004

p.123, 'We were playing . . .'
'La clave del Gol', *Fox Sports,* 18 September 2016

p.128, 'Never forget that a contract . . .'
Diego A. Maradona. *El Diego: The Autobiography of the World's Greatest Footballer.* Random House, London 2005

p.136, 'Three months after Goikoetxea's injury . . .'
Jorge Cyterszpiler, 'Aquest any cent!', TV3, 24 September 1999

p.139, 'Yes, but Maradona can't play . . .'
'Aquest any cent!', TV3, 24 September 1999

p.144, 'I am convinced it all started . . .'
Gabriela Cociffi, *Gente,* 10 January 1996

p.157, 'My mother used to make . . .'
*Destino Futbol: Ciudad Diego*, ESPN, 2013; Lukas Sepiurka, *El capitán de Nápoles*, 2020

p.169, 'He called [Oscar] Ruggeri . . .'
Álvaro Corazón Rural, *Jot Down*, January 2019

p.169, 'The Aerolineas Argentina . . .'
Diego A. Maradona. *El Diego: The Autobiography of the World's Greatest Footballer*. Random House, London 2005

p.170, 'Do you know what it was like . . .'
Diego Borinsky, '100x100', *El Gráfico*, January 2014

p.170, 'There were several meetings . . .'
Fernando Vergara, *La Nación*, 16 June 2016

p.173, 'The meeting in Barranquilla . . .'
Fernando Vergara, *La Nación*, 16 June 2016

p.176, 'We played a friendly . . .'
Ezequiel Fernández Moores, *Fútbol Pasión: La Argentina que reinó en México – Jorge Valdano*. Tranquilo Producciones, 2014

p.177, 'There was one thing . . .'
Diego Armando Maradona and Daniel Arcucci, *Touched by God: How We Won the Mexico '86 World Cup*. Penguin Books, 30 May 2017

p.180, 'We weren't sure . . .'
Diego Borinksy, '100x100', *El Gráfico*, May 2007

p.182, 'The Bulgarians were looking at us . . .'
Diego A. Maradona. *El Diego: The Autobiography of the World's Greatest Footballer*. Random House, London 2005

p.184, 'Bilardo wanted to show us . . .'
Christian Rémoli, *1986: La historia detrás la Copa*, Koala Contenidos, Argentina 2016

p.189, 'We went through the usual . . .'
Diego Armando Maradona and Daniel Arcucci, *Touched by God: How We Won the Mexico '86 World Cup*. Penguin Books, 30 May 2017

p.206, 'But Jorge, you were ahead . . .'
*El Gráfico*, July 1996

p.207, 'Michaels Owen's dive . . .'
Fernández Moore, *1986: La historia detrás de la Copa*, Christian Rémoli, Koala Contenidos, Argentina 2016

p.209, 'I swear on my life . . .'
Diego Maradona, *Crónica*, 23 June 1986

p.209, 'I was thinking . . .'
Diego A. Maradona. *El Diego: The Autobiography of the World's Greatest Footballer*. Random House, London 2005

p.209, 'As an experience . . .'
Jorge Valdano, *El País*, 13 June 2020

p.212, 'None of them likes . . .'
Jorge Valdano, *Marca*, 12 July 1996

p.216, 'If you talk to all my teammates . . .'
Diego Borinsky, '100x100', *El Gráfico*, January 2014.

p.217, 'I didn't care . . .'
Diego A. Maradona. *El Diego: The Autobiography of the World's Greatest Footballer*. Random House, London 2005

p.226, 'Neapolitans will understand . . .'
*Corriere della Sera*, September 1986.

p.228, 'I wonder if this is . . .'
Bruno Passarelli, *El Gráfico*, 7 October 1986

p.228, 'I didn't like Diego at first . . .'
*Gente,* December 1986

p.238, 'Dad! . . .'
Gabriella Cociffi, *Gente,* September 1996

p.241, 'I was a drug addict . . .'
Gabriella Cociffi, *Gente,* September 1996

p.244, 'Rest assured . . .'
Maradona interview by Maurizio Constanzo, *'L'intervista',* Tele 5 Italia, 26 January 2017

p.246, 'Naples may be very beautiful . . .'
Bernard Bloch, *'Napoli corner: Maradona y el Napoli',* Canal+ documentary, 1987

p.247, 'Think he'd sign . . .'
Jon Smith, *The Deal.* Constable & Robinson, 2016

p.248, 'And what about you? . . .'
Matías and Nicolás Gueilburt, *Cóppola: el representante de Dios,* Canal Infinito, 2010

p.260, 'One day in Naples . . .'
TyC Sports channel

p.262, 'The next day . . .'
Diego Borinsky, '100x100', *El Gráfico,* 16 March 2020

p.263, 'Some of our team . . .'
Maradona interviewed by Alejandro Fantino on *Mar de Fondo,* TyC Sports, December 2004

p.266, 'It's all done . . .'
Diego A. Maradona. *El Diego: The Autobiography of the World's Greatest Footballer.* Random House, London 2005

p.266, 'It had all been set up . . .'
Diego Borinsky, '100x100', *El Gráfico,* 2007

p.269, 'Because I left Villa Fiorito . . .'
Diego A. Maradona. *El Diego: The Autobiography of the World's Greatest Footballer.* Random House, London 2005

p.269, 'They tried to buy me . . .'
Diego Armando Maradona and Daniel Arcucci, *Touched by God: How We Won the Mexico '86 World Cup,* Penguin Books, 30 May 2017

p.277, 'It's a lie . . .
Gabriella Cociffi, *Gente,* September 1986

p.279, 'There has been a black hand . . .'
Gonzalo Bonadeo, *Súper Deportes del Mundo,* TyC Sports, November 1991

p.294, 'It all started with . . .'
Interview by Álvaro Corazón Rural, *Jot Down,* January 2019

p.295, 'We were so happy . . .'
Maradona to Adrián Paenza, Canal 13, 31 June 1994

p.305, 'They used Maradona . . .'
Carlos Fren interviewed by Maximiliano Uria, *Clarín,* 12 October 2018

p.315, 'Diego ended up exhausted . . .'
Matías and Nicolás Gueilburt, *Cóppola: el representante de Dios',* Canal Infinito, 2010

# PICTURE CREDITS

The author and publisher are grateful to the following for permission to reproduce photographs:

Katherine Balmer (kbalmer@shutterstock.com): 1 (above); 10 (below); 13 (above)
Lee Curran (lee@alamy.com): 6 (below); 9 (above); 11 (below); 12; 13 (below)
Stephen Kirkby (stephen.kirkby@gettyimages.com): 1 (below); 2; 3 (above); 3 (below); 4; 5; 6 (above); 7; 8; 9 (below); 10 (above); 11 (above); 14; 15 (above); 15 (below); 16 (above); 16 (below)

# INDEX

Maradona is DM throughout.